Two-Bit Culture: The Paperbacking of America

America's Hidden History

A Nation Rising

The Hidden History of America at War

In the Shadow of Liberty

More Deadly Than War

Strongman

Great Short Books: A Year of Reading—Briefly

THE DON'T KNOW MUCH ABOUT® SERIES

Don't Know Much About History

Don't Know Much About Geography

Don't Know Much About the Civil War

Don't Know Much About the Bible

Don't Know Much About Mythology

Don't Know Much About the American Presidents

THE
WORLD
IN
BOOKS

52 Works of Great Short Nonfiction

Kenneth C. Davis

SCRIBNER

New York   London   Toronto   Sydney   New Delhi

Scribner

An Imprint of Simon & Schuster, LLC

1230 Avenue of the Americas

New York, NY 10020

Copyright © 2024 by Kenneth C. Davis

The Scripture quotations contained herein are from the New Revised Standard Version Bible, copyright © 1989 by the Division of Christian Education of the National Council of the Churches of Christ in the U.S.A., and are used by permission. All rights reserved.

First Scribner hardcover edition October 2024

SCRIBNER and design are trademarks of Simon & Schuster, LLC

Simon & Schuster: Celebrating 100 Years of Publishing in 2024

For information about special discounts for bulk purchases, please contact Simon & Schuster Special Sales at 1-866-506-1949 or business@simonandschuster.com.

The Simon & Schuster Speakers Bureau can bring authors to your live event. For more information, or to book an event, contact the Simon & Schuster Speakers Bureau at 1-866-248-3049 or visit our website at www.simonspeakers.com.

Manufactured in the United States of America

10 9 8 7 6 5 4 3 2 1

Library of Congress Cataloging-in-Publication Data has been applied for.

ISBN 978-1-6680-1559-9
ISBN 978-1-6680-1561-2 (ebook)

To all the librarians, writers, readers,
booksellers, publishers, teachers, and others
who defend the freedom to read

6. Do not overwrite. Rich, ornate prose is hard to digest, generally unwholesome, and sometimes nauseating.

—William Strunk Jr. and E. B. White,
The Elements of Style

Why are we reading, if not in hope of beauty laid bare, life heightened and its deepest mystery probed?

—Annie Dillard, *The Writing Life*

Dead writers and living Gods became my truest friends, and I prefer to be alone with them.

—Amit Majmudar, *Godsong*

Contents

     Timothy Snyder.   358

The Origin of Others | Toni Morrison   363

Under a White Sky: The Nature of the Future |
     Elizabeth Kolbert   370

     AFTERWORD: What Is Not Here and What I Learned   375

     APPENDIX I:
          My Ten Favorite Great Short Nonfiction Books   383

     APPENDIX II:
          52 More of the Great Short Books That Make Us Think   385

     Acknowledgments   387

     Notes   389

"Books Are Weapons in the War of Ideas"

In May of 1933, the Nazis burned books. And not a few. Across Germany, books were incinerated by the thousands. Under watchful Nazi eyes, obedient students gathered before large bonfires to consign to the flames the works of such German writers as Karl Marx, Erich Maria Remarque, and Nobel Prize winner Thomas Mann, along with books by Ernest Hemingway, Jack London, and Helen Keller. These public spectacles were carried out by Hitler's acolytes, chanting "fire oaths" with the near-orgiastic fervor that had once accompanied the burning of witches and heretics. In the most notorious of these book burnings, some forty thousand people assembled in Berlin to hear Reich Minister of Propaganda Joseph Goebbels proclaim, "No to decadence and moral corruption!" before they threw books into a massive conflagration.

Across America today, another daunting spectacle is taking place under the guise of morality. The country has been swept by a partisan-driven wave of book banning, censorship, and yes, in some places, threats of book burning. School and public libraries are being purged of certain books, sometimes following a single complaint, usually about books regarding sexuality, gender, the Holocaust, and/or racism—many by writers of color. Librarians have quit in disgust or been fired; others have been viciously harassed online or physically threatened. Under the pretext of "parental rights," the highly coordinated grievances against books have multiplied alongside a spreading attempt to scrub American history classes of anything that might cause some students to feel "shame."

Are you frightened? I am. There is nothing new about censorship in America: attacks on books and writers are older than the nation itself. But something is different about this well-organized and highly partisan onslaught. It is about more than a few books that are claimed to be unfit for young readers. It is a purge of ideas. A rising chorus of voices has sought to powerfully counter these modern American book banners. The stakes could not be higher.

Nearly a century ago in Berlin, the "decadence and moral decay" of Thomas Mann, the "soul-shredding overvaluation of sexual activity" of Sigmund Freud, the "literary betrayal of our soldiers" in Remarque's World War I classic *All Quiet on the Western Front*, and the "falsification of our history and disparagement of its great figures" justified the destruction of literature. These distant echoes from 1933 should serve as a bright, flashing red light for us. The demise of Germany's constitutional democracy was swift and sweeping. As a further warning, we might recall the words of German playwright Heinrich Heine, whose work was tossed into the bonfires in 1933: "Where they burn books, they will also ultimately burn people."

As a historian, I look to the past to understand the present. And here is what I see. During World War II, while the Nazis burned books and people, the United States made a remarkable decision to give books away. Under a plan launched in 1943 by a consortium of American publishers known as the Council on Books in Wartime, millions of Armed Services Editions were printed and distributed for free to Americans at war. Members of the armed services were encouraged to read more books. Intended as a morale boost, the program introduced men and women in uniform to a wide selection of stories and ideas from a broad array of writers. Handed out to Americans serving on battleships, bombers, and in barracks around the globe, the Armed Services Editions were published under a simple motto: "Books Are Weapons in the War of Ideas."

Today we are in a new War of Ideas. Like all wars, this one is about control, fear, and power. The opponents of books have decided that some books contain ideas that disturb a carefully ordered world, which is today predicated on sexism, racism, and white supremacy. To them, books are dangerous. These enemies of books want to limit the spread of ideas for a simple reason: books make us think.

So, first they come for the books.

This battle over books is profoundly disturbing to me. For many years, I have lived a life in books. Books made me who I am. An avid library goer from childhood, a voracious reader, a former bookseller, and a writer, I have long advocated for reading, learning, and knowing. I have always tried to champion the power of books to sharpen critical thinking, question easy assumptions, and facilitate the spread of knowledge. I believe that open books open minds.

In my first book, *Two-Bit Culture: The Paperbacking of America* (1984), I wrote about the democratization of reading in America through the revolutionary introduction of mass-produced and -distributed paperbacks, all sold for twenty-five cents, or "two bits." In *Two-Bit Culture*, I identified consequential books that educated the public and shaped our culture because they were widely available and affordable. The "paperback generation" was part of a true sea change in reading and thinking.

To win this current War of Ideas we need first to acknowledge how much books matter. How they educate, inform, and inspire. We need to fight for the right to read what we want to read. And, perhaps most importantly, we simply need to read more books.

But which books? Where do we begin? There are millions to choose from—at least for now. If you seek some guidance, I am here to help.

In the spirit and style of my previous book *Great Short Books: A Year of Reading—Briefly*, a compilation of short novels, welcome to a compendium of some of the most consequential but concise nonfiction ever written. *The World in Books* offers a selection of fifty-two short but provocative works of nonfiction. Here you will discover a curated collection of some of the world's most influential and profound thinkers and writers and their consequential ideas. All of these fit into a roughly two-hundred-page limit, with a few occasional exceptions. Many are much shorter. This means, Gentle Reader, that each of these selections could easily be read in a week's time or less, making for another "Year of Reading—Briefly."

In compiling this collection, I highlighted books that provide insight, inspiration, and illumination. They range across many important ideas, issues, and isms—racism, fascism, sexism, socialism, and authoritarianism among them—along with religious freedom, creativity, and the climate crisis. Together, these fifty-two entries comprise a rich intellectual adventure, while also underscoring what has always been for me an article of faith: books matter.

That may seem obvious on its face. But a little publishing history is in order. Once upon a time in much of the Western world, there was only one set of permitted books and one accepted truth. Most of these books were in Latin, which meant few people could read them. And they were very expensive, which also limited their availability. For the most part, these books asserted the sole truth of Christianity as decreed by the Church in Rome.

The Renaissance and the spirit of humanism changed that. Bringing to light ideas from ancient sources that clashed with Christian orthodoxy, along with books increasingly written in common languages such as Italian, German, and English, the Renaissance and humanism were fueled by the revolutionary advent of Gutenberg's press around 1440. Johannes Gutenberg's movable type completely altered the trajectory of history by mass-producing books, which made them vastly less expensive than the medieval era's handwritten, illuminated manuscripts. By the end of the fifteenth century, hundreds of presses across Europe were producing hundreds of thousands of books.

The books being more widely printed and shared did not necessarily propose *new ideas*. The Renaissance and the flowering of humanism came about because people learned about *old ideas*—very old ideas from ancient Greece, ancient Rome, and the Arabic world. Many had been suppressed because they had been considered pagan heresy. But with the increased availability of books, and the growth of European universities, literacy and education exploded. Once the exclusive purview of the aristocrat and the cleric, books became available to the many. The result was the dynamic burst of creativity and thought in Western civilization's arts, writing, philosophy, the sciences—and religion. The printed word was central to Europe's next great movements, the Reformation and Age of Reason.

It is this simple: open books open minds.

That is an obvious and glorious truth.

But why focus again on short books?

Reading books is a fundamental skill and valuable pleasure that has sadly fallen victim to the pressures of our times. The recent years of pandemic and political chaos have wreaked havoc on our ability to focus and read. But these events only exacerbated a deeper issue: the impact of the internet. It is the subject explored in a provocative book titled *The Shallows: What the Internet Is Doing to Our Brains* by author Nicholas Carr, who diagnosed this vexing modern problem:

> Over the last few years I've had an uncomfortable sense that someone, or something, has been tinkering with my brain, remapping the neural circuitry, reprogramming the memory. My mind isn't going—so far as I can tell—but it's changing. I'm not thinking the way I used to think. I feel it most strongly when I'm reading. I used to find it easy to immerse myself in a book or a lengthy article. . . . The deep read that used to come naturally has become a struggle.

Carr is not alone in that struggle. It is a commonly shared problem as we bury our faces in screens. But in confronting this technological assault on our ability to focus, amid the deluge of crises we confront, one of the most useful things we can and must do is read. When I previously wrote about the therapeutic value of reading, I was unaware that this activity has a name: Bibliotherapy.

The idea can be traced to the ancient Greeks, as *New Yorker* writer Ceridwen Dovey explains, "who inscribed above the entrance to a library in Thebes that this was a 'healing place for the soul.'" Dovey continues: "For all avid readers who have been self-medicating with great books their entire lives, it comes as no surprise that reading books can be good for your mental health and your relationships with others, but exactly why and how is now becoming clearer, thanks to new research on reading's effects on the brain."

While the "Bibliotherapy" described by Dovey focuses on novels, I argue that reading nonfiction conveys similar advantages. Recent studies confirm that reading books provides mental stimulation and other healthful benefits. In a January 2023 *New York Times* article on regaining focus and concentration, Dana G. Smith explained: "Try deep reading (on paper). Traditionally, our brains tended to read print materials more slowly, in part because we were more likely to go back and double-check what we just read. That extra time lent itself to sophisticated mental processes like critical analysis, inference, deduction and empathy."

These are attributes we all sorely need to cultivate. So, think of reading nonfiction as another form of fitness. Reading short books, I contend, is like the "high-intensity interval training"—quick bursts of vigorous activity—that we are now told is the most efficient way to stay fit. I would suggest, to extend the exercise analogy, that an athlete aspiring to run a marathon starts training with short runs. Brief nonfiction, then, provides a form of mental and psychological workout that prepares us to bring our brains into peak condition.

Short nonfiction engages us, makes us think, helps us refocus, and primes us for longer, more challenging efforts.

But where to start? That is what this book is about.

Moving in chronological order from ancient times to modern days, this collection takes us from some of the earliest known books to our own times—from the Bible to James Baldwin, from Machiavelli to Toni Morrison. I hope these entries will carry readers on an exciting voyage that includes many of the greatest books, writers, and ideas of all time. But Gentle Reader, travel through these selections in any order you choose. Think of this collection as a wonderful book buffet at a great all-night diner: you can eat as much as you like and even go for dessert first.

I will quickly admit that the task of winnowing down this collection was daunting. Even by limiting my field of vision to books of no more than two hundred pages, the array of choices—like the menu at that twenty-four-hour diner—was overwhelming. After culling centuries' worth of consequential books, the final choices are presented in the following format:

- the book's title, date of composition, author, specific edition and translation cited, and page length

- a brief sample, which may consist of the opening words or another memorable excerpt

- a biography situating each author in the times in which they lived

- a concise "Why You Should Read It" commentary

- a final section suggesting "What to Read Next"—either books by the same author or related works, many of a similar length.

So, what is here? You will find works ranging from the earliest recorded literature to modern writers, from *Gilgamesh* and the *Bhagavad Gita* to Dante to Joan Didion. I set out to include an equal number of works by writers identified as male or female—with the recognition that some of these selections have unknown or legendary authors. That said, we must acknowledge that until fairly recently in recorded time few women were taught to read or write. Women's voices have largely been silenced through-out history, an argument made in one of the selections, Virginia Woolf's *A Room of One's Own.*

These wide-ranging readings were chosen to provoke questions and reflection. How, for instance, do Aristotle's thoughts on writing resonate today? Why did an ancient Hindu poem influence Thoreau and Gandhi? What can we learn from an observer of Mussolini's Italy in a time of rising authoritarianism? The collection moves on to modern times, probing works that address such issues as civil rights, women's rights, and the threat of autocracy. And did I mention sex?

This meant returning to familiar works as well as discovering new books. Included are some classics you may have read and would benefit from revisiting now, and those you wish you had read but never did. Perhaps you were assigned one of Plato's dialogues in Philosophy 101. But you may have missed *The Symposium*, a lively narrative set at an Athenian drinking party in which the central subject is "eros"—desire. See, I told you there would be sex.

With offerings ranging from *The Art of War* to *All About Love*, you will encounter a mélange of classic philosophy and contemporary wisdom—along with some powerful history and poignant memoirs. In this way, *The World in Books* offers a progression through intellectual history in palatable portions. But this is not your freshman-year Western Civ textbook. Nor is it meant to supplant Dr. Eliot's Five-Foot Shelf of Books, so-named for Harvard president Charles W. Eliot who compiled a collection of classic literature that any educated person should read. (It filled fifty volumes!)

No, this is intended as a lively illumination of the ideas and people that have shaped thought and history from the earliest times to our own—presented without pedantry. It adds up to what I would call the thinking-driven life.

How, you may ask, did I choose? Besides length, I had four essential considerations:

- Consequence: What was the book's impact?

- Timeliness: Do the ideas speak to us today?

- Literary value: Is the writing richly rewarding?

- Accessibility: Does the language resonate with modern readers?

Most of the included works ring all four bells. But my selection process placed slightly more weight on the first two of these: consequence and timeliness. As I culled the possibilities, I became convinced that books that address our present world deserve greater attention. I moved from the general goal of presenting a wide range of thought and experience to exploring works that speak specifically to the crises we now confront. We live in a time when religious intolerance and fundamentalism, racism, sexism, authoritarianism, and the cloud of climate catastrophe dominate our lives. Increasingly, I turned to books that speak to these issues.

For example, James Baldwin's *The Fire Next Time*, a blistering indictment of America's racism written in 1963, could easily have been written in 2023. And in a time of heightened nuclear tensions, John Hersey's *Hiroshima* offers searing lessons about the cost of atomic warfare that are as powerful now as when they appeared in 1946.

I will be the first to admit that this is an audacious undertaking. I know that some will skim the table of contents and shriek, "How could you leave out _____ [fill in the blank]?" But that is the nature of any subjective list. Keep in mind my guiding principles of length, consequence, timeliness, literary value, and accessibility. And I suggest many other works—some that missed the cut—in the "What to Read Next" sections; the afterword also provides an extended list of more recommended great short nonfiction.

I set out to provide a year-long reading plan that was broad in both the time it covered as well as the ideas it presents. My selection process was also clearly guided by my passions and preferences. Ultimately, the books chosen reflect my judgment of what is profound, provocative, and poses a challenge to our accepted ideas and assumptions. To borrow from French Enlightenment philosopher René Descartes, "I read, therefore I think."

"Je pense, donc je suis"—"I think, therefore I am"—was written by Descartes in his 1637 *Discourse on the Method*. Descartes coined this bedrock tenet of Western thought along with its later Latin equivalent, *"Cogito, ergo sum."* The phrase has since become a foundational principle of Western philosophy: one must be a thinking entity to have a thought or, for that matter, a doubt.

Overcoming the hurdles presented by this selection process meant operating with some essential ground rules. Chief among these was sticking to nonfiction—even though it might be argued that works like the *Bhagavad Gita* and *Utopia* are essentially works of fiction. A related issue is that "nonfiction" might preclude poetry. But I bent this guideline by acknowledging that the earliest poetry was, in fact, a form of nonfiction. In the ancient world, poetry was first spoken, not written, and only later set down on clay, papyrus, parchment, and other writing materials. Among the included verse works are the Chinese classic *Tao Te Ching* and the poetry of Sappho of Lesbos—chosen in part as the rare sample of a woman's writing preserved from the Greek Classical period.

The next ground rule was grasping some of the foundational texts of world religion and philosophy. To do so meant viewing the Bible not as one book, but a collection of many books, and choosing to include two of them: Genesis for the Old Testament and the Gospel of Luke in the New Testament. Similarly, I include a single sura as an excerpt from the Qur'an (Koran) to introduce readers to Islam's sacred text. No reasonably educated person should be ignorant of what the fundamental works underlying world faiths actually say.

These examples speak to another significant challenge: translation. Over the centuries, many of these works have been translated many times. My ground rule here was to rely upon recent, widely accepted English translations with the understanding that every *translation* is also an act of *interpretation*. In many cases, I point to alternative versions.

And that brings me to my final—and perhaps most arbitrary—rule: to include books that engage modern readers. First and foremost, I sought works that make us think—but also those that provide a degree of reading pleasure.

Honestly, many of us recall that our class reading assignments could often be a slog. Without singling out specific examples, quite a few of the books I encountered in my sifting process may have once been consequential and timely. But some of these "classics," I found, were more like "museum pieces" composed in dense, dated prose that rendered them impenetrable. Mary Wollstonecraft's *A Vindication of the Rights of Woman*, a bedrock work in feminist history, fell into the category of books well past their "freshness date." If part of the point is to read for pleasure, the writing must be pleasing. But by all means, read Wollstonecraft if you choose.

During my year of reading great short nonfiction, I sought writing that arouses the imagination and intellect. We all know that we must eat our vegetables, but they can still be appealing. Broccoli can be boiled away to a limp lump. Or it can be beautifully prepared and plated. Achieving such an appetizing presentation, with minimal jargon, is my goal.

Against the challenges posed by the troubling times in which we live, I also moved through my reading in more personal terms. After a writing career of more than forty years, I recognize that each book I begin may be my last. As I approach my seventies, the questions that many writers ask of their work—"Is it any good?," "Does it matter?"—become even weightier. Coincidentally or not, I found myself drawn to books about examining life—and death—especially in a post-pandemic world. As Socrates supposedly said at his trial for impiety and the corrupting of youth, "The unexamined life is not worth living."

Confronting mortality is not a personal exercise in fatalism. Instead, it is a recognition that life and death are linked and the work we do must somehow count. When we begin to inventory our lives—to search for meaning—we are forced to ask: What have I accomplished? Did I succeed as a writer, a spouse, a parent, a human being? But this is not a memoir. I will only underscore the fact that many of the works I encountered helped me ponder such solemn questions.

All of these books—some very ancient, some contemporary—challenge assumptions regarding profound questions of how we should be in the world. I believe, perhaps more than ever, that it is possible—and never too late—to change, if we choose. I came away from my readings more convinced that learning, questioning, and thinking must be ongoing if we are to be that so-called change in the world.

Of course, one rationale for this project is to broaden our individual educations and become familiar with some landmarks in literary history. But this project goes beyond the notion of throwing out titles to impress the guests at a cocktail party or answering that *Jeopardy* stumper. We stand at a moment in history that requires informed, questioning, thinking people. The times demand a new Renaissance, a new humanism, that challenges orthodoxy and introduces powerful ideas. It is a moment that confirms H. G. Wells's dire 1920 prediction in *The Outline of History* that "human history becomes more and more a race between education and catastrophe."

Educating ourselves is the fundamental and central solution to averting such a catastrophe. By posing questions, expanding our knowledge base, and thinking for ourselves we can actually challenge those who would erase facts and science with propaganda and misinformation. "Only the educated are free," wrote the enslaved Stoic philosopher Epictetus, who greatly influenced the *Meditations* of Marcus Aurelius, a Roman emperor included here.

It is for enduring ideas like these that reverberate in our time that we must rediscover ancient classics and explore modern wisdom. This is what makes great literature timeless. We learn from its lessons, even after thousands of years. And that is especially true while we struggle through a War of Ideas.

During World War II, a wartime poster, depicting a Nazi book burning, featured a quote from President Franklin D. Roosevelt:

Books cannot be killed by fire. People die, but books never die. No man and no force can put thought in a concentration camp forever. No man and no force can take from the world the books that embody man's eternal fight against tyranny. In this war, we know, books are weapons.

In bringing together this extraordinary array of writings, offering historical context without encyclopedic dullness, and connecting the past to the present, the history to the headlines, I hope I have provided a rich reservoir of contemplation, insight, inspiration, resistance, and perhaps even a glimmer of truth—which, as we are told, "shall set you free."

THE
WORLD
IN
BOOKS

"Bitterly Gilgamesh wept for his friend Enkidu"

The Epic of Gilgamesh

— CIRCA 2000 BCE —

Author Unknown

New York: Penguin Books, 1972; translated with an introduction by N. K. Sandars; 128 pages

---

NOTE: This is a prose version, written at the suggestion of legendary Penguin Books founder Allen Lane and first published in 1960. I used it for its accessibility and readability. But there are numerous verse translations including *The Babylonian Gilgamesh Epic*, critical ed. and cuneiform texts, translated and edited by Andrew George, London: Oxford University Press, 2003; *The Epic of Gilgamesh*, 2nd Norton critical ed., translated and edited by Benjamin R. Foster, New York: W. W. Norton, 2019, with extensive notes and essays; and more recently, *Gilgamesh: A New Translation of the Ancient Epic*, translated from the Akkadian by Sophus Helle, New Haven, CT: Yale University Press, 2021.

OPENING WORDS

I will proclaim to the world the deeds of Gilgamesh. This was the man to whom all things were known; this was the king who knew the countries of the world. He was wise, he saw mysteries and knew secret things, he brought us a tale of the days before the flood. He went on a long journey, was weary, worn-out with labour, returning he rested, he engraved on a stone the whole story.

When the gods created Gilgamesh they gave him a perfect body. Shamash the glorious sun endowed him with beauty, Adad the god of the storm endowed him with courage, the great gods made his beauty perfect, surpassing all others, terrifying like a great wild bull. Two thirds they made him god and one third man.

SUMMARY

We begin at the beginning.

Considered the oldest epic poem in world literature, *The Epic of Gilgamesh* tells the story of a semidivine king named Gilgamesh, who may have been based on an actual historical figure in one of the world's first cities, Uruk in ancient Mesopotamia (modern Iraq), but who can also be considered the world's first superhero. Perfectly formed, possessing superhuman powers and knowledge, larger than life, and with an ego to match, he fits the mold of many other heroes of legend, myth, and literature, such as Hercules, King David of the Bible, or King Arthur of the stories of the Knights of the Round Table.

Ruling over the kingdom of Uruk, Gilgamesh is nearly godlike in his wisdom: he knows all, sees mysteries and secret things; he is unmatched in strength. Despite these gifts, he sets off on a series of adventures, in search of first enlightenment and eventually immortality. Older by far than the Homeric epics and the recorded stories of the Hebrew Old Testament, this tale of his journey takes us through a series of "hero's quests" that mark this epic poem as a landmark in world literature.

But his arrogance is equal to his wisdom and strength. And he takes women as he chooses. "His lust leaves no virgin to her lover, neither the warrior's daughter nor the wife of the noble." To punish his unseemly behavior, the gods create Enkidu, part man, part beast, formed from clay, who lives among the animals. A prototype Frankenstein monster with prodigious sexual endurance, Enkidu leaves the wilderness to challenge Gilgamesh to a fight. Both supernaturally strong, Gilgamesh and Enkidu brawl in the city streets until their match ends in a draw and the pair become friends.

Yes, *Gilgamesh* is the first "buddy movie"—or perhaps "the first queer love story," as author and Cambridge University Fellow Robert Macfarlane wrote in the *New York Review of Books* in 2022, a suggestion that has elicited considerable serious scholarship. Homoeroticism is an ancient theme and comes into play when discussing such heroes as Homer's Achilles and Patroclus or the Bible's David and Jonathan, two other pairs of warrior-comrades. These ancient tales remind us that the view of same-sex love in the ancient world was markedly different from that of the condemnation found in Judeo-Christian views, a subject further explored in this collection in Plato's *The Symposium* (see entry).

Angry over the failure of their plan to rein in Gilgamesh, the gods send the Bull of Heaven to punish both Enkidu and Gilgamesh. But the pair again confounds the gods. Together, they defeat the bull and dismember it, hurling its thigh—or severed penis, in another translation—at the goddess of fertility and sex, Ishtar. Responding to this new affront, the gods strike Enkidu with a fatal illness. Grieving for his beloved Enkidu, Gilgamesh sets off to find the secret of immortality and encounters the survivor of a great flood—yes, there is a flood story in *Gilgamesh* that is older than the Noah story in Genesis. Gilgamesh seeks a plant that will allow him to live forever. Will Gilgamesh discover that missing piece that will make him like a god?

ABOUT THE AUTHOR: UNKNOWN

Nothing can be said about the author of these epic poems, which predate Homer and the Bible, because nothing is known. Like the Bible (see Genesis entry), *The Epic of Gilgamesh* was more likely the work of many authors in the oral tradition before being set down centuries later. "The poem we call *Gilgamesh* is based on copies of a work assembled over a millennium after the earliest stories were written in Old Babylonian," explains historian Michael Schmidt. ". . . A specific scribe, editor, collator, poet is given credit for bringing it all together. He may have also been an exorcist, magician, diviner, priest, or seer; or a combination of these not unrelated vocations. . . . He is certainly not what we would regard as an *author* or a *poet*. His contribution was curatorial."

So how did the world's oldest written story come to us? It is an intriguing tale of archeology and human passion. A set of fragmented clay tablets, inscribed in cuneiform, one of the earliest known forms of writing, was discovered in the ruins of a temple in Nineveh, capital of the ancient Assyrian Empire, and brought to London in the mid-nineteenth century. There these shards of ancient writing remained until George Smith, a young printer, studied the tablets in the British Museum on his lunch break and cracked the code of the language inscribed on them. He was eventually given a position in the museum. Smith created the first English translation of one of the fragmented tablets of *Gilgamesh* and, in 1873, he published an article titled "The Chaldean Account of the Deluge," an episode from *Gilgamesh* trumpeting a story of a great flood that mirrored the flood account in Genesis.

Smith's revelation about the existence of a flood account that predated the story of Noah and his ark made international headlines. Newspapers began to sponsor expeditions to find further pieces of the story. Smith himself was sent by the British Museum to excavate an Assyrian site and died of dysentery in August 1876 during that trip. Since Smith's first translation, many other fragments of *Gilgamesh* have turned up and multiple translations now exist of what is considered the world's oldest story.

WHY YOU SHOULD READ IT

I'll be honest here. My Akkadian isn't great.

So, why read this ancient text when we don't really know why—or for whom—it was written? I first encountered *Gilgamesh* in writing my earlier books about the Bible and mythology, for the simple reason that, like many before me, I was fascinated by the idea that there was another flood account from the ancient Middle East. Raised on the story of Noah's ark from childhood Sunday school lessons, I experienced one of those "Why didn't they tell us that?" moments.

Gilgamesh explores themes that have driven storytelling from its very beginnings to modern times. It is an essential hero's quest: a series of adventures and trials aimed at gaining knowledge and power; in the case of Gilgamesh, he seeks the ultimate power of immortality. This is a reflection of the powerful desire of humans to be like gods, prevalent throughout mythology. It is also a story about friendship and loss. It is a story of the quest for meaning. In a recent version, translator Sophus Helle writes: "One reason for the epic's appeal is that it lures the reader in with a mix of wild energy and sober reflection. Gilgamesh the hero is youthful and rash, but Gilgamesh the epic is much more melancholic, full of meditations on death and the burden of community."

For these reasons, this ancient work—still being investigated and retranslated as new fragments turn up—remains such a subject of deep fascination. A 2003 edition of *Gilgamesh* is based on more than 180 fragments. And as recently as 2015, an Iraqi museum reported the discovery of twenty missing lines of poetry. In other words, there may be more *Gilgamesh* yet to be discovered. As new discoveries open up ancient mysteries, we must continue to explore the connections between myths and folklore that have influenced the sacred stories people have told for thousands of years. Storytelling is one key to what makes humans different from other creatures, and there are many stories, like this, that people have told for longer than we know.

Including *Gilgamesh* in this book represents the first case of an arbitrary bending of my rules. Like the *Bhagavad Gita* and other epic poems across the ancient world, *Gilgamesh* is essentially a work of fiction. But as with other legends, myths, fables, and fairy tales told by people across human time, it is fiction that gets at truth. Myths, after all, are not simply "make-believe." They have always been a culture's sacred stories, meant to convey a vision of truth. And like much of the greatest literature, it speaks to us over the centuries.

"Why does *Gilgamesh* continue to concern us? One reason is the durability of its central preoccupations," Robert Macfarlane wrote. "Ecocide, poor governance, toxic masculinity, fear of death, invasion, insomnia: Gilgamesh's themes could be transcribed from yesterday's newspaper."

WHAT TO READ NEXT

There is no sequel. Sorry. If *Gilgamesh* intrigues you, I would suggest an excellent—but short—deep dive into the history of the work and its many translations over time, *Gilgamesh: The Life of a Poem*. Michael Schmidt's work, cited earlier, offers a fascinating history of how the poem came to be and how it has been viewed over history and continues to be revitalized today.

To explore further the mythology and literature of ancient Mesopotamia, the so-called Cradle of Civilization, I suggest *Inana: Queen of Heaven and Earth*, by Diane Wolkstein, and *Inana: Lady of Largest Heart*, by Betty De Shong Meador, which explore the goddess Ishtar. Some of the poems about this goddess are attributed to a priestess named Enheduanna, credited as the first named author in history. *She Who Wrote: Enheduanna and Women of Mesopotamia ca. 3400–2000* tells her story and provides a rich visual introduction to the society from which *Gilgamesh* emerged. Another way to explore these ancient stories is through the work of Joseph Campbell in such books as *The Power of Myth* or *The Hero with a Thousand Faces*, or through Harvard professor Maria Tatar's 2021 book, *The Heroine with 1001 Faces*, which deals specifically with the traditional absence of women in male-centric hero quests and the important history of "heroism."

"The man said, 'The woman whom you gave to be with me,
she gave me the fruit from the tree and I ate.'"

The Book of Genesis

— CIRCA 1000 BCE (?) —

Author Unknown

The New Oxford Annotated Bible, *New Revised Standard Version, edited*
by Bruce M. Metzger and Roland E. Murphy, New York: Oxford University
Press, 1991; 68 pages, double columns

OPENING WORDS

In the beginning when God created the heavens and the earth, the earth was
a formless void and darkness covered the face of the deep, while a wind from
God swept over the face of the waters. Then God said, "Let there be light"; and
there was light. And God saw that the light was good; and God separated the
light from the darkness. God called the light Day, and the darkness he called
Night. And there was evening and there was morning, the first day.

In any discussion of reading "the Bible," we must begin with two basic questions: "What is the Bible?" and "Which Bible?" So, before summarizing Genesis and discussing who wrote it, a quick overview of the "Good Book" and how it came to be.

A compendium of many shorter books—how many depends on which version of the Bible you're reading—the Bible is believed by many to be the divinely inspired Word of God. But a Hebrew Bible differs from a Roman Catholic or Greek Orthodox Bible, which differs from a Protestant Bible in the number and ordering of books. So again, "Which Bible?"

The first five books of the Bible, known in Judaism as the Torah and to others as the Five Books of Moses, were passed down orally by nomadic tribespeople for centuries before being inscribed on scrolls in archaic Hebrew. These stories and laws were first set down in Jerusalem around 1000 BCE, approximately during the reigns of King David (circa 1000–960 BCE) and King Solomon (circa 960–922 BCE). Over several centuries, these were supplemented with books of history, poetry, philosophy, and prophecy. These ancient writings have since been edited, translated—and sometimes mistranslated—revised, published, and republished in myriad versions over the millennia.

In other words, the story of the Hebrew Bible, or TANAKH—an anagram of the Hebrew words for Law or Instruction, Prophets, and Writings—or the Christian Old Testament, is complex and still in dispute. Scholars disagree about when the Hebrew canon—meaning those books selected as sacred and divinely inspired—was first established; some argue for a date of 140–40 BCE and others say it was not fixed until the second century CE. The complete collection of books that made up the Hebrew scriptures was translated into Greek, in a version known as the Septuagint, in the first and second centuries BCE in Egypt. This Greek version became the basis for what Christians later called the Old Testament.

After the life and death of Jesus, the Hebrew scriptures were extended by various accounts and letters written near the end of the first century CE, recording Jesus's ministry and miracles and the founding of the Christian church, first as an offshoot or sect of Judaism. Composed by people without firsthand knowledge of Jesus, in Greek and Aramaic—a form of Hebrew spoken by Jesus—these writings later became Christianity's New Testament. The question of which New Testament books would be considered canonical—accepted by early Christian authorities as divinely inspired—was debated at the Council of Nicaea in 325 CE. The Roman emperor Constantine, who decriminalized Christianity in 313 CE, commissioned fifty copies of the Bible in 331 CE.

After Christianity became Rome's official religion in 380 CE, a Latin translation of both Old and New Testaments was ordered by Pope Damasus. Begun in 382 CE by Jerome, a Christian cleric who was later sainted, it became known as the "Vulgate," from a Latin word for a commonly used language. The Vulgate became the official Bible of Christianity for much of the next thousand years. Complete Bibles and collections of portions of the Bible were created in the form of illuminated manuscripts—intricately hand-copied and lavishly decorated books, available only to a few.

But, as I point out in my introduction, the development of movable type in Europe changed everything. Printed Bibles became more widely available. First produced in 1455 CE, Gutenberg's most famous creation remains the Gutenberg Bible, a Latin edition. Among the world's most priceless objects, forty-nine of these Bibles are known to exist, although only twenty-one of them are complete. The rapid spread of printing led to a boom in European literacy, which increased demand for Bibles. And people could read the Bible for themselves.

"The printing press had now become the collaborator and vehicle of the Protestant spirit," wrote historian and Librarian of Congress Daniel J. Boorstin. "And so it opened the path to a popular scriptural theology—and the Reformation." During the Protestant Reformation, the Bible was produced in commonly spoken languages, including Martin Luther's German-language Bible (1522–1534 CE) and early English translations such as the Tyndale Bible of 1525. Denounced as a heretic by men such as Thomas More (see entry), William Tyndale was strangled before being burned at the stake. In 1611, the most renowned English translation was issued as the King James Version. Described by prominent eighteenth-century cleric and scholar Robert Lowth as "the noblest monument of English prose," the King James Version has immeasurably influenced English language and literature ever since.

It later became clear that this widely quoted English "Authorized Version" contained errors of translation and interpretation. Many people are surprised to learn, for instance, that Moses and the Israelites did not actually cross the "Red Sea," but the "Sea of Reeds"—a mistranslation of the original Hebrew later immortalized by Hollywood in *The Ten Commandments*.

In other words, the story of the Bible is a meandering tale of many translations, interpretations, and decidedly human editorial decisions—not all widely agreed upon. The edition cited here, the New Revised Standard Version of *The New Oxford Annotated Bible*, is the one I was introduced to in college while studying the literature and history of the Bible. It is the result of extensive research and scholarship into the earliest known texts of the Bible by respected experts from a variety of faiths and offers valuable explanatory notes and editorial material about these ancient writings. For that reason, I recommend it. An alternative translation, also available from Oxford University Press, is the *Jewish Study Bible*, which features the Jewish Publication Society TANAKH translation.

SUMMARY

Spoiler alert! This story, which begins when God creates everything, does not end well. Adam and Eve are tossed out of Paradise. Their son Abel is done in by his older brother, Cain. Most of humanity drowns in the Flood, with the exception of Noah, his family, and an ark full of animals.

And we're just getting started. The first of the Bible's Five Books of Moses, Genesis offers a catalog of catastrophes. After wiping out most life on earth in the Flood, God repopulates the world. But when men attempt to build the tower of Babel reaching to the heavens, God frustrates this human attempt to be like gods and "confuses their language" as punishment— a legendary explanation for the world's many spoken languages. God then scatters humanity across the earth. Later a nomadic shepherd called Abram (later Abraham) is told by God to sacrifice his son Isaac, and he almost does. Esau is cheated out of his inheritance by his twin brother, Jacob. And Joseph has serious sibling rivalry issues with his eleven brothers and is sold into slavery.

In other words, the fifty chapters of Genesis cover a lot of ground and contain some of the most significant stories in religious history and Western tradition. Through highly dramatic narratives, Genesis recounts the history of the world, beginning with the Creation and the Fall of Man, and underscoring God's special relationship with the Jewish people who are descended from Abraham. He is promised by God that he will be the father of a great nation in whom "all the families of the earth shall be blessed."

Following the generations of Abraham's descendants—with the destruction of Sodom and Gomorrah thrown in there—Genesis concludes with the extended account of Joseph, famed for his "coat of many colors," or "a long robe with sleeves," according to the New Revised Standard Version. Sold into slavery by his jealous brothers, Joseph rises to become a trusted advisor to the Pharaoh.

Facing famine in their homeland, Joseph's brothers travel to Egypt, to be reunited with Joseph, and eventually bring their father, Jacob, and the people of Israel to live there. Genesis closes with Joseph's death at the age of 110, but with the expectation that these people will return one day to the land that God had promised to Abraham, Isaac, and Jacob.

ABOUT THE AUTHOR: UNKNOWN

While commonly described as the Books of Moses, the first five books of the Bible—Genesis, Exodus, Leviticus, Numbers, and Deuteronomy, and known as the Torah ("Law" or "Teaching") in Judaism—were not written down by Moses. We may logically assume that Moses, whose life story begins in Exodus, could not write of his own death or other events that occurred after his demise.

So, then, who wrote Genesis?

Centuries of archeology, scholarship, and research have concluded that the earliest sacred writings of Judaism were part of an ancient tradition passed along orally well before they were set down, just as the epic poems of Homer were sung before they were written. The process of recording these books dates to approximately 1000 BCE, based on stories that may go back another thousand years, drawing on legends, narratives, and folktales from Egypt, Mesopotamia, and other early civilizations.

Long-standing scholarly consensus holds that the earliest Hebrew scriptures were composed by five principal authors, or perhaps schools of writers and editors. Widely taught at leading religious and divinity schools, this concept is based on several distinctive writing styles and themes identified throughout the Five Books of Moses. Scholars commonly designate these "authors" by letters. In rough chronological order, they are:

- J, or the Jahwist: the oldest presumed source, dated between 950 and 750 BCE, known as J, for the German word *Jahwe*, translated in English as "Yahweh" and source of the English word "Jehovah," as well as its connection to Judah, one of two ancient monarchies. In his best-selling 1990 *The Book of J*, literary critic Harold Bloom contended that J was female. Besides contributing to the Books of Moses, Bloom argued, J may have also written an epic poem called the "Song of Deborah" found in the book of Judges. For these contributions, Bloom placed J alongside Homer, Shakespeare, and Tolstoy as a literary genius.

- E, the Elohist: so-named because this author preferred to use the word *Elohim* for God and may have been active between 850 and 800 BCE.

In *The Bible: A Biography*, biblical scholar and author Karen Armstrong writes: "The J and E authors interpreted the saga of Israel very differently, and later editors made no attempt to iron out these inconsistencies and contradictions. Subsequently historians would feel at liberty to add to the JE narrative and make radical alterations."

- D, the Deuteronomist: thought to have worked between 700 and 600 BCE, responsible, as you might guess, for the book of

Deuteronomy—fifth of the Five Books of Moses—and some of the later historical books of the Old Testament. Some scholars assert that D was the Hebrew prophet Jeremiah who lived from circa 650 BCE to 570 BCE.

- P, the Priestly source or author: Credited with "In the beginning," the P contribution is composed in formal language, and is especially interested with ritual observations and the duties of the ancient Jewish priesthood. Highly concerned with laws and religious observances, these sections are thought to have been written from 550 to 500 BCE.

- R, the Redactor or Editor: a group that took the existing strands of the texts and wove them together, probably around 400 BCE.

WHY YOU SHOULD READ IT

Whether you accept that Genesis is the "Word of God," or that it was composed and edited by a variety of authors over centuries, or that it is a collection of folktales and mythical stories told by a wandering ancient people to explain their world, you cannot dismiss its central place in world history, literature, and language.

Genesis is significant, first, as a foundational text for two of the world's principal monotheistic religions, Judaism and Christianity. Just as significantly, the narrative includes an account of Ishmael—Abraham's firstborn son—making Judaism's patriarch an ancestor of the prophet Muhammad, honored as the forerunner of Islam. For these reasons alone, an educated person must understand these stories and appreciate their impact.

Beyond recognizing its central significance in world religion, read Genesis for its amazing storytelling and lasting imprint on culture. Simply put, its stories are among the most important ever told and are at the center of much of Western history's intellectual traditions, literary themes, and religious tenets.

Many people have heard these stories told or mistold, or perhaps have seen Hollywood versions, without actually having read them. So read them for yourself. And to do that, you must begin at the beginning, with the Creation—both of them.

Yes, the book of Genesis contains two Creation accounts, separate and unequal. These two versions differ in literary style, details, and the order of the Creation. The first account in chapter 1 contains the familiar opening lines—cited earlier—and a six-day Creation, concluding with the appearance of humanity, male and female, at the same time, and unnamed:

in the image of God he created them;
male and female he created them.

After this, on the seventh day, God rests.

What follows is a very different rendering, which tells of Adam being made and Eve following later, the temptation of Eve by the serpent, and the first couple eating of the fruit of the tree of the knowledge of good and evil—no, not an apple. Scholars view these two variant accounts as clear evidence of different sets of authors, with the first account attributed to the Priestly source (P).

The second version is credited to J, whose narrative is thought to be the older, more folkloric version set in the Garden of Eden, a word meaning "delight." In the J version, a very human God walks about the garden in the cool of the day. Out of this garden flow four rivers, two of them identified as the Tigris and Euphrates in ancient Mesopotamia. In J's version, the order of creation is different, with man created before the animals and woman created later, formed from a rib a taken from the man. She is later tempted by the serpent to eat from the tree and shares the fruit with the man.

When an angry God asks the man if he has eaten the fruit, Adam doesn't hesitate to fatefully point a finger: "The woman whom you gave to be with me, she gave me the fruit from the tree and I ate."

Clearly, these Creation stories influenced the course of history and were central to cementing the second-place status of woman in powerful religious traditions. Various interpretations of other Genesis stories have also had enormous impact. They include the mistaken interpretation that

Canaan—the son of Noah's son Ham—was cursed to serve his brothers. In later interpretations, Canaan was said to be the ancestor of Africans and this "curse" was used as the biblical justification for the enslavement of Africans. Another is the tale of the legendary cities of Sodom and Gomorrah, destroyed by God for their "wickedness." Many scholars have refuted the idea that the "wickedness" of Sodom was a metaphor for homosexuality— hence the word "sodomy"—but for centuries this biblical tale served as the basis of viewing same-sex love as sinful.

WHAT TO READ NEXT

The obvious answer is to move on to the immediate sequel, the book of Exodus. The second book of the Bible introduces Moses after the people of Israel have been transformed in Egypt into a people in bondage. Born to a Hebrew mother, Moses is set afloat in a basket after the Pharaoh calls for all newborn Hebrew males to be thrown into the Nile. Rescued by the Pharaoh's daughter, Moses is raised as a prince of Egypt. After learning his true identity, Moses is directed by God to lead his people out of captivity, which he does in a series of miraculous events now marked as Passover. Following a long sojourn in the wilderness, Moses delivers the Ten Commandments.

In other words, this is also among the most significant narratives in history. Like Genesis, the book of Exodus describes events at the core of both Judaism and Christianity, and that are significant in Islam as well.

Beyond these two essential books of the Bible, you could read the Old Testament, or Hebrew Bible, in its entirety. But it can be rough sledding.* By all means, read the Psalms and Proverbs, for the richness of their language alone. And the Prophets, both major and minor, have provided spiritual sustenance and a source of faith for centuries. But if you prefer to cherry-pick, I recommend a few relatively short books from Hebrew scripture:

---

* In *Don't Know Much About the Bible* (New York: William Morrow, 1998), I offer a book-by-book summary of all of the books in both the Old and New Testaments, with an emphasis on their meaning, historical context, and impact on the course of human events.

- Ruth: a brief, charming tale of a woman who accepts the God of Israel, in a story emphasizing faith and familial loyalty

- Job: which raises the thorny problem of why bad things happen to good people and probes faith in the midst of suffering, a fairly universal theme

- Ecclesiastes: a philosophical treatise that also poses questions of existential weight about the meaning of human existence and opens with the despairing declaration that "all is vanity"—the author's way of asking what the point of life is

- Song of Solomon (Song of Songs): a collection of richly sensuous love poems exchanged between a man and woman that is said to represent the relationship between God and his people but does so in very evocative, often erotic language

In other words, there is a lot more to the Bible than your childhood religious education might have offered, if you had one. And if you did not learn about the essential stories and the language of the Bible, these books will certainly make you reconsider some of your assumptions—and perhaps gaze up at Michelangelo's paintings in the Sistine Chapel with different eyes.

"Who knows doesn't talk."

Tao Te Ching
(The Book of the Way)

— CIRCA 400 BCE —

Lao-tzu (Attributed)

Tao Te Ching: A Book about the Way and the Power of the Way, *Ursula K. Le Guin with J. P. Seaton, Boulder, CO: Shambhala, 1997; 126 pages. Among many other translations, I have also referred to* Tao Te Ching: A New English Version, *translated by Stephen Mitchell, New York: Harper Perennial Modern Classics, 2006; and* Tao Te Ching: The Tao and the Power, *translated by John Minford, New York: Viking, 2018*

OPENING WORDS

The way you can go
isn't the real way.
The name you can say
isn't the real name.

SUMMARY

In eighty-one succinct—but sometimes perplexing—verse entries, *Tao Te Ching* presents ancient Chinese wisdom about living a life of meaningful contemplation. Translated very roughly as "the way of integrity," *Tao Te Ching* celebrates living with honor, virtue, and what is now in vogue as "mindfulness." *Tao Te Ching* is also the basis for what would become Taoism (also spelled "Daoism"), a religion and philosophy that traditionally emphasizes living in harmony and balance with the energy that is within and guides everything in the universe.

Taoism, according to one recent translator, John Minford, "emphasized inner freedom, meditation, and the Self-Cultivation of the individual, surrender to the spontaneous rhythms of nature, primordial intuition, and exploration of the mysteries of the human condition and the wonders of the cosmos, listening to the silent music of the Tao."

These seemingly simple nuggets of Lao-tzu's teachings can be puzzling. For instance, in the third verse—"Hushing" in the late novelist and essayist Ursula K. Le Guin's version—Lao-tzu states:

When you do not-doing,
nothing's out of order.

On this central ideal of Tao, Ursula K. Le Guin comments: "Over and over Lao Tzu says *wei wu wei*: Do not do. Doing not-doing. To act without acting. Action by inaction. You do nothing yet it gets done. . . . The whole book is both an explanation and a demonstration of it."

In his translation, Stephen Mitchell dismisses the notion that "doing not doing" means passivity and discusses Lao-tzu's central concept as similar to entering the "zone": "A good athlete can enter a state of body-awareness in which the right stroke or the right movement happens by itself, effortlessly, without any interference of the conscious will. . . . The game plays the game; the poem writes the poem; we can't tell the dancer from the dance. . . . Nothing is done because the doer has wholeheartedly vanished into the deed."

At its heart, the ancient wisdom of *Tao Te Ching* lays out a path of living harmoniously, with a serene and generous spirit—as the last lesson says: "Wise souls don't hoard; the more they do for others the more they have."

ABOUT THE AUTHOR: LAO-TZU

Very little can be said with certainty or authority about the person who composed *Tao Te Ching*. Just as we have names but no real identities for the original authors behind *Gilgamesh*, Genesis, or the *Iliad* and the *Odyssey*, *Tao Te Ching* may have been compiled by multiple Chinese scholars over time and then attributed to the legendary Lao-tzu. Modern consensus holds that the work was first compiled around 400 BCE by one "Laozi," a philosopher whose name translates simply as "old master."

In one widely told ancient legend, the philosopher Laozi departs the kingdom of the Zhou dynasty and comes to a pass at the entrance to the state of Qin. In this apocryphal story, the guardian of the pass begs Laozi to write a book for him. Laozi writes a book in two sections of five thousand characters, in which he sets down his ideas about the Dao (literally "Way") and the *de* (its "virtue"). Then he disappears, according to ancient Chinese accounts.

"Nothing about it is certain," writes Le Guin, "except that it's Chinese, and very old, and speaks to people everywhere as if it had been written yesterday."

WHY YOU SHOULD READ IT

Laconic and sometimes mystifying, *Tao Te Ching* might sound to some like one of the most memorable lines in the *Star Wars* saga: When Yoda explains the Force to young Master Luke, he says, "Do. Or not do. There is no try."

So read it, as Le Guin did, for "the profound modesty of the language that offers what so many people for so many centuries have found in this book: a pure apprehension of the mystery of which we are part."

In the twenty-first century, when it seems that "*doing*" is what most occupies so many of us, this is a paradoxical instruction. Many people raised in a Western tradition are far more familiar with the "Thou shalt" and "Thou shalt not" approach to proper living. Alan Watts, a writer given much credit for introducing Eastern thought to America, once explained: "The West has no recognized institution corresponding to Taoism because our Hebrew-Christian spiritual tradition identifies the Absolute—God—with the moral and logical order of convention. This might almost be called a major cultural catastrophe, because it weights the social order with excessive authority."

Much to ponder. But "just do." That is the point. Read it to help develop awareness of ourselves and our surroundings, one of the central ideas in *Tao Te Ching*. It is not surprising, then, to find that Lao-tzu is cited often in *Wherever You Go, There You Are*, Jon Kabat-Zinn's best-selling book on mindfulness, first published in 1994.

The book forms the basis for Daoism, which became a powerful force in several Asian countries. But like other religions, Daoism was banned in China after the Communist takeover in 1949. However, it is now recognized as one of five faiths permitted in China—the others are Buddhism, Islam, Catholicism, and Protestantism—though all are strictly monitored by the Chinese government, according to the Council on Foreign Relations. Daoism is still widely practiced in Taiwan, Korea, and other Asian nations.

WHAT TO READ NEXT

Among the many available versions is translator Stephen Mitchell's popular *Tao Te Ching: A New English Version*. Mitchell's often differs from Le Guin's, underscoring the contrast between translation and interpretation; Mitchell cites the fact that more than one hundred English versions of *Tao Te Ching* had been produced by 1986. The Le Guin edition provides a list of some of the other notable translations made through history. Both Mitchell and

Le Guin emphasize that they have produced *versions*. In comparing these two without any sense of written or spoken Chinese, I was drawn to the poetic sensibility of Le Guin's interpretation.

Another and important corollary text in Chinese history to explore is *The Analects* of Confucius, a collection of aphorisms and wisdom brought together in 497 BCE by students of the most famous and influential Chinese philosopher besides Lao-tzu. According to legendary accounts, Confucius met Lao-tzu and acknowledged him as the Master. The teachings of Confucius are more focused on a moral code of proper behavior, with an emphasis on wisdom, self-knowledge, courage, and sincerity. Among his renowned sayings is "Do not impose on others what you yourself do not desire" (*Analects*, book 15, 24), the Confucian version of the Golden Rule.

I would also point to two other works of short nonfiction worth investigation. *The Way of Zen* by Alan Watts is important for its role in the introduction of Zen Buddhism, with its roots in Taoism, to Western readers in 1957. And *You Are Here: Discovering the Magic of the Present Moment* is one of many works by the late Thich Nhat Hanh, among the most prominent proponents of Buddhist thought and practice in recent history. A key figure in the modern mindfulness movement, Thich Nhat Hanh died in 2022 at age ninety-five.

"Some people live as though they are already dead," he wrote. "There are people moving around us who are consumed by their past, terrified of their future, and stuck in their anger and jealousy. They are not alive; they are just walking corpses. If you look around yourself with mindfulness, you will see people going around like zombies. Have a great deal of compassion for the people around you who are living like this. They do not know that life is accessible only in the here and now."

"You will have memories
Because of what we did back then
When we were new at this,"

Stung with Love:
Poems and Fragments

— CIRCA 610–570 BCE —

Sappho

New York: Penguin Books, 2009; translated with an introduction and notes
by Aaron Poochigian and with a preface by Carol Ann Duffy; 102 pages

---

NOTE: Since the discovery of additional fragments of Sappho's poetry in 2012, translating Sappho for a modern audience is something of a scholarly cottage industry. Among the more recent editions are *Sappho: A New Translation of the Complete Works* by Diane J. Raynor and André Lardinois, Cambridge, UK, Cambridge University Press, 2014.

EXCERPT

Sweet mother, I can't take shuttle in hand.
There is a boy, and lust
Has crushed my spirit–just
As gentle Aphrodite planned.

SUMMARY

Poignant, personal, and often erotic, these are the poems of Sappho, one of the few women of the Classical Greek era whose writings have survived the centuries. Elegant and refined, both sensual and sensuous, Sappho's verses plumb the heights and depths of passion and intimacy, fused with the fragrances and sensory delights of Lesbos, a large island in the Aegean Sea.

Whether describing a scene from the Trojan War from a woman's perspective or expressing the pain of unrequited love and the torturous delights of the lover and the beloved, Sappho's poems still speak plainly to us today—

You will have memories
Because of what we did back then
When we were new at this,

Yes, we did many things, then—all
Beautiful . . .

Timeless sentiments. "However," as translator Aaron Poochigian notes, "we are left to wonder just what beautiful things the speaker and addressee 'did back then' when they were young."

Writing in archaic Greek, Sappho may have created some ten thousand lines of poetry, but only about one hundred poems and poetic fragments are known today; at least 90 percent of her work has been lost. Imagine if instead of 154 Shakespearean sonnets, we possessed only 15—or only four of some forty plays attributed to him. "The greatest problem for Sappho studies is that there's so little Sappho to study," writes Daniel Mendelsohn in the *New Yorker*. "It would be hard to think of another poet whose status is so disproportionate to the size of her surviving body of work."

Frustratingly slim, this collection contains bits and pieces of two-thousand-year-old songs. And songs they were. Today we read Sappho in lines on a page, but her words were intended to be accompanied by a lyre, a handheld stringed instrument. This is, in essence, what "lyric poetry" means—words meant to be set to music and sung to the lyre. There is still debate over whether Sappho's "lyric poetry" was meant to be sung publicly or in private, and by one performer or a chorus.

There is no debate about her impact. For more than two thousand years, the work of the Greek lyric poet Sappho has inspired lovers, as well as other poets and writers. Even in ancient times, Sappho was renowned to other poets of the Greek and Roman Classical periods. Coming down through the ages, her collections of poems or mere fragments have inspired, besides other poetry, many myths and misconceptions about one of the few women artists from that time whose work has survived.

ABOUT THE AUTHOR: SAPPHO

In 1972, lesbian feminist activists Sidney Abbott and Barbara Love wrote a book called *Sappho Was a Right-On Woman*. Addressing both feminism and lesbianism, the title became a rallying cry among women on the barricades of the fledgling gay rights movement of the 1970s as well as mainstream feminism. Posters heralding the phrase helped make a modern icon of this somewhat mysterious Greek poet who lived more than two thousand years ago.

Yet, for a person whose name and birthplace have become part of the language, Sappho of Lesbos largely remains a cipher, an enigma. Her identity and life are concealed in the mists of a lost history. A mythology, fueled by centuries of speculation—and ancient snark—has sprung up around her life and work, leaving few certainties. She was, as critic Daniel

Mendelsohn wrote, "the seventh-century-B.C. lyric genius whose sometimes playful, sometimes anguished songs about her susceptibility to the graces of younger women bequeathed us the adjectives 'sapphic' and 'lesbian' (from the island of Lesbos, where she lived)."

But what else can we know? Scholarly agreement, including the chronology in the edition cited here, places her birth around 630 BCE and death around 570 BCE, in Mytilene on the island of Lesbos, the third-largest island in the Aegean Sea, near the coast of modern Turkey, and renowned for its wine and olive oil. A member of an aristocratic family, Sappho had three brothers, one of whom was a wine exporter who sailed to Egypt. One of her poems mentions a daughter, but according to some modern translators, the ancient Greek word can also be interpreted as "child" or "slave."

Beyond such basics, much of Sappho's life remains a legend. "No other woman from early antiquity has been so talked about, and in such conflicting terms. The sources are as sparse as the legends are manifold, and any attempt to distinguish between the two virtually hopeless," wrote Judith Schalansky in the *Paris Review*. "Every age has created its own Sappho. Some even invented a second in order to sidestep the contradictions of the stories: she was variously described as a priestess in the service of Aphrodite or the Muses, a hetaera,* a man-crazed woman, a love-crazed virago, a kindly teacher, a gallant lady; by turns shameless and corrupt, or prim and pure."

Sappho apparently lived much of her life in Mytilene. But during a time of political turmoil, she and her family fled or were exiled to Syracuse, in Sicily. Even her appearance is debated. One ancient source described her as beautiful; another, according to Schalansky, said she was "ugly, being dark in complexion and of very small stature."

---

* A *heataira* (Greek) or *hetaera* (Latin) was " a class of professional independent courtesan of ancient Greece. . . . Usually living fashionably alone, or sometimes two or three together, the *hetairai* enjoyed an enviable and respected position of wealth and were protected and taxed by the state." *Encyclopedia Britannica*.

At some point, Sappho returned from exile and founded a school or gathering place for girls, again according to Schalansky, as either "a women's circle in Mytilene, which may have been a cultish community set up to honor Aphrodite, a symposium of fellow females bearing an erotic attachment to one another, or a marriage preparation school for daughters of noble birth: no one knows for sure."

Nor is there even certainty about her sexuality. Was Sappho of Lesbos a lover of women? Not so fast, according to Daniel Mendelsohn. "However exalted her reputation among the ancient literati . . . Sappho was known primarily as an oversexed predator—of men," he writes. "This, in fact, was the ancient cliché about 'Lesbians': when we hear the word today we think of love between women, but when the ancient Greeks heard the word they thought of blow jobs. In classical Greek, the verb *lesbiazein*—'to act like someone from Lesbos'—meant performing fellatio, an activity for which inhabitants of the island were thought to have a particular penchant. Comic playwrights and authors of light verse portrayed Sappho as just another daughter of Lesbos, only too happy to fall into bed with her younger male rivals."

In fact, among the most popular and lasting legends of Sappho's love life was one about her passion for a handsome young boatman called Phaon, which supposedly led her to jump off a cliff. There is no evidence to support such a story. Sappho's life, like much of her verse, exists only in fragments.

WHY YOU SHOULD READ IT

Read it first for pleasure in the beauty and sensuality of Sappho's poetry. She employed recurring images of flowers, bright garlands, naturalistic scenes, altars smoking with incense, and perfumed oils for the hair and body. All of these were elements of rituals in devotion to Aphrodite, the ancient Greek goddess associated with love, lust, passion, and procreation. Yes, we are back to sex.

Sappho's lyrics also offer a distinct view of life in this extraordinary time, as Greece emerged as a center of culture in the Mediterranean world.

Consider, as Judith Schalansky writes in the *Paris Review*, "There are not many surviving literary works older than the songs of Sappho." She lived and wrote in a time not far from the recording of some of the earliest books of the Bible. But her point of view is distinct. Lyrical, romantic, and sensual, Sappho presents an extraordinary contrast to the tales of sin, murder, deception, and a punishing deity found in the book of Genesis (see entry).

In her pioneering work *Goddesses, Whores, Wives, and Slaves*, Sarah B. Pomeroy commented: "As a poet, she was inventive, using new poetic structures and meters, but she was a self-conscious artist too, often addressing herself. Although so little of her poetry survives, the power of her writing is great enough to show that she merits the praise she earned from antiquity, when Plato called her the tenth Muse, to the present." So, read it because it is among the earliest known existing remnants of a female artist. It is *lyrical poetry*, echoing the very human experience of love and desire that has animated poetry—and all literature—for all time.

WHAT TO READ NEXT

It is impossible to recommend more of Sappho's work, simply because none has yet been found. We must content ourselves with tantalizing bits and pieces currently available and hope that some enterprising archeologists eventually turn up some more stray mummy wrappings that add to the Sapphic library.

Unfortunately, there is sparse work by any women of the Classical era. Of a handful of known names from earlier periods in history, little writing survives. Other women who wrote were forgotten or ignored. So, to follow up on Sappho, I would suggest the Song of Solomon, mentioned after the discussion of Genesis (see entry). Contrast the love song considered "divinely inspired" in both Judaism and Christianity with the passionate verses of this Greek poet.

Finally, I suggest comparing the work of Sappho to that of American poet Emily Dickinson, whose fragmentary poems, many critics contend, evoke the lyrics of Sappho. "We know that the letters Emily Dickinson wrote to her friend and future sister-in-law Susan Gilbert had a series of passionate passages deleted from them, prior to publication, by her niece Martha, Gilbert's daughter, who omitted to indicate these deletions," Judith Schalansky writes. "One of these censored sentences, from June 11, 1852, reads: 'If you were here—and Oh that you were here, my Susie, we need not talk at all, our eyes would whisper for us, and your hand fast in mine, we would not ask for language.'"

"Warfare is the art of deception."

The Art of War

— LATE 6TH CENTURY BCE(?) —

Sun Tzu or Sun Tzi (Attributed)

New York: Norton, 2020; translated by Michael Nylan; 157 pages

OPENING WORDS

Arms are a vital matter for the ruling house, says Master Sun. As the arena of life and death, as the path to survival or ruin, this subject merits due reflection. Hence the five considerations that must always be kept before you when gauging the strength of the two sides and investigating the true conditions, so as to arrive at a good grasp of the situation: (1) the Way; (2) the heavens; (3) the earth; (4) the field commander; and (5) the regulations.

The "Way," by definition, refers to whatever allows the people and their superior to be of one will, and therefore willing to live or die with him, undeterred by danger.

SUMMARY

An ancient Chinese text, considered the earliest known guide to war and military science, *The Art of War* lays out fundamental rules for tactics and strategy on the battlefield. Some twenty-five hundred years old, the book continues to be widely read by world leaders, military commanders, and businesspeople—and is still considered essential reading at such places as the U.S. Military Academy at West Point.

In ten concise chapters—in Michael Nylan's translation—Sun Tzu discusses such concepts as the first calculations before going to battle, initiating and planning a battle, "attacks with fire," and the use of spies. In discussing the "Nine Kinds of Ground," for instance, Sun Tzu advises to "never attack the enemy on ground worth fighting for," advice that has been wisely followed—and foolishly ignored—many times throughout history.

Perhaps more important than its practical and tactical advice for navigating the battlefield is Sun Tzu's broader message of understanding the enemy and knowing oneself:

Know the enemy and your own,
And victory is in sight.

As Nylan writes, this sense of knowing who we are is "perhaps the most profound message derived from The Art of War."

ABOUT THE AUTHOR: SUN TZU

Translated variously as Sunzi or Sun-tzu, also spelled Sun Wu, the author of *The Art of War* is widely thought to be a military strategist and commander who served the Chinese state of Wu between 770 and 476 BCE. However, some scholars, including Nylan, contend that the text may have been written later, between 475 and 221 BCE, when China was divided into six or seven warring states.

Nylan further argues that the text is more likely a "composite" of wisdom accumulated over time and that Sun Wu is closer to a legend than an identifiable historical figure. Long credited with leading a great victory by deploying mass infantry in battle, instead of using noblemen in chariots, Sun Wu was a legendary hero, but he may not have existed at all or was a real person whose exploits were later greatly magnified. Nylan dismisses the "hero narrative" as lacking strong historical evidence. So add Sunzi to the ranks of those part-legendary warriors through history, such as the biblical King David or the legendary King Arthur, who were based on actual people and later draped in fabulous tales.

WHY YOU SHOULD READ IT

Most likely, Gentle Reader, you are not preparing to deploy troops, either to defend your land or to conquer a neighbor. You may not need, for instance, to follow this specific requirement for:

a thousand four-horse light chariots;
a thousand leather-clad carts;
ten thousand armored soldiers;
enough provisions for a thousand leagues.

And you are also not likely—like *The Sopranos'* Tony Soprano—to be fretting about the correct strategy for dealing with your Mob enemies. After an episode aired in which Tony told his therapist, Dr. Jennifer Melfi, that he had read Sun Tzu at her recommendation, the book was suddenly in wide demand. One publisher even issued an edition whose cover trumpeted: "As featured on *The Sopranos.*"

Since I was preparing for none of these eventualities, I first read *The Art of War* as a fascinating historical document. Studied by military tacticians throughout history, Sun Tzu has been notably influential for many centuries and is worth knowing on that basis alone.

The Art of War appeared in the West in the late eighteenth century, when it was translated into French by a Jesuit priest, and it is thought that Napoleon may have read the work. Military historians have suggested that it influenced his breakthrough approach to European warfare, although this conclusion is somewhat speculative.

The book clearly influenced military leaders over the centuries, though its impact is historically and morally complex. In 2014, retired Japanese admiral Fumio Ota wrote: "Europe first discovered Sun Tzu during the late 18th century. Wilhelm II, the emperor of Germany, supposedly stated, 'I wish I could have read Sun Tzu before World War I.' General Douglas MacArthur once stated that he always kept Sun Tzu's *The Art of War* and Walt Whitman's *Leaves of Grass* on his desk. At the end of the Cold War, the United States borrowed from Sun Tzu when it created 'competitive strategy,' which aimed to attack the Soviets' weaknesses with American strengths. This is exactly Sun Tzu's meaning when he said an 'Army avoids strength and strikes weakness.'" Ota argues that *The Art of War* still is studied by and influences the Chinese military.

But there is some ambiguity about the book's intent. As Nylan comments, "Like the general public, military men and textual scholars have long debated whether the ultimate message of *The Art of War* text is prowar or antiwar. By some accounts, Ho Chi Minh, his general Giap [Communist leaders of North Vietnam] and Mao Zedong scoured the text in order to plot their next strategic moves (although not a few dispute these claims). At the same time, the text urges upon its followers the notion that it is better to outthink the enemy than to fight him, in part because of the devastating costs of war." In other words, in offering strategy, the real advice offered is the importance of war as a last resort.

Apart from its intrinsic historical interest, *The Art of War* also offers intriguing insights into human psychology, which is one reason business leaders still flock to it. According to a 2015 *Business Insider* article, a tech CEO threatened with a hostile takeover by a rival CEO purchased copies for his company's team to gird for a business battle. "It's a smart book," opined *Business Insider* before distilling its advice for corporate leaders. "It's also poetic, repetitive, and arcane."

True, it does suffer a bit from being overly aphoristic. But the book highlights the fundamental importance of self-knowledge—another example of timeless wisdom.

WHAT TO READ NEXT

There are no other known writings by Sun Tzu, but anyone interested in military history and other influential theories on strategy for leaders might look to Niccolò Machiavelli's 1519 work by the same name. Unlike Machiavelli's more famous work, *The Prince* (see entry), this book was published during his lifetime. It offers a series of dialogues between Florentine aristocrats and humanists on the tactics of war and the author's belief in the importance of a citizen army, or militia, instead of reliance on untrustworthy mercenary forces.

Another influential text on military matters is *On War* (1833) by Karl von Clausewitz—admittedly, a much heavier lift than Sun Tzu or *The Prince*. It is notable for the author's famous dictum "War is not merely a political act, but also a political instrument, a continuation of political relations, a carrying out of the same by other means."

*"So if I had my way I wouldn't want to go too far in drinking and
I wouldn't advise anyone else to do so, especially when you've
still got a hangover from the night before."*

The Symposium

— CIRCA 385–370 BCE —

Plato

*New York: Penguin Books, 1999; translated with an introduction and notes
by Christopher Gill; 90 pages*

EXCERPT

Then Agathon, who happened to be lying on his own on the bottom couch,
said, "Come and lie down beside me, Socrates, so that, by contact with you,
I can share the piece of wisdom that came to you in the porch. It's clear you
found what you were looking for and have it now; otherwise you wouldn't have
stopped."

Socrates sat down and said, "How splendid it would be, Agathon, if wisdom was the sort of thing that could flow from the fuller to the emptier of us
when we touch each other, like water, which flows through a piece of wool from
a fuller cup to an emptier. If wisdom is really like that, I regard it as a great

privilege to share your couch. I expect to be filled up from your rich supply of fine wisdom. My wisdom is surely inferior—or rather, questionable in its significance, like a dream—but yours is brilliant and has great potential for growth. Look at the way it has blazed out so fiercely while you're still young; it was on display the other day, with more than thirty thousand Greeks there to see it."

SUMMARY

If it was called "Frat Party"—or even "Cocktail Party"—you probably wouldn't pay much attention to this essential piece of Classical Greek philosophy. But no, it is called a symposium, which may summon an image of tweedy professors, bespectacled intellectuals, and other wordy academics discussing weighty questions of existentialism, literature, and language in lofty terminology.

Told by Plato—one of the three greatest Greek philosophers, along with Socrates and Aristotle—this book is composed as a series of conversations at a lively drinking party in late fifth-century BCE Athens. It kicks off with a classic Athenian smackdown by Socrates of Agathon, a poet who has just won a prize and is also hosting the dinner. Soon after, "they then poured libations, sang a hymn, and performed all the other customary rituals, and turned to drinking." Then the men start talking about just how much they have had to drink. Not exactly the way I remember Philosophy 101.

As these Greek men, in loose tunics, recline on couches and drink some more, what follows is a discussion about love or, more precisely, eros—desire—or Eros, the god of love, and eventually, in particular, love between men.

As translator and editor Christopher Gill explains, "A marked feature of the *Symposium*, as of other early and middle Platonic dialogues, is the emphasis on sexual (or at least erotic) relations between males. . . . It is now accepted that 'homosexuality' is a modern, post-Freudian category. In ancient Greek culture, as in some others, there is a widespread assumption that male sexual and erotic desire may be directed, in a non-exclusive way, at males as well as females."

With its witty repartee among well-known Athenians of the time—
Plato's mentor, Socrates, sits center stage—it reads as if it could be performed as a drama. The scene is set as the men finish eating, have their hands
washed, then send the "flute girl" off to play for the women. Each of the
seven dinner companions, including the noted playwright Aristophanes, will
offer thoughts on love. Finally, Socrates sets everyone on the path toward
some universal truth by relating his conversation with Diotima, a legendary
priestess, who explains the highest form of love to Socrates:

> And why is reproduction the object of love? Because reproduction is
> the closest mortals can come to being permanently alive and immor-
> tal. If what we agreed earlier is right, that the object of love is to have
> the good *always*, it follows that we must desire immortality along
> with the good.

Diotima is not just talking about children. She goes on to explain that
men can be pregnant "in their minds" and bring forth wisdom and other
kinds of virtue by finding "a mind that is beautiful, noble, and naturally
gifted." She later continues: "People like that have a much closer partnership with each other and a stronger bond of friendship than parents have,
because the children of their partnership are more beautiful and more
immortal."

On this lofty note, a drunken gate-crasher, Alcibiades—a prominent
Athenian general—barges in on the arm of a flute girl, accompanied by
more drunken men. More drinking and a final speech by Alcibiades follow,
after which most of the men fall asleep and Socrates departs.

ABOUT THE AUTHORS: PLATO—AND SOCRATES

How to reduce twenty-five hundred years of debate and entire libraries
filled with books on Greek philosophy to a few pages of essentials about
Plato and Socrates?

Let's start with Socrates, teacher of Plato, who wrote *The Symposium*.
Born around 470 BCE, when Athens was reaching the height of its power

and prestige as a center of cultural, political, and economic growth, Socrates is widely regarded as the founder of Western philosophy and rational inquiry. The Athens of his day was in its Golden Age: some of the most influential figures in Greek theater, history, and medicine all lived from around 480 BCE to 404 BCE.

But in 431 BCE, during this time of relative peace, prosperity, and prominence, Athens entered a war with rival city-state Sparta. Known as the Peloponnesian War, it would continue for nearly thirty years; Athens was also devastated by an unidentified plague in 430 BCE, eventually bringing an end to that glorious era.

A veteran of the long wars between Athens and rival Sparta, Socrates had been a hoplite, or a soldier, in the Athenian infantry. Said to be stoic, fearless, and quite ugly, he was credited with saving the life of the Athenian general Alcibiades—the drunken character who appears at the conclusion of *The Symposium* and discusses his love for Socrates. Bravery in battle—not his philosophy—initially brought Socrates fame.

By the time he was in his late thirties, Socrates had a following among young Athenians impressed by his personality and views of life. Among these was the idea that everything we see, from a chair to such concepts as courage, goodness, or beauty, is illusory—mere shadows that represent a more perfect and changeless form of such ideas. To Socrates, the pure essence of these ideals was accessible only to the mind—and only logic and reason could reveal them. His chief antagonists were the masters of public speaking called Sophists, itinerant teachers who were less interested in seeking the truth than being paid to teach young Athenians the art of persuasion through rhetoric and oratory.

Claiming he was driven by a divine inner voice, Socrates never wrote anything. But he was certainly written about. One of his first literary appearances is in the play *Clouds* by Aristophanes, called the Father of Comedy, who is also one of the speakers in *The Symposium*. *Clouds*, mentioned in the dialogue, was written while Socrates was alive, and mocks him as one of the Sophists, a professional teacher who runs a "Think Factory" where young Athenians learn rhetoric to "make the weaker argument the stronger."

Most of what is known about Socrates's philosophy comes down through the dialogues composed by Plato, the second of the great Athenian philosophers. Socrates's greatest student—and the most significant witness to his life and thought—Plato was born into a wealthy, prominent, and influential Athenian family in 428 or 427 BCE. He became a follower and friend of Socrates. Once an aspiring playwright, Plato made Socrates his primary character, as he does in *The Symposium*.

It is easy to see why. "'The Socrates of Plato's works professes an exclusive commitment to making his fellow Athenians 'better' by urging them to examine their values and actions systematically, on the grounds that 'the unexamined life is not worth living, (*Apology* 38a),'" writes Professor Elizabeth Watson Scharffenberger, a specialist in Athenian culture. "He exhorts them to think and act in consistently virtuous, just, temperate, and courageous ways, even if such behavior endangers material prosperity and life itself (for example, *Apology* 29c–30b); he argues that the welfare and health of the soul are more important than any consideration of material comfort."

In many of Plato's dialogues, it is difficult to determine whose views are being presented: Do they belong to Socrates, or is the character of Socrates merely a mouthpiece for Plato's ideas? "So a halo of ambiguity surrounds the life of Socrates," as historian Daniel Boorstin put it. "The scholars' 'Socrates Problem' allows each of us to have our own Socrates. Besides the biographical memoir Plato had to invent a new literary form—the dialogue—to communicate the meaning of Socrates. . . . Then he used his dramatic talent to interpret a philosopher whose message could be carried only in the spoken word. For a philosopher whose mission was the discovery of ignorance, the Socratic dialogues provided a convenient vehicle."

And in those dialogues, Socrates made enemies. Like many gadflies who challenge authority and ask hard questions, Socrates irked the powerful. While he was friends with one of the so-called Thirty Tyrants who took control of Athens in 404 BCE after the city surrendered to Sparta, he refused to go along with the actions of these oligarchs, who were responsible for putting many Athenians to death.

In 399 BCE, Socrates was tried in Athens for "impiety and corrupting the youth." In his defense, he rebutted some but not all of these charges, making his famous declaration about "the unexamined life." Convicted, he might have chosen to escape or to suggest another form of punishment. Instead, Socrates drank the poison hemlock and died.

After the death of his mentor, Plato left Athens and traveled to Syracuse, an ancient city settled by Greeks on the island of Sicily. Inspired by Socrates, Plato sought a cure for the ills of society through inquiry. He arrived at the conclusion that society could not be fixed until philosophers were kings and kings were philosophers.

Returning to Athens in the early 380s BCE, Plato founded a school where he taught these ideas to the sons of wealthy Athenians. It was near a grove of trees named for Academus, a mythological Greek hero, and would come to be known as the Academy, the first formal site of philosophical teaching and considered the forerunner of the university. His most renowned student was Aristotle, who would later start a school of his own called the Lyceum.

Clearly drawn from Socrates, Plato's writings and teachings emerged as the basis for what was later called Platonism—a belief in eternal realities called Forms that existed apart from the changing things of the physical world. Explaining Plato's belief in the "sublime power of the intellect," philosopher Luc Ferry writes: "To attain a successful life—one which is at once good and happy—we must remain faithful to the divine part of our nature, namely our intellect. For it is through the intellect that we attach ourselves, as by 'heavenly roots,' to the divine and superior order of celestial harmony." Plato went on to write the philosophical dialogues, many featuring Socrates, that became the foundation of Western philosophy. The exact date and circumstances of Plato's death around 347 BCE remain unclear; in some accounts he died at a wedding feast and in another in his bed while a young girl played the flute.

While the grove of his Academy was destroyed by the Roman general Sulla in 86 BCE, Plato's "school" lasted some nine hundred years until the Christian emperor Justinian shut it down in 529 CE. Dismissed as "pagan" and mostly lost for centuries, Plato's work was not completely forgotten during the early Christian era. The Christian philosopher Augustine was influenced by certain of Plato's ideas, such as his argument for a "divine craftsman" in the dialogue *Timaeus* and the immortality of the individual soul. But it would take the rediscovery of many ancient Greek texts during the Renaissance to bring about a complete rebirth of the ideas of Socrates and Plato, among other significant Greek classics in mathematics, astronomy, and other sciences.

WHY YOU SHOULD READ IT

The Symposium is a perfect example of what I like to consider a "stepping-stone" book. It is short, relatively accessible, and deeply provocative. It may then lead to longer, more challenging works.

But first, it is a provocative discussion of sex, gender, and human instincts.

Its central subject—*eros*, desire, love—is about as universal as it gets. *The Symposium* raises essential questions about the meaning of "love"— a concept thought of very differently over time, from the most basic sexual desire to Christianity's "the greatest of these is love" and on to bell hooks's modern examination in *All About Love* (see entry). In other words, these ancient Athenians were discussing ideas that still confound us today.

We are in a moment when questions of gender conformity and sexual identity have moved from the academic world of biology, sociology, and psychology to a very open and angry political arena. When some people talk about a return to a "classical Western education," the relationship between older and younger Athenian men—the "lover" and the "beloved"—may not be what they have in mind.

As translator Christopher Gill writes, "The *Symposium*, together with some other Platonic and non-Platonic evidence for this period, gives special prominence to what we can call the 'erotic-educational' relationship. This is one between an older and a younger male, in which the older initiates the younger into 'virtue,' as understood in male citizen circles."

The Symposium offers a challenge to many contemporary views on gender roles, sex in society, and the place of same-sex love in Athens— and by extension, ancient Greece. As the men deliver their speeches, *The Symposium* explores ideas—both profound and profane—about the nature of love as a response to beauty and a cosmic force. Eventually, they lead to the views of Plato's mentor, Socrates, who advocates for an ideal of spiritual love.

Read it also to grasp what is known as the "Socratic method," the form of inquiry that Socrates used—framing himself as an ignorant questioner, then leading his students through a quest for objective truth. As Luc Ferry explains:

> Socrates proceeds to ask his interlocutors a stream of questions, usually to show that they are contradicting themselves, that their initial ideas or convictions do not hold water, and that they must reflect more if they are to get any further. . . . He makes a show of not knowing. He likes to play the innocent—let's say there is an Inspector Columbo side to his personality. But in truth he knows exactly where the interview is heading. This is not a level playing field: Socrates is pretending to be equal, whereas he has the advantage, that of the master over his pupil.

In a time when meaning-making was dominated by ancient superstitions about all-powerful gods, these Greeks began the greatest transformation in history—in which reason replaced faith in deities and Creation myths as the cause of all things.

It is this spirit of relentless questioning, so clearly displayed in *The Symposium*, that matters a great deal today. We need people who ask hard questions. Philosopher and writer Martha C. Nussbaum, one of the foremost authorities on Socrates, agrees on why Socrates matters:

> In a democracy fond of impassioned rhetoric and skeptical of argument, he lost his life for his allegiance to this ideal of critical questioning. Today his example is central to the theory and practice of liberal education in the Western tradition. . . . One of the reasons people have insisted on giving all undergraduates a set of courses in philosophy and other subjects in the humanities is that they believe such courses . . . will stimulate students to think and argue for themselves,

rather than defer to tradition and authority—and they believe that the ability to argue in this Socratic way is, as Socrates proclaimed, valuable for democracy.

The Socratic ideal, however, is under severe strain in a world bent on maximizing economic growth.

WHAT TO READ NEXT

Perhaps the next best choice is to read how Socrates defended himself. His courtroom speech is found in Plato's *Apology*, a dialogue often collected with other works by Plato, who was an eyewitness to the speech. Summarizing what Socrates said at his trial, professor of ancient philosophy M. M. McCabe explains the essence of his defense:

> Is it that life has its value when it just goes on for a very long time, without the things in it that make it valuable; or does it consist in the things that make it valuable? That's an agenda that Socrates proposes not only for Plato, but for every ethical theorist afterwards. You must explain what it is for a life to have value: until you can do that your ethical theories are empty and void.

Once through *Apology* and other shorter dialogues, you may try the heavy lifting in the most central of Plato's works in which Socrates is featured. It is not a short book. But *The Republic* is essential. It begins by asking what justice is and why the wicked often seem happier. It includes "The Allegory of the Cave," in which Socrates describes prisoners chained within a cave who can only see the shadows cast by a fire on the wall. Plato's most famous work is indispensable in any discussion of what kind of government is best.

"*The Republic* is really exploring what it would be to have good political rule," says Princeton professor Melissa Lane. "There are two desiderata: you want to have people who have the right moral character, who aren't wanting to get power in order to feather their own nests or to execute their enemies. That's very fundamental. You want people who are reluctant to rule. You also want people who understand the good, who understand the goals of rule, because if you're ruling, you're ruling for some purpose."

Moving on to contemporary work, I recommend University of Chicago professor Martha C. Nussbaum's *Not for Profit*. It is a timely and valuable book that makes a compelling case for the importance of the liberal arts, increasingly under fire. In a 2016 preface to it, she writes: "*Not for Profit* focuses on citizenship. I argue that the humanities and arts provide skills that are essential to keep democracy healthy."

And finally, another contemporary recommendation is *Rescuing Socrates: How the Great Books Changed My Life and Why They Matter for a New Generation*. It was written by Roosevelt Montás, who immigrated to America from the Dominican Republic, went to public schools in Queens, New York—where his mother worked a minimum-wage garment factory job—and then graduated from Columbia University, where he teaches. He writes:

> Every year, I witness Socrates bringing students—my high school students as well as my Columbia students—to serious contemplation of the ultimately existential issues his philosophy demands we grapple with. My students from low-income households do not take this sort of thinking to be the exclusive privilege of a social elite. . . . Socrates whispers to them not to mistake these marks of privilege for true expressions of merit and to find in their own intellectual integrity a source of self-worth and self-respect that surpasses any material advantage their peers might have over them.

*"In stories, what is impossible but believable is preferable
to what is possible but unconvincing."*

The Poetics (How to Tell a Story)

— 335 BCE —

Aristotle

How to Tell a Story: An Ancient Guide to the Art of Storytelling for
Writers and Readers, *Princeton, NJ: Princeton University Press, 2022; translated and introduced by Philip Freeman; 244 pages in a bilingual edition
including the original Greek*

OPENING WORDS

In this book we are going to discuss the craft of poetry—that is, of storytelling—
of all kinds, along with the power each kind of poetry can have. We will also
examine how to put together plots of high quality, the number and nature of
the parts that make up a story, and other topics of this sort.

Let us begin, as is natural, with basic principles.

Epic and tragic poetry, as well as comedy, dithyrambic poetry, and most
music played on pipes and lyre—these are all a kind of *imitation*.

But these arts differ from one another in their imitation in three ways—namely, they use different media, different objects, or different manners.

SUMMARY

Thank you, Aristotle. My work here is done.

Like every excellent teacher, the great Greek philosopher Aristotle starts out with the basics and explains exactly what he is going to teach you. Here he is going to tell you everything you need to know about telling stories. In this recent translation by Philip Freeman, a professor of humanities at Pepperdine University, the rules for writing laid down by Aristotle more than two thousand years ago are clearly organized and introduced with excellent explanatory notes. Subtitled *An Ancient Guide to the Art of Storytelling for Writers and Readers*, this is a master class in the art of poetry and drama whose rules might also apply to any kind of writing that aspires to art.

And let's face it: instead of using Aristotle's original—*Poetics*—titling this book *How to Tell a Story* makes it quite a bit more intriguing.

The "dithyrambic poetry" cited earlier—I looked it up so you don't have to!—refers to an early form of performance art: songs and dance publicly performed in rites honoring Dionysus, the god of wine, merriment, and theater, known as Bacchus to the Romans. "Dionysian" and "Bacchanalian" then meant fairly wild parties, or Classical "raves." The classics of Greek theater, including the works of Aristophanes, Euripides, and Sophocles, emerged later from these cultic rituals.

Explaining Aristotle's use of the Greek words for "poetry" and "poet," translator Philip Freeman notes: "These words can be limiting to modern readers since they have a more restricted use in our culture than in ancient Greece, where the medium for the presentation of most stories, including drama, comedy, and epic, was poetic verse, often accompanied by music."

Aristotle will explain, in Freeman's translation, such topics as: "Where Does Storytelling Come From?"; "The History of Tragedy"; "Plot Is the Most Important Thing"; and, in one of my favorite sections, "It's Not about You—Why Writers Should Stay out of the Story." "Homer deserves praise above other poets for many reasons," Aristotle explains, "but most of all because he knows when not to use his own voice. A storyteller should say as little as possible as a narrator."

ABOUT THE AUTHOR: ARISTOTLE

Aristotle was born in 384 BCE, in northern Greece, in what was then part of the ancient kingdom of Macedonia. His father, Nicomachus, was the physician to King Amyntas of Macedonia, the grandfather of Alexander the Great. At the age of seventeen, after the deaths of his parents, Aristotle moved to Athens to study at Plato's Academy. Becoming Plato's student, and later his colleague, he remained at the Academy for twenty years. (See preceding entry *The Symposium* for more on Plato.)

While Aristotle was in Athens, Philip II, king of Macedonia and father of Alexander, went to war with Athens. The Greek city-state eventually surrendered and Philip became the Macedonian master of the Greek world.

During his long stay at the Academy, Aristotle acknowledged his debt to Plato. But he began to respectfully disagree with some of his mentor's teachings. In particular, Aristotle distanced himself from Plato's theory of Forms—the concept that idealized forms of all things existed in a nonphysical essence outside the real world. After Plato's death in 347 BCE, Aristotle traveled for several years, eventually landing on the island of Lesbos, where he began to study marine life, a reflection of the fact that he was far more interested in the natural world—and what we would call the natural sciences—than in mathematics and Plato's purely philosophical approach. His approach represents a basic split in philosophy, still debated—how do we know what we know?: Do we gain knowledge by examining the world through rigorous rational questioning or by observation of that world?:

Even his works attacking Plato's theory of ideas reveal how deeply Plato had influenced him [comments Daniel Boorstin]. But he was not sympathetic to the emphasis on mathematics in the Academy, signaled by the legendary inscription over the entrance: "Only geometers may enter." "The moderns have turned philosophy into mathematics," Aristotle would later complain in the *Metaphysics*, "though they pretend one should study them for further ends.". . . Plato's grand other-worldly theme that denied the reality of the sensible world proved the perfect challenge, for Aristotle's practical spirit was obsessed with the range and variety of experience.

At the invitation of King Philip, Aristotle returned to Macedonia to become tutor to Philip's son Alexander, then a teenager. When Alexander became Macedonia's ruler and set out on his conquests of much of the known world, Aristotle returned to Athens. There he opened his own school, in 335 BCE, in a grove sacred to the god Apollo Lyceius. Known as the Lyceum, Aristotle's school placed a greater emphasis on the study of the natural world, rather than only the pure mathematics and philosophy instruction at Plato's Academy.

The distinction between the world views of the older Plato and younger Aristotle was made famous in a Renaissance painting by Raphael called *The School of Athens*. Hanging in the Vatican, near the Sistine Chapel, it depicts Plato pointing to the heavens as Aristotle gestures toward the ground—emphasizing the fundamental distinction in their approaches to philosophy. As historian Charles Freeman describes this contrast:

> Aristotle had arrived from northern Greece to study at Plato's Academy as a seventeen-year-old in 367 BC. He stayed there until 347 BC, gradually developing his own way of thinking, which moved well away from Plato's preoccupation with a "real" immaterial state of being towards the empirical study of the natural world. "There is something in all natural things," he once told his students when they showed disgust over a mound of decomposing cuttlefish that he assembled for them to study. "One should approach research on animals of whatever type without hesitation. For inherent in each of them is something natural and beautiful.

When Alexander the Great died in 323 BCE, Athens was no longer welcoming to Macedonians, including Aristotle. Knowing the fate of Socrates, who was tried and forced to drink hemlock by an Athenian court, Aristotle fled because, as Philip Freeman writes, "he would not let the Athenians sin against philosophy a second time as they had in killing Socrates."

Aristotle died in 322 BCE, in Chalcis on the Aegean island of Euboea. He left his library, including an enormous collection of his own writings, to his successor at the Lyceum. These included many of his surviving works, which are fundamental to modern philosophy and exerted tremendous influence on Western thought for centuries to come, from the medieval era to the Renaissance and down to modern times. Aristotle's known works— among them *The Politics*, *Ethics*, and *De Anima* (On the soul)—amount to about 1 million words. Scholars believe these represent only about 20 percent of his total output; the rest, at least 130 books, according to classicist Edith Hall, including the second book of *Poetics*, have been lost. (Speaking of lost books, Aristotle's *Comedy* is central to the complex medieval murder mystery in Umberto Eco's best seller *The Name of the Rose*.)

WHY YOU SHOULD READ IT

The first reason is pretty simple. Everyone should read some Aristotle at least once. He is the last figure in the triumvirate of Greek philosophers, along with Socrates and Plato, who have influenced—and in many ways dominated—Western thought for more than two thousand years. And I suppose if you are studying Greek—which I am not—this bilingual edition may be of great use in comparing the original to a clear, modern translation/interpretation.

How to Tell a Story, or *Poetics*, is a fairly gentle introduction to Aristotle. If you are a writer, or want to be a writer, or are a student of literature and drama, this accessible handbook is a fundamental source document. In a brief introduction to this book, Philip Freeman quotes the noted screenwriter and playwright Aaron Sorkin: "Rules are what makes (sic) art beautiful. . . . These rules also apply to writing. The rulebook is the *Poetics* by Aristotle. All the rules are there."

But a word of caution, here. Aristotle marks high on two of my benchmarks for inclusion in this series: consequence and timeliness. Aristotle's rules for writing have influenced writers throughout history—and still do. *How to Tell a Story* (*Poetics*), however, falls short on the questions of accessibility and reading pleasure. It can be rough sledding, at times. Keep in mind that Aristotle's writings read more like lecture notes than a carefully crafted piece of writing.

But as Professor Roosevelt Montás writes, "I read and loved Plato's dialogues in high school, but did not encounter Aristotle until my freshman year of college. That first encounter didn't go very well. Part of the problem was that the charm and beauty of Plato's writing had set the bar for what I expected of philosophy. . . . I warn my Contemporary Civilization students . . . that reading Aristotle can feel like chewing on cardboard. Don't expect enchantment from Aristotle."

Despite that warning—and, by the way, I don't think *Poetics* in this translation is quite as bad as a cardboard snack—give it a try. Reading Aristotle and gaining an acquaintance with his thinking is still a fundamental piece of a complete education. As Daniel J. Boorstin comments:

Aristotle's overwhelming influence was due not only to the amazing inclusiveness of his surviving works but also to his emphasis. While Plato had put him on the paths of philosophy, it was his reaction against Plato that gave him his distinctive appeal and explained how he suited the future of the West. Plato's appeal had been the charm of the ideal, the enduring, and the changeless. But Aristotle's interest in nature and experience led him to focus on a world of motion, change, and time. . . . For Aristotle, then, there was no real world of the static. When he saw the chicken, he imagined its coming from the egg. When he saw an egg he imagined a chicken.

WHAT TO READ NEXT

Aristotle wrote. A lot. And long. Many of his other most important and influential works are deep dives. You might next try *De Anima* (On the soul), a pioneering work on human consciousness in which he holds that all living things have a soul, which is their essence.

Rescuing Socrates, a 2021 book by Professor Roosevelt Montás, provides an accessible discussion of Aristotle, Plato, Socrates, and other philosophers. In it, he offers a powerful argument for studying the works of these men and the other so-called Great Books. Another excellent and relatively short introduction to Aristotle can be found in Edith Hall's 2019 book, *Aristotle's Way: How Ancient Wisdom Can Change Your Life*. In it, Hall writes:

When you read Aristotle describing people who are mean with money, or quick to anger, you see all-too-recognizable human types who behave just the same today. He is also a fine role model for people at any time of life. Not only did he make a success of his own life, family and friendships, but he even managed to survive the most turbulent political events to achieve his personal ambition . . . of founding an independent university and getting most of his ideas down on papyrus.

*"Know what your duty is
and do it without hesitation."*

The Bhagavad Gita

— 400 BCE–200 CE (?) —

Vyasa (Attributed)

New York: Harmony Books, 2000, Bhagavad Gita: A New Translation*;
translated by Stephen Mitchell with appendix by Mohandas K. Gandhi;
221 pages*

Note: There are many alternative translations of this ancient text. I have
also referred to *The Bhagavad Gita: A New Translation, Contexts, Criticism,* New York: Norton, 2015, translated with an introduction by Gavin
Flood and Charles Martin, 167 pages; and *Godsong: A Verse Translation
of the Bhagavad-Gita, with Commentary,* translated by Amit Majmudar,
New York: Alfred A. Knopf: 2018, 210 pages.

EXCERPT

The whole universe, all things
animate or inanimate,
are gathered here—look!—enfolded
inside my infinite body.

SUMMARY

Commonly translated from Sanskrit as "The Song of God," "The Song of the Blessed One," or the "The Song of the Lord," the *Bhagavad Gita* is an ancient foundational text of Hinduism. Often referred to simply as the *Gita*, and composed sometime between 400 BCE and 200 CE, it is a dialogue in verse between Arjuna, a warrior prince preparing for battle, and his friend and charioteer Krishna, who is revealed to be an avatar, or incarnation, of the god Vishnu.

While this book, or poem, stands alone, it exists as a relatively brief episode within the *Mahabharata*, a much longer Hindu epic. Written in Sanskrit, the *Mahabharata* is the longest known poetic saga, with "almost 100,000 couplets—about seven times the length of the *Iliad* and the *Odyssey* combined," according to *Encyclopedia Britannica*.

Like Homer's *Iliad*, the *Mahabharata* describes a war, in this case a dynastic struggle between two groups of warring cousins. These families are fighting over succession—now there's a timely topic—to the throne of the North Indian kingdom of Bharata. Unlike the lengthy fight for the Iron Throne in *Game of Thrones* or Homer's ten-year Trojan War or even the four seasons of HBO's saga of the Roy clan, *Succession*, this battle lasts only eighteen days. The narrative portrays the lives and deaths of heroes, battles, military strategy, and diplomacy in this war. In Hindu tradition and literature, the *Mahabharata* is considered as significant as Homer's *Iliad* and *Odyssey*, the Bible, or the works of Shakespeare are in Western literary traditions.

The *Gita*, on the other hand, consists of a mere seven hundred numbered verses, divided into eighteen chapters. As it opens, the opposing sides in the *Mahabharata* war stand ready to begin battle. But Prince Arjuna, hero of one of the warring families, despairs at the thought of having to kill his opponents who are, in this case, also his kinsmen. "After Hamlet," Arjuna is "literature's greatest ditherer," wrote critic Parul Sehgal in the *New York Times*, who also described the *Gita* as "an apologia for war embraced as a classic of pacifism. A holy book admired by scientists."

Refusing to fight, Arjuna lays down his bow. His friend and charioteer Krishna then counsels Arjuna that he must do his duty as a warrior and noble person. As their dialogue continues, Krishna will eventually reveal himself to be an avatar, a human incarnation of the Hindu deity Vishnu. He will instruct Arjuna on the essential battle within the soul of the individual. This conversation makes the book an essential text of Hinduism.

ABOUT THE AUTHOR: VYASA

Like the Greek bard Homer, Moses of the Five Books of Moses, Sun Tzu, and Lao-tzu, the poet Vyasa is a legendary figure. The notion of a traditional author's biography simply does not apply to the person called Vyasa.

The name literally translates as "Arranger" or "Compiler" in Sanskrit, the ancient Indo-Aryan language of classical Hinduism. Said to have lived around 1500 BCE, Vyasa was a legendary sage credited with composing the longer *Mahabharata*. "But there is general scholarly consensus that in its original form it was an independent poem," translator Stephen Mitchell writes of the *Gita*, "which was later inserted into its present context, Book Six of India's national epic, the Mahabharata."

In his 2018 translation, *Godsong*, Amit Majmudar writes: "Did Krishna 'really' sing it? Did Vyasa, the poet of the *Mahabharata*, transcribe it? Does Vyasa even exist, or is he like Homer, a construct? Was the Gita written centuries later by that omnipresent genius, Anonymous? . . . None of this matters to our experience of the Gita."

WHY YOU SHOULD READ IT

In his classic account of the making of the atomic bomb, historian Richard Rhodes described what happened when the first atomic bomb was successfully tested in New Mexico's desert on July 16, 1945. Robert Oppen-heimer, the brilliant theoretical physicist who led the development of the weapon, recalled the moment that the Atomic Age opened, as recounted by Rhodes in *The Making of the Atomic Bomb*:

> We waited until the blast had passed, walked out of the shelter and then it was extremely solemn. We knew the world would not be the same. . . . I remembered the line from the Hindu scripture, the *Bhagavad-Gita*: Vishnu is trying to persuade the Prince that he should do his duty and to impress him he takes on his multi-armed form and says, "Now I am become Death, the destroyer of worlds." I suppose we all thought that one way or another.

Translator Stephen Mitchell renders this famous line, 11.32, as:

> *I am death, shatterer of worlds,*
> *Annihilating all things.*

Oppenheimer is one of a wide range of luminaries who have com-mented on the power and insights of the *Gita*. Ralph Waldo Emerson and Henry David Thoreau were also impressed by the work, which was first translated into English by Charles Wilkins in 1785. In the twentieth century, poet T. S. Eliot was profoundly influenced by the *Gita* and other Hindu texts. This inspiration is reflected in some of his most famous works, including *The Waste Land* and particularly *Four Quartets*. As translator Stephen Mitchell noted, T. S. Eliot ranked the *Gita* "second only to the Divine Comedy" as a philosophical poem in a 1929 essay on Dante.

One of the most consequential readers of the *Gita* was Mohandas K. Mahatma (Great soul) Gandhi, the man who led India to independence in 1947 through nonviolent civil disobedience. While it might seem con-tradictory for the great prophet of nonviolence to celebrate a poem about war, Gandhi wrote:

The author of the Mahabharata has not established the necessity of physical warfare; on the contrary, he has proved its futility. He has made victors shed tears of sorrow and repentance, and has left them nothing but a legacy of miseries.

In this great work, the Gita is the crown. Its second chapter, instead of teaching the rules of physical warfare, tells us how a perfected man is to be known. In the characteristics of the perfected man of Gita, I do not see any to correspond to physical warfare. . . . In Hinduism, incarnation is ascribed to one who has performed some extraordinary service to mankind.

In the second chapter that Gandhi has singled out, Krishna tells Arjuna:

Know what your duty is
and do it without hesitation.

The god then urges the mortal Arjuna to behave as a warrior must in this great battle, with the promise that heaven's gates will open to him for having done what is right.

First introduced to the book as a student, Gandhi eventually translated the *Gita* from its original Sanskrit into Gujarati, his native Indo-Aryan dialect, in 1929. He is said to have listened to a recitation of the *Gita* in the hours before an assassin shot him on January 30, 1948. And then, as Gandhi lay dying, the *Gita* was again read to him. Professor Uma Majmudar, a specialist in Gandhi, wrote: "No other book or scripture influenced Gandhi, shaped his character, and transformed his life as profoundly and permanently as did the Bhagavad Gita. Among the many books he read, 'Gita' alone became an unfailing source of strength and solace to him in the darkest hours of his life. As a spiritual reference book, the Gita was not only his constant companion, it was his 'eternal mother' whom he esteemed even more than his earthly mother."

To readers unfamiliar with Hindu theology and philosophy, and especially those raised within the traditions of Judeo-Christian religious thought, the notion of a "friendly," even benevolent, deity telling a man to kill his enemies as part of his duty might seem contradictory. Yet the Old Testament is filled with accounts of exhortations to kill whole nations as a sort of holy obligation. And both Christianity and Islam possess significant episodes of blood-soaked history.

Like many ageless works of religion and spirituality, the *Gita* is complex in its worldview and perhaps at times seemingly contradictory. Its subtleties demand careful rereading and study. But the effort is useful for its literary value and insight into a deeply influential exploration of an ancient faith. In a recent English translation, Amit Majmudar offers this rationale for reading the poem: "The Gita imagined a relationship in which the soul and God are equals. It's a relationship mostly missing from every other scripture: friendship."

Among the profound insights to be found in the *Gita* is the essence of the Hindu view of life and death. Sunita Puri, a palliative care physician and author, offered this compelling rationale for appreciating the work: "My parents, both Hindus, had taught me that understanding death as inevitable is necessary to appreciate the meaning and beauty of life. . . . The *Bhagavad Gita*, which my father had read to me as a child, emphasizes that change is the law of the universe. . . . I'd expected, partly as a result of my medical training, to change and control what wasn't necessarily mine to change and control. How might I doctor my dying patients differently if I remembered that everything worldly—a painstakingly crafted mandala, a sky ablaze with color, our fragile human lives—is also temporary and subject to change?"

WHAT TO READ NEXT

For the daring, there are complete versions of the *Mahabharata*, as well as abridged editions, including a Penguin Classic, in which the *Bhagavad Gita* appears. Besides the complete *Mahabharata*, two other essential pieces of Indian literature are the Rigveda, a collection of Sanskrit hymns, and the *Ramayana*, another epic poem. Dated to about 500 BCE, written in Sanskrit, and attributed to the sage Valmiki, the *Ramayana* tells the story of Rama, a prince whose father exiles him because of a dispute over a throne.

Like Homer's *Iliad*, the *Ramayana* is largely about a war over a woman. Its central plot is about the conflict between Rama and Ravana, a demonic king who abducts Sita, Rama's beloved wife. Enlisting the aid of an army of monkey soldiers led by Hanuman, a monkey general, Rama goes to war to rescue his wife.

"Do not judge, and you will not be judged; do not condemn,
and you will not be condemned. Forgive, and you will be forgiven;
give, and it will be given to you."

The Gospel According to Luke

— CIRCA 65–85 CE —

Author Unknown

The New Oxford Annotated Bible, *New Revised Standard Version, edited
by Bruce M. Metzger and Roland E. Murphy, New York: Oxford University
Press, 1991; 47 pages*

EXCERPT

In the sixth month the angel Gabriel was sent by God to a town in Galilee
called Nazareth, to a virgin engaged to a man whose name was Joseph, of the
house of David. The virgin's name was Mary. And he came to her and said,
"Greetings, favored one! The Lord is with you." But she was much perplexed
by his words and pondered what sort of greeting this might be. The angel
said to her, "Do not be afraid, Mary, for you have found favor with God. And
now, you will conceive in your womb and bear a son, and you will name him

Jesus.* He will be great, and will be called the Son of the Most High, and the Lord God will give to him the throne of his ancestor David. He will reign over the house of Jacob forever, and of his kingdom there will be no end."

NOTE: A BRIEF HISTORY OF THE NEW TESTAMENT

The Gospel according to Luke is a book in the New Testament of the Christian Bible. So, again, we begin with that basic question: "Which Bible?" Library and bookstore shelves groan under the weight of competing versions of the "Good Book" or "Greatest Story Ever Told," accepted as holy scripture by Christians, including many who consider it "infallible"—that is, fully trustworthy—or "inerrant," meaning free from any errors.

As previously noted in the entry on Genesis, the earliest books of the Bible—those that Christians call the Old Testament—were passed down orally for centuries before being inscribed in archaic Hebrew. These sacred writings would have been familiar to Jewish people living in the Roman world around the time of the birth of Jesus—a date that cannot be fixed with any certainty, just as the precise date of Jesus's death is unknown.

The New Testament is concerned with the life, death, and teachings of Jesus, the central figure in the New Testament and in Christianity. It opens with the four accounts of Matthew, Mark, Luke, and John, all followers of Jesus. Jesus himself left no known writing. There are precious few references to his life and death outside the biblical record, and none are contemporaneous. Among the early communities of Jesus's followers, accounts of his life, teachings, and miraculous deeds were circulated orally.

As time passed, these narratives were recorded on scrolls written mostly in Greek and some Aramaic—a variant of Hebrew, which Jesus would have spoken. Many of these "books" codifying the teaching of Jesus, along with the letters written by early Christian leaders and other first-century Christian writings, were copied by hand and circulated widely among ancient

---

* Jesus is the Greek form of the Hebrew name Joshua.

communities across Middle East and the Mediterranean world. Unlike the
Hebrew scriptures, which span many centuries, these books cover less than
a century in time.*

Eventually, twenty-seven of these writings would be fixed as "canonical"—
officially recognized as sacred texts—and become Christianity's New Testament. They include:

- the four Gospels, from the Anglo-Saxon *gōd-spell*, for "good tidings"—
  Matthew, Mark, Luke, and John—which recount the birth and life of
  Jesus, his teachings, miraculous acts, death, and resurrection. Although
  Mark is placed second, it is widely considered to be the earliest
  Gospel, composed around 70 CE—a significant date as it followed
  the Romans destroying the Temple in Jerusalem after suppressing a
  Jewish revolt.

- the Acts of the Apostles, describing the establishment of the early
  Christian church.

- twenty-one letters—or Epistles—written to be shared among the
  early Christian communities. It should be noted that while the
  Epistles follow the Gospels in the ordering of these books, many
  were probably written before the Gospels were composed.

- a final book, Revelation, offering an apocalyptic vision—from the
  Greek *apokalypsis*, "revelation"—of the ultimate return of Jesus Christ
  and setting forth God's will for the future, thought to be written
  during the reign of the Roman emperor Domitian (81–96 CE).

There are some five thousand Greek manuscripts known to contain
all or part of the New Testament, some of them copies made as late as the

---

* For a more complete history and summary of the books in the New Testament, see *Don't
Know Much About the Bible* (New York: William Morrow, 1998).

Middle Ages. During the second century, many early churches had begun to recognize some of these writings as divinely inspired and authentic. Other "gospels" and letters were set aside as lacking authority, or were even considered dangerous heresies (see *The Gnostic Gospels* entry). In the fourth century, a series of church councils, such as the First Council of Nicaea in 325, began selecting which books were canonical. Shortly after that, Emperor Constantine commissioned fifty Bibles in 331, but the formal list was still not set. In 367 CE, Athanasius, the Bishop of Alexandria, Egypt, named the twenty-seven books that are now recognized as the New Testament and used the word "canonized" to describe them.

After the Roman Empire was Christianized, a Christian cleric named Jerome, who was later sainted, began a Latin translation of both Old and New Testaments in 382 CE. Known as the "Vulgate"—a Latin word for a commonly used language—Jerome's version became the standard of the Roman Church. (It should be noted that the Eastern churches had various different lists of the approved Gospels.) During the Protestant Reformation, more than one thousand years later, the Bible was translated into commonly spoken languages, including Martin Luther's German version—which changed the ordering of the New Testament books—and English-language translations, the most prominent being the King James Version of 1611. These various translations from Hebrew and Greek to Latin and then to other commonly spoken languages, and the decisions made over centuries to exclude some writings as noncanonical, led to errors and inconsistencies over which biblical scholars still argue.

"The Christian scriptures were written at different times, in different regions and for very different audiences," biblical historian Karen Armstrong writes, "but they shared a common language and set of symbols, derived from the [Hebrew] Law and the Prophets. . . . They brought together ideas that originally had no connection with one another—son of God, son of man, messiah and kingdom—into a new synthesis. The authors did not argue this logically but simply juxtaposed these images so repeatedly that they merged together in the reader's mind."

SUMMARY

The Gospel of Luke depicts the life, teachings, and miraculous works of Jesus, who is presented as the divine-human Savior, or Messiah. Beginning with the birth of Jesus's cousin, John the Baptist, the gospel offers a comprehensive account of the major events in Jesus's life, beginning with his birth in a Bethlehem stable to Mary and Joseph where the child was laid "in a manger, because there was no place for them in the inn."

It is all here, a life told in episodes. Luke's version continues with Jesus's circumcision and presentation in Jerusalem's Temple, his boyhood, and then his adult baptism by John when a heavenly dove descended on Jesus and a voice said, "You are my Son, the Beloved, with you I am well pleased."

This divine moment of recognition is followed by the Temptation, as Jesus is confronted by the devil during forty days in the wilderness. Luke then provides a genealogy of Jesus's lineage dating back to Adam, the first man, and goes on to recount Jesus's activity in the region of Galilee where he gathers twelve disciples and begins his relatively brief ministry as an itinerant teacher and healer. The book culminates in Jesus's journey to Jerusalem for the final week of his life. Building to its account of the Last Supper and Jesus's crucifixion, burial, and resurrection—celebrated as the Christian holiday of Easter—the Gospel of Luke concludes as Jesus is "carried up into heaven."

ABOUT THE AUTHOR: UNKNOWN

Who was Luke? As with many of the books of the Bible, there is precious little evidence to say who actually wrote the Gospel of Luke. Though attributed to a man named Luke, the work is considered anonymous by biblical scholars because what little is known of and accepted about him comes only from Christian traditions. Early Christians held that Luke was a physician—translated from the Greek for "one who heals"—and a friend of the Apostle Paul, a Syrian Jew known as Saul who persecuted early Christians until he underwent a miraculous conversion.

As Paul, he became Christianity's most successful promoter, especially in the non-Jewish world, and wrote fourteen of the twenty-one New Testament Epistles, or letters. Two of these mention Luke, called "the beloved physician" and a Gentile convert. Luke may have traveled with Paul on his wide-ranging missionary travels to centers of the early Christian church.

Whoever composed Luke's Gospel was well educated and wrote in the polished style of Classical Greek literature. That same author is credited with compiling the Acts of the Apostles, which together with the Gospel of Luke account for about one-quarter of the New Testament. The Acts of the Apostles describes events after the resurrection in which Jesus's followers begin to form what would emerge as a new faith separate from Judaism. It is widely thought that these two books, Luke and Acts, were meant to be read together, but the later compilers of the New Testament inserted the Gospel of John between them to keep the four Gospels together.

WHY YOU SHOULD READ IT

Why Luke? Why not Matthew, Mark, or John?

Many Christians grow up hearing the New Testament stories of the life of Jesus as a seamless narrative, told in countless Christmas pageants and Hollywood histories. They are unaware that significant differences exist in what are called the Gospels. But they do. The author of Luke presents what is perhaps the smoothest, most readable, and most comprehensive account of the life and ministry of Jesus.

The fact that Luke's author was attempting to address a largely non-Jewish—or Gentile—audience may be one reason the Gospel of Luke is so accessible. Luke's text also possesses the ring of historical authenticity, citing Jesus's age—"about thirty"—when he began preaching. For these reasons, if you are going to read only one Gospel, Luke is a good place to start.

Besides narrating Jesus's life, numerous miracles, teaching stories, and parables—such as the Good Samaritan and the Prodigal Son, both exclusive to Luke—Luke's version of Jesus's words offers the essence of Christian faith in a dramatic and highly detailed narrative.

Luke includes episodes of Jesus's final journey to Jerusalem not found in the other Gospels. His three final chapters, devoted to the events leading up to Jesus's arrest, trial, and execution, are followed by an account of the resurrection, the empty tomb, and Jesus's subsequent appearance to his followers. For those unfamiliar with these events, or their centrality to Christianity, Luke provides a skillful rendering of the final days of Jesus of Nazareth.

WHAT TO READ NEXT

The obvious answer is to read the other three Gospels: Matthew, Mark, and John. Matthew and Mark generally agree with Luke on details in Jesus's life, and together these three narratives are known as the "Synoptic Gospels," from the Greek word *synoptikos*, for "viewing together." While they describe many of the same events, these narratives offer the slightly differing perspectives of each Gospel's author, sometimes with differing emphasis. But despite their similarities, these Gospels also have some significant disparities. Read and compare.

The Gospel of John, however, differs markedly from the other three in both its literary style and some of the events it catalogs. Its opening lines, referred to as "The Prologue," are poetic and mysterious: "In the beginning was the Word, and the Word was with God. He was in the beginning with God" (John 1:1–2). This opening passage clearly connects Jesus ("the Word") back to the Creation in Genesis.

How these Gospels differ serves to remind us that the Bible is a book of faith—not journalism, history, or biography. And there is no question that these books changed the world.

"Learn to ask of all actions, 'Why are they doing that?'
Starting with your own."

Meditations

— DATED TO THE 170S CE —

Marcus Aurelius

New York: Modern Library, 2003; a new translation, with an introduction,
by Gregory Hays; 191 pages

EXCERPT

When you wake up in the morning, tell yourself: The people I deal with today
will be meddling, ungrateful, arrogant, dishonest, jealous, and surly. They are
like this because they can't tell good from evil. But I have seen the beauty of
good, and the ugliness of evil, and have recognized that the wrongdoer has a
nature related to my own—not of the same blood or birth, but the same mind,
and possessing a share of the divine. And so none of them can hurt me. No one
can implicate me in ugliness. Nor can I feel angry at my relative, or hate him.
We were born to work together like feet, hands, and eyes, like the two rows of

teeth, upper and lower. To obstruct each other is unnatural. To feel anger at
someone, to turn your back on him: these are obstructions.

SUMMARY

A series of ethical, spiritual, philosophical, and practical reflections composed by a sitting Roman emperor, *Meditations* has come down through
the centuries as a source of wisdom, insight, and real-world guidance.
Written in a style similar to journal entries—and perhaps not meant to
be read by others, as translator Gregory Hays suggests—these thoughts
and personal admonitions offer general prescriptions on how to comport
oneself in the world.

The twelve books in *Meditations* begin with "Debts and Lessons"—notes
of gratitude to the author's family and mentors, and then his schooling. It
serves as the most autobiographical of the "meditations," in contrast to the
later books, which explore large ethical and philosophical questions about
living correctly and doing what is right. The two following books are "On the
River Gran, among the Quadi" and "In Carnuntum"; the remaining books
are numbered 4 through 12.*

Meditations does not progress toward some cosmic final answer but
instead collects the themes, concerns, and questions that preoccupy Marcus
Aurelius. Many of these reflections might be summed up in these lines
from book 8:

> For every action, ask, How does it affect me? Could I change my mind
> about it?
>
> But soon I'll be dead, and the slate's empty. So this is the only
> question: Is it the action of a responsible being, part of society, and
> subject to the same decrees as God?

---

* Valuable and necessary notes explaining Greek traditions, Roman history, place-names,
and contemporary personalities are provided in this edition.

In all of his "meditations," Marcus Aurelius draws deeply on a school of ancient Greek philosophy called Stoicism that enjoyed wide prominence in Roman life. Founded in Athens by Zeno of Citium around 300 BCE, Stoicism holds that the universe is a logical system. "The basic assumption of Stoicism was that extreme emotion, possibly destructive emotion, was to be shunned; the wise man would free himself from anger, jealousy, and other distracting passions and live in a state of calm and contemplative peace," critic Robert Hughes explains in his history of Rome. ". . . only in this way could he see what was true and guide his actions appropriately."

For Trekkies, think Mr. Spock in a toga. Logic rules.

ABOUT THE AUTHOR: MARCUS AURELIUS

If the sum of your knowledge of the Roman emperor Marcus Aurelius comes courtesy of the film *Gladiator*—love it, by the way—stop right there. That is the Hollywood history in which Marcus Aurelius is done in by his son and successor, Commodus. It ain't necessarily so.

Marcus Aurelius was born Marcus Annius Verus on April 26, 121 CE, in Rome during the reign of the emperor Hadrian. At Marcus Verus's birth, his paternal grandfather was a member of the patrician class and served in official roles, including as consul, the highest elected office, in imperial Rome and his maternal grandmother was the heiress to an enormous fortune. One of his aunts—his father's sister—was married to the future emperor; Marcus was eventually named his successor and would take the name Caesar Marcus Aurelius Antoninus Augustus.

In plain terms, he was born to privilege and power at the center of Rome near the peak of its supremacy in the ancient world—the period known as Pax Romana. This was a two-hundred-year-long run of relative peace and prosperity that ended not long after Marcus Aurelius died.

Tutored in the classics of Greek and Roman literature, Greek rhetoric, Latin oratory, and Roman law, Marcus became emperor at age forty, when Antoninus died on August 31, 161 CE. Once emperor, Marcus honored his uncle's wishes with the appointment of his younger adopted brother, Lucius Verus, as co-regent.

Traditionally cast as one of the "good emperors"—so named by Niccolò Machiavelli—Marcus Aurelius ruled Rome for nineteen years, until his death in March 180 CE. While persecution of Christians in Roman provinces grew during his reign, there is no evidence to suggest that Marcus was personally responsible for the policy. Illegal since the early second century, Christianity faced greater official persecution later in the second century when Marcus ruled. But as editor and translator Gregory Hays argues, "Marcus himself was no doubt aware of Christianity, but there is no reason to think that it bulked large in his mind."

Although Marcus had no military experience, Roman armies would fight a long series of wars during his reign, part of an effort to stabilize the empire against growing threats from restive regions. As often happens during far-flung conflicts, these wars had unintended consequences. In fighting the Parthians (in what is now Armenia), co-regent Verus and his troops may have brought back the first devastating pandemic to strike Rome. Known as the Antonine Plague, some evidence suggests that it was smallpox, and it was responsible for as many as 10 million deaths over the course of several years; Verus, who died in 169, may have been among its victims.

During an ongoing series of battles with Germanic tribes, Marcus Aurelius died of unknown causes in his military quarters on the Danube in 180 CE. His eighteen-year-old son, Commodus, named co-regent three years earlier, succeeded his father. While it made for a good plot line in *Gladiator*, there is no evidence Commodus committed patricide. Commodus himself was assassinated in 192.

WHY YOU SHOULD READ IT

Why read the two-thousand-year-old musings of a Roman emperor? Marcus Aurelius was a "philosopher king"—Plato's ideal ruler, combining political skill with knowledge. Aurelius set out to answer an ancient philosophical question—how to be good—in a very practical manner. He sought to understand how to confront a world that seems to be conspiring against one's best intentions. *Meditations* is his self-reflective guide to self-improvement—as translator Gregory Hays writes, these entries were "composed to provide a momentary stay against the stress and confusion of everyday life: a self-help book in the most literal sense." Read Marcus Aurelius to see how a man who may have been the most powerful individual of his time—certainly in the world controlled by Rome—responded to the trials and problems he confronted.

Starting with the fundamental proposition that nothing in life is permanent, *Meditations* is, in part, a call to live intentionally and humbly. "And this too:," he writes in book 7, "you don't need much to live happily. And just because you've abandoned your hopes of becoming a great thinker or scientist, don't give up on attaining freedom, achieving humility, serving others, obeying God."

These are ideas—how to behave in the face of stress and difficulty, pandemic and war—represented elsewhere in this collection by a wide variety of books and writers, such as the *Bhagavad Gita*, *The Book of the Way*, Thoreau, and Viktor Frankl.

Lao-tzu said, in Ursula K. Le Guin's interpretation:

Need little,
want less.

I think it fair to say that Marcus Aurelius would have agreed with his Chinese predecessor in his *Meditations*. And in the nineteenth century, Thoreau (see entry) echoed these ideas about simplicity in *Walden*. But he put it more plainly: "Beware of all enterprises that require new clothes."

Marcus Aurelius was concerned with profound questions, perhaps during dark times in his own life. These are all questions of life's meaning, dealing with pain and disappointment, and acting morally. All of his notions of a simple existence, a life of integrity and contemplation, correct actions, and cultivating patience, honesty, and humility were virtues similar to those extolled by the Greek philosophers he studied, as well as an ancient Chinese philosopher and a man who left society to live beside a New England pond.

They are part of the reason we read classic wisdom today. It never gets old. And it can still speak to us.

Game to go deeper into Stoicism? Recently back in vogue, Stoicism has acquired new currency in our time of turbulence because it is highly practical, less dependent upon the intervention of a deity, and more individually driven. For a generation of "Nones"—those who no longer identify with any organized religion—Stoicism is less concerned with why the world is as it is than what one does about it. Also, as Thoreau would appreciate, it does not require new clothes.

If so, I recommend you try another of the Stoics currently in fashion, the Roman writer and philosopher Seneca (circa 5 BCE–65 CE), who lived about a century before Marcus Aurelius. Some of his writings have been recently issued in a brief volume called *On the Shortness of Life*. In it, Seneca counsels:

> Life is long enough, and a sufficiently generous amount has been given to us for the highest achievements if it were all well invested. But when it is wasted in heedless luxury and spent on no good activity, we are forced by death's final constraint to realize that it has passed away before we knew it was passing. So it is: we are not given a short life but we make it short.

Among the most important influences on Marcus Aurelius was an enslaved teacher and thinker named Epictetus. Try his *Discourses and Selected Writings*, which presents his Stoic ideas in a fairly accessible modern translation that is a must for anyone interested in seriously exploring Stoicism. And a contemporary interpretation of Epictetus can be found in Sharon Lebell's 1995 book, *The Art of Living: The Classical Manual on Virtue, Happiness, and Effectiveness*, drawn from the writings of Epictetus and interpreted in highly contemporary language.

"We gave Moses the Scripture and We sent messengers after him in succession. We gave Jesus, son of Mary, clear signs and strengthened him with the holy spirit."

The Qur'an: "The Cow"

— CIRCA 633–645 CE —

Muhammad (Attributed)

New York: Oxford University Press; 2016; a new translation by M. A. S. Abdel Haleem; 33 pages out of a total 464

EXCERPT

This is the Scripture in which there is no doubt, containing guidance for those who are mindful of God, who believe in the unseen, keep up the prayer, and give out of what We have provided for them; those who believe in the revelation sent down to you [Muhammad], and in what was sent before you, those who have firm faith in the Hereafter. Such people are following their Lord's guidance and it is they who will prosper. As for those who disbelieve, it makes no difference whether you warn them or not: they will not believe. God has sealed their hearts and their ears, and their eyes are covered. They will have great torment.

SUMMARY

Considered Islam's supreme authority, the Qur'an—once more commonly anglicized as "Koran"—is the source of the creeds, rituals, ethics, and laws at the heart of the faith of Islam, which is translated as "surrender" or "submission" to the will of God. The Qur'an is believed to have been divinely revealed to the Prophet Muhammad over twenty-one years by Jibril, typically translated as Gabriel—the messenger angel who appears in the Hebrew scriptures and in the New Testament, announcing the birth of John the Baptist and Jesus. The Qur'an, which is simply translated in English as "recitation" or "reading," is divided into 114 chapter-like units called suras (or surahs).

"The Cow" is the second and longest of these suras, which are roughly organized by length in descending order. Like the other suras, this one is named for a conspicuous word in its central narrative. (Among others are "Women," "Jonah," "Thunder," and "The Cave" in which these words are significant.) In this case, the title refers to the cow in an account that mirrors a story recorded in the biblical book of Exodus. In the Qur'an version of this episode, Moses tells the Israelites to slaughter a cow, beginning an exchange in which the people ask Moses to describe exactly what kind of cow they must sacrifice. In another echo of Exodus, "The Cow" recounts how God saved the Children of Israel from Egypt's Pharaoh by parting the sea and then gave Moses the extensive set of laws to distinguish right from wrong and dictate everyday behavior.

These reverent references to events at the heart of Judaism in this opening section of the Qur'an may come as a surprise—or perhaps a revelation—to people who have no idea that Old Testament figures such as Moses and the patriarchs Abraham, Isaac, and Jacob appear prominently in Islam's holy book. In the same way, Christians whose familiarity with Islam is limited to the long history of enmity between the two faiths may be surprised at the invocation of the names of Jesus and Mary.

While the entirety of the Qur'an is directed toward the faithful, "The Cow" is also specifically addressed to "believers" who are provided with elaborate instructions about prayer, dietary rules, pilgrimage, charity, and other sacred obligations of Islam—divine guidance that leads, they are told, to prosperity. Yet among the concluding words of "The Cow" is a passage of wisdom and encouragement that may seem quite similar to that of other beliefs: "God does not burden any soul with more than it can bear: each gains whatever good it has done, and suffers its bad."

To be clear, this entry is a discussion of the Qur'an in an English translation of a book written, and meant to be read and recited, in Arabic. With all due respect, I cite translator M. A. S. Abdel Haleem,* who writes in his introduction:

> This translation is intended to go further than previous works in accuracy, clarity, flow, and currency of language. It is written in a modern, easy style, avoiding where possible the use of cryptic language or archaisms that tend to obscure meaning. The intention is to make the Qur'an accessible to everyone who speaks English, Muslims or otherwise, including the millions of people all over the world for whom the English language has become a lingua franca.

ABOUT THE AUTHOR: MUHAMMAD

According to Islamic belief, the Qur'an was revealed to the Prophet Muhammad by the angel Gabriel, beginning in 610 and ending with Muhammad's death in 632 CE. According to historian Karen Armstrong, "The Quran was revealed to Muhammad verse by verse, *surah* by *surah*, during the next twenty-one years, often in response to a crisis or question that had arisen in the life in the little community of the faithful." But just as we can say with some authority that Vyasa did not write the *Bhagavad Gita*, Moses did not write the book of Genesis, and Lao-tzu did not write *Tao Te Ching*, it

---

* Born in Egypt and an expert in the Qur'an and Arabic, M. A. S. Abdel Haleem has been, since 1995, Professor of Islamic Studies at the University of London's School of Oriental and African Studies. With a doctorate from the University of Cambridge, he is also the editor of the *Journal of Qur'anic Studies* and in 2008 was made an Officer of the Order of the British Empire. He provides valuable explanatory notes throughout this English-language edition.

would be historically appropriate to say that the founding prophet of Islam did not write what became the text of the Qur'an.

Islamic tradition holds that the words were *revealed* to Muhammad, who then *recited* them to his followers. Muhammad's recitations were memorized by his ardent disciples—just as Jesus wrote nothing, yet his words and deeds were recorded by his own devoted followers. With each of the Prophet's new revelations, those around Muhammad would learn them and then recite them to others.

Muhammad "was meticulous in ensuring that the Qur'an was recorded," according to translator M. A. S. Abdel Haleem. The complete text of the Qur'an was later compiled from these various written versions following the Prophet's death, just as the gospels and letters of the New Testament were only written down and collected well after Jesus's death.

So, who was this Prophet? While some of Muhammad's biography has been layered in myth and legend, there are many early sources to provide a reasonable sense of the factual history.

It is widely agreed that Muhammad was born around the year 570 CE, in Mecca, then a center of trade on the Arabian Peninsula and now considered Islam's holiest site. At the time of Muhammad's birth and early life, the various Arab tribes were divided among nomadic herders and more settled traders. They practiced a variety of polytheistic religions all ruled by a high god called Allah (simply "God" in Arabic), whom many Arabs believed to be the same God worshiped by the Jews and Christians living in bordering lands. Muhammad's home of Mecca, however, was a significant center for a variety of polytheistic worship cults.

In his introduction, M. A. S. Abdel Haleem notes: "The Hajj pilgrimage to the Ka'ba in Mecca, built, the Qur'an tells us, by Abraham for the worship of the one God, was practiced but that too had become corrupted with polytheism." And, according to Karen Armstrong, "There was also spiritual restlessness in Mecca. . . . Arabs knew that Judaism and Christianity, which were practiced in the Byzantine and Persian empires, were more sophisticated than their own pagan traditions. Some had come to believe that al-Lah (whose name simply meant 'the God') was the deity worshiped by Jews and Christians, but he had sent the Arabs no prophet of their own and no scripture in their own language." Muhammad would change that.

Muhammad's father died before his birth and his mother died when he was six. His grandfather cared for him but died when the boy was eight years old. Muhammad was then entrusted to the family of an uncle, Abu Talib, who took Muhammad on his first trade journey when he was twelve years old. According to historian Karen Armstrong, "The young Muhammad was well-liked in Mecca. He was handsome, with a compact, solid body of average height. His hair and beard were thick and curly, and he had a strikingly luminous expression and a smile of enormous charm, which is mentioned in all the sources. . . . He inspired such confidence that he was known as al-Amin, the Reliable One."

Working as a trader for a wealthy merchant, Khadija bint Khuwaylid, a widow and distant relative fifteen years his senior, Muhammad impressed her with his honesty and character. When Muhammad was about twenty-five, Khadija proposed marriage, and they wed in 595. She would become his ardent supporter and a revered figure in Islam.

They lived in Mecca, where Muhammad sought retreat in some nearby caves between lengthy caravan trips. In the year 610, during a retreat during the ninth month of the Arabic lunar calendar, when blood feuds were suspended in pre-Islamic times, Muhammad was given the first of these revelations, initiating his role as Prophet. Fasting during this ninth month, Ramadan, become one of the pillars of Islam. In what is described as an overpowering moment, Muhammad was approached by an angel, shown a piece of silk with words inscribed on it, and told to read. He did not know how to read. The angel squeezed Muhammad, repeating the command to "recite" twice, and then recited to Muhammad the first two lines of the Qur'an.

These revelations continued, but it was another two years before Muhammad began to preach what had been revealed to him. He was given divine instruction to spread the words he heard, which ultimately included the creeds, rituals, ethics, and laws of Islam. Muhammad initially encountered hostility from the tribal leaders who clung to their own polytheistic beliefs and resented being told to abandon their traditional gods. This initial

ridicule led to ostracism and then an outright boycott of Muhammad and
his clan. Eventually, in the year 615, Muhammad sent his clansmen and
other followers to seek refuge from persecution in the Christian kingdom
of Abyssinia (Ethiopia). Then, in 620, the year after his wife and uncle—his
closest supporters—both died, Muhammad experienced an event called the
Night Journey and Ascension to Heaven, during which the angel Gabriel
accompanied Muhammad to Jerusalem and then to Heaven.

"Muhammad was transported on a winged horse to the rock where
Abraham nearly sacrificed his son Ishmael," explains Bruce B. Lawrence
in a recent history, *The Koran in English.* "It was a great rock in an ancient
city, Jerusalem. Jerusalem was the abode of prophets, from Abraham to
David to Jesus. And it now hosted another prophet, the Arab Prophet
Muhammad. Dazzled, he was transported from that rock up to heaven."
In Islamic tradition, it is Ishmael rather than Isaac who is going to be
sacrificed by Abraham before God intervenes and a ram is substituted.
The site, known as Al-Aqsa, is one of the holiest sites in Islam and sits on
Jerusalem's Temple Mount, making it one of the holiest sites in Judaism,
and revered by Christians as well.

After encountering Adam, Jesus, John the Baptist, Abraham, and other
biblical figures, Muhammad was taken to the Divine Throne, accompanied
by the angel Gabriel. With the advice of Moses, Muhammad was able
to negotiate the number of times the faithful must pray from an initial
admonition of fifty down to a daily recital of five prayers. The time of
this journey and ascent is marked as one of the Islamic calendar's most
significant dates.

Following this event, Muhammad continued to attract new believers in Yathrib, an important trading town north of Mecca, who offered
sanctuary to the Prophet. Many of his earlier followers later moved from
Abyssinia to Yathrib, an event marked as the Migration (Hijra, or Hegira),
later adopted as the start of the Islamic calendar. Yathrib would become
known as Medina, the City of the Prophet. Monogamous until his wife
Khadija's death, Muhammad later took numerous wives, often as a means
of forging political ties. Among these wives was his favorite, the third and
youngest, Aisha.

Over more than twenty years, Muhammad continued receiving divine revelations, which he recited to his followers who memorized and then recorded them. But many of the leaders of the Meccan establishment were threatened by Muhammad and his new religion. Muhammad and his followers posed a risk to the established religious traditions and the prosperity these traditions brought to Mecca, already a significant destination for pilgrims before Islam was established. What began as ridicule and ostracism evolved into outright persecution of Muhammad's followers. In 622, the Prophet and many Muslim families left Mecca for Medina and the Meccan leaders vowed revenge. These conflicts between Muhammad's followers and other Arabs ultimately led to outright warfare, in which Muhammad emerged as a military leader. Following a series of thirty-eight battles, fought between 624 and 631, the entire Arabian Peninsula accepted Islam and the warring tribes were united under Muhammad.

In 632, Muhammad made a final pilgrimage to Mecca, where he received the last revelation of the Qur'an. Soon after, he complained of a severe headache and died on June 8 in Medina in the arms of Aisha, considered his second and most beloved wife after his first, Khadija. His place of leadership was taken by a series of leaders—first, Abu Bakr, the father of Aisha. He was followed by 'Umar, 'Uthman, and 'Ali, the four leaders referred to as the Rightly Guided Caliphs. In 633, Abu Bakr ordered that the various recorded versions of Muhammad's revelations be collected into one volume. In 645, 'Uthman commissioned the copying and distribution of copies of the Qur'an. Under the leadership of these four men, Islam spread far beyond Arabia and, by the end of its first century, stretched across North Africa to Spain.

WHY YOU SHOULD READ IT

I will reiterate a point made in my introduction: no reasonably educated person should be ignorant of what the fundamental works underlying world faiths actually say.

For those unfamiliar with the Qur'an, I suggest reading it to learn about the foundation of one of the world's major religions. And, perhaps,

also in a spirit of increasing tolerance—a goal made increasingly urgent
by recent events in the Middle East. It is fair to say that Thomas Jefferson
might have been motivated by these same ideas when he acquired an English
translation of Islam's holy book while still a student at William and Mary
in 1765. Part of Jefferson's personal library, it was included in the Jefferson
collection purchased by the nation to restock the Library of Congress after
it was burned by the British in the War of 1812.

According to Peter Manseau, religion curator at the National Museum
of American History, "Historians have attributed the third president's ownership of the Muslim holy book to his curiosity about a variety of religious
perspectives. It's appropriate to view it that way. Jefferson bought this book
while he was a young man studying law, and he may have read it in part to
better understand Islam's influence on some of the world's legal systems."
Among Jefferson's greatest contributions is the fundamental toleration of
all religions that he believed in and attempted to codify: eventually his
views found their way into the First Amendment to the U.S. Constitution.

For many, especially in the Western world, this need to understand
is undeniably meaningful when it comes to the Qur'an. So much of the
world's recent death and destruction is rooted in the conflict between Judaism, Christianity, and Islam. And of course, many who speak in anger at
the Qur'an too often speak in ignorance. We often fear what we don't
understand.

In its essence, the Qur'an lays out a highly prescribed set of strict behav-
iors for believers, with an emphasis on justice, equity, and compassion—
and submission or surrender, the very meaning of the word *islam*. But as a
religious text, the Qur'an also expands upon many of the messages of the
Hebrew and Christian scriptures, emphasizing that Muhammad was another
in this line of prophets, from Noah, Abraham, and Moses through Jesus.
As translator Haleem notes, "The Qur'an stresses that all these prophets
preached the same message and that the Qur'an was sent to confirm the
earlier messages."

And historian Karen Armstrong echoes this when she comments:
"Hence Muhammad never asked Jews or Christians to accept Islam, unless
they particularly wished to do so, because they had received perfectly valid

revelations of their own. The Quran insists strongly that 'there shall be no coercion in matters of faith,' [Quran 2: 256] and commands Muslims to respect the beliefs of Jews and Christians, whom the Quran call *ahl al-kitab*, a phrase usually translated 'People of the Book' but which is more accurately rendered 'people of an earlier revelation.'"

From a cultural perspective, the Qur'an is recognized as the greatest masterpiece in Arabic literature. Again, historian Armstrong emphasizes Muhammad's literary gifts: "He was also creating a new literary form and a masterpiece of Arab prose and poetry. Many of the first believers were converted by the sheer beauty of the Quran, which resonated with their deepest aspirations, cutting through their intellectual preconceptions in the manner of great art, and inspiring them, at a level more profound than cerebral, to alter their way of life."

From a purely historical perspective, like the Old and New Testaments, *Tao Te Ching*, and the *Bhagavad Gita*—already discussed—the Qur'an has been one of the most profoundly influential books in history, all the more reason for those unfamiliar with it to gain some insight into its development and meaning.

WHAT TO READ NEXT

Like the Torah and the rest of the Bible, the Qur'an has inspired centuries of scholarly investigation and interpretation. The best brief work of nonfiction I can recommend for those who wish to further explore the Qur'an, Islam, and the life of its prophet is Karen Armstrong's 2006 biography, *Muhammad: A Prophet for Our Time*. A highly respected historian of religion and author of such best-selling works as *A History of God: The 4,000-Year Quest of Judaism, Christianity, and Islam*, Armstrong has written a concise, readable life of the prophet.

Contending that centuries of Christian propaganda have distorted the life and message of Muhammad, which worsened in the wake of September 11, 2001, and the destruction of the World Trade Center, Armstrong writes: "We can no longer afford to indulge this type of bigotry, because it is a gift to extremists who can use such statements to 'prove' that the Western world is indeed engaged in a crusade against the Islamic world. Muhammad was not a man of violence. . . . Muhammad literally sweated with the effort to bring peace to war-torn Arabia. His life was a tireless campaign against greed, injustice, and arrogance. He realized that Arabia was at a turning point and that the old way of thinking would no longer suffice, so he wore himself out in the creative effort to evolve an entirely new solution." Also of value is Armstrong's *Islam: A Short History*, a concise and readable account that carries through to contemporary times.

Another relatively brief recent work of a far more scholarly, yet still accessible, nature is *The Koran in English: A Biography*, a 2017 book by Bruce B. Lawrence, professor emeritus of religion at Duke University.

And finally, a book I plan to explore is *God in the Qur'an*, published in 2018 by Jack Miles. It was described by author Mustafa Akyol in the *New York Times* as "a highly readable, unbiasedly comparative and elegantly insightful study of the Quran." Miles is the Pulitzer Prize–winning author of *God: A Biography*, another book in the realm of religious history that I highly recommend.

"Let me say that whenever she appeared anywhere, the hope of her wondrous greeting emptied me of all enmity and kindled instead a flame of charity that inspired me to forgive whoever had offended me."

Vita Nuova

— CIRCA 1293 (FIRST PRINTED EDITION 1576) —

Dante Alighieri

New York: Penguin Books, 2022; dual-language edition with parallel text, translated with an introduction and notes by Virginia Jewiss; 182 pages

EXCERPT

Nine times already since my birth had the heaven of light, revolving, returned to nearly the same point in its orbit when the glorious lady of my mind—she was called Beatrice even by many who did not know her name—first appeared to my eyes. She had already been in this life long enough for the heaven of the fixed stars to move one-twelfth of a degree east, so she appeared to me near the beginning of her ninth year, and it was near the end of mine when I first saw her. She was dressed in a modest and becoming crimson—that noblest of colors—and girded and adorned in a manner befitting her tender age.

SUMMARY

Italy's most renowned and beloved poet—*il Sommo Poeta*, or the Supreme Poet—Dante is a towering figure not only in Italian literature but in all of Western letters. His three-part masterwork, *The Divine Comedy*, is considered one of the most significant literary works in history.

But well before he set down his epic journeys through Hell, Purgatory, and Paradise, Dante Alighieri wrote *Vita Nuova* (New life), his *libello*—or "little book." Breaking from Latin as the standard language of poetry and mixing prose and poetry in a Tuscan vernacular that even the "donkey men" could understand, the work describes Dante's first sighting, at the age of nine, of his beloved Beatrice, an ethereal figure slightly younger than Dante at the time. Translator Virginia Jewiss notes: "The encounter—the first episode Dante deems worthy to be recorded—is described in cosmic terms, as if the heavens had aligned to bring them together."

This chance glimpse, along with another nine years later, provokes the vision that inspired *Vita Nuova* as well as the three epic poems of *The Divine Comedy*, in which Beatrice is a central figure.

"From then on," Dante writes, "I swear, Love was lord of my soul."

To recount all that befalls Beatrice and the lovestruck Dante would count as a spoiler. Suffice it to say that the forty-two brief chapters—each in this edition with the original Italian facing the English translation—offer unique insight into the mind of the poet as well as the medieval notion of courtly love, a sometimes secret, highly respectful, and even devoutly spiritual form of adoration for a woman. Courtly love was considered equivalent to divine love.

"In the Middle Ages, a sign of true love was that you did *not* have sex or physical contact with the object of your affection," writes scholar and literature professor Joseph Luzzi. "Love for the unattainable woman taught virtue and lifted the soul. Turning love into sex was the equivalent of reducing the most sublime emotion to the tyranny of the body and its unslakable desires."

As with Dante's Beatrice, the courtly lady might well have no idea of the admirer's adoration. She served as a subject of praise for the removed lover to demonstrate his poetic skill, or explore philosophy and religious concepts, in the practice of lauding her, as Dante does in this sonnet:

My lady carries Love within her eyes,
whence everything she looks on is ennobled;
all turn her way whenever she walks by;
and he who's greeted by her starts to tremble. . . .

Translator Virginia Jewiss uses the term *prosimetrum* to describe Dante's mixed use of poetry and prose. Writing in the Tuscan vernacular that was later used by Petrarch and Boccaccio, Dante broke the stranglehold of formal Latin, which could be understood by only a few.

ABOUT THE AUTHOR: DANTE ALIGHIERI

The greatest of medieval poets, Dante Alighieri was born between May 21 and June 20, 1265, in Florence, then a republic in an Italy divided among contending city-states and still dominated in matters of politics and religion by the Vatican. These were the early days of Florence's burgeoning wealth as a trading and financial center, as it flowered to become one of Italy's most important and powerful cities and, later, the pulsing center of the Renaissance.

Dante's father was a moneylender—a profession technically against the law at the time, when loaning money at interest was considered "usury" and forbidden by the Church. To skirt the rules, moneylenders like Dante's father, and such bankers as the Medici family, disguised their services and made generous donations to church and civic organizations. Such philanthropy seemed to wipe away sin. While not in the cream of Florentine society, Dante grew up in a family of some means and political connections, claiming ancestry from ancient Romans and a warrior in the First Crusade.

Then, at a festival in the spring of 1274, by traditional accounts, nine-year-old Dante locked eyes with a beautiful girl he would immortalize as Beatrice. In that moment, Dante the boy became Dante the poet.

Little is known about Dante's education, but he later spent time with the learned monks in Florence. He also became a member of a group of Tuscan poets, who were beginning to write in what is called *dolce stil novo*—the sweet new style—emphasizing divine love. He would see Beatrice again as a teenager and began writing the poems that would be included in *Vita Nuova*.

The object of his fervor has traditionally been identified as Beatrice Portinari, the youngest daughter of a wealthy banker named Folco Portinari. In 1287, Beatrice married another high-ranking Florentine banker, Simone Bardi. Known to friends as Bice, she died in 1290, at age twenty-four.

By then, Dante's father had also died, leaving him some property, and he had married Gemma Donati, with whom he would have four children. Much of Dante's biography after this point is complicated by the bewildering thickets of political machinations between competing forces within Florence, which eventually led to open warfare. In 1289, twenty-four-year-old Dante fought in a battle giving his family's party, the Guelphs, control of the city. While continuing to shape *Vita Nuova*, completed sometime before 1295, Dante had also entered Florence's political fray. After winning a series of lower elected posts, Dante was elected a prior—one of the city's six highest elected officials—in 1300.

But just two years later, again resulting from political intrigues and papal politics, Dante was charged by a new Florentine government on trumped-up charges of corruption, fraud, and other crimes. For his failure to appear in court, Dante was then sentenced to death in absentia. He never returned to Florence. "Exile would make him, in his own words, *macro*, lean from hunger and want," writes Joseph Luzzi, "as he ranged throughout the Italian Peninsula looking for a home and a way to earn his bread—literally and figuratively." (The ban would not be rescinded until 2008 by a city council vote in Florence.)

During these wanderings, Dante was dependent upon the hospitality of various families in different regions of Italy. He continued to write letters and canzoni—longer poems—addressing the political situation in Italy, always complicated by relationships and conflicts with a changing cast of Popes and European monarchs vying for power. But by 1306, Dante had begun the work of composing the *Commedia* and he would use its first part, *Inferno*, to extract literary revenge on many of his Florentine enemies by consigning leading figures in Florence to the various depths of hell. As manuscripts of this work began to circulate in a time before mass printing, Dante's fame grew. He eventually completed the work in the city of Ravenna, where he spent the rest of his life.

"*The Divine Comedy* became a staple of cultural life from the moment Dante died in 1321 in Ravenna, where to this day his corpse remains interred—much to the chagrin of Florence," notes Luzzi. In 1353, the city that had banished Dante organized a lecture series in honor of the "Supreme Poet." The first to deliver this lecture was Boccaccio, author of the *Decameron*, the 1353 collection of one hundred stories also written in vernacular Italian, narrated during the Black Death and another foundational work of Western literature.

WHY YOU SHOULD READ IT

Dante's *Vita Nuova* is more than an extraordinary piece of writing. His combination of poetry and prose signaled an important literary development that also offers insight into the working mind of one of literature's greatest geniuses. Written before *The Divine Comedy*, and first published in hand-copied manuscripts rather than printed books, Dante's *Vita Nuova* used allusions to sacred texts and compared his beloved Beatrice to Christ in ways that were unacceptable to the Catholic church. A censored edition appeared in print in 1576, more than three centuries after Dante's death in 1321, and it was not published in English until 1843, when American writer Ralph Waldo Emerson completed a translation that is credited with helping introduce Dante to America. In 1861, the poet and painter Dante Gabriel Rossetti made a much-admired translation, the first to be published in Britain.

Besides Emerson and Rosetti, *Vita Nuova* has inspired other poets and writers. And there is a simple reason. How often does a great poet tell us what he is thinking as he composes his poetry? That may be why the great twentieth-century poet T. S. Eliot called *Vita Nuova* "a work of capital importance for the discipline of the emotions." While Eliot often alludes to Dante in his poetry, his poem "Ash-Wednesday" was specifically inspired by *Vita Nuova*. Other writers moved by Dante's "memoir" of unattainable love include the French poet Charles Baudelaire and Jorge Luis Borges in his short story "The Aleph," about the death of another Beatriz.

But beyond these and other writers influenced by Dante, Italy's great poet is exploring in *Vita Nuova* essential questions about love—a subject treated numerous times elsewhere in this collection, from Plato to bell hooks—and more specifically spiritual love, which may be unreachable in this life.

The book also represents a milestone in the progression of Europe out of the Middle Ages toward the era of humanism and the Renaissance, the extraordinary period in which the rediscovery of ancient literature and artwork contributed to a remarkable outburst of creativity and intellect. "Fixing a date for the beginning of the Renaissance is impossible, but most scholars believe its stirrings had begun by the early 1400s," noted historian William Manchester. "Although Dante, Petrarch, Boccaccio, Saint Francis of Assisi, and the painter Giotto de Bondone—all of whom seem to have been infused with the new spirit—were dead by then, they are seen as forerunners of the reawakening."

Finally, count *Vita* as another prime example of what I call stepping-stone books. It is much easier to take on this brief, accessible introduction to Dante's work than to attempt to plunge into the three parts of *The Divine Comedy*.

WHAT TO READ NEXT

For the courageous, it may be time to take up *Inferno*, *The Divine Comedy's* first book. Its opening lines are among the most famous in Western literature:

> *Midway on our life's journey, I found myself*
> *In dark woods, the right road lost. To tell*
> *About those woods is hard—so tangled and rough*

The first book in a three-part travel epic, *Inferno* is a weighty and power-fully influential vision of the Christian belief in an afterlife in which people are judged for their acts on earth. In Dante's one hundred cantos (more than fourteen thousand lines), the three parts of *Divine Comedy*, the poet recounts his journeys through the realms of the dead: the Inferno, Purgatory, and Para-dise. He is first guided on the way through by the Roman poet Virgil—author of the epic account of Rome's founding, the *Aeneid*. They traverse nine rings of Hell, each representing a level of punishment for the damned until they finally reach the bottom of the pit and Satan. In the second part, the two poets climb the seven levels of Mount Purgatory, each stage representing one of the Deadly Sins, where sinners must wait until they are purged of their sins and allowed to continue to heaven. Finally, in the last section, Dante is reunited with Beatrice, who guides him through the nine heavens of Paradise before reaching the tenth where God dwells with the angels.

In *The Reopening of the Western Mind: The Resurgence of Intellectual Life from the End of Antiquity to the Dawn of the Enlightenment*, historian Charles Freeman summarizes the significance of Dante's epic masterwork:

> The *Divine Comedy* is, of course, deeply rooted in Catholic theology.... It is also a superb work of literature, notable for its relentless probing into the nature of good and evil, the ultimate ends of life and the supremacy of spiritual values. Virtually every theological issue of the day is touched upon and Dante's own emotions, from disgust to exul-tation, are expressed. There are many moving moments when Virgil tries to comfort him in the face of the horrors that they encounter in hell. Poetically, the sense of order and evolution towards its end and the vivid nature of Dante's writing and insights mean that the journey, even in Paradise, is never dull. It also offers an early insight into the future development of western Christianity after 1300 in revealing a growing distinction between spirituality and the church hierarchy that seems to have abandoned it.

Having made it through Dante, consider another significant document of the Middle Ages, a series of letters, available in various editions as "The

Letters of Abelard and Heloise." A prominent twelfth-century theologian, Peter Abelard was hired to tutor Heloise, the niece of a powerful official at the cathedral of Notre-Dame. They fell in love, were secretly married, and conceived a child. Heloise's uncle forced her into a nunnery and had Abelard castrated.

Although they were never reunited, the pair continued a correspondence that transformed their professions of earthly love into a deeper spiritual bond. Both were philosophers and scholars whose writings about religion and affairs of the heart were deeply influential. The words of Heloise about matters of theology and the role of women in the Church have made her an early champion of feminism. Their ill-starred love story served as the basis of the successful play *Abelard and Heloise* by Ronald Millar.

"The prospective bride, no matter whether she's a spinster or a widow, is exhibited stark naked to the prospective bridegroom by a respectable married woman, and a suitable male chaperon shows the bridegroom naked to the bride."

Utopia

— 1516 —

[FIRST ENGLISH TRANSLATION, 1551]

Thomas More

New York: Penguin Books, 2003; translated with an introduction and notes by Paul Turner; 135 pages

EXCERPT

Utopia was originally not an island but a peninsula. However, it was conquered by somebody called Utopos,* who gave it its present name—it used to be called Sansculottia—and was also responsible for transforming a pack of ignorant savages into what is now, perhaps, the most civilized nation in the

---

* In this translation, "Utopos" is equivalent to "nobody," and "Sansculottia" means "no breeches," as the former inhabitants of the peninsula went naked.

world. The moment he landed and got control of the country, he immediately
had a channel cut through the fifteen-mile isthmus connecting Utopia with
the mainland, so that the sea could flow all round it. Fearing it might cause
resentment if he made the local inhabitants do all the work, he put his whole
army on the job as well.

SUMMARY

Thomas More was, by every account, a man with a sharp wit, even joking
with the executioner on the scaffold before he was beheaded for opposing Henry VIII. "Gallows humor," indeed. So, let's start with the word—
"Utopia"—Thomas More's first little joke. It is derived from Greek and can
either mean "the good place," or as more commonly translated, "no place."
As translator Paul Turner points out, "its meaning (Noplace) should be
borne in mind throughout."

Opening with an invented and obscure "Utopian Alphabet," *Utopia* is
divided into two books. In the first of these, book 1, More describes events
that happened in 1515, while he was on a diplomatic mission. Book 2 presents
More's imagined world, an idealized "Noplace" with no poverty, ample provi-
sion for the aged, meaningful work for all, and complete religious tolerance.
And where prospective bride and groom got to see each other naked before
marrying. Clearly, "Noplace" did not exist.

Book 1 is intended to give *Utopia* the ring of historical authenticity.
It presents an exchange of letters and dialogues between Thomas More, a
rising star in the court of Henry VIII, and several other men—actual figures
known to More—on the subjects of royal marriages and wool. Yes, wool!

Wool was serious business in More's England. Thousands of peasants
had been forced off their farms, which were converted to more lucrative
sheep pastures by the aristocrats who owned the land. That transformation
led to mass starvation and widespread thievery, punishable by hanging. As
many as seventy thousand people were hanged during Henry's reign.

Against this historical background, More introduces the fictional
Raphael Nonsenso (in this translation; Raphael Hythlodaeus in More's
original Latin). With another nod to historical authenticity, Nonsenso is

said to have sailed on three of Amerigo Vespucci's recent voyages to the New World but remained on an island off the coast of America for five years.

In book 2, Nonsenso describes a carefully ordered island society that is completely contrary to More's England. In Utopia, all property is communal, everyone wears the same simple clothing, and jewels and gold—used for chamber pots—are worthless. All Utopians work, but only six-hour days: "They never force people to work unnecessarily," explains Nonsenso, "for the main purpose of their whole economy is to give each person as much time free from physical drudgery as the needs of the community will allow, so that he can cultivate his mind—which they regard as the secret of a happy life."

There are many other perks. Every person receives universal healthcare and free childcare, and there is freedom of religion—a considerable irony as More was a staunch Catholic who later persecuted Protestants. Another irony—given More's future role in the life of Henry VIII—divorce is allowed in Utopia, "by mutual consent . . . on grounds of incompatibility."

Utopia raises a large question: Was Thomas More really suggesting a perfect communal—even communistic—society? Or does the underlying idea that this is a tale told by a man named Nonsenso and Utopia is "no place" mean More was merely mocking these "utopian" ideals?

ABOUT THE AUTHOR: THOMAS MORE

Saint or villain? Depends on which literary version of Thomas More you accept. In *A Man for All Seasons*, a 1960 play by Robert Bolt and later an award-winning film, More is a humanist and martyred hero of conscience. In the more recent novels by Hilary Mantel, commencing with *Wolf Hall*, More is an unyielding heretic hunter who burns Protestants at the stake.

Whichever of these Thomas More may have been, his end was the same: he was beheaded in 1535 for treason. He was later sainted by the Catholic church, yet in the Soviet Union More would be memorialized as a prophet of socialism.

His complex story begins on February 7, 1477 or 1478, in London, where Thomas More was born the eldest son of a barrister—a specialized lawyer who gives expert legal opinions in courts and tribunals. In 1490, More became a page on the staff of the archbishop of Canterbury, lord chancellor under Henry VII. More later went to Oxford and studied law, establishing a reputation as a brilliant barrister himself.

Around the turn of the century, More began mixing with scholars interested in a revival of classical literature. This period of European history—the dawn of the Renaissance, Reformation, and Western humanism—was greatly inspired by the rediscovery of lost Greek and Latin texts. Largely concealed during the medieval era, these works were carried to Europe by scholars fleeing Constantinople after its fall to the Ottomans in 1453. With the advent of the printing press, they become more available. Scholarly Europe was beginning to celebrate humanity as "the measure of all things."

At about this time, Thomas More also lived in or near a monastery, though he didn't take monastic vows. A devout Catholic, he wore a "hair shirt," a coarse undergarment made from animal skin—goat in More's case—meant to be worn as a form of penance. He also performed self-flagellation. More was also introduced to Desiderius Erasmus, one of the leading humanist scholars of the period. In 1505, Erasmus came to live with Thomas More and they became devoted friends.

A turning point for More came when Henry VII died in 1509. His eldest son and heir, Prince Arthur, had died at age fifteen two years earlier, a few months after marrying Catherine of Aragon, daughter of Spain's monarchs, Isabella and Ferdinand. After Henry VII's death, seventeen-year-old Henry took the throne as Henry VIII. He then married Catherine, his dead brother's widow and six years his senior. Following three stillborn infants and the death of a son at seven weeks, Catherine gave birth to a girl named Mary—England's future queen—in February 1516.

By that time, More had risen in politics to become a member of Henry's court and was dispatched to the Netherlands, where he wrote *Utopia*. More later became secretary and confidant to Henry VIII. At the time, Henry adamantly opposed the ideas of Martin Luther, the German priest who rejected what he called the abuses of the Catholic church. With More's help, Henry wrote a response to Luther for which he was named Defender of the Faith by Pope Leo X. Later, More wrote arguments refuting many of Luther's ideas as heresy as well as attacking Luther personally. More also objected to the translation of the Bible from Latin into English.

In 1529, Thomas More rose to become Henry's lord chancellor, the most powerful man in England after the king. But More's ascension was short-lived. A devout Catholic, he challenged Henry VIII when the king sought a divorce from Catherine so he could marry Anne Boleyn. The most consequential royal breakup in history brought disaster for More. After Henry severed ties with the Vatican and adopted the title of "Supreme Head of the Church and Clergy" in 1531, Thomas More refused to affirm Henry's divorce from Catherine, resigning his office in 1532.

When Henry married Anne Boleyn—who gave birth to the future Queen Elizabeth—More refused to attend Boleyn's coronation as queen. In addition to denying the king's supremacy, More refused to accept the Act of Succession, favoring Anne Boleyn as queen and her children as heirs to Henry's throne. For denying the Supremacy of the King in 1534, More was charged with high treason and imprisoned in the Tower of London. In 1535, he was tried and sentenced to a traitor's death by half-hanging and then being drawn-and-quartered and burned—a fate that the king commuted to a much swifter beheading. The same fate befell Anne Boleyn, second of Henry VIII's six wives, a year later.

Utopia was not published in English until sixteen years after More's death.

In 1886 Thomas More was beatified—proclaimed "blessed," a step toward sainthood in the Catholic church—and he was canonized as a saint in 1935.

WHY YOU SHOULD READ IT

There are many reasons to read *Utopia*. To list a few—

- It is a landmark of Western literature. While some traditional "Great Books" by "Dead White Men" have been dismissed, don't toss out Thomas More.

- It is an intriguing, provocative, and entertaining vision of a perfect society that prompts consideration of the way we live now. Who are we? What do we value most? What is an "ideal" world?

- Its title has permanently entered our language. The word "utopia" stands for an ideally perfect place, especially in its social and moral aspects. Of course, its opposite is "dystopia."

- *Utopia* is an influential book that has inspired other satirical classics in a genre that includes *Gulliver's Travels* (1726), *Candide* (1759), and modern "dystopias" including *Nineteen Eighty-Four, Brave New World*, and *The Handmaid's Tale*, among others.

- Its main character Utopos, founder of Utopia, is modeled on Plato's "philosopher king," connecting us to a significant philosophical antecedent.

Finally, read *Utopia* to consider another question its author inspires: Is Thomas More a hero of Catholicism? Or communism?

"Some have argued that More was genuinely concerned with the poverty and corruption of England and, as a young man whose convictions were still evolving, was trying to imagine how society might be better run," writes historian Charles Freeman. "It might even be that More had composed a satire on idealism, expecting the reader to realize that he is setting out the impossible."

That leaves the big question. Was More's "Noplace" achievable? Is a more perfect world possible after all?

WHAT TO READ NEXT

There are two essential figures in Thomas More's life and times whose work deserve mention. First is Desiderius Erasmus, the Dutch philosopher who numbers among the most significant humanists and is the author of *In Praise of Folly* (1509). Written while he lived in More's home, the book—

whose Latin title can be read as *In Praise of More*—is a sharp satire, attacking superstition, many European traditions, and, most tellingly, the practices of the Catholic church—to which Erasmus remained faithful.

The second is Martin Luther, one of More's chief adversaries. Luther's Ninety-Five Theses, which may have been nailed to the door of a church in Wittenberg, Germany, in 1517, led to the Protestant Reformation. They appear in *The Ninety-Five Theses and Other Writings* and are essential to understanding how Luther's words began a theological revolution that reshaped Christianity and world history.

Another fascinating document of this era is *The Four Voyages*, which collects Christopher Columbus's logbook, letters, and other dispatches. It offers revelations about the man whose trips to the Americas changed the course of history. It was the opening of this New World in voyages by Columbus, Vespucci in particular—who is named in the text—and others that provided Thomas More with part of the inspiration for *Utopia*.

*"Therefore one must be a fox in order to recognize traps,
and a lion to frighten off wolves."*

The Prince

— 1532 —

Niccolò Machiavelli

New York: Penguin Books, 2004; translated by George Bull; 113 pages

EXCERPT

From this arises the following question: whether it is better to be loved than
feared, or the reverse. The answer is that one would like to be both the one
and the other; but because it is difficult to combine them, it is far better to
be feared than loved if you cannot be both. One can make this generalization
about men: they are ungrateful, fickle, liars, and deceivers, they shun danger
and are greedy for profit; while you treat them well, they are yours. They would
shed their blood for you, risk their property, their lives, their sons, so long, as I
said above, as danger is remote; but when you are in danger they turn away. . . .
Men worry less about doing an injury to one who makes himself loved than to
one who makes himself feared.

SUMMARY

The first modern work of "realpolitik," *The Prince* is a treatise on how to acquire power, create a state, and hold on to it. Written more than five hundred years ago by an astute Florentine diplomat and historian, it is a handbook of succinct advice that has been studied by kings and dictators, captains of industry, and Mafia dons who desire the secret of getting power and keeping it.

First circulated in manuscript in 1513, *The Prince* opens with a fawning request to "Your Magnificence"—Lorenzo II of the powerful Medici family. Machiavelli asks the lord of Florence to excuse him—"a man of low and humble status"—for daring to "discuss and lay down the law about how princes should rule." It is a strange plea, considering the Medici had just thrown Machiavelli in jail and had him tortured on suspicion of conspiracy in a murder plot. Once freed from prison but out of a job, Machiavelli retreated to his family farm to lick his wounds and write the book he hoped might restore his position with Florence's first family.

In clear and fairly simple language—though with some admittedly obscure historical reference points—Machiavelli lays out twenty-six sections in this rule book for rulers with direct headlines: "How Many Kinds of Principality There Are and the Ways in Which They Are Acquired," "How Princes Should Honor Their Word," "How Flatterers Must Be Shunned," and "Cruelty and Compassion," the section cited in the preceding excerpt.

Using examples from ancient and recent history during a turbulent era on the Italian Peninsula, when it was far from a nation, Machiavelli was writing about the Italy that existed in his time. With a dozen independent kingdoms, dukedoms, small republics, some major city-states, and the Papal States controlled by the Pope, it was a confusing, volatile, and often violent landscape. Various Popes, Italian noblemen, and European monarchs vied for control of a fractured Italy. The turbulence reached international crisis in September 1494, when the ambitious King Charles of France lay claim to the Kingdom of Naples and crossed the Alps with thirty thousand soldiers. The French threat forced the contending Italian powers to choose sides and the conflict raged. Florence chose the French.

Against this chaotic and dangerous historical and political background, Machiavelli would go on to offer counsel on how the wise Prince should govern most effectively. Whether his intended audience, the Medici rulers of Florence, ever read his words is a matter of conjecture. But certainly, many others throughout history did.

Along with his guided tour through a gallery of good and bad "princes" over centuries, mingled with pointers on armies, strategies, and fortresses, Machiavelli peppers the book with the aphoristic wisdom that would bring him admiring readers and harsh criticism for centuries to come. Typical of this acumen is: "And here it has to be noted that men must be either pampered or crushed, because they can get revenge for small injuries but not for grievous ones. So any injury a prince does a man should be of such a kind that there is no fear of revenge."

Machiavelli did not coin the phrase "the end justifies the means." He just wrote the quintessential handbook on how a ruler, especially a new prince, might employ immoral or bad methods as long as the result was good—at least, for the prince. As historian Ross King concludes, "Machiavelli has long enjoyed an eminent reputation drastically at odds with the one-dimensional image of the dishonest and manipulative stage villain. . . . Machiavelli was an advocate of republicanism and liberty . . . a complex thinker whose writings belie the popular view of him as the messenger of a simple doctrine of conquest through iniquitous stratagems."

ABOUT THE AUTHOR: NICCOLÒ MACHIAVELLI

Born in Florence on May 3, 1469, Niccolò Machiavelli was a member of a once-prominent and relatively wealthy family that had fallen from grace. Machiavelli later wrote he was born in poverty. His father, Bernardo Machiavelli, a doctor of the law, was barred from holding office in Florence as a debtor. Yet he still owned a property in Florence near the famed Ponte Vecchio bridge and Niccolò grew up on his father's farm outside Florence. Little is known of his early youth and education, except that his father possessed an extensive library and that the young Machiavelli was well-read and educated by local Florentine masters of the humanist school. He learned Latin and probably knew some Greek.

Machiavelli came of age in a city at the height of its cultural influence: Florence was one of the centers of book publishing and a hotbed of the art and intellectual ferment of the Italian Renaissance. Under Lorenzo de' Medici—merchant banker, patron of the arts, and the powerful ruler of Florence known as Lorenzo the Magnificent—this Florence celebrated humanism by rejecting the Bible as the source of all knowledge and reviving the classics of Greece and Rome. Artists such as Michelangelo, Ghirlandaio, and Botticelli, all active during Machiavelli's lifetime, were moving away from strictly religious subjects in their artwork. And Michelangelo's *David* was placed in the city's central square in 1504. Machiavelli would become a friend and colleague of Leonardo da Vinci.

But like his Florentine compatriot Dante, two centuries earlier, Machiavelli lived in unsettled and treacherous times. France, the Holy Roman Empire, the Vatican, and the various Italian city-states and kingdoms— Milan, Venice, and Naples, among them—were in near-continuous battles for control of all or parts of a divided Italy. After Lorenzo's death in the epochal year of 1492, the Medici lost power and were exiled from the city.

They were replaced for a time by the fire-and-brimstone Dominican preacher Girolamo Savonarola, who despised the humanist mania for Greek and Roman antiquity then celebrated in Florence. Savonarola was notorious for the "bonfire of the vanities," in which great artworks—including tapestries, paintings, and books by Dante, Petrarch, and Boccaccio—were consigned to the flames in the public square. After Savonarola lost favor with the Pope, he was hanged in 1498 as a heretic—confessing after undergoing the strappado, in a which a prisoner was hoisted in the air by ropes attached to the wrists and then suddenly dropped to the floor.

With Savonarola removed from the scene, Florence returned to a republican government. And at twenty-nine, Machiavelli was appointed to a post as Second Chancellor, responsible for domestic reports and the city's correspondence. Styling himself as the Florentine Secretary, he held this position until 1512, while serving as an envoy of the republic, dispatched to meet Popes and the crowned heads of Europe. Altogether, during his

fourteen years in office, Machiavelli embarked on more than forty diplomatic missions.

While serving as secretary and envoy, Machiavelli also organized a militia
force of Florentine citizens, arguing against the use of mercenaries—a theme
he would underscore in *The Prince*. During a lingering conflict with the
neighboring city of Pisa, he collaborated with Leonardo da Vinci on an
elaborate but failed plan to divert the Arno River to deprive Pisa of water.
Machiavelli later led a successful militia army in defeating Pisa. But a few
years later, his poorly armed militiamen suffered a disastrous defeat in battle
at Prato. Florence fell once more to the Medici, backed by a Spanish army
allied with Pope Julius II. The Medici rode into the city in September 1512,
ending Florence's democratic rule.

Suspected in a conspiracy against the Medici, Machiavelli was imprisoned and tortured, subjected like Savonarola to the strappado. After his
release under papal amnesty, Machiavelli withdrew to his family farm south
of Florence where he wrote *The Prince*—his vain attempt to curry favor with
the Medici, Florence's power brokers—and another much longer historical
work, *Discourses on Livy*. Livy was a prominent historian of the Roman
republic, which Machiavelli admired. This book is more concerned with
how to preserve republics, a subject not discussed in *The Prince*. It was his
Discourses rather than *The Prince* that influenced America's founders, John
Adams among them, for its insight into republican ideals.

Machiavelli kept busy with more than his writing, according to writer
Ondine Cohane, who followed in the author's footsteps five centuries later:
"The bust of Machiavelli in the Palazzo Vecchio is a relief thought to be
taken from his death mask. It shows a rather brooding face, a thin-lipped
and sharp-boned figure. In fact I had imagined before my visit to his hamlet
that he was a man of few passions besides work and politics. But on my tour
I learned how he was a man of huge appetites: In addition to his own seven
legitimate children, he managed to be something of a Tuscan Casanova,
enjoying women all over Italy, and he drank copiously, too: 'After dinner, I
go back to the inn: here are the innkeeper, and usually a butcher, a miller,
and two bricklayers. In their company I roguify myself all day,' he wrote."

After failing to win a post under the Medici, Machiavelli turned to writing poetry and for the theater. His bawdy comedy, *The Mandrake*, proved the most successful work of his career, and was eventually performed in the papal court. With this literary success, he returned to Medici favor and received a papal commission to write a history of Florence. Remarkably, he did not balk at describing how the Medici family had crushed all political opposition.

During another crisis, when the army of the Holy Roman Emperor Charles was occupying much of Italy, Machiavelli was credited with reinforcing Florence's fortifications so successfully that the invaders bypassed the city. Ragged and hungry, these mercenaries violently sacked Rome in May 1527. "In the ensuing chaos, the Medici regime in Florence was overthrown; the republic was restored; the Great Council was reinstated," writes Claudia Roth Pierpont. "This was everything that Machiavelli had hoped for even when he appeared to be on the other side. . . . As a Medici supporter, he found himself once again unemployed, subject to the same sort of political suspicions as when the Medici had first returned."

Having sided with the Medici, Machiavelli was once again out of work and out of favor. He returned to his farm, where he fell ill with a stomach disorder. Machiavelli died on June 21, 1527, after receiving last rites, at the age of fifty-eight. He was buried in Florence's Santa Croce church, where there is now a monument above his tomb, erected in 1789.

Both of Machiavelli's most important books were published only after his death, the *Discourses on Livy* in 1531 and *The Prince* in 1532. In 1559, *The Prince* was placed on the first papal Index of Prohibited Books, where it remained until 1890.

WHY YOU SHOULD READ IT

There are a few names and adjectives derived from names in this collection, like Utopia and Orwellian, that have become part of the language. Add "Machiavellian" to the list. Ever since *The Prince* was published, its advice and author have been considered shockingly immoral—one reason that his name became shorthand for cutthroat cunning, duplicity, and a win-at-all-costs mentality in politics and business.

But as biographer Ross King and others have argued, Machiavelli gets something of a bad rap. Over time, scholars and historians have debated whether Machiavelli was truly advocating for no-holds-barred political manipulation or merely describing the reality he saw. *The Prince* is a valuable book because it is among the first works of political science; Machiavelli is a meticulous observer of statecraft. He was also an astute reader of human nature, so his most notable work is valuable for his insights into sociology and the psychology of leaders and followers—not always predictable. While his recommendations to the Prince often emphasized a bare-knuckled sense of authority, Machiavelli also understood the value of "soft power." He counseled: "A prince should also show esteem for talent, for actively encouraging able men, and honouring those who excel in their profession."

There is little question that *The Prince* is a landmark piece of historical literature for its place in establishing an influential set of rules for governing. These rules have been used by a variety of forces—for good and ill. It may have been read by Henry VIII and his influential counselor Thomas Cromwell. Machiavelli influenced Enlightenment thinkers, like Rousseau, who found his ideas a basis for political liberty. Later Italian patriots, who would eventually unite Italy in the nineteenth century, saw him as a passionate prophet of Italian unification.

But *The Prince* is also one of the books that signal the great turning point in Western history when humanism, the Renaissance, and the Reformation altered the course of events. It was the era that signaled a break with centuries of rule by Church and kings, an era in which the ancient Greek ideal—"Man is the measure of all things"—replaced an orthodoxy of thought and opened the way for practical philosophers such as Machiavelli to rewrite the rule books. But Machiavelli was also writing from the real experience of corruption and political instability he had witnessed and—barely—survived. As historian Charles Freeman writes, "The jaded Machiavelli was critical of his more philosophical contemporaries who underestimated the need for coercion."

Machiavelli and his most famous work are, then, somewhat ambiguous. As biographer Ross King writes, "The key to some of the ambiguities may lie in the nature of the man himself. Machiavelli's numerous undertakings—

diplomat, playwright, poet, historian, political theorist, farmer, military engineer, militia captain—make him, like his friend Leonardo, a true Renaissance man. Yet, like Leonardo, who denounced the 'beastly madness' of war while devising ingenious and deadly weapons, Machiavelli is awash in paradoxes and inconsistencies."

After it was published in 1532, *The Prince* was condemned by many over the centuries, according to Claudia Roth Pierpont of the *New Yorker*, as the "Stratagems of Satan." Machiavelli was accused of inspiring Henry VIII to challenge the Pope and, decades later, of inciting the massacre of Protestants in France. "Wherever a sovereign usurped power from the church or the nobility," wrote Pierpont, "whenever ostentatious deceit or murderous force was used, Machiavelli was spied in the shadows, scribbling at his desk amid the olive groves, his quill dipped in a poison so potent that it threatened the power structures of Europe." But, Pierpont adds, "Machiavelli no more invented political evil by describing it than Kinsey invented sex."

That said, *The Prince* remains one of the most widely read books in Western history. It does, however, break a few of my rules for this collection. Though it certainly has been and remains consequential, *The Prince* is infused with references to biblical figures (Moses, King David), historical rulers (from ancient Greece, Carthage, and Rome), and contemporary Italian leaders—including a bevy of popes and the notorious Cesare Borgia—who may seem obscure. Machiavelli's historical name-dropping may pose a challenge, but his message is highly relevant. Stay with it and you may even consider using Machiavelli as an entrée to learn more about some of the famous and tarnished men he singled out.

As a historian, I pondered what Machiavelli would make of some of the modern world's students of his advice about being more feared than loved. Hitler and Stalin are both said to have studied *The Prince*, which certainly does not qualify as an endorsement.

On the other hand, when I consider the greatest of American political leaders, few fit the "Machiavellian" mold. Abraham Lincoln and Franklin D. Roosevelt, two of the American presidents I most admire, certainly understood power and its uses, and both had enemies and detractors in their day. But in leading the nation through its greatest crises—the Civil War for Lincoln and the Great Depression and World War II for FDR—these men, I think it is fair to say, were more loved than feared. What would Machiavelli say?

WHAT TO READ NEXT

For serious scholars of political science, Machiavelli's *Discourse on Livy* is considered by historians to be his more significant work—though it is about four times the length of *The Prince*.

For an excellent brief biography of Machiavelli and his times, I recommend *Machiavelli: Philosopher of Power*, written by Ross King, a leading historian of the Italian Renaissance. I would highly commend two of King's other works that brilliantly depict this miraculous era: *Brunelleschi's Dome: How a Renaissance Genius Reinvented Architecture* and *Michelangelo and the Pope's Ceiling*, a riveting account of the creation of the masterpiece on the ceiling of the Vatican's Sistine Chapel.

"I had often before this said, that if the Indians should come,
I should chuse rather to be killed by them than be taken alive . . ."

The Sovereignty and
Goodness of God

— 1682 —

Mary Rowlandson

The Sovereignty and Goodness of God *by Mary Rowlandson with Related*
Documents, Boston: Bedford/St. Martin's, 1997; edited with an introduction
by Neal Salisbury; 184 pages

EXCERPT

On the tenth of February 1675,* Came the *Indians* with great numbers upon
Lancaster. Their first coming was about Sun-rising; hearing the noise of some

---

* This was the date on the old Julian calendar, then used in England and its colonies; the
date would be February 20, 1676, under the Gregorian calendar, later adopted in England
and America. Spelling, grammar, and punctuation per original text.

Guns, we looked out; several Houses were burning, and the Smoke ascending to Heaven. There were five persons taken in one house, the Father, and the Mother and a sucking Child, they knockt on the head; the other two they took and carried away alive. There were two others, who being out of their Garison upon some occasion were set upon; one was knockt on the head, the other escaped: Another there was who running along was shot and wounded, and fell down; he begged of them his life, promising them Money (as they told me) but they would not hearken to him but knockt him in head, and stript him naked, and split open his Bowels.

SUMMARY

If your history of colonial New England leapfrogs from the Pilgrims and the legendary first Thanksgiving in 1621 to a brief stopover for the Salem Witch Trials in the 1690s and then a tea dump in Boston Harbor in 1773, then you—like many Americans—have some large, blank spaces to fill. That's where Mary Rowlandson comes in.

The Sovereignty and Goodness of God is her vividly gripping, first-person account of nearly three months spent in captivity among Native people during King Philip's War, a brutal conflict that raged across New England in the late seventeenth century. That said, Rowlandson's book must be read for what it was: Puritan propaganda meant to inflame anti-Native sentiment and celebrate Rowlandson's exemplary religious devotion.

In 1676, a full century before the American Revolution began, a scorched-earth war between Native people and Anglo-American colonists ravaged the New England countryside for months. In the midst of this fighting, thirty-eight-year-old Mary Rowlandson thought that she and her three children would be secure in their refuge, a well-stocked "garrison house" in Lancaster, a frontier settlement in central Massachusetts.

But, as she graphically describes, a party of Wampanoag, Nipmuck, and Narragansett warriors swept into the village in February 1676. Rowlandson's large house, where thirty neighbors had sought safety, was set ablaze. As the wooden structure went up like kindling, Mary Rowlandson had to choose between certain death inside and a possible death outside.

Fleeing the burning house, she and her children were taken hostage along with some two dozen other Anglo-American settlers—mostly women and children—and marched off to an uncertain fate. She was separated from two of her children and another later died in her arms.

Trudging through the wilderness in a bitterly cold New England winter, Mary Rowlandson tells of being held by a Native force led by Metacom, a prominent chief known to Anglo-American colonizers as King Philip. He was the son of a very famous father in American history: Massasoit was sachem, or chief, of the people who helped the English settlers survive their first year in 1621 and joined that legendary Thanksgiving feast. Though highly subjective, Rowlandson's account paints a very different picture of relations between the Native nations and the colonizers, a story our schoolbooks leave out.

ABOUT THE AUTHOR: MARY WHITE ROWLANDSON

Mary Rowlandson's story is a fitting follow-up to that of Thomas More, whose execution in 1535 was reflective of the religious and political strife that tore apart England, and much of Europe, for more than a century. Born in England around 1637, Mary White Rowlandson was about two years old when her parents came to America as part of the Great Migration that brought fleets of English Puritans to the Massachusetts Bay Colony. The Puritans were a dissident group who wished to "purify" the Protestant Church of England—somewhat different from the other sect of "Pilgrims," Separatists who sought to completely break from the state church. In the 1630s, thousands of Puritans left their English homes for a new life in America, largely as a result of the religious conflicts that bloodied Europe during the Protestant Reformation.

In a mass movement commencing in 1630 and lasting a decade, more than twenty thousand Puritans sailed for America, bringing their severe form of Calvinist Christianity with them. While there was a brief period of uneasy peace between the indigenous people and the Puritans, this formidable influx of English colonists, armed with considerable firepower, soon encroached on Native American homelands, hunting grounds, and sacred territory. The Puritans also began to vigorously convert the indigenous people to Christianity, and specifically their Puritan vision. The White family, including two-year-old Mary, was part of this great Puritan wave, eventually settling and prospering in the Massachusetts frontier outpost of Lancaster.

In 1656, at about age nineteen, Mary White married Joseph Rowlandson, Lancaster's minister, a prominent figure in a colony where religious leaders also controlled the government. In 1676, during Metacom's or King Philip's War, Rowlandson was taken captive, as described in her account. Remaining with her captors for nearly three months, she was eventually ransomed and reunited with her husband and two surviving children.

A year after Mary Rowlandson's rescue, she and her husband moved to Connecticut, where he led another church. After Joseph Rowlandson's death in 1678, Mary began to record her experiences in captivity. Her autobiographical narrative was published in Cambridge, Massachusetts, in 1682, one of the most personal accounts of the clash of these two worlds—Native American and English Puritan.

A sensation in both America and England, the book quickly became a best-selling piece of anti-Indian, Puritan propaganda. In it, Mary Rowlandson wrote: "I remember in the night season, how the other day I was in the midst of thousands of enemies, & nothing but death before me. . . . Oh! The wonderful power of God that mine eyes have seen . . . that when others are sleeping mine are weeping."

Remarried and then widowed again in 1691, Mary Rowlandson lived as a respected community leader in Wethersfield, Connecticut, until her death in 1711.

WHY YOU SHOULD READ IT

Once among the most famous people in America, Mary Rowlandson, with the war in which she was caught, was eventually erased from history books. The brutal era of King Philip's War, with its ultimate destruction of entire Native nations, was not included when generations of schoolchildren learned about the settlement of New England, even though the conflict was far more significant than the so-called first Thanksgiving.

So, read Mary Rowlandson to illuminate a period in which the Native people of New England, pressed by waves of English arrivals, were losing their lands to unscrupulous settlers. Their traditions were also lost to Puritan missionaries who between 1660 and 1663 produced the first complete Bible printed in North America. To propagate Christianity among the indigenous people, whose religious traditions were considered "heathen," it was translated by a Puritan minister, John Eliot, into Natick, an Algonquin language; one thousand copies were printed in Cambridge, Massachusetts.

The narrative also provides a graphic and historically accurate picture of Mary Rowlandson's capture and grueling life as a hostage. Her memoir is considered the first "Indian captivity narrative"—which would emerge as a popular genre in early American literature—as well as the first North American publication by a living woman, and something of an early "best seller" as well. "It is a powerful rendering of a cross-cultural encounter under the most trying and extreme of circumstances," writes Neal Salisbury, editor of this edition, "in which the protagonist/author finds the very boundaries of her cultural identity being tested."

Read it finally as a piece of what I call America's hidden history. Metacom's War would go down as seventeenth-century New England's single greatest calamity, the deadliest war in the history of European settlement in North America. In the space of little more than a year, a third of the hundred or so towns in New England were burned and abandoned. The destruction and loss of life on both sides was catastrophic, far beyond the casualties in other American wars. In his National Book Award–winning *Mayflower*, historian Nathaniel Philbrick summarized the devastation this way:

Plymouth Colony lost close to 8 percent of its men.

But the English losses appear almost inconsequential when compared with those of the Indians. Of a total Native population of approximately 20,000, at least 2,000 had been killed in battle or died of their injuries; 3,000 had died of sickness and starvation, 1,000 had been shipped out of the country as slaves, while an estimated 2,000 eventually fled to either the Iroquois to the west or the Abenakis to the north. Overall, the Native American population of southern

New England had sustained a loss of somewhere between 60 and 80 percent.

Neither a standard history nor journalism, Rowlandson's book is a primary source document for historians, but is still a personal memoir and must be read that way. It was written for a white, English Christian audience to emphasize the superiority of her faith. But it remains a compelling document that reminds us that history is the story of real people and not a rote recitation of dates, battles, and speeches. As Professor Elaine Showalter described Rowlandson's ordeal:

> Step by painful step, she was being removed from her life as a pious Puritan matron and entering the harsh world of the Narragansetts, where she found that her will to survive was stronger than her fear or grief. She surprised herself with her endurance and ability to adapt. She ate food that previously would have disgusted her, including raw horse liver and bear meat. Regarding the Indians as savages, she also learned to acknowledge their humanity, and to negotiate and bargain with them.

WHAT TO READ NEXT

Mary Rowlandson wrote nothing else. But her remarkable account is an entryway to more about this overlooked, and often sanitized, era in American history, as well as the genre of "captivity narratives." For more historical context on the world of Mary Rowlandson, I recommend Lisa Brooks's *Our Beloved Kin: A New History of King Philip's War*, winner of the 2019 Bancroft Prize in history; *The Name of War: King Philip's War and the Origins of American Identity* (1998) by Harvard historian and *New Yorker* contributor Jill Lepore; and Nathaniel Philbrick's best-selling *Mayflower* (2006), cited earlier. None of these is short, but all provide a much richer and more realistic picture of colonial New England than most Americans ever receive.

The wider subject of "captivity narratives" is explored in *Women's Indian Captivity Narratives* (1988), a collection edited by Kathryn Derounian-Stodola that presents a variety of these experiences—far from unusual in America, well into the nineteenth century. Among these is the story of Mary Jemison, taken as a child from frontier Pennsylvania. She chose to remain with her Seneca captors, later marrying two successive Seneca men. She would become famed as "The White Woman of the Genesee." A similar significant account is documented in *The Unredeemed Captive: A Family Story from Early America* (1994) by John Demos. It describes the 1704 capture of Eunice Williams, a young woman from Deerfield, Massachusetts. Like Mary Jemison, Eunice Williams chose to remain with her Mohawk captors and marry one of them.

A later counterpoint can be found in *Life Among the Piutes: Their Wrongs and Claims*. Written in 1883 by Sarah Winnemucca, the book is the first published by a Native American woman and is valuable for its description of Northern Paiute life and the impact of white settlement.

An excellent overview of indigenous American history is presented in the prizewinning *An Indigenous Peoples' History of the United States* by Roxanne Dunbar-Ortiz. She writes: "To say that the United States is a colonialist settler-state is not to make an accusation but rather to face historical reality, without which consideration not much U.S. history makes sense, unless Indigenous peoples are erased. But Indigenous nations, through resistance, have survived and bear witness to this history."

"Lies have dominated people for a long time."

Treatise on Toleration

— 1763 —

Voltaire

New York: Penguin Books, 2016; translated with an introduction and notes by Desmond M. Clarke,; 164 pages

EXCERPTS

Reason is gentle and humane, and it encourages toleration; it eliminates discord, reinforces virtue and is more effective in persuading people to obey the law than force is in winning their compliance. One should also not underestimate the ridicule with which all sensible people regard religious enthusiasm in our time. This ridicule is a powerful barrier against the excesses of all religious sects.

The law of intolerance is therefore absurd and barbaric. It is the law of the jungle and, indeed, it is even worse because wild animals kill others only to eat, while we human beings are exterminating each other for the sake of a few paragraphs.

SUMMARY

In 1761, a French merchant named Jean Calas was falsely accused of murdering his son in the largely Catholic town of Toulouse. Calas was a French Protestant, or Huguenot, and his alleged motive was that his son was converting to Catholicism; after being tortured, and under threat of his family members being tortured as well, Calas supposedly confessed to the crime and was executed on March 10, 1762.

A year later, the poet, playwright, novelist, and essayist Voltaire anonymously produced *Treatise on Toleration*, an impassioned work calling for a spirit of religious tolerance written in the belief that the execution of Calas was a grave injustice. Convinced of the man's innocence, Voltaire argued that the religious hostility of the Catholics who controlled Toulouse was responsible for his wrongful death. "If an innocent Huguenot could be so unjustly tortured and executed at the instigation of a Catholic mob in Toulouse," translator and editor Desmond M. Clarke writes of Voltaire's thinking, "then no one was safe and it was time to re-examine the laws and customs of France that discriminated systematically against the Huguenot minority."

In a series of brief chapters, Voltaire lays out his arguments for toleration of religious belief and freedom of conscience, referencing contemporary events and the nation's bloodstained history. Voltaire would have been keenly aware of the 1572 massacre of thousands of Huguenots—perhaps as many as thirty thousand across the country—murdered in a paroxysm of violence known on St. Bartholomew's Day.

Voltaire traces the violence brought about by religious conflicts in France, where the line between church and state was nonexistent. But Voltaire also questions assumptions and church orthodoxy about the Bible and religious traditions that had emerged over more than a thousand years of Christianity. Like many Deists—Benjamin Franklin and American presidents Washington, Jefferson, Madison, Monroe, and Lincoln among them—Voltaire did not abandon Christianity. But he was an advocate of freedom of speech, freedom of religion, and the separation of church and state. Nearing the conclusion of *Treatise*, Voltaire writes: "I sow a seed that may in due course produce a harvest. Let us wait as long as is necessary for the king's bounty, the wisdom of his ministers and the spirit of rationality that is beginning to shed its light everywhere."

ABOUT THE AUTHOR: VOLTAIRE

Voltaire is the author of one of my favorite books, *Candide*, published in 1759. One of freshest and funniest books I have ever read, it reflects his willingness to take on the most sacred of cows—church and state. He spent much of his life in witty, withering attacks on such institutions.

Voltaire was born François-Marie Arouet on November 21, 1694, the son of a reasonably well-to-do official in the French legal system. Beginning studies at the Jesuit Collège Louis-le-Grand, young Arouet acquired a classical education and developed a love for theater and literature, as well as a growing skepticism of religion.

After being dismissed from a diplomatic post in Holland over an amorous misadventure, he returned to Paris and began to write poems. His work was widely popular. But he crossed a line when he satirized a French nobleman, and he was held for a time in the Bastille.

With ambitions of becoming France's next great dramatist, he turned to theater after his release from jail. Voltaire saw his first play, the tragedy *Oedipus*, performed to great success in 1718 at the Comédie-Française. He had by then adopted the pen name Voltaire, derived from an anagram of his birth name. According to the Voltaire Foundation: "Voltaire is an anagram of 'Arouet l(e) j(eune)' (in the 18th century, *i* and *j*, and *u* and *v*, were typographically interchangeable) . . . but the play on the verb *volter*, to turn abruptly, evokes a playful or 'volatile' quality which foretells the quick style, pervasive humour and irony that make Voltaire such an important figure in the history of the Enlightenment."

After a near-fatal case of smallpox, Voltaire once again faced trouble over his penchant for poetically satirizing the nobility. After being beaten and, once again, briefly jailed, he left in 1726 for England, where he met Alexander Pope and Jonathan Swift and became familiar with some of the leading English writers and thinkers of the day, including Swift, Isaac

Newton, and John Locke—men at the center of this era of great intellectual ferment. They were upending centuries-old views of nature, astronomy, religious authority, and the concept of absolute monarchy.

Returning to Paris, Voltaire made his first fortune by curious means. Pooling money with several other men, he was able to buy all the tickets in a French lottery. Voltaire repeated the strategy until he gathered a small fortune, which he then invested wisely.

Soon after his return to France, Voltaire wrote *Letters Concerning the English Nation*. Composed in English, the book celebrated England's Parliament, Quakerism, inoculation against smallpox, and the achievements of Isaac Newton. (Voltaire is also credited with spreading the legendary story of Newton being inspired by a falling apple.) In Desmond M. Clarke's description of this collection of letters—actually a series of essays—they "praised the innovative and creative energy of the British scientific and political opinions in contrast with the conservative tyranny that resulted from the close co-operation between the Catholic Church and the royal court in France."

The book appeared in France as *Lettres philosophiques*. Condemned in June 1734, the book was publicly burned in Paris, and its publisher arrested. Also facing arrest, Voltaire fled Paris, settling with his lover, Madame du Châtelet, in Champagne. A mathematician and physicist, she wrote scientific treatises and translated Newton's work into French while tutoring Voltaire in the natural sciences. They were together, living and working with great mutual respect, by all accounts, for some twelve years. Madame du Châtelet began an affair with another poet in 1748 and, after giving birth to a daughter, died at age forty-two in September 1749. By then, Voltaire had begun a relationship with his niece, Marie Louise Mignot, who remained with Voltaire for the rest of his life.

In 1751, he published *Age of Louis XIV*, a significant work of history in which he extolled the "Sun King" for ushering in an era of artistic, scientific, and literary achievement rivaling the great ages in Greece, Augustan Rome, and the Italian Renaissance.

Voltaire wrote *Candide* in 1759 in a château near Geneva. Then he embarked on the campaign to exonerate the executed shopkeeper, Jean

Calas, resulting in the publication of *Treatise on Toleration* in 1763—
anonymous because all publications at the time had to be approved by the
French royal court.

That book was followed a year later by *The Pocket Philosophical
Dictionary*—also anonymous—a series of brief essays, arranged alpha-
betically, on such subjects as atheism, free will, and, of course, toleration.

"Voltaire wanted to write a book which would shock and which would
change minds," wrote Nicholas Cronk, director of the Voltaire Foundation
at the University of Oxford, "above all he wanted to reach out to a wide
readership, so portability was essential: small books are cheaper—and easier
to hide if the police come looking for them." Predictably, "the book was
promptly condemned in Paris . . . and burned by the public executioner in
Geneva. It was also placed on the Index of books prohibited by the Catholic
Church until the Index was abolished in 1966."

In 1778, Voltaire returned to Paris for the production of one of his final
plays, *Irène*. He died there on May 30, at the age of eighty-three. Voltaire's
body was smuggled out of Paris by admirers who feared that he would be
refused burial by Church authorities. Voltaire's remains were eventually
returned to Paris and interred in the Panthéon, a mausoleum for distinguished French citizens, in July 1791.

WHY YOU SHOULD READ IT

In a collection of writers and thinkers whose work changed history, Voltaire
must be placed among the first rank. Unlike many other philosophers,
Voltaire wrote to be read not by just the learned and scholarly. His wit, wisdom, and language were meant to be accessible to all. "*The Treatise*," writes
Desmond M. Clarke, "was much more like the work of a campaigning
journalist, and it focused primarily on the way in which French Catholics
treated fellow citizens who were Calvinists [Protestants]."

Its influence was far-reaching in the Age of Revolution that followed.
Religion and monarchies were shaken in the Enlightenment's wake. Voltaire
and Benjamin Franklin were close friends, and Voltaire's ideas about natural
rights profoundly influenced members of America's Founding Generation,

including John Adams, Thomas Jefferson, and George Washington, who ordered a translation of Voltaire's writing after the Revolution. (Washington also sat for a life mask by the French sculptor Antoine Houdon famed for crafting statues of Voltaire.)

In the republic born after France's violent revolution, Voltaire's belief in a natural right to freedom of thought and religion was enshrined by France's first legislature. The August 1789 Declaration of the Rights of Man and the Citizen proclaimed: "The free communication of ideas and opinions is one of the most precious of the rights of man. Every citizen may, accordingly, speak, write, and print with freedom, but shall be responsible for such abuses of this freedom as shall be defined by law."

Despite these achievements, Voltaire has contemporary critics who believe that streams of racism and anti-Semitism course through his work. Exploring the racial prejudices of Enlightenment thinkers like Kant, Hume, and Voltaire, Professor Laurie Shrage wrote in the *New York Times* that Voltaire considered Jews—or "Adamites—in his wording, "a major menace to European civilization, since they kept infecting it with what he considered the horrible immorality of the Bible. Voltaire therefore insisted that Europe should separate itself from the Adamites." Shrage went on to ask: "Should those who teach their works and ideas in the 21st century share them without mentioning the harmful stereotypes these thinkers helped to legitimize?" It should be pointed out that in *Treatise on Toleration*, Voltaire cites an earlier church council's dictum: "Let no one do any violence to the Jews."

In addition to his problematic views on Jews, Voltaire also wrote disparagingly of Africans, and although critical of the slave trade, he invested in a French trading company and profited from African slavery. For these reasons, a statue honoring Voltaire in Paris was defaced with red paint in 2020 and later removed, ostensibly for cleaning. (As of this writing it has not been replaced.)

As students of American history know, we are constantly confronted by contradictions in history. A closer look at so-called Great Men can often reveal their imperfections. Martin Luther profoundly changed history but was an outspoken anti-Semite; America's Founding Generation particularly embodies that sort of contradiction: many of the men who were devoted to the ideals of "life, liberty, and the pursuit of happiness" and that "all men are created equal" enslaved people or otherwise profited from the African slave trade. This was an inconvenient truth in America, ignored in American schoolbooks for a very long time. At least forty of the fifty-six signers of the Declaration of Independence were enslavers, as were Washington, Madison, and Monroe. The list, of course, includes Thomas Jefferson, who kept a bust of Voltaire at his Monticello home. That historical fact, which some would try to whitewash in the teaching of American history, is too important to leave out when we tell the story.

The same is true for Voltaire.

WHAT TO READ NEXT

Read Voltaire's *Candide* (1759). Fast-paced and very comical, it is an excellent fictional counterpoint to his nonfiction. A rollicking tour-de-force of Voltaire's world, it features the young hero Candide, who suffers through the Inquisition, wars, imprisonment, and deadly earthquakes in the belief that he lives in the "best of all possible worlds." In grand comic fashion, Voltaire's picaresque acidly sketches, and then destroys, many of the great institutions of his time.

But for readers who desire more Enlightenment wisdom of the nonfiction variety, some suggestions. First, I point to *A Discourse on Inequality* (1755) by Jean-Jacques Rousseau, which argues that man was better off in a state of nature than in civilized society. Rousseau also wrote *The Social Contract* (1762), which famously opens: "Man was born free, and everywhere he is in chains." Rousseau's book is credited with helping bring about the French Revolution a generation later.

"Just as Voltaire sought a common vision for all mankind, to be fulfilled in 'civilization,'" concludes Daniel Boorstin, "so Rousseau, having witnessed the varied spectacle of war and civilization in the enlightened Europe of his day, envisioned a liberated mankind. . . . If men would only return to their natural bliss, they would be free to fulfill their human possibilities."

Another central thinker of this era is Englishman John Locke, whose brief but radical *Letter Concerning Toleration* (1689) and *Second Treatise of Government* (1690) influenced Voltaire. While neither can be counted pleasure reading, they were profoundly influential, especially to America's Founding Generation. In particular, Thomas Jefferson would borrow significant words in the Declaration of Independence on Locke's work. For instance, Locke's phrase "the pursuit of property" was changed—for the better, perhaps—to "the pursuit of happiness."

"My own mind is my own church."

The Age of Reason:
Being An Investigation of True
and Fabulous Theology

— 1794 —

Thomas Paine

Mineola, NY: Dover, 2004; 208 pages; edited by Moncure Daniel Conway; other available editions include collections such as Thomas Paine: Collected Writings, *New York: Library of America, 1995*

EXCERPT

I believe in one God, and no more; and I hope for happiness beyond this life.

I believe the equality of man, and I believe that religious duties consist in doing justice, loving mercy, and endeavouring to make our fellow-creatures happy.

But, lest it should be supposed that I believe many other things in addition to these, I shall, in the progress of this work, declare the things I do not believe, and my reasons for not believing them.

I do not believe in the creed professed by the Jewish church, by the Roman church, by the Greek church, by the Turkish church, by the Protestant church, nor by any church that I know of. My own mind is my own church.

All national institutions of churches, whether Jewish, Christian, or Turkish, appear to me no other than human inventions set up to terrify and enslave mankind, and monopolize power and profit.

SUMMARY

If the Bible is the "Divine Word of God," why does it contain so many historical errors and contradictions? This question troubled Voltaire, and it also really bothered Thomas Paine, the most influential pamphleteer and propagandist of the American Revolution. But Paine's polemic *The Age of Reason* raised the stakes.

Composed in part while Paine was jailed in the Bastille during the French Revolution, facing the prospect of the guillotine, the pamphlet offers his reasoned assault on organized religion and its role in society. Attacking the fundamentals of Christianity and elevating reason and science, it is a summation, etched in acid, by a humanist and freethinker whose ringing declaration "I believe in one God, and no more" stands as the essence of Deism. As historian Eric Foner notes, Paine's tirade caught on: "Reprinted in countless editions, the pamphlet became the most popular Deist work ever written."

An outgrowth of the Enlightenment, Deism is a religious view that holds faith in a God who formed the universe and established rationally comprehensible moral and natural laws but no longer intervenes in human affairs through miracles. It also rejects most organized faiths, with their rules and artificial hierarchies, as a corruption of faith in divine Providence.

Deists such as Paine dismissed biblical "revelation," believing that religious truth could be found only through human reason and that religious laws should align with nature's laws. In his argument, Paine exposed the flaws he found in his examination of both the Old and New Testaments.

He begins with the very process by which the Bible was produced:

When the church mythologists established their system, they collected all the writings they could find, and managed them as they pleased. It is a matter altogether of uncertainty to us whether such of the writings as now appear under the name of the Old and the New Testament, are in the same state in which those collectors say they found them; or whether they added, altered, abridged, or dressed them up.

Be that as it may, they decided by *vote* which of the books out of the collection they had made, should be the WORD OF GOD, and which should not.

These very human decisions, in Paine's mind, had nothing to do with the Creator. "The Almighty," concluded Paine, "is the great mechanic of the creation, the first philosopher, and original teacher of all science."

ABOUT THE AUTHOR: THOMAS PAINE

Witness to and key participant in the American Revolution and the French Revolution, Thomas Paine was born in Thetford, England, on February 9, 1737.* His father was a Quaker and a corset maker; his Anglican mother was the daughter of a local attorney and kept house. With only a paltry education, Paine was apprenticed at the age of thirteen—to his father—but ran away to join the navy during the Seven Years' War, fought from 1756 to 1763 and known in America as the French and Indian War. Paine later found work as an excise official, a government officer charged with hunting smugglers and collecting taxes on liquor and tobacco.

That career ended abruptly when Paine nettled his employers by writing an argument in favor of raising the pay of excise agents like himself. Not just angling for a raise, he intended to expose the corruption in the excise service. He also sought to alleviate the crushing poverty of the English laboring class. Whether it was his father's Quakerism, the tenor of the times, or

---

* Because of changes to the calendar after England shifted to the Gregorian dating system in 1752, Paine's birthdate is also listed as January 29, 1736, in the "Old Style."

simply Paine's personality, he demonstrated a penchant for speaking "truth to power" that would mark his entire life, land him in endless trouble, and keep him in perpetual poverty.

Paine's fate turned in London in 1774. There he met Benjamin Franklin, America's most prominent man of the day. Famed for his writing, practical inventions, and scientific discoveries, Franklin was in London to argue for American causes. Urging Paine to move to America, Franklin provided him with a letter of introduction to a Philadelphia printer. Shortly after landing in the city in November 1774, Paine was given work in a printing house.

His arrival in Pennsylvania was timely. Philadelphia was a hotbed of political change and Paine arrived shortly before the conflict between the American colonies and the British passed the tipping point. The first shots were fired in Massachusetts in April 1775. As the Continental Congress hesitantly debated a complete break with England, Paine took up the patriot cause. Arguing for complete American independence as a fundamental principle rather than merely rebelling against unfair taxes as some American patriots did, he laid out his case in *Common Sense*, anonymously published in January 1776.

"Of more worth is one honest man to society and in the sight of God, than all the crowned ruffians that ever lived," Paine wrote. The brief pamphlet sold more than five hundred thousand copies within a few months. (It is estimated that equivalent number of sales in contemporary America, considering the relative population of the country in 1776, would be more than 15 million copies.) Paine's pamphlet is widely credited with swinging American opinion in favor of independence. But *Common Sense* was also a welcome breath of fresh air in the stuffy air of political discourse. As Eric Foner notes, "It also revealed Paine as a brilliant, innovative stylist, capable of breaking with time-honored traditions of political writing to forge a new language that would reach out to a mass audience."

An equally significant contribution came through a series of essays published under the heading *The American Crisis* between 1776 and 1783. The first of these pamphlets, *The American Crisis. Number I*, published in Philadelphia on December 19, 1776, remains a landmark piece of American literature:

These are the times that try men's souls: The summer soldier and
the sunshine patriot will, in this crisis, shrink from the service of
his country; but he that stands it NOW, deserves the love and thanks
of man and woman. Tyranny, like hell, is not easily conquered; yet
we have this consolation with us, that the harder the conflict, the
more glorious the triumph. What we obtain too cheap, we esteem too
lightly: — 'Tis dearness only that gives every thing its value.

Written as George Washington's demoralized, ill-equipped Continental
Army was in retreat, Paine's call to action was a lightning bolt of inspiration.
General Washington ordered his officers to read Paine's rousing words to
the troops. Committed to supporting the American effort throughout the
war, Paine went to France on a diplomatic mission in 1781, returning with
money, clothing, and ammunition that contributed to the success of the
War for Independence.

With the Revolution over, Paine was again in poverty. While his patri-
otic works had sold hundreds of thousands of copies, he refused to accept
any profits. He petitioned the Congress for financial assistance and was
given some money and title to a farm in New Rochelle, New York.

Returning to England in 1787, Paine was drawn into a sharp debate
over France's ongoing Revolution, which had begun in 1789. On March
13, 1791, Paine published *Rights of Man*, which created an immediate furor.
Paine defended the French Revolution and denounced the evils of poverty,
illiteracy, unemployment, and war. In the book, he also outlined a plan for
popular education, relief of the poor, pensions for the elderly, and public
works for the unemployed. Funded by a gradual income tax, Paine's program sounds very much like the blueprint of modern progressive American
politics—not very different from the New Deal policies enacted under
Franklin D. Roosevelt during the Great Depression.

At the time, however, British authorities were unimpressed. The book
was banned and its publisher jailed. Indicted for treason, Paine was tried
in absentia, found guilty of seditious libel, and declared an outlaw. *Rights
of Man* was ordered permanently suppressed.

Paine had arrived in revolutionary France in 1790, the year before the book's publication, where he hailed the abolition of the monarchy. Declared an honorary French citizen, he was elected to the National Convention. But Paine argued against the execution of Louis XVI and deplored the Reign of Terror that had taken hold in France with a series of massacres and mass executions. This time, Paine's outspokenness landed him in more than hot water. For his criticism of the new regime, Paine was arrested and imprisoned from December 28, 1793, to November 4, 1794. While awaiting execution, he was spared only when someone failed to correctly mark his cell. Paine was released through the intervention of the American Minister to France, the future American president James Monroe.

While in prison, however, Paine wrote a letter excoriating then-president George Washington, America's most beloved hero, for failing to sufficiently assist him. Later published in a newspaper in 1796, the letter sharply criticized Washington: "Monopolies of every kind marked your administration almost in the moment of its commencement. The lands obtained by the Revolution were lavished upon partisans; the interest of the disbanded soldier was sold to the speculator . . . In what fraudulent light must Mr. Washington's character appear in the world, when his declarations and his conduct are compared together!"

This was a public bridge burning from which Paine would never recover. He returned to America in 1802 at Thomas Jefferson's invitation. But having publicly criticized George Washington, Paine discovered that his Revolutionary contributions a quarter century earlier had been forgotten. In poverty and poor health, worsened by his drinking, Paine was regarded as an atheist and largely abandoned by his friends and former allies.

Thomas Paine died in disgrace, shunned by many in the nation he had helped create. The Quaker church refused to bury him after his death in New York City's Greenwich Village in 1809. He was buried on his farm in New Rochelle, New York. A British admirer later had his remains exhumed to be returned to his native England and placed in a mausoleum honoring Paine. The plan failed. "The bones then were passed to a day laborer," according to Library of Congress reference librarian Heather Thomas, "then a furniture dealer, then oblivion."

WHY YOU SHOULD READ IT

As a student of American history, a skeptic of religious orthodoxy, and a person who aligns with the label of "Freethinker," I have always admired Thomas Paine. A "Forgotten Founder," he would be overshadowed by more celebrated heroes, such as Washington, Jefferson, and Franklin, all of whom shared some of Paine's views on religion and politics.

Read *The Age of Reason* for his systematic debunking of religion and, particularly, the powerful institution of Christianity. Paine condemned the hypocrisy of a church that, "with the assistance of some old stories . . . has set up a system of religion very contradictory to the character of the person whose name it bears. It has set up a religion of pomp and of revenue in pretended imitation of a person whose life was humility and poverty."

Read it because it continues the intellectual, political, and religious ferment that began in the contentious time of Thomas More, nearly three centuries earlier, and continued through the time of Voltaire, animating the Enlightenment spirit that turned the Age of Reason into an Age of Revolution. The old hierarchies of church and monarchy tumbled because of thinkers like Thomas Paine.

Read it, then, because of Paine's profound influence. "More than any other individual, Paine in his revolutionary internationalism, his rationalism and faith in human nature, his defiance of existing institutions, epitomized the radical cast of mind," Eric Foner writes. "His ideas and personal example have continued to inspire those who believe that the modern world has betrayed, not fulfilled, the high hopes for a just social order raised during Paine's Age of Revolution."

WHAT TO READ NEXT

For more Thomas Paine, try *Common Sense*, the anonymous pamphlet published in 1776 that is credited with forging popular support for the cause of American independence, and *The American Crisis*, the collected pamphlets he wrote bolstering support and raising funds for the American cause. Both *Common Sense* and *The American Crisis* series count as great short nonfiction.

For other works focused on the founding of the Republic, I suggest *The Constitutional Convention: A Narrative History from the Notes of James Madison* by Edward J. Larson and Michael P. Winship, an accessible presentation of the debates that led to the drafting of the U.S. Constitution in 1787; *The Autobiography of Benjamin Franklin*, written by America's greatest celebrity of the day; and *A Narrative of A Revolutionary Soldier* by Joseph Plumb Martin, the Revolutionary War as experienced by a young man who enlisted in George Washington's Continental Army when he was a teenager and remained through the victory at Yorktown in 1781.

For those interested in a deeper dive into the ideas of Paine and other secularists in American history, I recommend *Freethinkers: A History of American Secularism* (2004) by journalist and author Susan Jacoby. The early period of the beginning of the American Republic is also covered in my book *A Nation Rising: Untold Tales from America's Hidden History* (2010), which presents a series of episodes that offer a version of the period from 1800 to 1850 that the textbooks leave out.

"You have seen how a man was made a slave;
you shall see how a slave was made a man."

Narrative of the Life of Frederick Douglass, an American Slave

— 1845 —

Frederick Douglass

New Haven, CT: Yale University Press, 2001; 148 pages

OPENING WORDS

I was born in Tuckahoe, near Hillsborough, and about twelve miles from Easton, in Talbot county, Maryland. I have no accurate knowledge of my age, never having seen any authentic record containing it. By far the larger part of the slaves know as little of their ages as horses know of theirs, and it is the wish of most masters within my knowledge to keep their slaves thus ignorant. I do not remember to have ever met a slave who could tell his birthday.

SUMMARY

Seven years after escaping to freedom, Frederick Douglass published an account of his life in bondage as a child and young man. In eleven riveting chapters, he recounts a cruel, violent existence up until the time he broke free. In direct language, the narrative relates his birth on a plantation to an enslaved woman from whom he was soon separated and his upbringing in the cabin of his enslaved grandmother, who cared for the children of younger women.

Douglass did not soften the harsh realities he was subjected to and witnessed: his was stark testimony to the beatings and degradation meted out to family members and other enslaved people:

> Before he commenced whipping Aunt Hester, he took her into the kitchen, and stripped her from neck to waist, leaving her neck, shoulders, and back, entirely naked. He then told her to cross her hands, calling her at the same time a d—d b—h. After crossing her hands, he tied them with a strong rope, and led her to a stool under a large hook in the joist. . . . He made her get upon the stool, and tied her hands to the hook. . . . He commenced to lay on the heavy cowskin.

This was strong medicine for abolitionists; Douglass did not pander to delicate sensibilities. The brutal picture he painted was colored by suggestions of the sexual domination of enslaved women that was central to American slavery.

A fleeting moment, and perhaps the promise of a better life, comes as Frederick is sent from his birthplace in Talbot County on Maryland's eastern shore to Baltimore, at seven or eight, to serve Hugh and Sophia Auld, caring for their son, Tommy. At first sight, Mrs. Auld presents "a white face beaming with the most kindly emotions." She begins to teach Frederick the alphabet. But this education was cut short. When Hugh Auld saw his wife teaching the young boy to read, he quickly ended the lessons. Douglass understood early that ignorance was key to the white man's dominance and that reading was the key to freedom. He set about teaching himself how to read and write.

After being moved to several other farms, Douglass was sent to work in Baltimore's shipyards when he was about eighteen. There he planned his escape with the help of Anna Murray, a Black freedwoman. They were reunited and married in New York City before moving on to New Bedford, Massachusetts. The narrative concludes as Douglass addresses an abolitionist meeting in 1841. It was the opening act of an unparalleled career as speaker, writer, and publisher, propelling Frederick Douglass to become the most influential abolitionist of his day and one of the most compelling and significant figures in American history.

ABOUT THE AUTHOR: FREDERICK DOUGLASS

Born Frederick Augustus Washington Bailey to Harriet Bailey, an enslaved woman, Douglass did not know his birthday, as he wrote. In later years, he chose to mark it on February 14 because his mother called him "my little Valentine." He is believed to have been born in 1817 or 1818. He also wrote that he did not know his father, but that he was a white man.

Separated from his mother, who was hired out to work twelve miles away, Frederick saw little of her before her death when he was about seven. As a boy, he went through a succession of Talbot County, Maryland, households and farms until he worked in his teens at a Baltimore shipyard. He managed to escape in 1838 with papers and a sailor's uniform provided by Anna Murray.

Settling in New Bedford and taking the name Douglass as an alias to avoid capture, he began to read *The Liberator*, William Lloyd Garrison's influential abolitionist weekly. While attending an antislavery meeting in Nantucket in 1841, he was encouraged to speak to the largely white audience about his life. Immediately, he was hired as a lecturer, using his own story to condemn slavery.

After four years on the lecture circuit, Douglass published the *Narrative* in 1845. It was written to rebut the skepticism that such an articulate Black man could be a fugitive from slavery—another manifestation of the racist prejudice that Douglass continued to face as a free man. But Douglass brought the receipts, offering specific evidence of his life in slavery and singling out specific names of those who "owned" him. He left out only the details of his own escape so as not to endanger the chances of others trying to make their way to freedom.

Attesting to its veracity was a preface by William Lloyd Garrison and an introductory letter by Wendell Phillips, both prominent abolitionists. An immediate success, the book was translated into French, German, and Dutch. "In six years, twenty-one editions of the book had been published in the United States, the United Kingdom, and Europe . . . and by 1853, at least 30,000 copies had been sold," according to this edition's introduction.

With this notoriety, Douglass faced the prospect of reenslavement under existing law. Leaving the United States, he spent two years in England and Ireland, where he lectured widely, promoting the sale of his book to abolitionists abroad. After his freedom was purchased by English abolitionists, Douglass in 1847 returned to Rochester, New York, where he began to publish his own newspaper, the *North Star*. The title referred to the advice given to those attempting to escape slavery—"follow the North Star." Eventually, he and Garrison, close allies for several years, split over tactics and philosophy. Garrison believed that the U.S. Constitution, with its compromises on slavery, demanded "disunion" and a new constitution. Douglass had come to accept the view that the Constitution, while flawed, should be viewed as an "antislavery" document and that Congress should end slavery. (The two men eventually reconciled after the Civil War in 1873.)

As an ardent proponent of women's suffrage, Douglass was the only Black man present at the July 1848 Seneca Falls Convention, the birthplace of the women's rights movement. In 1852, he delivered one of his most famous orations, "What to the Slave is the Fourth of July?" In this stinging speech, made on Independence Day in Rochester, Douglass excoriated Americans celebrating the nation's founding while slavery continued. In 1855, Douglass published *My Bondage and My Freedom*, a second volume of autobiography that raised the subject of segregation in the North.

As the nation moved toward Civil War, Douglass met secretly in 1859 with John Brown, the radical abolitionist planning an ill-fated raid on a federal armory in Harpers Ferry, Virginia (now West Virginia). Brown wanted Douglass to join him in this armed rebellion against slavery, certain that the famed abolitionist would help attract other Black people to take part in a mass uprising. Convinced that Brown's plot was suicidal, Douglass refused to join the venture; it failed completely in October 1859. Brown was executed in December 1859.

Accused of conspiring with John Brown, Douglass fled the country once more, for first Canada and then England, where he lived until April 1860. He would not publicly reveal that he had met with John Brown for twenty years.

By the time the Civil War broke out in April 1861, Douglass had become the most famous and widely traveled orator in the nation. He also emerged as a vocal critic of President Lincoln for his refusal to allow Black men to join Union armies. "We are striking the rebels with our soft white hand," he said, "when we should be striking them with the iron hand of the black man which we keep chained behind us."

Once Black men were allowed to enlist with the creation of the Bureau of Colored Troops in May 1863, Douglass became an active recruiter, encouraging Black men to join Union armies. These segregated regiments were known as United States Colored Troops (USCT). Fearing that these soldiers might seek revenge on their former masters, the Bureau created an ordered structure for training, drilling, and equipping large numbers of emancipated Black men. More than 160,000 men served in the USCT, led by white officers. Douglass's two sons joined the Massachusetts Fifty-Fourth Infantry (made famous in the film *Glory*). Advocating for equal pay for the U.S. Colored Troops, Douglass met with President Lincoln on three occasions, including the day of Lincoln's second inauguration in March 1865, weeks before Lincoln was assassinated.

After the war, Douglass's Rochester home was burned down in a suspected arson. Frederick and Anna Douglass moved to Washington, D.C. As the postwar Reconstruction Amendments ended slavery, made citizens of emancipated Black people, and gave Black men the vote, Douglass was far from satisfied. He continued to press for the rights of Black people and women and against the rising tide of lynchings. Without his consent or knowledge, his name was placed in nomination as vice president on the 1872 Equal Rights Party ticket with Victoria Woodhull as the presidential candidate. Douglass was later named U.S. Marshall for the District of Columbia, the first Black man to hold the position, and later the first recorder of deeds in D.C., an official position responsible for public records relating to real estate and property rights. A third volume of his autobiography, *The Life and Times of Frederick Douglass*, was published in 1881 (revised in 1892).

After the death of his wife Anna in 1882, Douglass married Helen Pitts, a white woman twenty years younger, provoking considerable criticism and controversy from family members as well as Black and white critics of intermarriage. To those who claimed that Douglass had betrayed his race, he said, "What business has the world with the color of my wife?"

In 1895, after attending a women's rights convention in Washington, Douglass suffered a massive heart attack and died at home on February 20, aged seventy-seven or seventy-eight. His home, Cedar Hill, is a National Historic Site in the Anacostia section of Washington, D.C.

WHY YOU SHOULD READ IT

In a time of debate over how and what students should learn about the nation's history of slavery, Douglass's book remains one of the foundational texts that should be read in every school and by every American. It cuts through politics, academic arguments, and textbook language about amendments, compromises, and proclamations to make slavery what it is first and foremost—a human story.

Published seven years before Harriet Beecher Stowe's *Uncle Tom's Cabin* shocked the nation with its fictional depiction of slavery's inhumanity, Douglass's book, and his life, underscored what I have called America's Great Contradiction—that a nation "conceived in liberty" was also born in shackles. Of the two books, Douglass's autobiographical *Narrative* has best stood the test of time. Unquestionably influential in its day, *Uncle Tom's Cabin* both is now viewed as overly sentimental and has been widely critiqued by such writers as Richard Wright and James Baldwin for its stereotypical treatment of Black characters. Douglass's *Narrative* stands as an intensely personal account of the life of an enslaved person, from a childhood born in bondage, being separated from his mother, and the violence and degradation he faced. It remains a landmark of great power—as searing and timely today as when it was written.

With his scorching portrayal of the daily degradation and brutality faced by enslaved people, Douglass rendered an unmistakable judgment on the crime against humanity called slavery. In particular, he called out the false "slaveholding religion of this land" as distinct from the "Christianity of Christ." He wrote: "I therefore hate the corrupt, slaveholding, women-whipping, cradle-plundering, partial and hypocritical Christianity of this land."

His realization that the desire of masters to keep enslaved people ignorant and illiterate is also a profound lesson at a time when powerful forces seek to suppress books and writers.

Narrative of the Life of Frederick Douglass, an American Slave remains one of the greatest and most significant autobiographies in American history.

WHAT TO READ NEXT

You might consider the two later volumes in Douglass's eventual autobiographical trilogy: *My Bondage and My Freedom* (1855) and *Life and Times of Frederick Douglass* (1892). All three books are available individually and have also been collected in a single edition by the Library of America. There are also other crucial works referred to as "slave narratives" that are part of the important literature written by formerly enslaved people. These include the memoirs of Solomon Northrup, Harriet Jacobs (see entry), and Ellen and William Craft. Another important work is *The Interesting Narrative of the Life of Olaudah Equiano*, published in 1789, the first published personal account of a man taken from Africa into slavery.

A very short work of nonfiction from the post–Civil War period is *A Colored Man's Reminiscences of James Madison*, appearing first in a magazine in 1863 and published as a book in 1865 by Paul Jennings. Born enslaved on James Madison's Montpelier plantation, Paul Jennings was taken to the White House as an enslaved valet when he was about ten. He witnessed the burning of Washington, D.C., by the British in 1814 during the War of 1812 and was with James Madison at his death as his personal servant. Eventually emancipated, he wrote this memoir, considered the first published personal account by anyone who has worked in the White House.

Recent years have also seen a wealth of highly readable, outstanding historical literature documenting slavery and emancipation. Among these is David W. Blight's Pulitzer Prize–winning biography, *Frederick Douglass: Prophet of Freedom* (2018).

To that, I add several extraordinary works of recent scholarship: *The Hemingses of Monticello: An American Family* (2008), Annette Gordon-Reed's Pulitzer Prize–winning masterpiece about the relationship between the young enslaved woman Sally Hemings, her family, and Thomas Jefferson; *The Slave Ship: A Human History* (2007) by Marcus Rediker, a vivid description of the horrifying violence and terror of transporting enslaved captives from Africa to the Americas; *Bury the Chains: Prophets and Rebels in the Fight to Free an Empire's Slaves* (2005) by Adam Hochschild, a narrative account of the abolition movement in England; Edward E. Baptist's *The Half Has Never Been Told: Slavery and the Making of American Capitalism* (2014), documenting how slavery was transformed into big business after the end of the foreign slave trade created a profitable domestic slave trade; and Manisha Sinha's expansive *The Slaves' Cause: A History of Abolition* (2016).

To this list I would humbly add my 2016 book, *In the Shadow of Liberty: The Hidden History of Slavery, Four Presidents, and Five Black Lives*, which presents the stories of five individuals enslaved by Presidents Washington, Jefferson, Madison, and Andrew Jackson. Paul Jennings is one of those five.

"The history of all hitherto existing society is the history of class struggles."

The Communist Manifesto

— 1848 —

Karl Marx and Friedrich Engels

New York: Penguin Books, 2011; Introduction by Marshall Perman; translated by Samuel Moore; 104 pages

OPENING WORDS

A spectre is haunting Europe—the spectre of Communism. All the Powers of old Europe have entered into a holy alliance to exorcize this spectre: Pope and Czar, Metternich and Guizot, French Radicals and German police spies.

Where is the party in opposition that has not been decried as Communistic by its opponents in power? Where the Opposition that has not hurled back the branding reproach of Communism, against the more advanced opposition parties, as well as against its reactionary adversaries?

SUMMARY

Rarely has a brief piece of writing been as consequential in history as *The Communist Manifesto*. From its first lines, which describe the great European powers conspiring to destroy any attempts to organize workers for social and economic justice, this slim declaration laid out the basic ideas that drove the growth of international communism in the twentieth century.

Its authors, Karl Marx and Friedrich Engels, worked on it for about six weeks—from the middle of December 1847 to its publication as an anonymous pamphlet in January 1848. Writing it as the platform of the newly formed Communist League, they first stated their fundamental proposition: that the history of society was "a history of class struggles."

In the first of the manifesto's four sections—"Bourgeois and Proletarians"— they wrote: "Freeman and slave, patrician and plebian, lord and serf, guildmaster and journeyman, in a word, oppressor and oppressed, stood in constant opposition to one another." This conflict could end, they wrote, only with a complete transformation of society or "in the common ruin of the contending classes."

For Marx and Engels, the division of classes was a matter of who owned or controlled the means of production (the "bourgeoisie") and those who produce and provide service to that dominant class ("proletarians"). In a note to the 1888 English edition, Engels explained these terms: "By bourgeoisie is meant the class of modern Capitalists, owners of the means of social production and employers of wage labour. By proletariat, the class of modern wage-labourers who, having no means of production of their own, are reduced to selling their labour power in order to live."

The manifesto concludes by asserting that victory for the working classes—the "proletariat"—would put an end to class society as it existed. The dominant class controlled not only material production but also the production of ideas and was consequently able to control the political system. Such systems were inherently unequal and maintained through oppressive laws and the fact that, to put it simply, "the rich got richer." In the manifesto, Marx and Engels put forth a series of immediate measures as first steps toward a vision of communism, including a progressive income tax, the

abolition of inheritances, and free education for all children. It closes with
the ringing words and a challenge that transformed modern times:

The proletarians have nothing to lose but their chains. They have a
world to win.
WORKINGMEN OF ALL COUNTRIES, UNITE!

ABOUT THE AUTHORS: KARL MARX AND FRIEDRICH ENGELS

Karl Heinrich Marx and Friedrich Engels must be counted among modern
history's most influential people.

Let's begin with Marx. Philosopher, economist, historian, and journalist
Karl Heinrich Marx was born on May 5, 1818, in Trier, Prussia (in what
is now Germany). He was the son of a successful attorney and a mother
descended from a line of rabbis. Both parents were Jewish, but Marx's
father converted to Christianity; being a Jew was a social and professional
liability at the time and so Karl Marx was baptized as Christian. Beginning
his university studies in Bonn in 1835, he transferred to the University of
Berlin a year later to study law and philosophy. Marx went on to receive
his doctoral degree from the University of Jenna in 1841.

As a student, Marx was already involved in progressive, left-wing political movements when he began contributing to *Rheinische Zeitung*, a liberal
democratic newspaper published in Cologne. After becoming its editor in
1842, Marx met Friedrich Engels, born in Prussia on November 28, 1820,
to a wealthy cotton manufacturer who owned mills in the industrial area
around Manchester, England. In his school years, Engels began to adopt
the radical ideas of the republican revolutions that were sweeping across
Europe in the mid-nineteenth century.

When he was twenty-two, Engels was sent to his father's textile factory in Manchester in the hopes that he would abandon his radicalism
and join the family business. There Engels met Mary Burns, a factory
worker with similarly radical opinions. They began a relationship that
lasted until her death in 1863, but they never wed as they both opposed
the institution of marriage. In 1845, Engels wrote *The Condition of the*

Working Class in England, an influential work describing the squalid lives of factory workers.

Meanwhile, under pressure and official censorship, Marx resigned from *Rheinische Zeitung*, and the Prussian authorities eventually shut down the paper. In June 1843, Marx had married Jenny von Westphalen, whose well-off Prussian family had both military and governmental connections and objected to the marriage. A few months later, the couple moved to Paris, a center of more radical working-class European protest. Marx became more involved with the Parisian working classes and, in 1844, he and Engels renewed their friendship, which would last the rest of their lifetimes.

In 1847, Marx and Engels took part in the London meeting of the first congress of the Communist League, merged from several existing parties. Tasked with writing the League's platform, they produced *The Communist Manifesto* in early 1848. The year it appeared saw a series of republican revolts against European monarchies that began in Sicily and spread across Italy to France, Germany, and the Austrian Empire. All of these attempts to bring about democratic reform were crushed by the "holy alliance" of old Europe's powers described in *The Communist Manifesto's* opening words.

Marx always lived in relative poverty with his wife and young children in a two-room flat in Soho, London. The couple had seven children, but only three lived to adulthood. Supported by the wealthy Engels, Marx devoted himself to research in the British Museum while writing *Das Kapital*, a massive synthesis of economic and political history, the first volume of which was published in 1867. During this period, he and Engels also wrote newspaper articles, including those published in the United States in the *New-York Daily Tribune*, a progressive paper founded by abolitionist Horace Greeley.

In poor health for many years, Karl Marx died a "stateless person" on March 14, 1883, and was buried in Highgate Cemetery in London. After Marx's death, Engels continued to edit the work of his collaborator and published two further volumes of *Das Kapital*. Engels also published his own significant works in the areas of anthropology and sociology before his death of throat cancer in August 1895, at the age of seventy-four.

WHY YOU SHOULD READ IT

This is simple. *The Communist Manifesto* is one of the most consequential works of modern times. What its two initially anonymous authors laid out in a twenty-three-page pamphlet—later published in multiple German, Russian, Polish, Italian, and English editions whose separate prefaces are included in this edition—is "one of the four best-selling books of all time," according to an information service allied with the German Federal Foreign Office. "Both the *Manifesto* and *Das Kapital* [Marx's later book] are UNESCO World Heritage documents."

Appearing first, *The Communist Manifesto* lay the groundwork for revolutionary movements, and inspiration to people as diverse as Mussolini, Lenin, Stalin, and Mao Zedong—meaning it also became the source of much of the twentieth century's conflicts. The Communist governments that grew out of the class struggle predicted by Marx and Engels eventually came to dominate much of Asia and Eastern Europe under the Soviet Union, stretching from Korea to Cuba. Many of these regimes, especially those in Eastern Europe, collapsed after the fall of the Berlin Wall in 1989 and the dismantling of the Soviet Union a few years later.

Today, the words "socialism," "Marxism," and "communism" are tossed around like political hand grenades, with little regard for—or understanding of—their real meanings. Although the United States has come a long way from the Cold War fear that made the words "socialism" and "communism" strike dread in American hearts and minds, they are still "dirty words" in American politics.

The ideas of Marx and Engels were adopted—and some would say brutally transformed—by such Communist leaders as Lenin, Stalin, and Mao, who turned these economic ideas into murderous, authoritarian one-party states. In *The Twilight of Democracy*, Pulitzer Prize–winning writer and authoritarianism expert Anne Applebaum writes: "Unlike Marxism, the illiberal one-party state is not a philosophy. It is a mechanism for holding power."

So set aside preconceptions. Read what Marx and Engels actually wrote and believed. It is instructive—and even surprising. "Marx hates capitalism, but he also thinks it has brought about immense real benefits, spiritual as well as material," writes Marshall Berman in his introduction, "and he wants the benefits to be spread around and enjoyed by everybody, rather than monopolized by a small ruling class. That is very different from the totalitarian rage that typifies radicals who want to blow it all away."

The ideas Marx and Engels laid out have taken a different path in many modern Western nations where the notion of democratic socialism has been adopted in varying degrees, rejecting the pure communism of Marxist-Leninists. But as the widening inequality gap in a modern, globalized, and increasingly technologically sophisticated world is growing exponentially, so is discontent with work and a capitalist system that does not equitably share the wealth, which, it is widely argued, is generated by labor. One man who made this argument was a reader of Karl Marx, who in 1861 wrote: "Labor is prior to and independent of capital. Capital is only the fruit of labor, and could never have existed if labor had not first existed. Labor is the superior of capital, and deserves much the higher consideration."

Those are the words of Abraham Lincoln. Of course, such sentiments would have no place in the modern version of Lincoln's Republican Party. Karl Marx would probably not be surprised.

WHAT TO READ NEXT

In a book about short books, it is hard to recommend Marx's other major work, *Das Kapital* (*Capital: A Critique of Political Economy*). First published in 1867, it eventually filled three volumes—the second in 1885 and third in 1894, both edited by Engels—ranging to thousands of pages. Arguing that capitalism would create ever-increasing inequities, this monumental work predicted an eventual system of common ownership of the means of production. In Marx's view, as historian Daniel Boorstin explains, "to secure the maximum profit, the capitalist paid the worker only enough for his subsistence. Surplus value, then, is the value produced beyond what he is compensated. Thus the capitalist's profit came from exploiting the worker."

In 1861, President Abraham Lincoln put it this way: "Capital is only the fruit of labor, and could never have existed if labor had not first existed. Labor is the superior of capital, and deserves much the higher consideration."

Another of the most consequential of all works related to Communist history was not included here. But it must be mentioned. Though very consequential, *Quotations from Chairman Mao Tse-Tung* (his name is now transliterated as Mao Zedong) has lost timeliness and falls way short as an appealing or pleasurable literary landmark. Produced by the Foreign Language Press in Beijing (then Peking) in 1966, it is a collection of writings and aphorisms by the man who was inspired by Marx and dominated the Chinese Communist Party almost from its beginnings. Bound in red covers, it became famed simply as the "Little Red Book."

For years, *Quotations from Chairman Mao Tse-Tung* was required reading in China and millions of copies were distributed to the Chinese people and published around the world. Drawing on the words and writings of Chairman Mao—known to the Chinese as "the Great Helmsman"—from the 1920s until the early 1960s, the book is organized into several loosely defined divisions: "The Communist Party," "Serving the People," "Unity," and "Discipline." Among its most memorable adages is:

> A revolution is not a dinner party, or writing an essay, or painting a picture, or doing embroidery; it cannot be so refined, so leisurely and gentle, so temperate, kind, courteous, restrained and magnanimous. A revolution is an insurrection, an act of violence in which one class overthrows another.

First conceived as a simple version of Mao's ideas and admonishments to be distributed to the Red Army, it is one of the most widely published books in the world after the Bible and Qur'an. Held aloft by members of the youthful Red Guard during the violent era of the Cultural Revolution that bloodied China during the 1960s, the book has lost its once-powerful grip on twenty-first-century China. Mao remains a revered figure in China, but his words are now viewed there with nostalgia. Clearly of historical consequence, it reads like mere political cant and no longer carries the weight it once did.

You can read more about Mao and his rise to power in my book *Strongman: The Rise of Five Dictators and the Fall of Democracy* (2020).

*"Unjust laws exist: shall we be content to obey them, or shall we endeavor
to amend them, and obey them until we have succeeded,
or shall we transgress them at once?"*

Civil Disobedience

— 1849 —

Henry David Thoreau

New York: Penguin Books, 2017; in Walden and Civil Disobedience; *with
an introduction by Kristen Case; 28 pages with notes*

OPENING WORDS

I heartily accept the motto,— "That government is best which governs least";*
and I should like to see it acted up to more rapidly and systematically. Carried
out, it finally amounts to this, which I also believe,—"That government is best
which governs not at all"; and when men are prepared for it, that will be the

---

* "A close version of this motto appears as the masthead for the *United States Magazine and
Democratic Review* and in Emerson's essay on 'Politics.'" "Notes for 'Civil Disobedience,'"
in Henry David Thoreau, *Walden and Civil Disobedience* (New York: Penguin Books,
2017), 307.

kind of government which they will have. Government is at best but an expedient; but most governments are usually, and all governments are sometimes, inexpedient. The objections which have been brought against a standing army, and they are many and weighty, and deserve to prevail, may also at last be brought against a standing government.

SUMMARY

At under thirty pages—including notes—this is among the shortest of the "great short books" included here. Technically, Thoreau's "Civil Disobedience" is not a book but an essay. I highlight it, however, for its consequence, timeliness, and literary value as well as its accessible readability.

First delivered as a lecture under the title "Resistance to Civil Government," this work—Thoreau's most famous after *Walden*—has profoundly influenced generations of those who sought to protest injustice—Mahatma Gandhi and Martin Luther King Jr. chief among them.

It was presented at the Concord Lyceum in late January 1848, about a week before the end of the war between the United States and Mexico. Thoreau's speech expressed his complete opposition to both the war and slavery, which undergirded the conflict with Mexico. The Mexican-American War, declared by the United States in April 1846, was an act of unprovoked territorial expansion that would open up vast new areas to slavery's westward spread in the United States. A staunch abolitionist, Thoreau opposed both the aggressive land grab and slavery—which would ultimately lead to America's Civil War. He objected to a nation that was based on enslavement and was moving toward an empire based on conquest.

While "Civil Disobedience" recalled the founding principles of the United States and its rebellion against a monarch, Thoreau was not setting out to provoke outright armed revolution. This was not a call to arms or the barricades. In his essay, Thoreau is calling for "disobedience"—a willful noncompliance with unjust laws in an unjust state—by its citizens. He balked at providing support to a state, or a religious institution, in which he did not believe. And so, he committed an act of civil disobedience. He had stopped paying what was then called a poll tax, required of every adult, regardless of income. For his refusal, Thoreau was jailed for a night, which he describes as "prison" in the essay.

Thoreau concludes: "There will never be a really free and enlightened State, until the State comes to recognize the individual as a higher and independent power, from which all its own power and authority are derived, and treats him accordingly."

ABOUT THE AUTHOR: HENRY DAVID THOREAU

Born on July 12, 1817, in Concord, Massachusetts, Thoreau was the son of a pencil maker. Named David Henry at birth, he later decided to reverse his first and middle names and call himself Henry David. Thoreau was sent to Concord Academy and graduated from Harvard in 1837. He briefly taught at a school in a village near Concord, resigning after a few weeks because he refused to administer corporal punishment. After working briefly in his father's pencil-making business, Thoreau and his brother, John, opened a grammar school of their own in Concord in 1838. Offering a progressive program of education, including nature walks, the school operated for only three years before John became fatally ill. He died from lockjaw in Thoreau's arms in 1842.

While still at Harvard, Thoreau had befriended Ralph Waldo Emerson, already an established lecturer, philosopher, and writer. Emerson's *Nature*, published in 1836, laid out some of the early ideas of New England's Transcendental movement—an outgrowth of Unitarianism, itself an offshoot of Christianity, that emphasized people's inherent goodness, which was only corrupted by institutions and organized religion. Transcendentalists saw divinity in everyday experiences and the natural world.

Emerson also encouraged Thoreau to write, and he began a journal that he would keep for the rest of his life. The two men were at the center of a group of writers and thinkers gathered around Concord that included Bronson Alcott, Margaret Fuller, and Nathaniel Hawthorne. Thoreau also began to contribute poetry and essays to the *Dial*, a magazine founded by Emerson and other Transcendentalists and first edited by Margaret Fuller.

After living with the Emersons, Thoreau was encouraged by poet Ellery

Channing to go out to the woods to live by himself. Thoreau built a hut near Walden Pond, on land owned by Emerson, where he lived for a little over two years. During that time, he was jailed for refusing to pay six years of unpaid poll taxes, as described in "Civil Disobedience," and was released only when someone—perhaps his aunt—paid the back taxes against his wishes. Thoreau also wrote and self-published *A Week on the Concord and Merrimack Rivers*, an account of a canoe trip he had taken with his brother, John. It sold only a few hundred copies before the printer dumped the remaining unsold books on Thoreau's doorstep.

Returning to his parents' home in 1848, Thoreau remained there for the rest of his life. While he continued to write essays and his journals, his most famous work *Walden; or, Life in the Woods* (later shortened to *Walden*) was published in 1854. That same year, he delivered a lecture, later published as "Slavery in Massachusetts," about the capture and reenslavement of a man named Anthony Burns, a runaway whose 1854 arrest and trial under the Fugitive Slave Act caused abolitionists to riot in Boston. Thoreau denounced slavery and excoriated the governor and his fellow citizens of Massachusetts for their failure to do what was just: "The law will never make men free; it is men who have got to make the law free. They are the lovers of law and order who observe the law when the government breaks it."

In 1859, Thoreau's father died and he became more involved in the family's pencil business. At the same time, the country's crisis over the slavery issue was growing dangerously contentious, violently capped by the failed attack of radical abolitionist John Brown and his small band on the federal arsenal in Harpers Ferry, Virginia. After Brown was arrested, Thoreau delivered a speech in Concord, "A Plea for Captain John Brown," on October 30, 1859. Later printed, it was one of the first and most vociferous defenses of the fiery abolitionist who was hanged on December 2, 1859. "I hear many condemn these men because they were so few," Thoreau wrote of Brown and his compatriots. "When were the good and the brave ever in a majority?"

Suffering from tuberculosis—his sister Helen had died from the disease in 1849—Thoreau fell ill in 1860 and traveled to Minnesota in hopes that the climate might improve his health. He later returned to his mother's home, where he died on May 6, 1862, of tuberculosis; he was forty-four years old. In eulogizing Thoreau, his mentor and friend, Ralph Waldo Emerson, said:

> The country knows not yet, or in the least part, how great a son it has lost. . . . His soul was made for the noblest society; he had in a short life exhausted the capabilities of this world; wherever there is knowledge, wherever there is virtue, wherever there is beauty, he will find a home.

WHY YOU SHOULD READ IT

In negotiating the correct response to an unjust government and unjust laws, Thoreau's concept of "nonviolent resistance" inspired many other protest movements in the twentieth century. But if only two people had been influenced by Thoreau's ideas, his place in history and that of "Civil Disobedience" would be secure.

Both Mohandas K. "Mahatma" Gandhi and Dr. Martin Luther King Jr. acknowledged Thoreau's influence in shaping their decisions to pursue nonviolent protest. For Gandhi, it was in achieving India's independence. For King, it was the Civil Rights Movement. In his autobiography, King wrote:

> When I went to Morehouse as a freshman in 1944, my concern for racial and economic justice was already substantial. During my student days I read Henry David Thoreau's "On Civil Disobedience" for the first time. Here, in this courageous New Englander's refusal to pay his taxes and his choice of jail rather than support a war that would spread slavery's territory into Mexico, I made my first contact with the theory of nonviolent resistance. Fascinated by the idea of refusing to cooperate with an evil system, I was so deeply moved that I reread the work several times.
>
> I became convinced that noncooperation with evil is as much a moral obligation as is cooperation with good. No other person has been more eloquent and passionate in getting this idea across than Henry David Thoreau.

In selecting "Civil Disobedience," I thought it spoke more decisively than the alternative, *Walden*, to this historical moment. In a sense, Thoreau's two most famous works present seemingly opposing responses to the threats posed by the modern world's gross injustice, rising authoritarianism, and political dissonance: retreat from society or engage, as he advocated in "Civil Disobedience." Critic Rebecca Solnit described these two divergent personas: "Thoreau the rebel, intransigent muse to Gandhi and Martin Luther King, and that other Thoreau who wrote about autumnal tints, ice, light, color, grasses, woodchucks, and other natural histories."

It would be a mistake to think that Thoreau could not bridge the two. As Rebecca Solnit put it, "You head for the hills to enjoy the best of what the world is at this moment; you head for confrontation, for resistance, for picket lines to protect it, to liberate it. Thus it is that the road to paradise often runs through prison, thus it is that Thoreau went to jail to enjoy a better country, and thus it is that one of his greatest students, Martin Luther King Jr., found himself in jail and eventually in the way of a bullet on what got called the long road to freedom, whose goal he spoke of as the mountaintop."

In an introductory essay to the edition cited, Professor Kristen Case discusses the profound issues of debt, inequality, racism, and "a deeply damaged planet" confronted today by young people in particular. She comments: "Thoreau's writings have renewed significance: They suggest the value of unsettling the settled, and of asking ourselves how we should live when the inherited answers are no longer acceptable."

WHAT TO READ NEXT

Walden is an obvious must. Thoreau's account of his two-year stay in a small cabin reflected his search for simplicity and self-reliance. "The mass of men lead lives of quiet desperation," he wrote. "What is called resignation is confirmed desperation." And later he writes: "I went to the woods because I wished to live deliberately, to front only the essential facts of life, and see if I could not learn what it had to teach, and not, when I came to die, discover that I had not lived."

I would also recommend Ralph Waldo Emerson's 1836 book-length essay *Nature* for its influence and impact, first of all on Thoreau, who read it while a student at Harvard. Emerson argues that the divine can be found in nature and that the world creates too many distractions. While Emerson's language and approach are far more scholarly than Thoreau's, this long essay lays out many of the fundamental ideas that would collectively be called Transcendentalism. "The happiest man," Emerson writes, "is he who learns from nature the lesson of worship."

On the specific question of civil disobedience, my first suggestion is Dr. Martin Luther King Jr.'s *Why We Can't Wait*. Published in 1964, the year King was awarded the Nobel Peace Prize, it was written after the 1963 Birmingham, Alabama, campaign—a series of nonviolent demonstrations that were met with fury, fire hoses, and police dogs. Arrested during these demonstrations in April 1963, King wrote his famous "Letter from Birmingham Jail" while behind bars in solitary confinement. This book expands on the themes in that letter.

A more recent exploration of the history of civil disobedience in America is the highly praised 2013 book *Civil Disobedience: An American Tradition* written by Lewis Perry.

Thoreau and *Walden* in particular have had enormous influence on generations of American writers. Thoreau's work figures significantly in two other books I recommend to readers: Jon Krakauer's *Into the Wild* (1996) is a gripping exploration of the life of a young man, largely inspired by *Walden*, who died while trying to live alone in the Alaskan wilderness; John McPhee's *The Survival of the Bark Canoe* (1975) is the great journalist's account of the art and craft of building traditional birch bark canoes and includes a Thoreau-like trip into the wilds.

"I want to add my testimony to that of abler pens to convince the people of the Free States what Slavery really is. Only by experience can any one realize how deep, and dark, and foul is that pit of abominations."

Incidents in the Life of a Slave Girl: Written by Herself

— 1861 —

Harriet Jacobs

New York: Modern Library, 2021; with Introduction by Tiya Miles; 237 pages. This edition also includes an Introduction by Lydia Maria Child, who served as the book's original editor, and valuable historical and other reference notes as well as a commentary by Jean Fagan Yellin, whose research established Harriet Jacobs as the book's author and who later wrote a definitive biography of her. Other available editions of this work include a Norton Critical Edition published in 2019

OPENING WORDS

I was born a slave; but I never knew it till six years of happy childhood had passed away. My father was a carpenter, and considered so intelligent and skilful [sic] in his trade, that, when buildings out of the common line were to be erected, he was sent for from long distances, to be head workman. On condition of paying his mistress two hundred dollars a year, and supporting himself, he was allowed to work at his trade, and manage his own affairs. His strongest wish was to purchase his children; but, though he several times offered his hard earnings for that purpose, he never succeeded.

SUMMARY

Written in secret over several years and published in 1861 under the pseudonym "Linda Brent," this is the first-person account of a young woman born into slavery in North Carolina in the fall of 1813. With remarkable clarity of voice, scathing in her total contempt for slavery and disgust with enslavers, Harriet Jacobs tells of her girlhood, motherhood at sixteen, hiding from her enslavers for several years, and her escape to freedom and eventual emancipation in the North.

Addressed principally to the white women of its time, the book is a landmark in the category of slavery narratives, and American literature at large, as well as a searing coming-of-age story in a society in which young women such as Harriet Jacobs were legal "property." Her tales of the sexual violence that she and other enslaved women endured were meant to jolt the conscience of her readers—and they do.

The narrative begins with a brief preface: "Reader, be assured, this narrative is no fiction. . . ." Yet until fairly recently, the book was thought to be fiction written by a white woman—like one of its most famous literary predecessors, *Uncle Tom's Cabin*, written by Harriet Beecher Stowe in 1852. The notion that a white woman had created the narrative was grounded in the racist presumption that no Black woman could write such a book.

To summarize Jacobs's account is to risk detracting from the power of her writing and do an injustice to her story, so I proceed cautiously. At heart, it is a narrative of her relatively happy childhood, spanning from a "mistress" who taught her to read and write—only later made illegal in North Carolina—until she was willed to become the property of a small child and fell into the power of a man identified as "Dr. Flint," a man of considerable cruelty. After Linda turned fifteen, Flint began to intimidate her sexually: "My master began to whisper foul words in my ear," she recorded. "Young as I was, I could not remain ignorant of their import." Harriet managed to elude Flint as his wife looked on jealously, enraged by her husband's obvious interest in the girl.

To avoid an actual assault by Flint, Harriet agreed to sexual relations with "Mr. Sands," another white man. As historian Tiya Miles writes in this edition, "Making this decision to protect her body from one white man by giving it to another was Jacobs's bid to protect her core self from Flint's tyrannical sway."

In her teens, Harriet would bear two children by Sands: Joseph, born around 1829 (birthdates of enslaved people often went unrecorded), and Louisa, born around 1832. Both, of course, were born enslaved and the vindictive Dr. Flint tells her, "These brats will bring me a handsome sum of money one of these days." Soon after, Harriet made an initial escape from Flint's home, remaining hidden for several years in an attic crawl space in the home of her free grandmother.

In 1842, Harriet escaped all the way to the North, leaving behind her enslaved children. She eventually encountered sympathetic abolitionists, eventually to become an outspoken abolitionist herself. At the urging of a Quaker abolitionist and feminist, Harriet Jacobs wrote the story of her life. With the Civil War looming, Jacobs published the book to promote the cause of emancipation with a shocking dose of reality.

ABOUT THE AUTHOR: HARRIET JACOBS

Born in 1813 in Edenton, North Carolina, Harriet Jacobs was enslaved at birth but, as she writes, was barely aware of her status. She was the "property" of the owner of a tavern, a seemingly kindly woman who taught Harriet to sew, read, and write and promised to free the girl one day. But she reneged after Harriet's mother died. Harriet's father, Elijah Knox, an enslaved carpenter, attempted to purchase Harriet and her brother John but failed to do so before his death in 1826. Upon the death of the tavern owner, Harriet was "willed" to the woman's three-year-old niece whose father, Dr. James Norcom ("Dr. Flint" of *Incidents)*, became her de facto owner.

These are the earliest of the "incidents" laid out by Jacobs in her narrative, published in 1861. Nearly twenty years earlier, in 1842, Harriet had escaped slavery by boat to Philadelphia, aided by antislavery groups. Proceeding on to New York, she found work as a nanny to the family of a popular magazine writer, Nathaniel Parker Willis. Harriet would remain close to the family for years, although the Willis family allowed her to leave her job on several occasions when she got word that Dr. Norcom was looking to recapture her. Taking refuge in Boston, she was reunited with her brother John, who had also escaped. She also eventually connected with her two children who had been purchased by their father, who eventually allowed them to go north. Harriet Jacobs was legally emancipated only when Nathaniel Willis's wife, Cornelia, purchased her freedom in 1852.

As her brother John became increasingly involved with famed abolitionist William Lloyd Garrison's antislavery work, Harriet joined him in Rochester, New York, where Frederick Douglass (see entry) published his abolitionist newspaper *North Star*. Harriet met the Quaker abolitionists Amy and Isaac Post. Amy encouraged Harriet to write her story. Harriet initially wrote only an outline, which she sent to Harriet Beecher Stowe of *Uncle Tom's Cabin* fame, hoping that the world-renowned author might take on the story and give it notoriety. Stowe declined. But following the death of her beloved grandmother, Harriet Jacobs chose to write the book herself. She had also read a defense of slavery by Julia Tyler, wife of former president John Tyler, claiming America's enslaved were happy. Jacobs wrote a letter published in the *New York Tribune*, refuting Tyler and signed "A Fugitive Slave." After years of work, and with the editorial assistance of abolitionist Lydia Maria Child, the book was published in January 1861, months before the Civil War began in April.

Almost from the outset, the book was believed to have been written by a white person. The widely presumed author, Lydia Maria Child, had in fact edited Harriet Jacobs's writing. In an introduction, Child wrote:

"At her request, I have revised her manuscript; but such changes as I have made have been made mainly for purposes of condensation and orderly arrangement. I have not added any thing to the incidents, or changed the import of her very pertinent remarks."

After the Civil War broke out in April 1861, she began to do relief work for the "contrabands," enslaved people who had escaped from slaveholding but were technically not free, and wrote about her experience for William Lloyd Garrison's *The Liberator*. The fame brought by her book allowed her to build a network of abolitionists to support her relief work and she attended major antislavery conferences with fame gained by the book.

During the Civil War, Jacobs continued to call for complete emancipation. While profoundly significant, Abraham Lincoln's 1863 Emancipation Proclamation did not free all the enslaved but applied only to enslaved people in the states that were in rebellion and over which Lincoln had no control. Full emancipation did not come until the ratification of the Thirteenth Amendment in December 1865. Jacobs later founded a school for Black children, with her daughter, now trained as a teacher, as its leader in Alexandria, Virginia. Jacobs and her daughter also traveled to Savannah, Georgia, after the city fell to Union troops, to organize relief efforts for the emancipated people there.

Later in life, Harriet Jacobs and her daughter struggled financially and had to operate boardinghouses and take odd jobs, in first Cambridge, Massachusetts, and later Washington, D.C., where in 1877 she encountered the destitute widow and children of her former enslaver and supported them. It was there, in Washington, that Jacobs died on March 7, 1897.

WHY YOU SHOULD READ IT

While not perhaps as well-known as the other notable Harriets of the era—Harriet Beecher Stowe and Harriet Tubman, famed for her work on the Underground Railroad—Harriet Jacobs is certainly deserving of wider recognition and a wider audience. Alongside *Narrative of the Life of Frederick Douglass* (see entry), published in 1845, her book stands as a classic of American literature. And it certainly should be counted as more significant than the much more famous—if now largely unread—*Uncle Tom's Cabin.*

"Publication of this book marked, I think, a unique moment in our literary history," writes historian and Harriet Jacobs biographer the late Jean Fagan Yellin, who passed away in July 2023. "*Incidents* defied the taboos prohibiting women from discussing their sexuality—much less their sexual exploitation—in print." Jean Fagan Yellin was able to scrupulously document and establish the authorship of Harriet Jacobs, publishing an authoritative edition of *Incidents* in 1987 and a full biography of its author, *Harriet Jacobs: A Life*, in 2004.

At the time Yellin's edition documenting the veracity of *Incidents* was published, Harvard professor and historian Henry Louis Gates Jr. wrote:

> Jacobs's narrative is a bold and gripping fusion of two major literary forms: she borrowed from the popular sentimental novel on one hand, and the slave narrative genre on the other. Her tale gains its importance from the fact that she charts, in great and painful detail, the sexual exploitation that daily haunted her life—and the life of every other black female slave. In the character of the unrelentingly evil Dr. Flint, and in the hard choices that his vulgar pursuit forces Jacobs to make, she graphically renders the sexual aspect of economic exploitation in a manner unimaginable before. Whereas the black male slave narrators' accounts of sexual brutality remain suggestive, if gruesome, Jacobs's . . . charts in vivid detail precisely how the shape of her life and the choices she makes are defined by her reduction to a sexual object, an object to be raped, bred or abused.

I include *Incidents in the Life of a Slave Girl* in a time when the history of American slavery has shockingly and disconcertingly become a partisan dividing line. With some politicians seeking erasure of a past that they think will make children feel "ashamed," the testimony of a book like this becomes all the more necessary. As I write this, a set of educational standards has been introduced in Florida that, according to the *Washington Post*, "say students should learn that enslaved people 'developed skills' that 'could be applied for their personal benefit.'" Anyone who reads the account Jacobs offers can see that there was no "upside" to slavery, a crime against humanity of unspeakable proportions.

"I read the first annotated edition of *Incidents* in an African-American literature course my junior year in college," writes Harvard historian Tiya Miles. "It was 1990, and Jean Fagan Yellin, a literary historian, had snatched the book from obscurity and decades of academic dismissal just three years prior. . . . I remember grasping my copy, the same one I hold today, and not wanting to let Jacobs go when her dreams were still incomplete. Harriet Jacobs's account of bondage and the bittersweet realities of freedom broke my young heart and changed the trajectory of my life. Her courage moved me to follow her lead as a writer and educator, to answer in my own small way the call she extends to all of us, her trusted readers."

WHAT TO READ NEXT

Several other memoirs of formerly enslaved people are listed in the entry on Frederick Douglass's *Narrative*. To those I would add *The Narrative of Sojourner Truth* (various editions), the memoir of an enslaved woman who escaped and successfully sued for the freedom of her son. She went on to become a prominent speaker in the cause of abolition and women's rights. *Ain't I a Woman* collects some of the speeches given by Truth and is another worthy book for the To-Be-Read list in its expression of the lives of enslaved women, especially in a moment when such valuable documents are being erased from certain school studies in this country.

*"The entire system of the judiciary of this country
is in the hands of white people."*

On Lynchings

— 1892, 1895, 1900 —

Ida B. Wells-Barnett

Mineola, NY: Dover, 2014; 163 pages

OPENING WORDS

Wednesday evening May 24th, 1892, the city of Memphis was filled with excitement. Editorials in the daily papers of that date caused a meeting to be held
in the Cotton Exchange Building; a committee was sent for the editors of the
"Free Speech" an Afro-American journal published in that city, and the only
reason the open threats of lynching that were made were not carried out was
because they could not be found. The cause of all this commotion was the
following editorial published in the "Free Speech" . . .

Eight negroes lynched since last issue of the "Free Speech" one at Little
Rock, Ark., last Saturday morning where the citizens broke (?) into the pen-
itentiary and got their man there; three near Anniston, Ala., one near New

158

Orleans; and three at Clarksville, Ga., the last three for killing a white man, and five on the same old racket—the new alarm about raping white women. The same programme of hanging, then shooting bullets into the lifeless bodies was carried out to the letter.

SUMMARY

Among books that document stark moments in the history of man's inhumanity to man, this may be one of the most challenging to read. It provides a grueling account of the horrific treatment of Black people, largely but not exclusively in the Jim Crow South where unlawful beatings, torture, shootings, and lynching became a commonplace public entertainment in the late nineteenth century—and continued for decades.

After the lynching of three of her friends and neighbors in 1892 by a white mob in Memphis, Ida B. Wells (Wells-Barnett after a later marriage) spoke out by writing the *Free Speech* newspaper editorial cited earlier. Soon after, she was forced to flee the city. Wells then determined to set out on a one-person campaign to investigate and document the widespread lynching of Black people, usually men accused of raping white women—a common accusation that Wells's reporting showed to be completely unfounded. "Nobody in this section of the country believes the threadbare old lie that Negro men rape white women," Wells wrote. Her dogged journalism was incredibly courageous as she set out to examine and detail every horrific instance of lynching she could find.

This single volume collects three separate pamphlets—*Southern Horrors: Lynch Law in All Its Phases* (1892); *A Red Record: Tabulated Statistics and Alleged Causes of Lynchings in the United States 1892–1893–1894* (1895); and *Mob Rule in New Orleans: Robert Charles and His Fight to the Death* (1900). Wells was a pioneering journalist who documented the scourge of lynching in late nineteenth-century America. Her work was meticulously researched and documented, and she hoped to shine a light on the murderous plague of lynchings and other tortures Black Americans were subjected to—and not only in the former Confederacy. "'If this work can contribute in any way toward proving this, and at the same time arouse the conscience of the

American people to demand for justice to every citizen, and punishment by law for the lawless, I shall feel I have done my race a service,'" she wrote after fleeing Memphis, in a preface to the first report. "'Other considerations are minor.'" Her work won the admiration of, among many others, Frederick Douglass, who praised her reporting in 1892.

In concluding her first report, Wells wrote: "Nothing is more definitely settled than he [the Afro-American] must act for himself. I have shown how he may employ the boycott, emigration and the press, and feel that a combination of all these agencies can effectually stamp out lynch law, that last relic of barbarism and slavery."

ABOUT THE AUTHOR: IDA B. WELLS-BARNETT

To the list of other important American pamphleteers in American history— including Thomas Paine and Henry David Thoreau—let us add the name of Ida B. Wells. Born into slavery during the Civil War, she was considered the most famous Black woman in the United States during her lifetime. Then history largely erased her.

Wells was born enslaved in Holly Springs, Mississippi, in 1862. Her father, James Madison Wells, himself the child of a white man and an enslaved Black woman, was a carpenter and was often hired out, with his wages going to his owner (a scenario like that recounted in *Incidents in the Life of a Slave Girl*, see entry). Ida's mother, Elizabeth "Lizzie" Watterton, was born in Virginia as one of ten children and was eventually enslaved in the home of a man named Spires Bolling, where she met James. Both of Ida's parents were literate—a rarity—and they taught Ida to read.

Emancipated after the Civil War, Ida grew up during Reconstruction, the hopeful but short-lived period when Black men, including her father, were able to vote. Involved in local politics and highly enterprising, her father established his own carpentry business and was a trustee of what became Rust College, one of the historically Black colleges and universities, which Ida herself attended. In 1878, Wells's parents and an infant brother died of yellow fever and she was forced to provide for her seven remaining siblings. Lying about her age allowed a teenage Wells to work as a teacher while her grandmother tended the younger family members. At night and on weekends, Ida continued her own education.

Wells began teaching shortly after the controversial, tainted election of 1876 gave Republican Rutherford B. Hayes the presidency. Granted the victory by a presidential commission that decided the fate of contested slates of electors from several states, Hayes pledged to withdraw federal troops from the former Confederate states. Once in office, Hayes effectively ended Reconstruction. A Supreme Court decision nullifying the Civil Rights Act of 1875 further strengthened the hands of white southerners, ushering in the era of white supremacist laws that sought to eliminate Black votes and cement segregationist policies in place for generations to come.

Seeking opportunity, Ida Wells moved to the home of an aunt in Memphis in 1879 with two of her sisters and was again hired as a teacher. While Memphis remained a bastion of Jim Crow, the city did have a thriving, educated Black community with its own businesses. But five years after settling in Memphis, Ida Wells was told to leave the "ladies car" on a train for the segregated car for Black people. Long before Rosa Parks refused to give up her bus seat, Ida Wells stood her ground. She was forced from the train, sued, and won a settlement from the railroad company. On appeal, however, the Tennessee Supreme Court overturned the award in 1887, ordering Wells to pay the court costs.

By then, Ida Wells had begun to write about her experiences under the pen name "Iola" for *The Living Way*, a Black weekly church newspaper. She continued writing for other Black newspapers, including the *Free Speech and Headlight*, becoming part-owner of the paper in 1889 and later shortening its name to *Free Speech*.

Her life took a horrific and fateful turn in 1892, when three of her neighbors and friends were lynched outside Memphis. One was the Black owner of a grocery that competed with a white-owned business whose owner fired up a mob to kill the three men. Wells wrote the angry editorial (cited earlier) that brought down the wrath of the mob on *Free Speech* and Wells. The paper's offices were ransacked and Wells's life was threatened.

Leaving Memphis, she moved to New York, where she wrote for the *New York Age* and began her pioneering work as an investigative journalist—

well before the term "investigative journalist" even existed. Wells's articles appeared in the more than two hundred Black weeklies then in circulation in the United States and were often reprinted abroad. The first of her pamphlets, *Southern Horrors: Lynch Law in All Its Phases*, was published in 1892. "Her goal was to question a stereotype that was often used to justify lynchings—that black men were rapists," wrote Caitlin Dickerson in the *New York Times*. "Instead, she found that in two-thirds of mob murders, rape was never an accusation. And she often found evidence of what had actually been a consensual interracial relationship."

In 1895, Wells married Ferdinand L. Barnett, a widower who was a lawyer, civil rights activist, and owner of the *Chicago Conservator* in Chicago. That year, she published her second pamphlet, *A Red Record*. And in the following year, she was among the founders of the National Association of Colored Women, which promoted Black suffrage as well as other civil rights. In 1909, she was among the founders of the National Association for the Advancement of Colored People (NAACP), becoming a member of its executive committee. But she left the organization, disillusioned by its white leadership and skeptical of its effectiveness.

Partly for this reason, Wells fell from national prominence, her place taken by activists such as W. E. B. Du Bois (see entry). "Despite her ebbing influence," concludes Caitlin Dickerson, "she continued to organize around causes such as mass incarceration, working for several years as a probation officer, until she died of kidney disease on March 25, 1931, at 68."

Though her fame and extraordinary accomplishments were impressive, her death was somewhat overlooked. In 2018, however, she received a full obituary in the "Overlooked" series of the *New York Times* focusing on remarkable people whose deaths—and lives—had not been acknowledged. That same year, Congress Parkway, a prominent street in her adopted city of Chicago, was renamed in her honor. And in 2020, Ida B. Wells was posthumously awarded a special Pulitzer Prize citation: "For her outstanding and courageous reporting on the horrific and vicious violence against African Americans during the era of lynching."

Wells had visited the White House in 1898 to lobby President William McKinley to pass anti-lynching legislation. Her efforts failed, blocked by segregationists in the Senate. But in 2022, President Biden signed a bill making lynching a federal crime. At the bill's signing both President Biden and Vice-President Kamala Harris recognized the work Ida B. Wells had done more than a century before. One of her descendants, great-granddaughter Michelle Duster, spoke at the signing event: "She carefully chronicled names, date, locations and excuses used to justify lynchings. She wrote articles and pamphlets and gave speeches about the atrocities. . . . Despite losing everything, she continued to speak out across this country and Britain about the violence and terror of lynching."

The Spires Bolling House in Holly Springs, Mississippi, in which her parents were enslaved and where Ida B. Wells was born enslaved, is now a historic site and the location of the Ida B. Wells-Barnett Museum.

WHY YOU SHOULD READ IT

This is easy. Wells's work is a groundbreaking piece of journalism that exposed the long history of violence against Black Americans. It is also important to recognize a towering figure in the early Civil Rights Movement who was largely erased from the history of the period. While it may be difficult for some to face up to the horrors that she documented, this piece of reckoning may be more necessary than ever. As mentioned in the previous entry, we are in the midst of a time when the teaching of American history, as it relates to the history of Black people in America in particular, is under attack by political forces that would erase such subjects as "divisive concepts."

Responding to this wave of partisan legislation, the American Historical Association, a professional organization of scholars and teachers, released a statement expressing "horror" at the assumptions behind such bills as a "frontal attack on academic freedom." The association's statement continued:

> This is not merely an escalation of the "history wars" that have ebbed and flowed across the American landscape—and indeed, in other nations as well; the United States is hardly exceptional in this

regard. Like the proponents of more conventional "divisive concepts" legislation, advocates of this particular assault especially fear the implications of the state's youth learning that slavery and racism have enduring legacies. The idea that racism is a central aspect of American historical development—and its enduring presence in institutions, cultures, and practices—is well within the mainstream of historical scholarship, however much we might disagree about dynamics, relationships, and models of change.

Like *Incidents in the Life of a Slave Girl*, Wells-Barnett's work is a must read for a number of reasons. Both are books whose authors had largely been ignored or forgotten by history—perhaps in no small part because they were women. But both provide intimate and unforgettable witness to large pieces of American history that have too often been left to historians. There is no question that the work in this collection of pamphlets is searing and uncomfortable. But some writing is not meant to make us feel comfortable. This is the sort of book that should be required reading for all of us—because it should make us squirm. It should certainly not be locked away in a closet of unspeakable things. Ida B. Wells was a truth teller.

WHAT TO READ NEXT

The two most famous and recognizable Black voices of Ida B. Wells's lifetime, W. E. B. Du Bois and Booker T. Washington, are discussed in *The Souls of Black Folk* (see following entry).

Of a more contemporary nature is *Just Mercy: A Story of Justice and Redemption* by Bryan Stevenson, founder of the Equal Justice Institute, an organization dedicated to defending the rights of the wrongly condemned and unjustly imprisoned, many of them minorities. Reflecting on the larger question of America's mass incarceration rates, the book became a national best seller in 2014 and is one of the most acclaimed and important books of recent years.

In the author's words, "It is about how easily we condemn people in this country and the injustice we create when we allow fear, anger, and distance to shape the way we treat the most vulnerable among us." In 2018, the Equal Justice Institute opened the National Memorial for Peace and Justice in Montgomery, Alabama. The museum focuses on the legacy of slavery with an emphasis on segregation, lynching, and other forms of racial terror. I think of Stevenson's book as a modern complement to the work of Ida B. Wells-Barnett in its focus on the gross inequities of a system that often falls far short of any sense of true justice and remains unquestionably tilted against people of color.

Finally, for a more complete picture of this extraordinary woman's life and achievements, I point to *Ida: A Sword among Lions* (2008), an eight-hundred-page critically acclaimed biography of Wells-Barnett by Professor Paula Giddings. In it, Giddings makes clear how few writers of the time or soon after acknowledged Wells-Barnett's groundbreaking work, adding: "Subsequently, the NAACP marginalized Wells-Barnett's contributions, even while it adopted her strategies and perspectives."

"We have no right to sit silently by while the inevitable seeds are sown
for a harvest of disaster to our children, black and white."

The Souls of Black Folk

— 1903 —

W. E. B. Du Bois

New York: Penguin Books, 1996; 247 pages, including notes

OPENING WORDS

Herein lie buried many things which if read with patience may show the strange meaning of being black here in the dawning of the Twentieth Century. This meaning is not without interest to you, Gentle Reader; for the problem of the Twentieth Century is the problem of the color-line.

I pray you, then, receive my little book in all charity, studying my words with me, forgiving mistake and foible for sake of the faith and passion that is in me, and seeking the grain of truth hidden there.

I have sought here to sketch, in vague, uncertain outline, the spiritual world in which ten thousand thousand Americans* live and strive."

SUMMARY

Collecting essays and sketches first published in the *Atlantic Monthly* in 1903, this work stands as both a landmark in American literature and a foundational work in sociology. It was written by W. E. B. Du Bois, one of the most prominent, influential people of the twentieth century, who addresses "the problem of the color-line."

Against the extreme racial barriers of his day, Du Bois explores the social, political, and moral hurdles confronting Black Americans at the dawn of a new century. Its opening, "Of Our Spiritual Strivings," laid out what Du Bois called the metaphor of the "veil," the fundamental difficulty Black Americans confronted:

It is a peculiar sensation, this double-consciousness, this sense of always looking at one's self through the eyes of others, of measuring one's soul by the tape of a world that looks on in amused contempt and pity. One ever feels his twoness,—an American, a Negro: two souls, two thoughts, two unreconciled strivings; two warring ideals in one dark body, whose dogged strength alone keeps it from being torn asunder.

A key chapter is "Of Mr. Booker T. Washington and Others," which presents dueling visions of Black America at the turn of the century. Educator Booker T. Washington was the era's other most prominent Black figure, famous for delivering an 1895 speech known as the "Atlanta Compromise."

---

* According to documents of the 1900 U.S. Census, "the number of negroes in the United States is . . . nine and one-fifth million (9,204,531) . . . ," which the Census Bureau acknowledged was most likely an undercount. It also recognized that "between 11 and 16 per cent of the negro population have . . . some degree of white blood." "Negroes in the United States," https://www2.census.gov/prod2/decennial/documents/03322287no8ch1.pdf#[0,{%22name%22.

In it, Washington called for accommodation with whites, in essence, accepting segregation and disenfranchisement.

"Every chapter in Du Bois's book forms a segment of a complex argument," writes professor and editor Donald Gibson, "an argument deriving from the political, philosophical, psychological, and temperamental differences between him and Booker T. Washington."

Du Bois assails what he called Washington's "programme of industrial education, conciliation of the South, and submission and silence as to civil and political rights." The highly educated Du Bois insisted on securing for all Black Americans the right to vote, civic equality, and a broad education according to ability, rather than instruction aimed only at vocational training.

In "The Sorrow Songs," the closing chapter, Du Bois writes of the power of the Negro spiritual and examines "these weird old songs in which the soul of the black slave spoke to men." He goes on to conclude:

> Your country? How came it yours? Before the Pilgrims landed, we were here. Here we have brought our three gifts and mingled them with yours: a gift of story and song . . . ; the gift of sweat and brawn to beat back the wilderness, conquer the soil, and lay the foundations of this vast economic empire two hundred years earlier than your weak hands could have done it; the third, the gift of Spirit. . . . Our song, our toil, our cheer, and warning have been given to this nation in blood-brotherhood. . . . Would America have been America without her Negro people?

That question crescendos into a fitting coda to these essays.

ABOUT THE AUTHOR: W. E. B. DU BOIS

Of many significant writers profiled in this collection, W. E. B. Du Bois is among the most difficult to reduce to a brief summation. He was simply among the most influential and accomplished Americans of the twentieth century. Devoted to the cause of true freedom for Black Americans, W. E. B.

Du Bois was a scholar, historian, pioneering sociologist, educator, poet, and activist who went on to become a founding member of the NAACP. He was also the first Black man to receive a doctorate from Harvard.

On February 23, 1868, William Edward Burghardt Du Bois (pronounced "due-boyss," he insisted) was born in Great Barrington, Massachusetts. The Thirteenth Amendment had ended legal American slavery in 1865, but the family he was born into had already been free. His mother, Mary Silvina Burghardt, was part of Great Barrington's small free Black community. She was descended from Tom Burghardt, an enslaved man thought to have won his freedom by joining the Continental Army during the American Revolution. William's mixed-race father, Alfred Du Bois, was born in Haiti and settled in Great Barrington, marrying Mary in 1867. Two years after William was born, Alfred abandoned the family, sending mother and son back to live with her parents.

In *Souls*, Du Bois briefly discusses his childhood and the "revelation" of his race in an integrated schoolhouse where he was first confronted by the distinction his skin made:

> In a wee wooden schoolhouse, something put it into the boys' and girls' heads to buy gorgeous visiting-cards—ten cents a package—and exchange. The exchange was merry, till one girl, a tall newcomer, refused my card,—refused it peremptorily, with a glance. Then it dawned on me with a certain suddenness that I was different from the others; or like, mayhap, in heart and life and longing, but shut out from their world by a vast veil. I had thereafter no desire to tear down that veil, to creep through; I held all beyond it in common contempt, and lived above it in a region of blue sky and great wandering shadows. That sky was bluest when I could beat my mates at examination-time, or beat them at a foot-race, or even beat their stringy heads.

Du Bois did it through education. With money raised from neighbors in the town's First Congregational Church, he attended Fisk University, Nashville's historically Black institution of higher learning, graduating in

1888 with his first BA degree. While there, he taught during summers and came face-to-face with Jim Crow racism for the first time. Du Bois then attended Harvard, which did not accept his Fisk credits, working his way through school with summer jobs and scholarships. He graduated cum laude with a second BA degree in history and in 1891 received a scholarship to attend Harvard's graduate school in sociology.

In 1892, Du Bois won a fellowship allowing him to study in Berlin and travel around Europe. After returning, he completed his dissertation, *The Suppression of the African Slave-Trade to the United States of America, 1638–1870*, becoming Harvard's first Black Ph.D. recipient. From there, Du Bois moved on to a succession of academic posts, beginning with Ohio's Wilberforce University, where he married Nina Gomer, his student, in 1896. He next moved to Philadelphia as a researcher at the University of Pennsylvania. His fieldwork led to the 1899 publication of *The Philadelphia Negro*, a landmark work of sociology that refuted widely held prejudices about Black people in Philadelphia and generally.

The study was published after he had moved to teach at Atlanta University, a research university and another historically black school (later renamed Clark Atlanta University). Through his writings and lectures about Black America to expositions in Europe, Du Bois emerged as America's most prominent Black spokesperson, alongside Booker T. Washington, whose accommodationist policies sharply divided the two men.

Born enslaved in 1856, Booker T. Washington taught himself to read and, after emancipation, worked in coal mines and salt furnaces to earn money to attend Virginia's Hampton Institute, established to educate freedmen. At twenty-five, he was appointed to lead the Tuskegee Institute, which became the nation's leader in Black vocational training. Washington worked against racial hatred and bias, but he believed his people should gradually raise themselves up through hard work. His accommodationist view, which did not oppose the social order or strike at the white supremacy of Jim Crow, won favor among many white people and he attracted the support of wealthy industrial philanthropists such as Andrew Carnegie and John D. Rockefeller.

Du Bois had different ideas, arguing that Washington's strategy, which accommodated segregationist policies, did not demand the vote for Blacks, and accepted widespread voting restrictions, such as property requirements and literacy tests, that suppressed Black votes, would only perpetuate racism. In 1905, he cofounded the Niagara Movement, an organization dedicated to rebutting Washington. The movement faltered, in part because of Washington's popularity. But in time, the Niagara Movement became the forerunner of the interracial National Association for the Advancement of Colored People (NAACP), founded in 1909.

Du Bois played a central role in the NAACP's creation and also became editor of its magazine, *The Crisis*, which published photographs of lynching victims. It also led the protest against the 1915 movie *The Birth of a Nation*, a film glorifying the Ku Klux Klan that was shown in Woodrow Wilson's White House. Despite his pacifism and misgivings about the ongoing racism in the army and the Wilson administration, Du Bois took the lead in urging Black men to enlist after war was declared on Germany in April 1917.

After the war, as editor of *The Crisis*, he was a central figure in the Harlem Renaissance of the 1920s. But Du Bois became disillusioned as he felt that many whites were drawn to Harlem's cultural achievements as a form of voyeurism and that Black artists were not using their success to advance the cause of the masses.

In 1929, sixty-one-year-old Du Bois took part in a public debate, *Shall the Negro Be Encouraged to Seek Cultural Equality?*, with Lothrop Stoddard, a white proponent of the concept of a Master Race. Stoddard put forth ideas in his book *The Rising Tide of Color against White World-Supremacy*, soon to be promulgated in Nazi Germany. By all accounts, Du Bois demolished Stoddard, who was humiliated by the audience's mocking laughter. This event is brilliantly detailed in Ian Frazier's 2019 *New Yorker* article "When W. E. B. Du Bois Made a Laughingstock of a White Supremacist."

A socialist since 1911, Du Bois was a pragmatist in his politics, supporting Democrats or Republicans who might aid his crusade for greater civil rights for Black Americans. But after 1931, Du Bois and the NAACP leadership were at odds in part because Du Bois had begun to embrace Black separatism. Resigning from *The Crisis* and the NAACP, he returned to Atlanta University, where he wrote and published *Black Reconstruction*, a landmark work of history, in 1935.

In 1940, Du Bois published *Dusk of Dawn*, a second volume of auto-biography, and three years later, at age seventy-five, was abruptly fired or forced to resign by Atlanta University. It was a decision made, Du Bois believed, because of his confrontational approach to civil rights. Rejoining the NAACP, he was part of the delegation that attended the 1945 conference that established the United Nations. But his embrace of Marxism and association with socialism amid Cold War fears made him a target of the FBI. By mutual agreement, he resigned from the NAACP in 1948. The FBI did not relent and, in 1951, Du Bois was tried but acquitted as an agent of a foreign government due to his work for the Peace Information Center, a group trying to ban nuclear weapons.

Outraged by U.S. government McCarthy-era anti-communist policies, such as court decisions upholding legislation requiring communists to register with the government, and the seizure of his passport by the government, Du Bois joined the Communist Party in 1961, at age ninety-three. He moved soon after to Ghana with his second wife, Lola Shirley Graham. A Ghanian American composer and writer, Graham had married Du Bois after his first wife died in 1951.

W. E. B. Du Bois died in Ghana on August 27, 1963, the day before the famous March on Washington, where a moment of silence was observed in his honor. After Du Bois died, Martin Luther King Jr. said of him:

> One idea he insistently taught was that black people have been kept in oppression and deprivation by a poisonous fog of lies that depicted them as inferior, born deficient and deservedly doomed to servitude to the grave. . . . Dr. Du Bois recognized that the keystone in the arch of oppression was the myth of inferiority and he dedicated his brilliant talents to demolish it.

WHY YOU SHOULD READ IT

Written more than 120 years ago, *The Souls of Black Folk* is a fundamental document in understanding American history and the course of America's racial and social politics. At a moment when powerful forces are attempting to erase aspects of Black history from schoolbooks and squelch classroom discussion of America's racist past, the words of W. E. B. Du Bois stand as a testament to the importance of contemplating that history. It is more than fair to borrow from the Du Bois opening lines cited earlier and say: Gentle Reader, the problem of the Twenty-First Century is still the problem of the color-line.

WHAT TO READ NEXT

One of the other major works by Du Bois is *Black Reconstruction in America*. Anything but short, it is another essential scholarly work that refuted the then widely accepted idea that Reconstruction was a failure. Du Bois reframed the era as one in which formerly enslaved people made major strides toward democracy, only to be set back by the rise of Jim Crow and a new era of legal segregation.

I can also recommend the authoritative biography of Du Bois, a two-volume work by David Levering Lewis that won the Pulitzer Prize for Biography: *W. E. B. Du Bois: Biography of a Race, 1868–1919* (1994, winner of the Pulitzer, Bancroft, and Parkman Prizes); *W. E. B. Du Bois: The Fight for Equality and the American Century, 1919–1963* (2001, Pulitzer Prize).

As a counterpoint, I suggest *Up from Slavery* by Booker T. Washington. Acknowledged as a great orator and educational leader in his day, Washington was the ideological opponent of Du Bois. But the two men agreed that education held the key to a Black future.

Both *Up from Slavery* and *The Souls of Black Folk* are on the Modern Library list of 100 Best Nonfiction Books of the Twentieth Century. However, Washington's views about separation of the races have fallen from favor as Washington has. Yet an appreciation of Washington on the National Museum of African American History and Culture website notes:

> These two giants—Washington and Du Bois—underscore the fact that there was not a single linear path to achieving racial equality in the nation. The struggle required African Americans to both battle and accommodate the realities of segregation and discrimination to help future generations more fully realize the promise of America.

"The silence and darkness which are said to shut me in,
open my door most hospitably to countless sensations
that distract, inform, admonish, and amuse."

The World I Live In

— 1908 —

Helen Keller

New York: New York Review Books, 2003; edited with an introduction by
Roger Shattuck; 182 pages

OPENING WORDS

I have just touched my dog. He was rolling on the grass, with pleasure in
every muscle and limb. I wanted to catch a picture of him in my fingers, and
I touched him as lightly as I would cobwebs; but lo, his fat body revolved,
stiffened and solidified into an upright position, and his tongue gave my hand
a lick! He pressed close to me, as if he were fain to crowd himself into my hand.
He loved it with his tail, with his paw, with his tongue. If he could speak, I
believe he would say with me that paradise is attained by touch; for in touch
is all love and intelligence.

SUMMARY

Written in 1908, when Helen Keller had already attained international renown, this collection of essays gives us a perception of this remarkable woman that may differ from the familiar one left by the image of Helen Keller as a child. Left blind and deaf by illness in early childhood, the author, political rights activist, and disability rights advocate is today known largely to most people through the many versions of *The Miracle Worker*, the play and later film based on her childhood experience of learning to spell out words in the hands of her teacher, Annie Sullivan. The title was inspired by a remark attributed to Mark Twain, who knew and admired Keller and Sullivan. "Helen is a miracle, and Miss Sullivan is the miracle-worker," said Twain.

But this book, long out of print but now available, brings to light the adult Helen Keller, a woman who is intellectually curious and remarkably poetic in capturing the world she lives in but can only feel. Invoking comparison to Emerson and Thoreau, her essays describe how Keller experiences the world, touching on sensations and emotions, imagination, and broader themes of optimism, happiness, and satisfaction—and emphasizing her reality and experience as being as meaningful as any sighted, hearing person's:

> Most people measure their happiness in terms of physical pleasure and material possession. Could they win some visible goal which they have set on the horizon, how happy they would be! . . . If happiness is to be so measured, I who cannot hear or see have every reason to sit in a corner with folded hands and weep. If I am happy in spite of my deprivations, if my happiness is so deep that it is a faith, so thoughtful that it becomes a philosophy of life,—if, in short, I am an optimist, my testimony to the creed of optimism is worth hearing.

ABOUT THE AUTHOR: HELEN KELLER

What many of us learned about Helen Keller stops with her as a seven-year-old learning to communicate. But Keller's life was far more complex and intriguing. She was born Helen Adams Keller on June 27, 1880, in Tuscumbia, Alabama. Her father, Arthur Keller, was a newspaper editor who had served in the Confederate army during the Civil War. Her mother, Catherine, was the daughter of a Confederate general, and both parents had been born into Alabama's slaveholding elite.

Before turning two, Helen suffered a mysterious illness, thought to be a form of meningitis or perhaps scarlet fever, that left her blind and deaf. She also "reverted nearly to the state of a seriously wounded, untamed animal," as the late literary critic and scholar Roger Shattuck noted in an introduction to this edition. "This isolated creature survived five years of frustration and indulgence within her despairing family before finding release."

When she was six, Helen was examined by Alexander Graham Bell, the developer of the telephone. At Bell's suggestion, Joanna (better known as Anne or Annie) Sullivan, a twenty-year-old teacher with Boston's Perkins Institution for the Blind—directed by Bell's son-in-law—was dispatched to the family.

Under Sullivan's instruction, Keller had learned within months to feel objects and associate them with words spelled out by finger signals on her palm. She could read sentences by feeling raised words on cardboard and made her own sentences by arranging words in a frame. "Four months after Annie's arrival in Alabama," writes Shattuck, "Helen began writing to her aunts and uncles in childish block letters." A gifted teacher, Sullivan remained with Keller as governess, and later companion, from March 1887 until her death in October 1936.

By the time she was fourteen, Helen Keller was able to write a brief sketch of her life called "My Story" that appeared in a magazine in 1894—and is reprinted in this edition of *The World I Live In*. She later spent winters at the Perkins Institution learning Braille and began the slow process of learning to speak at Boston's Horace Mann School for the Deaf. Keller learned to lip-read by placing her fingers on the lips and throat of the speaker while the words were simultaneously spelled out for her.

Keller later enrolled in New York City's Wright-Humason School for the Deaf and at sixteen entered the Cambridge School for Young Ladies in Massachusetts. She won admission to Radcliffe College—the woman's college affiliated with Harvard—in 1900. With Sullivan at her side providing "hand lectures," Keller graduated cum laude in 1904.

While still a sophomore at Radcliffe in 1903, she wrote an autobiography, *The Story of My Life*, with the help of Sullivan and editorial assistant John Macy, a Harvard instructor who later married Sullivan. This autobiography first appeared in the *Ladies' Home Journal* in six installments in 1902 and went on to sell millions of copies worldwide in book form. It was the first of several books Keller would write, including *The World I Live In*, her collection of short essays published in 1908. Keller also began advocating for the blind in many major American magazines of the day, including *Ladies' Home Journal* and the *Atlantic Monthly*. With the aid of an interpreter, she began to lecture in 1913, often on behalf of the American Foundation for the Blind, for which she later established a large endowment fund.

Fewer people know about Helen Keller's radical politics. A pacifist and advocate for civil rights and the rights of the disabled, Keller cofounded the American Civil Liberties Union with Roger Nash Baldwin and other activists in 1920. She was an early supporter of the NAACP and an opponent of the rampant lynchings of the 1920s. She advocated for birth control—as well as eugenics, a theory of improving the human gene pool by discouraging reproduction among certain groups. Popular in the early twentieth century, it was a position from which she later retreated.

And she was, since 1909, a socialist. In a socialist newspaper, the *New York Call*, she addressed imprisoned socialist Eugene Debs as "Dear Comrade" in 1919. She wrote, "I write because I want you to know that I should be proud if the Supreme Court convicted me of abhorring war, and doing all in my power to oppose it. When I think of the millions who have suffered in all the wicked wars of the past, I am shaken with the anguish of a great impatience. I want to fling myself against all bruite (sic) powers that destroy life and break the spirit of man." Earlier, in 1912, she also joined the Industrial Workers of the World ("Wobblies"), a labor union movement that was later suppressed.

That is the Helen Keller left out of schoolbooks. "Some of the reason schools don't teach much about Keller's adult life is because she was involved in groups that have been perceived as too radical throughout American history," wrote Olivia B. Waxman in *Time*. "She was a member of the Socialist

Party, and corresponded with Eugene Debs, the party's most prominent member and a five-time presidential candidate. She also read Marx, and her associations with all of these far-left groups landed her on the radar of the FBI, which monitored her for ties to the Communist Party."

In 1933, the Nazis also deemed her writing unacceptable. Helen Keller's *How I Became a Socialist* and pacifist writings were among those burned in Berlin in May of that year. According to the United States Holocaust Memorial Museum, "Keller donated her German royalties to a fund for German war-blind veterans. Nonetheless, her socialist and anti-war writing was burned. Keller's open letter of protest, published in the *New York Times* and elsewhere, warned the German people that the burning of books could not eradicate ideas."

Keller traveled the world as an advocate for the disabled as well as her other causes. She met with every president from Grover Cleveland to Lyndon B. Johnson, who honored her in 1964 with the Presidential Medal of Freedom. After a series of strokes in 1961, Keller largely remained at her home in Connecticut until her death on June 1, 1968. Her ashes are buried at the Washington National Cathedral. In 1999, Keller was ranked by Gallup among the most admired people of the twentieth century.

WHY YOU SHOULD READ IT

While I had considered this title from the very beginning of my quest, it was only when I saw Annie Dillard refer to it in *The Writing Life* (see entry) that I was convinced I must include Keller's collection. "Once, in daylight, I glanced at a book on a stack's corner, a book I had presumably touched every night with my hand," writes Dillard. "The book was *The World I Live In*, by Helen Keller. I read it at once: it surprised me by its strong and original prose."

That, I suppose, is synchronicity of reading: one book, one writer, urging me on to another. Having read this deeply moving collection, I can only concur with Dillard's assessment; Keller's essays are "strong and original."

So read it for the pure literary pleasure. And read it also for Keller's unique insights about how we should all experience the world. But finally, read it also for the more complete picture of an extraordinary individual who may be sequestered by some in the limited frame of "disabled writer," as if her physical limitations are all that defined Keller. That is a disservice to Keller's work. As Roger Shattuck wrote in his introduction, "The reason why we find a convincingly human quality in *The Story of My Life* and *The World I Live In* reaches beyond our fascination with the disabled and the handicapped. These books display the redemptive power of language in certain cases, and the power of that language to reach us all."

As the record of her commitment to greater social justice certainly demonstrates, Keller was far more than a spokesperson for the disabled. In a 2015 appreciation on the 135th anniversary of Keller's birth, Sascha Cohen focused on the writer's radical activism: "She noticed the close relationship between disability and poverty, and blamed capitalism and poor industrial conditions for both. As Keller told the New York *Tribune* in 1916, blindness was 'often caused by the selfishness and greed of employers.' In her writings and speeches, Keller called for revolution rather than reform. She had no patience for compromise, and argued that charitable aid did more to assuage the guilt of the prosperous than to improve the conditions of vulnerable people's lives."

So read it for the remarkable insights of a woman who truly "felt" the world and set out to change it.

WHAT TO READ NEXT

For more about Keller, try her 1903 autobiography, *The Story of My Life*, which goes as far as the time she was a college student. Written while she was still at Radcliffe, the book described her remarkable early life and work with Annie Sullivan. It provided the source material for *The Miracle Worker*, which began as a 1957 teleplay by William Gibson, was performed on Broadway, winning a Pulitzer Prize, and then was filmed in 1962 with Anne Bancroft as Sullivan and Patty Duke as Helen, reprising their Broadway roles. It has since been reprised in film and on television.

"Like most uneducated Englishwomen, I like reading—
I like reading books in the bulk."

A Room of One's Own

— 1929 —

Virginia Woolf

New York: Harcourt Brace & Co., 1981; foreword by Mary Gordon; 114 pages

OPENING WORDS

But, you may say, we asked you to speak about women and fiction—what has that got to do with a room of one's own? I will try to explain. When you asked me to speak about women and fiction I sat down on the banks of a river and began to wonder what the words meant. They might mean simply a few remarks about Fanny Burney*; a few more about Jane Austen; a tribute to the Brontës

---

* Some of these names may require a word of explanation: Fanny Burney was an English satirical novelist whose first published work was the anonymous *Evelina* (1778); Haworth Parsonage was the family home of the Brontë sisters; Miss Mitford was Mary Russell Mitford, an author and dramatist; the more recognizable George Eliot was the pen name of Mary Ann Evans, who wrote seven novels; Mrs. Gaskell was an English novelist (*Mary Barton*, 1848) and the first biographer of Charlotte Brontë.

and a sketch of Haworth Parsonage under snow; some witticisms if possible about Miss Mitford; a respectful allusion to George Eliot; a reference to Mrs. Gaskell and one would have done. But at second sight the words seemed not so simple. . . . All I could do was to offer you an opinion upon one minor point— a woman must have money and a room of her own if she is to write fiction; and that, as you will see, leaves the great problem of the true nature of woman and the true nature of fiction unsolved.

SUMMARY

How can women be creative? What obstacles do women face as artists and writers? In October 1928, novelist Virginia Woolf was asked to speak on "women and fiction" before two student societies at Newnham College and Girton College, the first two colleges for women at England's Cambridge University. By the time she spoke, Woolf had already published several novels, including *Mrs. Dalloway* and *To the Lighthouse*. And she had a great deal to say.

Beginning with the plight of women writers, but moving on to the larger question of the purpose of fiction, Woolf expanded her two talks into this book, published a year later by the Hogarth Press—a publishing venture that Virginia Woolf and her husband, Leonard Woolf, owned and operated.

In *A Room of One's Own*, Woolf conjures an imaginary narrator considering the question of women in fiction as she sits beside a river. This imaginary woman—a surrogate for Woolf—walks across a grassy plot near a noted university when a man intercepts her. "His face expressed horror and indignation. . . . I was a woman. This was the turf; there was the path. Only the Fellows and Scholars are allowed here."

With this imagined scene as background, Woolf addresses the centuries of hurdles faced by women with creative ambitions. Woolf conjures the figure of Judith, a "wonderfully gifted" sister of William Shakespeare: "She was as adventurous, as imaginative, as agog to see the world as he was. But she was not sent to school. . . . She picked up a book now and then, one of her brother's perhaps, and read a few pages. But then her parents came in and told her to mend the stockings or mind the stew and not moon about with books and papers." Woolf's fictional Judith does not end up as acclaimed as her brother. Far from it.

Woolf moves on to a discussion on writing and assesses many writers—of both sexes. Then she introduces another imaginary writer, "Mary Carmichael," and describes reading her "first novel," *Life's Adventure* and its opening sentence. Woolf writes:

> "Chloe liked Olivia. . . ." Do not start. Do not blush. Let us admit in the privacy of our own society that these things sometimes happen. Sometimes women do like women.

It should be noted that Woolf's lover, Vita Sackville-West, was in the audience while Woolf gave her lecture.

In her concluding section, Woolf moves beyond "women and fiction" to speak more broadly of what makes for genius, arguing that the greatest writers express what she calls "androgyny." She writes: ". . . it is fatal for anyone who writes to think of their sex. It is fatal to be a man or woman pure and simple; one must be woman-manly or man-womanly. . . . Some collaboration has to take place in the mind between the woman and the man before the act of creation can be accomplished."

Woolf's work is, first, an impassioned call for women to have income and "a room of one's own." That alone justifies its literary and historical significance. But in this closing discussion of what constitutes "genius," Woolf takes her argument to a more universal height. She raises the bar to consider what constitutes literary greatness, without regard to gender.

ABOUT THE AUTHOR: VIRGINIA WOOLF

A novelist, essayist, and diarist whose work would profoundly influence modern literature, Virginia Stephen was born on January 25, 1882, in London. She was the second daughter of Leslie Stephen, a prominent figure in English letters, and Julia Jackson, the widow of a successful barrister. Virginia's mother had gained fame as a model for the Pre-Raphaelite school of British painters and for her aunt Julia Cameron, a pioneer of photography.

Both of Virginia's parents had been married previously but lost their spouses. With four children between them from their first marriages, the couple wed in 1878. They would have four of their own children: Vanessa, who would become a modernist painter; a son, Thoby; Virginia; and another son, Adrian. While raised in a highly progressive and literary environment in Victorian England, Virginia received little formal education and then endured a childhood and young adult life filled with tragedy and despair. As writer and publisher Nigel Nicolson records:

> Her mother died when she was thirteen [1895], and her half sister when she was fifteen [1897]. At twenty-two she lost her father [1904], and two years later her brother Thoby [1906]. Another half sister was mentally deranged. Virginia herself, while still quite young, suffered from periods of acute depression and even insanity. She was sexually abused by her half brothers when she was too young to understand what was happening. [Note: Bracketed dates were added.]

Following her father's death in 1904, Virginia and other members of the Stephen family moved to the "bohemian" Bloomsbury neighborhood, where an artistic and literary society later to be known as the Bloomsbury Group emerged. A hothouse of modernist thought in art, literature, and politics—along with remarkably liberal social and sexual attitudes—the Bloomsbury Group included art critic Clive Bell, who was in an open marriage with Virginia's sister Vanessa; the critic and gallerist Roger Fry and painter Duncan Grant, who both became Vanessa's lovers; novelist E. M. Forster; and economist John Maynard Keynes. Another member was essayist and civil servant Leonard Woolf, "a penniless Jew," as Virginia described him when he proposed. They married in August 1912.

In 1913, following her marriage, Virginia Woolf attempted suicide, the beginning of a near-complete breakdown that lasted for several years. Her first novel, *The Voyage Out* (1915), was published in that period and was followed by another suicide attempt. In 1917, Leonard purchased a hand printing press as a diversion for Virginia. The Woolfs established the Hogarth Press, which would publish T. S. Eliot and other significant modernists. The press also published some of Woolf's most significant work: *Mrs. Dalloway* (1925), *To the Lighthouse* (1927), *Orlando* (1928), and *The Waves* (1931), as well as *A Room of One's Own*.

In 1922, Virginia met Vita Sackville-West, an aristocrat and successful writer then better known than Woolf. They began a friendship that became a sexual relationship, lasting for several years.

As the 1930s moved toward World War II, Woolf found it increasingly difficult to write. Possibly suffering from bipolar disorder, and with a history of childhood sexual abuse, Woolf took five years to finish *The Years*. Her final novel and the most popular during her lifetime, it was published by the Hogarth Press in 1937, the same year that Vanessa's son Julian Bell was killed in the Spanish Civil War.

The loss of her nephew heightened Virginia's pacifism, expressed in *Three Guineas*, a book-length essay that condemned war and explored some of the themes raised in *A Room of One's Own*. "It was a pacifist's statement, but it was something more," comments Nigel Nicolson, who knew Virginia Woolf. He was the son of the British writers Harold Nicolson and Vita Sackville-West, who had become Virginia Woolf's lover by the time *A Room of One's Own* was written. "She wished to lay the blame for war on men and their treatment of women. She came near to saying that if women had a greater influence in the state, there would be no wars."

Deeply troubled by the loss of Julian and the war with Germany that had begun in 1939, Woolf's depression worsened. On March 28, 1941, Virginia Woolf walked down to the river Ouse, filled the pockets of her overcoat with stones, and drowned herself. She was fifty-nine years old.

WHY YOU SHOULD READ IT

A Room of One's Own has rightfully become a landmark in feminist literature. In some respects, it continues the argument set forth in Mary Wollstonecraft's *A Vindication of the Rights of Woman*, a groundbreaking work calling for equality for women and published in 1792, nearly a century before Virginia Woolf's birth. In it, Wollstonecraft argued for women to be educated equally with men, along with other demands for equality of rights. The book profoundly influenced the suffrage and early women's rights movements that emerged in nineteenth-century England and America.

More than a century later, Woolf was writing after women had won the vote, in the aftermath of World War I; the suffrage movement had accomplished many of its goals and women were attending university. But Woolf focused more narrowly on the difficulty—if not impossibility— for most women to create artistically because they were simply too poor. That, she argued, was largely because society had relegated women to the role of mother and little else. Novelist Mary Gordon notes in a foreword: ". . . women are poor because, instead of making money, they have had children," adding: "Moreover, they were uneducated; they had no privacy. . . . Yet even when they were freed from the practical impediments imposed upon their sex, they had no tradition to follow."

"It stated the case with overwhelming force, grace and humor," Nigel Nicholson wrote of *A Room*. "Since the book originated as lectures, its style was conversational, more like her letters than her diary. . . . She upbraids the male sex for its love of war and making money. She dwells on the disadvantages that women have endured. . . . They did not have a chance."

A Room of One's Own also has its critics, especially those who find Woolf's sentiments classist. In her introduction to this edition, Mary Gordon confronts this candidly. "Woolf is concerned with the fate of women of genius, not with that of ordinary women; her plea is that we create a world in which Shakespeare's sister might survive her gift, not one in which the miner's wife can have her rights to property," writes Gordon, continuing: "Her passion is for literature, not for universal justice."

Woolf discusses other writers, some notable (Galsworthy and Kipling) and others obscure—John Langdon Davies? But she returns to the need for women to have the means to create. "Intellectual freedom," writes Woolf, "depends upon material things. Poetry depends upon intellectual freedom."

Despite Gordon's justifiable criticism, Woolf's book still counts first as a clarion call for a reordering of society to allow women creative opportunities and liberate them from their confined roles. She even imagines a time, perhaps in a hundred years, when "the nursemaid will heave coal. The shopwoman will drive an engine."

This is no firebrand's call for equality of the sexes. Nor it is a cry to man the barricades. But it should be read for its wider purpose. Woolf cajoles the women in her audience, now given the educational opportunity denied to Judith Shakespeare, to create. Her insights into reading, and writing, are of a larger scope. They have little do with the notion of personal satisfaction. "Human happiness, the happiness of writers—questions by which we, in our age, seem enthralled—do not enter these pages," Mary Gordon notes. "What is important, what is essential, is that works of genius be created."

Imploring the young women, now free to vote and study at university, to write all kinds of books—"travel and adventure, and research and scholarship, and history and biography, and criticism and philosophy and science"—Woolf concludes with a plea that they write books that speak to what she called reality. In reading such books, Woolf contends, "one sees more intensely afterwards; the world seems bared of its covering and given an intenser life. . . . I find myself saying briefly and prosaically that it is much more important to be oneself than anything else."

That, to me, seems like valuable advice for any writer, regardless of gender.

WHAT TO READ NEXT

Where to begin? Getting through all of the works of Virginia Woolf would constitute far more than a year of reading. Famed today primarily as a novelist, Woolf was also a prodigious essayist, diarist, and correspondent. Her diaries alone fill six volumes; the *Collected Essays*, four volumes; and letters, another six volumes. There are also numerous book-length essays.

Foremost among these is *Three Guineas*, a longer work of nonfiction that followed the publication of *A Room of One's Own* in 1938. Focused on pacifism, it was inspired by the death of her nephew Julian Bell, who was serving as an ambulance driver with the Republican forces opposing General Franco's Fascists in the Spanish Civil War.

For Woolf's fiction, begin with *Mrs. Dalloway*. This landmark of twentieth-century literature records the seemingly ordinary events in the day of a woman who is planning a dinner party that evening. Next, try *To the Lighthouse* (1927), recounting the visits of a family to the Isle of Skye in Scotland over a decade. It is ranked #15 on the Modern Library list of 100 Best Novels. Then there is *Orlando: A Biography* (1928). Differing in style from her other fiction, it is one of Woolf's most popular books. Dedicated to her friend and lover Vita Sackville-West, it describes the adventures of a poet who changes sex from man to woman and lives for centuries.

Cited earlier, *A Vindication of the Rights of Woman* (1792) by Mary Wollstonecraft is an influential landmark. While now somewhat dated and not written in the easiest prose, it might be called a milestone in "proto-feminism." In it, Wollstonecraft argued for women to be educated equally with men, presaging Woolf's argument in *A Room of One's Own*. Mary Wollstonecraft is also notable as the mother of Mary Wollstonecraft Shelley, even more famous as the author of *Frankenstein, or the Modern Prometheus* (1818); Wollstonecraft died in 1797, eleven days after the birth of her daughter.

I read and heartily recommend a more recent take on Woolf's theme, Mary Beard's 2017 book, *Women and Power: A Manifesto*. Like *A Room of One's Own*, this slim volume began as a series of lectures by the noted classicist and best-selling author of *SPQR*. These talks were Beard's response to the barrage of harassment from so-called trolls that she received in response to her writing and speaking. In it, she articulates a stark polemic about the continuing and increasingly violent tone of the suppression of women's voices. "It is not *what* you say that prompts it, it's simply the fact that you're saying it," Beard writes, adding a graphic description of a tweet she had received threatening death and sexual violence.

Beard opens by discussing her own mother, who was able to have a career, marriage, and family yet was still frustrated by lack of opportunity for women. Beard writes: "I wanted to work out how I would explain to her—as much as to myself, as well as to the millions of other women who still share some of the same frustrations—just how deeply embedded in Western culture are the mechanisms that silence women, that refuse to take them seriously, and that sever them . . . from the centres of power. . . . When it comes to silencing women, Western culture has had thousands of years of practice."

"I may say that only three times in my life have I met a genius, and each time a bell within me rang and I was not mistaken. . . . The three geniuses of whom I wish to speak are Gertrude Stein, Pablo Picasso and Alfred Whitehead."

The Autobiography of Alice B. Toklas

— 1933 —

Gertrude Stein

New York: Vintage Books, 1990; 252 pages

EXCERPT

This was the year 1907. Gertrude Stein was just seeing through the press *Three Lives* which she was having privately printed, and she was deep in *The Making of Americans,* her thousand-page book. Picasso had just finished his portrait of her which nobody at that time liked except the painter and the painted and which is now so famous, and he had just begun his strange complicated picture of three women. Matisse had just finished his Bonheur de Vivre, his first big composition which gave him the name of fauve or a zoo. It was the moment Max Jacob has since called the heroic age of cubism. I remember not long ago hearing Picasso and Gertrude Stein talking about various things that had happened at that time, one of them said but all that could not have happened in that one year, oh said the other, my dear you forget we were young then and we did a great deal in a year.

SUMMARY

First, let us be clear. This is *not* the autobiography of a woman named Alice Babette Toklas, who was born into a Polish Jewish family in San Francisco in 1876. A few months after fire devastated San Francisco in 1907, Alice B. Toklas moved to Paris and, on September 8, 1907, met Gertrude Stein. That day marked the beginning of a remarkable relationship lasting nearly four decades. It is Gertrude Stein who is the actual author and central character in this "autobiography."

This faux memoir, told through the voice of Alice B. Toklas, is Stein's account of life in avant-garde Paris from the beginning of the twentieth century until about 1932. Almost from the time she moved to France in 1903, Stein, a well-to-do Jewish American Radcliffe graduate and aspiring writer, was the sun at the center of the Parisian art and literary world's solar system. Her salon, shared with her lifetime companion, Toklas, became a gathering place that would help shape art and literature in the new century.

Stein's book is a veritable "Who's Who" of the most significant artists and writers of the day. So, to provide some context to the preceding excerpt: Picasso's 1906–1907 portrait of Gertrude Stein now hangs in New York City's Metropolitan Museum of Art; the "strange complicated picture" is *Three Women* (1908), held by the Hermitage Museum in Russia and closely related to *Les Demoiselles d'Avignon* (1907), hanging at the Museum of Modern Art in New York; *Bonheur de Vivre* ("Joy of Life") is now in Philadelphia's Barnes Collection. *Fauve* is a French word for "wild beast" and would be used to characterize an entire school of painters who used wildly exuberant colors, sometimes straight from paint tubes, whose images exploded on the canvas far less realistically than the Impressionists' did. And finally, Max Jacob was a French writer who became Picasso's first friend in Paris and a central figure in the art scene of this period.

Among the many extraordinary people who feature in the book's postwar era are bookseller and James Joyce patron Sylvia Beach, novelist

F. Scott Fitzgerald, photographer-writer Carl Van Vechten, actor-singer Paul Robeson, and, perhaps most significantly, Ernest Hemingway. It was this postwar-era Paris that Hemingway describes in *A Moveable Feast* (see entry). But Stein's portrait of the city and its artists cemented its legacy well before Hemingway's version appeared.

These names—and many others, both famous and obscure—cascade through Stein's narrative, as the author, in the guise of Toklas, records the moods and sentiments of a time that shaped modern art in the twentieth century in the works of such giants of painting as Gauguin, Cézanne, Matisse, and Picasso. "Stein wrote *The Autobiography of Alice B. Toklas* in the fall of 1932 in a kind of paroxysm of desire for the fame and money that so far eluded her," wrote Janet Malcolm in a 2007 biography of the two women, *Two Lives: Gertrude and Alice*. ". . . Finally, at the age of fifty-eight, she decided to (so to speak) prostitute herself and write a book in regular English that would be a best seller. That it actually became one may be a measure of the genius Stein claims for herself throughout the book. What kind of a genius she was is hard to pin down."

ABOUT THE AUTHOR: GERTRUDE STEIN

Born on February 3, 1874, in Allegheny City, Pennsylvania (now part of Pittsburgh), Gertrude Stein was the youngest of five children of wealthy German-Jewish Americans, Amelia and Daniel Stein; her father was a successful merchant with extensive real estate holdings. When Gertrude was still an infant, she was taken by her parents to Europe with her two older brothers, Michael and Leo. After several years, the Steins returned to America, eventually settling in Oakland, California, after Gertrude's father became director of San Francisco's streetcar lines.

After the death of her mother when Gertrude was fourteen, and her father three years later, Gertrude and her brother Leo moved to Baltimore to live with a maternal aunt's family. After Leo went to Harvard, Gertrude decided to follow him. She entered the Society for the Collegiate Instruction of Women, later renamed Radcliffe College, where she studied psychology with the philosopher William James. There is an oft-told story that on examination day Stein wrote a note to Professor James: "'Dear Professor James, I am sorry but really I don't feel a bit like an examination paper in philosophy today.'" She left. William James replied the next day that he often felt the same way and gave her the highest grade in the course. After graduating magna cum laude in 1898, Gertrude Stein went to medical school, at the suggestion of William James, studying at Johns Hopkins from 1897 to 1902, but left, apparently out of boredom.

With Leo, Gertrude moved to London and then Paris in 1903, living at first with her brother, who was emerging as an accomplished art critic. They were soon followed by her other brother Michael and his wife, Sarah. Gertrude Stein and her brothers were among the first collectors of works by the Cubists and other avant-garde painters of the period, including most prominently Pablo Picasso, Henry Matisse, and Georges Braque.

Buying relatively inexpensive works by then largely unknown artists allowed them to amass what would become a collection of twentieth-century masterpieces and regularly draw crowds to their homes for viewings. As author James R. Mellow described the scene, "The walls of their atelier were hung to the ceiling with now-famous paintings, the double doors of the dining room were lined with Picasso sketches. In the early decades of the century, hundreds of visitors flocked to the display of vanguard art: many came to scoff, but several went away converted. It was a brilliant scene—and a historic one. For all intents and purposes, Leo and Gertrude Stein had inaugurated, at 27 Rue de Fleurus, the first museum of modern art."

Gertrude Stein later occupied the apartment on her own, until she was joined by Toklas in 1907, and created the salon where artists and, later, expatriate American writers mingled freely. At the same time, Stein was trying to craft her own experiments in literature, attempting to replicate what the Cubists were doing with painting. Her self-published *Three Lives* (1909)—widely considered her best work—is comprised of the stories of three working-class women; one of them Melanctha, a mixed-race woman.

Also published at her own expense, in 1914, *Tender Buttons* is a modernist experiment in verse that took Stein's unorthodox, experimental use of language even further. But unimpressed critics found it largely devoid of logic. Written between 1906 and 1908, *The Making of Americans* is a nine-hundred-page novel without dialogue or action. Understandably, it did not find a publisher until 1925.

In addition to her books, Stein wrote librettos for operas by Virgil Thompson, including *Four Saints in Three Acts* and *The Mother of Us All*, both well received. And in 1933, she wrote her most conventional and most successful book. *The Autobiography of Alice B. Toklas* was excerpted in the *Atlantic Monthly* in four issues. It became a runaway success for its portrait of Paris as the center of the artistic and literary universe, both before World War I and after. The cast of characters is sometimes as overwhelming as a phone book. (You do know what a phone book is, I hope.)

The book's popularity led to an American lecture tour in 1934 and 1935, as Stein returned to the country for the first time in thirty years. But audiences often found her unorthodox lecture style, like her writing, somewhat incomprehensible.

Returning to France as the world lurched toward another world war, Stein and Toklas moved to a country house. Ever since, Stein's political views before and during the war have generated criticism and controversy. Stein had praised General Francisco Franco during the Spanish Civil War—the war discussed at length in the entry on Orwell's *Homage to Catalonia*—and, writes Dartmouth professor Barbara Will, was a "committed supporter of Philippe Pétain, head of state of the pro-Nazi collaborationist Vichy regime in France during the Second World War." Adds Will: "Others have tried to ignore or justify equally inexplicable events: for example, Stein's endorsement of Adolf Hitler for the Nobel Peace Prize in 1934, or her performance of the Hitler salute at his bunker in Berchtesgaden after the Allied victory in 1945."

These are questions raised by journalist Janet Malcolm's 2007 book, *Two Lives*: "How had the pair of elderly Jewish lesbians escaped the Nazis? Why had they stayed in France instead of returning to the safety of the United States?" Stein's defenders have claimed that Stein's statements and behavior were examples of her deliberate outrageousness or merely part of a survival strategy for a pair of Jewish women living in occupied France. But the questions further complicate the portrait of a woman who certainly altered the course of artistic history and who seemed to revel in confounding social constraints.

Gertrude Stein died on July 27, 1946, after stomach surgery in France. Alice B. Toklas survived Stein by more than twenty years. In 1954, she wrote what became a 1960s cult classic, *The Alice B. Toklas Cookbook*, notorious in part for a recipe for hashish fudge. She published an actual autobiography, *What Is Remembered*, in 1963, which ends with Stein's death. Alice B. Toklas died in March 1967 and was buried in Paris, with Stein, in the famous Père Lachaise Cemetery.

WHY YOU SHOULD READ IT

As I explained in my introduction, I had a certain set of rules for books that I selected for this compendium. They had to be about two hundred pages or less; nonfiction; and timely, consequential, accessible, and pleasurable. For Gertrude Stein's *The Autobiography of Alice B. Toklas*, I broke—or at least bent—a couple of these guidelines. And how appropriate: after all, Gertrude Stein certainly counts among the most notable rule breakers in literary and artistic history.

The Autobiography of Alice B. Toklas, at some 250 pages, is well over the length limit. It also bends the basic definition of nonfiction a bit, as it clearly is not what it claims to be. Stein's penchant for grandiosity is on full display as she places the label of "genius" into the pen, or mouth, of Toklas to describe herself. That defies a pure definition of nonfiction. And while accessible, it is a bit of a challenge to navigate the catalog of names named.

Nonetheless, the book remains fascinating for the very reasons it was a success in 1933—the richly detailed, sometimes comical, and often revealing portraits of some of the twentieth century's most significant painters and other artists. Especially captivating is the concluding chapter, "After the War—1919–1932," in which Stein's relationship with Hemingway plays a central role. And it concludes perfectly with Gertrude Stein suggesting that Alice B. Toklas write an autobiography. When it appears that Toklas will not do so, Stein says, "You know what I am going to do. I am going to write it for you. . . . And she has and this is it."

WHAT TO READ NEXT

In 2007, journalist-essayist Janet Malcolm (see entry) wrote *Two Lives: Gertrude and Alice*, a far more traditional biography of these two women and their forty-year expatriate marriage. Malcolm focuses specifically on the question noted earlier: How had these two Jewish American lesbians managed to survive the war years in France?

The other obvious bookend to *The Autobiography of Alice B. Toklas* is another book in this collection, *A Moveable Feast*, by Ernest Hemingway. Stein features prominently in Hemingway's memoir of the period.

"This war, in which I played so ineffectual a part, has left me with memories that are mostly evil, and yet I do not wish that I had missed it."

Homage to Catalonia

— 1938 —

George Orwell

New York: Mariner Books, 2015; 196 pages, plus two appendices

EXCERPT

Together with all this there was something of the evil atmosphere of war. The town had a gaunt untidy look, roads and buildings were in poor repair, the streets at night were dimly lit for fear of air-raids, the shops were mostly shabby and half-empty. Meat was scarce and milk practically unobtainable, there was a shortage of coal, sugar, and petrol, and a really serious shortage of bread. Even at this period the bread-queues were often hundreds of yards long. Yet so far as one could judge the people were contented and hopeful. . . . Above all, there was a belief in the revolution and the future, a feeling of having suddenly emerged into an era of equality and freedom. Human beings were trying to behave as human beings and not as cogs in the capitalist machine.

SUMMARY

A full decade before producing his most famous works, the novels *Animal Farm* (1945) and *Nineteen Eighty-Four* (1949), George Orwell—pseudonym of Eric Blair—wrote this firsthand, first-person account of his experiences fighting in the Spanish Civil War. A conflict that raged between 1936 and 1939, the war was fought between leftist Republicans and the Nationalists, conservative, right-wing traditionalists led by Fascist general Francisco Franco and supported with planes and arms by Hitler and armaments and troops by Mussolini.

Homage to Catalonia is Orwell at his most brilliant—as both a journalist and a novelist—in describing the sights, sounds, smells, and sensations of wartime Spain, a brutal conflict with atrocities committed by both sides. After arriving in Spain, Orwell enlisted in a militia unit of the Workers' Party of Marxist Unity—known as POUM. His wife of a few months, Eileen, would soon join him. Orwell describes his scant military training in Barcelona, his boredom on the front lines, and, in a vividly memorable passage, getting shot in the throat:

> The whole experience of being hit by a bullet is very interesting and I think it is worth describing in detail. . . . There seemed to be a loud bang and a blinding flash of light all around me, and I felt a tremendous shock—no pain, only a violent shock, such as you would get from an electric terminal; with it a sense of utter weakness, a feeling of being stricken and shrivelled up to nothing. . . . I fancy you would feel much the same if you were struck by lightning.

While Mussolini and Hitler aided the Nationalists of Franco, other Western democracies—including the United States and England—stayed on the sidelines. When Joseph Stalin threw his support behind the Republicans, Spain's civil war developed into a proxy war between these powerful dictators. It also became the defining event in Orwell's political outlook and his future writing.

ABOUT THE AUTHOR: GEORGE ORWELL

George Orwell was born Eric Arthur Blair in British colonial India in 1903. He gained literary immortality under his chosen pen name: George for England's patron saint and its king at the time and Orwell from a river in East Anglia.

Son of an official in the British Opium Department, Eric Blair was sent in 1911 to an English boarding school, where he observed the sharp differences between British classes, an early recognition of England's stark social divisions. As the child of a family of relatively modest means, Orwell gained an early perception of class differences that would frame his worldview and writing. He completed his education at Eton, the famed boys' boarding school where the English nobility, including many members of the royal family, have been educated. Too poor to attend university after Eton, Blair joined the Imperial Police instead and was assigned to Burma (now Myanmar). While on leave in England in 1927, Blair resigned from the police, aiming to become a writer.

Moving to live among the working classes in East London and, for a time, Paris, Blair did menial jobs and began to write. A nonfiction account of this experience, *Down and Out in Paris and London*, was published in 1933 under his pen name. It was followed by an autobiographical first novel, *Burmese Days* (1934).

Orwell then went to northern England, where he lived with destitute miners, describing their lot in *The Road to Wigan Pier* (1937), recently selected by the *Guardian* as one of the one hundred best nonfiction books of all time. It was during this time that Orwell married Eileen O'Shaughnessy, described by a recent biographer as "a stellar student" whose tutors included J. R. R. Tolkien and who was studying for a master's in psychology when she met Orwell. As Anna Funder writes, "for mysterious reasons the biographers don't directly attribute to Eileen, his writing suddenly got much better."

Orwell was working as a part-time bookstore clerk and running a small grocery, but by the time the book was published he and Eileen departed for Spain. He enlisted in the anti-Fascist militia and Eileen worked in the headquarters of the political party that Orwell was fighting with. Like Orwell, leftist supporters from around the world, including Americans of the Abraham Lincoln Brigade, flocked to the Republican side. International journalists also came to cover the fighting. Among them was Ernest Hemingway (see *A Moveable Feast* entry), who turned his wartime experience into the novel *For Whom the Bell Tolls*, and writer Martha Gellhorn, Hemingway's future third wife.

Orwell and Eileen had to flee Spain after Joseph Stalin, who had recently completed a murderous purge of hundreds of Communist Party members in the Soviet Union, began to employ similar tactics to wrest control of the leftist opposition to Franco's forces. Stalinists issued arrest warrants for both George and Eileen Orwell. These experiences led to *Homage to Catalonia*, which Orwell himself considered his best book. According to Martha Gellhorn's biographer Caroline Moorehead, it sold only six hundred copies by the time of Orwell's death. His experience in Spain left Orwell with a lifelong dread of communism, particularly Stalin's brand.

Working as a journalist and broadcaster for the BBC during World War II, Orwell also completed *Animal Farm*, an anti-Stalinist allegory published shortly after the war ended in 1945. Orwell's thinly veiled, unmistakable criticism of Stalin was controversial; the Soviet Union's dictator was still viewed favorably in England as a crucial ally in the defeat of Hitler's Germany.

Still, it brought Orwell his first popular success. And in 1949, Orwell's dystopian masterpiece *Nineteen Eighty-Four* was published to even greater success. Not long after its release, George Orwell—Eric Blair—died of tuberculosis in London on January 21, 1950, at age forty-six.

WHY YOU SHOULD READ IT

Ranked as #42 on the Modern Library's 100 Best Nonfiction Books of the Twentieth Century, Orwell's Spanish war account is, first of all, a dazzling work of nonfiction narrative. At turns dreadful and comic, the intense scenes in the trenches as part of a "democratic army" are a riveting piece of reportage. But as Orwell learned, there was another war going on within the larger war: the struggle by Soviet dictator Stalin to wipe out any dissenters from his brand of world communism—including POUM, the Spanish communist party with whom Orwell fought. This experience led Orwell to the deep distrust of Stalinism that would color his work.

Recent critics note accurately that Orwell was a partisan observer with a limited perspective on the war. *Homage to Catalonia* is far from a comprehensive history of this significant moment, which was also a prelude to World War II. In the British *Guardian*, professor and historian Paul Preston calls the book "a vivid account of the experiences of a militiaman on 'a quiet sector of a quiet front' in Aragón, evoking the fear, the cold and, above all, the squalor, excrement and lice of the rat-infested trenches." Preston adds, however: "And yet Orwell's book makes it too easy to forget that the Spanish republic was defeated by Franco, Hitler, Mussolini, and the self-interest and pusillanimity of the British, French and American governments. His ignorance of the wider picture while in Spain was forgivable."

Orwell was a witness to the growing threats of Nazism and Soviet socialism under Stalin. This is what led him to later write: "The Spanish war and other events in 1936–7 turned the scale and thereafter I knew where I stood. Every line of serious work that I have written since 1936 has been written, directly or indirectly, *against* totalitarianism and *for* democratic Socialism, as I understand it. It seems to me nonsense, in a period like our own, to think that one can avoid writing of such subjects."

Orwell, above all else, was a truth teller, which brought him enemies and critics on both the left and right. As he later wrote about *Homage*, "I did try very hard in it to tell the whole truth without violating my literary instincts." In a 1952 introduction to the book written after Orwell's death, noted literary critic Lionel Trilling comments: "He told the truth, and told it in an exemplary way, quietly, simply, with due warning to the reader that it was only one man's truth. He used no political jargon, and he made no recriminations. He made no effort to show his heart was in the right place, or the left place. . . . He was interested only in telling the truth. . . . And what matters most of all is our sense of the man who tells the truth."

WHAT TO READ NEXT

Begin with Orwell's two fictional masterpieces, *Animal Farm* and *Nineteen Eighty-Four*, whether or not you have read them before. Landmarks of twentieth-century literature, they are as relevant today as ever.

Move on next to one of my favorites, *Why I Write*, a collection of essays written between 1931 and 1946. Reflecting Orwell's thinking as bombs fell on London during World War II, it shows the author at his acerbic and uncompromising best:

> But the British ruling class obviously could not admit to themselves that their usefulness was at an end. Had they done that they would have had to abdicate. For it was not possible for them to turn themselves into mere bandits, like the American millionaires, consciously clinging to unjust privileges and beating down the opposition by bribery and tear-gas bombs. After all, they belonged to a class with a certain tradition, they had been to public schools where the duty of dying for your country, if necessary, is laid down as the first and greatest of the Commandments. They had to *feel* themselves true patriots, even while they plundered their countrymen. Clearly there was only one escape for them—into stupidity.

The book also includes Orwell's blistering 1946 essay, "Politics and the English Language," a true must read. In it, the man who created "Newspeak," the language spoken in the fictional Oceania, wrote: "But if thought corrupts language, language can also corrupt thought."

I plan to eventually take on *The Road to Wigan Pier*, his investigation of the working classes of the industrial section of England during the Great Depression. Writer Robert McCrum comments: "The upshot of this uniquely strange book was a kind of creative liberation: Eric Blair, who was now unequivocally George Orwell, had found his voice and his identity. For the rest of his active life—barely 10 years—he would write as a British literary socialist. From this declaration of intent come his masterpieces: *Homage to Catalonia*, *Animal Farm* and finally, *Nineteen Eighty-Four*. It's arguable that without *The Road to Wigan Pier* none of these would have been possible."

"Yet so great is his personal ascendancy that his underlings—knowing that they themselves will be kicked away as soon as they cease to be useful—still retain their personal devotion to him [Mussolini]."

A Chill in the Air:
An Italian War Diary, 1939–1940

— 1940 (2017) —

Iris Origo

New York: New York Review Books, 2017; 184 pages

OPENING WORDS

Rome, March 27

The train is packed; a thousand *squadristi* are on their way to Rome. The *squadristi* are the Fascists *della prima ora*, those who belonged to the first squads of 1919. They are going home to celebrate the 20th Anniversary of the *Fasci* and to hear the Duce's speech tomorrow.

The six in our carriage are all middle-aged men—stoutish, with their black shirts bulging at the waist; their boots, too, have an air of being too tight for them.

204

SUMMARY

Found among family photos in a brown box marked "Unpublished" and written in the years 1939 and 1940, this journal appeared in print posthumously for the first time in 2017. It is the wartime diary of a British-born writer who lived in Mussolini's Italy with her Italian husband as the country moved uncertainly toward war as Hitler's ally.

Iris Origo's firsthand account commences in 1939, two decades after Mussolini's Fascist party was formed. Its opening scene depicts a train car filled with "Fascists *della prima ora*"—"of the first hour"—and Origo refers to these *squadristi* as the first members of Mussolini's Fascist party. The Fascists took power in 1922 after Mussolini—"the Duce"—was made prime minister by Italy's king and quickly brought the nation under one-party rule.

Like many of the Italians around her, including her husband, Antonio, Iris Origo lives in fretful suspense, waiting to learn if the world will be thrown once more into a catastrophic conflict. Memories of the Great War, in which Antonio fought and which ended in November 1918, are still fresh, and crippled veterans of the fighting twenty years earlier can be seen on the streets.

Origo's diary reveals an uneasy nation in which Mussolini has won the admiration of many Italians. Even the author begrudgingly acknowledges Il Duce's successes in modernizing and uniting a fractious Italy—still a relatively new republic. But as Mussolini hardens his authoritarian grasp and later falls in line with Hitler's Germany, Origo sees the shops of Florence plastered with notices reading: "*Il Duce ha sempre ragione*" ("The Duce is always right"), a reflection of the cult of personality that Fascist propaganda has created.

As the weeks pass, Origo feels a gathering sense of urgency, as the radio is filled with official Fascist party news that contradicts the optimism of her godfather, William Phillips, the American ambassador to Italy. His confidence that cooler heads will prevail is tempered for Origo by the reality of rationing and the reports Iris hears from worried mothers of young men being called up for military service. The unsettled mood continues right up to September 2, 1939, when she writes: "Went to bed not daring to hope again—and yet unable not to. Tomorrow at midday we shall know." She soon gets her answer, writing on the next day: "We know—and it is war."

Once Italy has joined Germany's war, Origo continues her account through the first year of the conflict, until August 1, and the birth of her daughter: "In the autumn of 1940 I began to work in the Prisoner's Branch of the Red Cross—and until the spring of 1943 had no more time for writing."

ABOUT THE AUTHOR: IRIS ORIGO

From her birth in 1902, London-born Iris Margaret Cutting lived in a Gilded Age world of wealth and upper-crust society that might have been torn from the pages of a novel by Edith Wharton, who knew her family. Iris's father, William Bayard Cutting Jr., was born into New York's old money elite, among the founders of the New York Public Library, with a fortune coming from railroads and shipping. Having graduated with honors from Harvard in three years in 1900, he entered the diplomatic service, first as a secretary to the U.S. ambassador in London. In 1901, Cutting married Lady Sybil Cuffe, the daughter of an English peer.

Not long after Iris was born, her father contracted tuberculosis and he began to travel widely with his family in search of healthier climates while continuing his diplomatic service. In 1908, William Cutting was deputy consul in Italy when an earthquake leveled Messina, killing more than eighty thousand people. Dispatched to the city, he earned praise for the assistance he provided in the recovery effort.

Planning to teach at Harvard, Cutting first took the family to Egypt, where he succumbed to tuberculosis in March 1910. In his will, Iris's father left instructions that she be brought up in a country other than England or the United States. He said he wanted his daughter "to grow up free from all this national feeling which makes people so unhappy. Bring her up somewhere where she does not belong, then she can't have it." He suggested Italy.

Her mother, Lady Cuffe, moved to Fiesole, outside Florence, purchasing the villa that belonged to the Medici, once the wealthiest and most powerful family in that city and patrons of the arts that flourished during the Renaissance. Their home became a meeting place for a charmed circle of expatriates and visitors that included neighbor and art historian Bernard Berenson and such writers as Henry James, Aldous Huxley, and Edith Wharton, a friend of Iris's father.

After traveling to both America and England to make her social debuts, Iris returned to Italy and fell in love with Antonio Origo, the son of an Italian nobleman. Also from a family of considerable wealth, Antonio was ten years Iris's senior. Against her mother's wishes, they married in the Medici Chapel in 1924. The couple then purchased a dilapidated fifteenth-century Tuscan estate called La Foce, in a remote valley called Val d'Orcia.

They made elaborate plans to restore those lands and rebuild some twenty derelict farms where impoverished families already lived. The aristocratic couple sought to bring the entire property back to working order. Iris and Antonio Origo were not afraid of hard work or dirty hands as they plowed fields and learned to reap by hand. They also built a school for the children who lived on the farms and Iris taught them how to read.

Iris and Antonio had one son, Gianni, who died in 1933 at age seven of meningitis. In the wake of this tragedy, a grieving Iris traveled to London where she met with the prominent literary figures of the day, including Virginia Woolf. Iris Origo turned to writing and produced a pair of biographies in 1935: a brief book about the daughter of the poet Byron born out of wedlock, *Allegra,* published by Leonard and Virginia Woolf's Hogarth Press; and *Leopardi*, a biography of Italian poet Giacomo Leopardi published by Oxford University Press. In 1938, Origo produced *Tribune of Rome*, a biography of a fourteenth-century Roman political figure, also published by Hogarth Press. Eventually, Iris Origo returned to Italy, where war was looming, as described in *A Chill in the Air*, the posthumously published diary.

She and Antonio spent the war years at La Foce, during which time she also gave birth to two daughters, Benedetta and Donata. These times are detailed in a second diary, published after the war in 1947, *War in*

Val d'Orcia, a popular and critical success. And after discovering love letters of the poet Byron and an Italian countess, Iris Origo wrote about their relationship in *The Last Attachment* (1949).

Splitting time between La Foce and Rome, she continued writing, including an acclaimed history, *The Merchant of Prato* (1957), a narrative account based on the notebooks of medieval merchant Francesco di Marco Datini. In addition to several other works, she published an autobiography, *Images and Shadows: Parts of a Life*, in 1970. Antonio Origo died in 1976. Iris Origo died at La Foce, aged eighty-five, on June 28, 1988.

WHY YOU SHOULD READ IT

First, I might say in my experience that most "war memoirs" tend to be written by men—and this entry fittingly follows one of the finest in Orwell. These accounts tend to be far more concerned with the experience of combat. So, it is both useful and refreshing to read this coming-of-war memoir, looking at events through the eyes of a woman who is both an acute observer of the world around her and a well-connected and thoughtful diarist.

Read it also because Origo is a gifted writer, as writer Alexander Stille noted in a 2018 review: "Here she demonstrates the same keen eye for telling detail: paunchy middle-aged Fascists squeezed into their old black-shirt uniforms for an anniversary celebration that has the air of a college reunion; a young expectant mother who prays to have a girl so the child will not be dragged off to war; the blank expressionless look of the local peasants, men who have mastered the art of hiding their feelings, as they listen to Mussolini's declaration of war."

But perhaps more significantly, this account focuses on how the approach of war feels. It is important to understand events, like these in 1939, that may seem clear with the perspective of history. But to Origo, living through these days, they appear far more uncertain and confused. "Trenchant, intelligent, and written with a cool head, the book records the months before Italy's descent into the Second World War, when Mussolini's relationship with Hitler was being presented to the Italian public via a campaign of misinformation, what we would now call fake news," wrote Cynthia Zarin in the *New Yorker*. "As the title indicates, it's a chilling read."

More important still is the book's value as an alarm bell. In 1939, the direction of history was not yet clear to many people—some of whom would pay dearly for their optimism. As Origo's diary entries move toward the inevitable, the book provides an important cautionary tale about how badly the signs of impending doom can be missed—or dismissed—when confronting Fascism or authoritarians. As Alexander Stille concludes, "The people Origo encounters represent a much broader range of views: from convinced anti-Fascists to unquestioning Fascists who repeat phrases like 'A good Italian's duty now is to have *no* opinions.' Most occupy a swampy middle ground: They are uneasy about the slide into war but accept the regime's argument that Italy has little choice but to fight."

Origo's book is included here because it provides—like *Homage to Catalonia*—another telling example of how vigilant we must be in a world filled with aspiring Mussolinis and Stalins. We cannot afford to sleepwalk through history.

WHAT TO READ NEXT

Although published first, in 1947, *War in Val d'Orcia: An Italian War Diary 1943–1944* is actually a successor to *A Chill in the Air* and makes a perfect follow-up. Somewhat longer than *A Chill in the Air*, it provides a similar day-by-day account of wartime life on the Origos' large Tuscan estate. In this acclaimed diary of the war years from 1943 to 1944, Iris Origo and her Italian husband take great risks in providing food and shelter to refugee children, escaped Allied prisoners of war, Jews desperate to avoid deportation, and Italian partisans fighting the Nazis occupying Italy and their Fascist allies. It is a remarkably moving document.

I also recommend *Naples '44*, British journalist Norman Lewis's classic account, in diary form, of the sometimes agonizing postwar occupation of that city and other parts of war-ruined Italy.

*"There the young were to be born of the darkness of the deep sea
and the old eels were to die and become sea again."*

Under the Sea-Wind

— 1941 —

Rachel Carson

New York: Penguin Books, 2007; with illustrations by Howard Frech; 184 pages

OPENING WORDS

The Island lay in shadows only a little deeper than those that were swiftly stealing across the sound from the east. On its western shore the wet sand of the narrow beach caught the same reflection of palely gleaming sky that laid a bright path across the water from island beach to horizon. Both water and sand were the color of steel overlaid with the sheen of silver, so that it was hard to say where water ended and land began.

SUMMARY

An eleven-page introduction to a government brochure about fisheries does not sound like an auspicious beginning for a timeless work of nonfiction. But that was the humble genesis of this paean to the sea and its wonders— the first book by Rachel Carson, one of the finest and most influential writers of the twentieth century. Composed as part of a 1936 assignment from the U.S. Bureau of Fisheries, Carson's essay eventually grew into a rich exploration of the world of birds, fish, and other wildlife that abound on beaches and shorelines and in the oceans.

Under the Sea-Wind is divided into three sections: book 1, "Edge of the Sea," follows migratory birds moving north to summer on the Arctic tundra before making their return journey south; book 2, "The Gull's Way," examines the same migratory patterns but focuses instead on the seasonal life cycles of ocean fish; and book 3, "River and Sea," brings together the connectedness of rivers and oceans primarily through the life cycle of the eel.

If this sounds all science-wonky, it is not. A trained zoologist, Rachel Carson grounds her work in sound marine biology and ornithology. But her writing is as poetically evocative as the opening lines of Genesis. Narrating the natural cycles of life and death, predator and prey, Carson celebrates the vastness of the sea and the array of creatures it sustains. She brings this complex, interrelated world to life with the thrill of page-turning fiction.

Departing from the formal traditions of scientific writing, Carson shows great skill in her ability to "personalize" the animal world. In each section, she introduces her "characters"—fish and birds are given names that make the reader care about them.

In book 1, two sanderlings, a type of sandpiper, are presented as Blackfoot and Silverbar and their exploits confronting danger touch a deep emotional chord. In book 2, Scomber—the scientific name for the mackerel—is the main character, facing constant threats as he morphs from one of forty or fifty thousand eggs dropped by a female fish to a single mackerel left to fend for himself in an unforgiving undersea world. And finally, in book 3,

Anguilla, a ten-year-old female eel, swims from the freshwaters of a river to a deep abyss in the Sargasso Sea to spawn.

But Carson does not sentimentalize or "Disneyfy" this natural world. This isn't *Bambi* or *Finding Nemo*. She creates an artful, exquisite rendering of a world hidden to most of us for whom "a day at the beach" implies something very different.

ABOUT THE AUTHOR: RACHEL CARSON

Born on May 27, 1907, in Springdale, in western Pennsylvania, Rachel Louise Carson was raised on a sixty-acre farm, the youngest of three children. Though her father sold insurance, she spent a childhood in the fields, and her mother, who tended the farm, taught her plant names and birdcalls. An avid reader, Rachel Carson was especially drawn to stories of the sea—even though she had never seen it and couldn't swim.

From an early age Rachel Carson began writing stories of the natural world around her, and at age ten had a story published in the *St. Nicholas Magazine*, a popular children's magazine. Biographer Linda Lear records Carson telling a group of women in 1954, "I can remember no time, even in earliest childhood, when I didn't assume I was going to be a writer."

After graduating at the top of a small high school class, Carson went to Pennsylvania College for Women (later Chatham University) to study English. Under the influence of Professor Mary Scott Skinker, Carson switched to a biology major and traveled with her mentor in the summertime to the Woods Hole Marine Biological Laboratory in Massachusetts. There she saw the ocean for the first time.

After graduating with honors in 1929, she went on to graduate work at Johns Hopkins, earning a degree in zoology in 1932. Planning to study for a doctorate, Carson was forced to find work as the Great Depression descended on the country. Her extended family—ailing father, mother, divorced sister, and two young nieces—moved to Baltimore to live with her. As the family's sole breadwinner, Carson took work in a laboratory and taught at Johns Hopkins and the University of Maryland. She earned extra money writing about the marine life of the Chesapeake Bay for the

Baltimore Sun, signing her work as R. L. Carson to disguise her gender. Her father died in 1935, and, according to historian Jill Lepore, "As the Depression deepened, they lived, for a while, on nothing but apples."

In 1936, at the suggestion of Mary Skinker, Carson got work as a freelance writer with the U.S. Bureau of Fisheries, scripting radio segments on marine life. Then she was asked to write an introduction to a Bureau publication. Neatly typed by her mother, her essay was called "The World of Waters." When Carson turned it in, her supervisor told her that her work would not do; it was too good. He recommended that she send it instead to one of the leading literary journals of the day, the *Atlantic Monthly*.

The magazine published Carson's essay as "Undersea" in September 1937. "It left readers swooning," writes Jill Lepore, "drowning in the riptide of her language, a watery jabberwocky of mollusks and gills and tube worms and urchins and plankton and cunners." By then, Carson had aced a Civil Service test and won a full-time job with the Bureau of Fisheries (later the U.S. Fish and Wildlife Service).

After "Undersea" was published, Carson was given a contract to expand the article into a book. Occupied with her government job by day, and a slow writer to begin with, she often worked late into the night. Carson obsessively wrote and revised to get the sound of the words right. "Conscious of the role of alliteration and rhythm to create atmosphere, she read pages aloud to herself before she had her mother read them back to her," writes biographer Linda Lear. "While Carson was at work, her mother typed the revisions so they would be ready for her daughter's nighttime labor. This was a pattern the two women held to with every piece Carson wrote, until her mother passed away in 1958."

With line illustrations by Howard Frech, a *Baltimore Sun* artist, the book was published in November 1941 to admiring reviews. A few weeks later, Pearl Harbor was attacked and *Under the Sea-Wind* fell victim to World War II. Despite the enthusiastic critical reception, the book went largely unsold as the nation mobilized for war. Carson spent the war years, in part, advising American housewives how to prepare cheap fish during periods of meat rationing.

Undeterred by the book's poor performance, Carson worked on a concept for a sequel about ocean ecology—a word not then widely used. When the new work was completed, the *Atlantic* declined to publish an excerpt. But William Shawn of the *New Yorker* read it with enthusiasm. In 1951, Carson's work appeared in three parts in the magazine, quickly winning comparison to John Hersey's 1946 *Hiroshima* as a work of nonfiction. Later published in book form, *The Sea Around Us* won the National Book Award, was translated into thirty languages, and became a runaway national best seller. Its success led the publisher to reissue *Under the Sea-Wind*, which also became a best seller at the same time, a true publishing rarity in its day.

Her newfound success allowed Carson to leave her government post to focus on writing. She also bought a small summer cottage on an island off Maine and wrote the third book in the trilogy: *The Edge of the Sea*, published in 1955, another best seller also first serialized in the *New Yorker*. It was on this island that Carson met Dorothy Freeman, a married woman with a grown son. The two women developed a deep and devoted friendship, known mostly through loving letters written over eleven years. Many of these letters were destroyed, but some were published in *Always, Rachel*, a 1995 book edited by Freeman's granddaughter. Whether their relationship was romantic is ambiguous, but Freeman was a devoted supporter of Carson's work and life.

By the time *The Edge of the Sea* appeared, Carson was already concerned with the impact of DDT, a chemical insecticide used to kill mosquitoes during the war first and then also by civilians. Carson connected insecticides and other chemicals increasingly used in 1950s America to the growing environmental destruction she observed. She began more in-depth research into the spread of these chemicals and their connection to biology, medicine, and especially the deaths of birds.

During this time, Carson's mother—and tireless typist—suffered a stroke and died in December 1958. As Carson continued her research on chemical use, a breast lesion was discovered. She had earlier had two breast lumps removed and in 1960 underwent a radical mastectomy. More lumps were later discovered on her ribs, followed by debilitating surgeries and injections, leaving her, at times, wheelchair bound. Working in great physical pain and against a grim prognosis of death in just a few months, she kept writing. She submitted a draft of her work to the *New Yorker* in January 1962. Under the title *Silent Spring*, Carson's last—and most influential—book appeared in three issues of the magazine in June 1962:

> Since the late nineteen-forties, when DDT began to be used widely, a process of escalation has been going on in which ever more toxic chemicals must be found. This has happened because insects, in a triumphant vindication of Darwin's principle of the survival of the fittest, have consistently evolved super-races immune to the particular insecticide used, and hence a deadlier one has always had to be developed—and then a deadlier one than that. It has happened also that destructive insects often undergo a "flareback," or resurgence, after spraying, in numbers greater than before. The chemical war is never won, and all life is caught in its crossfire.

Silent Spring became a best seller in 1962, spurring congressional hearings at which Carson testified and a pledge by President Kennedy to investigate DDT and other pesticides. Carson was featured in *The Silent Spring of Rachel Carson*, a one-hour television special that aired on CBS in April 1963. The book created worldwide awareness of the dangers of pollution and is credited with kick-starting the environmental movement, leading to passage of the Clean Air Act in 1963 and the Clean Water Act and the Endangered Species Act in 1972—among other landmark environmental legislation—and the creation of the Environmental Protection Agency in 1970. It unfortunately must be said today that some of these laws and agencies have been crippled or set back by recent administrations and powerful opposition by well-funded corporations and industry groups.

Rachel Carson did not live to see the broad impact of her work. Wracked by the cancer that had spread though her body and suffering from anemia and other related ills, she died of a heart attack on April 14, 1964, at her Maryland home. Her ashes were divided, half buried in Maryland beside her mother's remains and half scattered by Dorothy Freeman in the ocean waters off Maine.

"A work that aspires, however humbly, to the condition of art should carry its justification in every line." I often thought of this memorable charge from novelist Joseph Conrad as I read *Under the Sea-Wind*. It is an exacting standard. But as I delighted in Carson's first book, I considered it a rare work that reaches that lofty goal. Reading it makes clear why she has been called the "scientist-poet of the sea."

While I am a great advocate of the value of reading for "pleasure," many of the books in this collection cannot be classified as "pleasure reading." However, Rachel Carson's first book, which she considered her best, was certainly one of the most pleasurable books I read in my year of reading nonfiction—briefly.

Beyond that, however, Carson's book introduces two of what biographer Linda Lear calls "Carson's most enduring literary themes: the ecological relationships of ocean life that have endured for eons of time, and the material immortality that embraces even the tiniest organism."

These themes, perhaps more significant than ever, make Carson's first book so necessary and valuable. With its original subtitle *A Naturalist's Picture of Ocean Life*, Carson's exploration of chance survival and the constant struggle to exist in the natural world creates a dramatic stage on which she presents the central character—the sea—in her grand vision:

> To stand at the edge of the sea, to sense the ebb and the flow of the tides, to feel the breath of a mist moving over a great salt marsh, to watch the flight of shore birds that have swept up and down the surf lines of the continents for untold thousands of years, to see the running of the old eels and the young shad to the sea, is to have knowledge of things that are as nearly eternal as any earthly life can be.

Carson anticipated the challenges we now recognize in the existential threat posed by global warming and climate change. She is a poetic writer, part of the great American nature writing tradition of Thoreau and others, and also was one of the pioneers of what my daughter recently described to me as "environmental ethics"—a subject further explored in this collection by the concluding entry, Elizabeth Kolbert's *Under a White Sky*.

Sixty years after Rachel Carson's death, her concerns about the primacy of the sea—as well as the threats raised in *Silent Spring*—are more dire than ever. That is why Rachel Carson is high on the list of authors whose work is more than thought-provoking, but a rousing call to conscience.

WHAT TO READ NEXT

If you are taken by Carson's work in *Under the Sea-Wind*, as I was, move on to the sequels, *The Sea Around Us* and then *The Edge of the Sea*. All three books are available individually and have also been collected in a single volume by the Library of America.

The book for which Carson is best known, *Silent Spring*, belongs on any list of environmental must reads. To that I would add two recent books: *The Uninhabitable Earth: Life after Warming* by David Wallace-Wells and *Losing Earth* by Nathaniel Rich. Another recommendation given to me is historian Douglas Brinkley's 2022 book *Silent Spring Revolution: John F. Kennedy, Rachel Carson, Lyndon Johnson, Richard Nixon, and the Great Environmental Awakening*. I must note that at more than 800 pages, it is not a short book. Among older landmarks in the field is *Desert Solitaire*, a 1968 book about the canyonlands of Utah by Edward Abbey, a writer described as the "Thoreau of the American West" by fellow writer Larry McMurtry; many of the works of poet-novelist-essayist Wendell Berry, including *The Unsettling of America: Culture and Agriculture*; and the work of Bill McKibben, starting with *The End of Nature*, a modern classic that also first appeared in the *New Yorker*.

"The gods had condemned Sisyphus to ceaselessly rolling a rock to the top of a mountain, whence the stone would fall back of its own weight."

The Myth of Sisyphus

— 1942 —

Albert Camus

New York: Vintage International, 2018, translated from the French by Justin O'Brien; 138 pages

OPENING WORDS

There is but one truly serious philosophical problem, and that is suicide. Judging whether life is or is not worth living amounts to answering the fundamental question of philosophy. All the rest—whether or not the world has three dimensions, whether the mind has nine or twelve categories—comes afterwards. These are games; one must first answer.

SUMMARY

In the course of one remarkable year, in the midst of World War II, Albert Camus produced an extraordinary literary hat trick, what he called a "cycle" of three works: a play, *Caligula* (not staged until 1945); a novel, *The Stranger* (*L'Étranger*); and this profoundly influential philosophical essay, *The Myth of Sisyphus* (*Le Mythe de Sisyphe*).

Its title and central metaphor come from the Greek myth of a cunning man named Sisyphus who, when Death came for him, was able to chain up Death so that no one died. For this act of defiance, Sisyphus is punished by the gods of Olympus, fated to perpetually roll a boulder up a hill only to have it roll down each time. In this ancient legend, Camus saw a perfect metaphor for the persistent struggle against life's absurdity.

The story of Sisyphus forms only one small part of this slim volume. The French writer-philosopher also presents, in considerable depth, his view of a universe he repeatedly calls "absurd"—and weighs whether life has meaning and if suicide is an apt response:

> A world that can be explained even with bad reasons is a familiar world. But, on the other hand, in a universe suddenly divested of illusions and lights, man feels an alien, a stranger. His exile is without remedy since he is deprived of the memory of a lost home or the hope of a promised land. This divorce between man and his life, the actor and his setting, is properly the feeling of absurdity. . . .
>
> The subject of this essay is precisely this relationship between the absurd and suicide, the exact degree to which suicide is a solution to the absurd.

ABOUT THE AUTHOR: ALBERT CAMUS

Philosopher, journalist, novelist, essayist, and wartime member of the French Resistance, Albert Camus was among the most influential writers of the twentieth century. Born on November 7, 1913, to French parents in Algeria, then a French colony, Camus never knew his father, a farmworker who died in 1914 while fighting with a French battalion called Zouaves on the outskirts of Paris early in World War I. Illiterate and deaf, his widowed mother cleaned houses.

Camus and his elder brother Lucien were raised in a small apartment with their mother, their grandmother, and a paralyzed uncle. As Sarah Bakewell describes, "His family had no electricity, no running water, no newspapers, no books, no radio, few visitors at home, and no sense of the wider 'life-worlds' of others." At seventeen, Camus was diagnosed with tuberculosis and forced to abandon his love of swimming and playing goalkeeper for a soccer club.

Earning a scholarship to a prestigious lycée—equivalent to high school—set him on a path to higher education. Camus attended the University of Algiers and studied philosophy part-time while working odd jobs to earn money. But his illness prevented him from taking the prestigious French exam the agrégration in philosophy.

In his first visit to France, Camus went to the Alps in an attempt to improve his health. After returning to Algiers, he briefly joined the Communist Party but was more interested in writing and directing theater than in revolutionary politics. He later wrote for and edited an Algerian newspaper, published two early books in Algeria in 1937 and 1938, and wrote about French intellectualism and philosophy, including reviews of work by his contemporary Jean-Paul Sartre, whom he would later meet.

As fascism spread in Europe, Camus moved to France to work for a French newspaper, *Paris-soir*. With the outbreak of World War II in 1939, he attempted to enlist in the French army but was rejected because of his poor health. Camus left Paris during the Nazi occupation in 1940. With his wife, Francine Faure, a mathematician and pianist he married in December 1940, Camus returned to Algeria and taught school in the port city of Oran.

Advised to move to improve his health, he returned to France, landing in Nazi-occupied Paris in 1942. Working as a manuscript reader for Gallimard, a French publisher permitted to continue publishing by the Nazis, and living near the headquarters of the German military police, Camus joined the French underground in 1943. At enormous risk, Camus secretly wrote for and edited *Combat*, the banned newspaper of the French Resistance, while continuing his own work in drama, fiction, and essays.

In 1942, Gallimard published his novel *The Stranger*; later that same year, *The Myth of Sisyphus* was released. In 1943, Camus introduced himself to Jean-Paul Sartre at a Paris café. They knew each other's work and Camus joined the circle of French writers and intellectuals that included Simone de Beauvoir (see entry) and Sartre, who also wrote for *Combat*.

Camus published two more of his most consequential books in 1947: the novel *La Peste* (The Plague), about people battling an outbreak of bubonic plague, a metaphor for fascism, in the Algerian city of Oran; and the book-length essay *L'Homme révolté* (The Rebel*)*. Disillusioned with communism and Marxism, which Camus viewed as alternative forms of totalitarianism, he fell out with Sartre, Beauvoir, and other left-wing contemporaries.

After the publication of his novel *La Chute* (The Fall*)* in 1956, Camus became, at the age of forty-four, the second-youngest recipient of the Nobel Prize in Literature in 1957. In honoring Camus, the Nobel Committee said: "Inspired by an authentic moral engagement, he devotes himself with all his being to the great fundamental questions of life, and certainly this aspiration corresponds to the idealistic end for which the Nobel Prize was established. Behind his incessant affirmation of the absurdity of the human condition is no sterile negativism. This view of things is supplemented in him by a powerful imperative, a nevertheless, an appeal to the will which incites to revolt against absurdity and which, for that reason, creates a value."

Camus died tragically in a car crash, along with his publisher, Michel Gallimard, on January 4, 1960. He was forty-six years old.

WHY YOU SHOULD READ IT

First, an admission. Having read *The Myth of Sisyphus* as a college student many years ago, I was somewhat hesitant to include the book in this collection after rereading it. I thought it fell short of the mark in my desire to include books that are accessible to the general reader. It is without question a highly challenging book, in part because of the author's erudition, including references to a great many other works and writers, some of whom are prominent—Nietzsche, Kierkegaard, Heidegger, Kafka—and others who are more obscure.

But I say read it, slowly, carefully, and perhaps with an encyclopedia handy to check some of his literary and philosophical references. This is, after all, a fundamental work in twentieth-century philosophy. And it represents a crucial interpretation of existentialist thought—even though Camus rejected that term for himself—and the most basic question of meaning.

"The fundamental subject of 'The Myth of Sisyphus' is this," Camus later wrote about the essay, "it is legitimate and necessary to wonder whether life has a meaning; therefore it is legitimate to meet the problem of suicide face to face. . . . Although 'The Myth of Sisyphus' poses mortal problems, it sums itself up for me as a lucid invitation to live and to create, in the very midst of the desert."

"Camus represents also the philosophical movement called Existentialism, which characterizes man's situation in the universe by denying it all personal significance, seeing in it only absurdity," said Anders Österling in presenting Camus with the Nobel Prize. "The term 'absurd' occurs often in Camus's writings, so that one may call it a leitmotif in his work, developed in all its logical moral consequences on the levels of freedom, responsibility, and the anguish that derives from it. The Greek myth of Sisyphus, who eternally rolls his rock to the mountain top from which it perpetually rolls down again, becomes, in one of Camus's essays, a laconic symbol of human life. . . . For Camus, the essential thing is no longer to know whether life is worth living but *how* one must live it, with the share of sufferings it entails."

The book is at its best as Camus frames the fundamental questions of meaning and the appropriate response to a universe that seems to defy the very search for meaning. He answers these clearly and definitively when he writes: "Thus I draw from the absurd three consequences, which are my revolt, my freedom, and my passion."

WHAT TO READ NEXT

For those who have never read Camus, I suggest starting with his fiction, *The Stranger* and *The Plague* in particular. *The Fall*, his last completed novel, is another short book—which I have not yet read but plan to—written in the form of a monologue delivered by a Parisian exile in Amsterdam, and, as the title suggests, represents the expulsion from Eden.

The chief contemporaries of Camus, Jean-Paul Sartre and Simone de Beauvoir—and the existential school—are described at greater length in the discussion of Beauvoir's *A Very Easy Death* (see entry).

On this reading of Camus, I also saw a connection to the Stoic thought explored in this collection in discussing Marcus Aurelius and concentration camp survivor Viktor E. Frankl (see entries). I was pleased to read that Sarah Bakewell, an authority on existential thought as well as the Camus-Sartre-Beauvoir circle, also sees this relationship. "There's definitely an element of Stoicism in existentialism, particularly in Sartre, and also in Viktor Frankl's work," comments Bakewell. ". . . It's not just a matter of enduring or retreating into an inner realm in which you're free. In fact, it's not really about the inner realm at all, because the way you find meaning is not within, but through a purpose in the world, something that's outside you, something that is greater than you. . . . Existentialist philosophy doesn't bring despair and angst into our lives, it gives us a way of making sense, it's a way of discovering our own inner freedom."

"There, in the tin factory, in the first moment of the atomic age,
a human being was crushed by books."

Hiroshima

— 1946 —

John Hersey

New York: Vintage Books, 2020; "A New Edition with a Final Chapter
Written Forty Years after the Explosion"; 196 pages

OPENING WORDS

At exactly fifteen minutes past eight in the morning, on August 6, 1945, Japanese time, at the moment when the atomic bomb flashed above Hiroshima, Miss Toshiko Sasaki, a clerk in the personnel department of the East Asia Tin Works, had just sat down at her place in the plant office and was turning her head to speak to the girl at the next desk.

SUMMARY

An account of the aftermath of the use of the first atomic bomb on August 6, 1945, *Hiroshima* appeared in its entirety in a single issue of the *New Yorker*, dated August 31, 1946. A band on the magazine's cover explained: "This entire issue is devoted to the story of how an atomic bomb destroyed a city."

A veteran journalist and novelist who spent World War II as a combat correspondent, John Hersey—already winner of a Pulitzer Prize for Fiction—framed this unprecedented moment in world history in the most human of ways. He told the story of the unthinkable destruction through the narrative accounts of six people who survived the blast: Miss Toshiko Sasaki, an office clerk; Mrs. Hatsuyo Nakamura, a tailor's widow; physician Dr. Masakazu Fujii; the Reverend Mr. Kiyoshi Tanimoto, pastor of a Methodist church; Dr. Terufumi Sasaki, a young surgeon; and Father Wilhelm Kleinsorge, a German Jesuit priest.

As Hersey explained, "A hundred thousand people were killed by the atomic bomb, and these six were among the survivors. They still wonder why they lived when so many others died."

Hersey's narrative traced the lives of these six individuals for roughly one year after the bombing, noting that they sometimes encounter each other as they try to make sense of what has happened to them and their city. Originally planned to run as four *New Yorker* articles, Hersey's story instead appeared in its entirety in the August 31, 1946, issue and was an immediate sensation. The magazine sold out and the article was offered free to Book of the Month Club subscribers; it was published in book form later that year.

Writing in 2010, in celebration of the *New Yorker*'s eighty-fifth anniversary, Jon Michaud records: "After publishing 'Hiroshima,' [*New Yorker* founding editor] Harold Ross said, 'I don't think I've ever got as much satisfaction out of anything else in life.'"

Hiroshima was revised in 1984 to include an additional chapter recounting Hersey's return to Hiroshima nearly four decades later. In it, he recaps the fates of the original six survivors and intersperses a timeline of other nations that have successfully tested atomic weapons since 1945.

ABOUT THE AUTHOR: JOHN HERSEY

Long before the vogue for writing nonfiction using the tools of the novelist was dubbed "The New Journalism" in a 1973 essay collection edited by Tom Wolfe, John Hersey pioneered the style. His account of the devastation of Hiroshima used the power of description, realistic dialogue, personal stories, and scene-by-scene narrative drive rather than traditional journalism's mere reporting of facts. It was written, *New Yorker* writer Roger Angell later commented, "in a prose so stripped of mannerism, sentimentality, and even minimal emphasis as to place each reader alone within scenes laid bare of all but pain."

"What everybody knows about John Hersey is that he wrote 'Hiroshima,' the one widely read book about the effects of nuclear war," wrote Nicholas Lemann in a 2019 appreciation of Hersey's work. "Its place in the canon is assured, not only because it was a major literary achievement but also because reporters haven't had another chance to produce an on-the-scene account of a city recently blasted by a nuclear weapon. Yet Hersey was more of a figure than that one megaton-weighted fact about him would indicate."

Born on June 17, 1914, in Tientsin, China, John Richard Hersey was the son of Roscoe Hersey, who worked for the Young Men's Christian Association, and Grace Baird, a missionary. He spent most of his first ten years in China and spoke Chinese before he spoke English.

The family returned in 1924 to Briarcliff Manor in Westchester County, New York, where Hersey attended public school before going to Hotchkiss, a private school in Connecticut, on a scholarship as the son of missionaries. "The scholarship boys cleaned classrooms, waited on tables, and were in one sense in a separate social class," Hersey told the *Paris Review* in 1986. "But that seemed to me to be perfectly normal; in fact, in ways I saw it as an advantage. Waiting on tables, you were at the nerve center of gossip and understanding—you knew everybody, what they were like, what they were about."

After graduating from Yale, he won a fellowship to Clare College in Cambridge. Determined to become a journalist, he applied to *Time* magazine. But he failed to get past the magazine's "*Time* Test," which required writing a story in the magazine's signature style.

Instead, Hersey won a job as private secretary to Sinclair Lewis, winner of the 1930 Nobel Prize in Literature, who had just published *It Can't Happen Here*, a novel about fascism coming to America. Part of Hersey's job was copying pages of a play Lewis was writing. "Mr. Hersey later recalled that he worked intensively with Lewis," the *New York Times* would note, "without ever realizing that his employer had a serious drinking problem."

Hersey later said, "He was wonderfully important to me; I was able to see the life of a man totally given over to writing. Even though he was not producing important novels anymore, he was so gripped by what he was doing that it was very impressive to me. . . . He led an irregular life, but a life that was passionately devoted to his work. I was exposed to someone who lived for writing, lived *in* his writing, in a way." Hersey took the "*Time* Test" again, writing an essay on how rotten the magazine was. He got the job.

Joining the staff of *Time* magazine in 1937, Hersey was sent to Asia as the war approached. He reported on both the European and the Pacific theaters during World War II, seeing action up close as a front-line combat journalist. During a month's vacation from *Time*, he wrote *A Bell for Adano*, a novel describing the Allied occupation of Sicily, for which he won the 1945 Pulitzer Prize. Among its characters was an American general who was based on General George Patton, described by Hersey as "rather seriously deranged during the Sicilian campaign." As a reporter and novelist, Hersey was invoking comparisons to Ernest Hemingway, then America's most celebrated writer (see entry).

Hersey's second most significant article also ran in the *New Yorker*. In June 1944, the magazine published "Survival," his account of the sinking of a torpedo boat, PT-109, in the Pacific. The article helped secure the heroic credentials of John F. Kennedy, the future representative, senator, and president of the United States:

> Kennedy, who had been on the Harvard swimming team five years
> before, took McMahon in tow and headed for the PT. A gentle breeze
> kept blowing the boat away from the swimmers. It took forty-five

minutes to make what had been an easy hundred yards. On the way in, Harris said, "I can't go any farther." Kennedy, of the Boston Kennedys, said to Harris, of the same home town, "For a guy from Boston, you're certainly putting up a great exhibition out here, Harris." Harris made it all right and didn't complain any more. Then Kennedy swam from man to man, to see how they were doing.

After the atomic bomb was dropped and the war ended in August 1945, *New Yorker* managing editor William Shawn discussed the idea for an article on Hiroshima with Hersey, who was preparing for a postwar reporting trip to Asia. As Jon Michaud recorded in 2010, "Hersey traveled through China and then spent a month in Japan interviewing Hiroshima survivors before returning to the U.S. in June to write his report."

After the success of *Hiroshima*, Hersey was intent on writing fiction. *The Wall* (1950), one of the first novels about the Holocaust, used fictional characters and diary entries to tell a riveting account of the doomed uprising of Jews in the Warsaw ghetto, a landmark "nonfiction novel."

From 1965 to 1984, Hersey taught writing at Yale. During the Vietnam War, he became an outspoken opponent of the war and advocate of civil rights—neither especially popular positions when he took them. One of his final nonfiction books was *The Algiers Motel Incident* (1968), which described an event in Detroit during a period of violent rioting in 1967. Three Black men were killed and others beaten by members of the local and state police and the National Guard.

Hersey died on March 24, 1993, at his winter home in Key West, Florida, aged seventy-eight.

WHY YOU SHOULD READ IT

Widely ranked among the most important books of the twentieth century, *Hiroshima* offers a searing and unforgettable testimony of one of history's most significant events. Hersey's account changed the national argument about the morality of nuclear war, though he never discussed the much-debated decision to drop the atomic bomb on Hiroshima—and a second on Nagasaki a few days later. Instead, Hersey offered facts draped in very human stories. Readers are left to make their own moral judgments.

In a *New Yorker* appreciation of Hersey in 2019, Nicholas Lemann wrote: "Hersey had received his own call during the Second World War, which he was early in coming to understand primarily as a great catastrophe rather than an inspiring American triumph. He went to the scene, he tirelessly looked where most journalists didn't, and he found ways of writing about what he saw that gave his journalism an enduring power. In a long, relentlessly productive career, that's what stands out."

"I don't think I have an impulse to teach in my writing," Hersey told an interviewer. "I do have a deep need to try to understand. In my effort to understand, I may hope that I can help readers to understand more about life, more about the stressful events I'm writing about."

We should all read *Hiroshima* to "understand," as Hersey put it.

For writers, aspiring or otherwise, it is required reading. Calling the book "a portable master class in history, humanity, and journalism," Pulitzer Prize–winning journalist Jacqui Banaszynski wrote about rereading the book in 2020, seventy-five years after the bomb was dropped:

> But it has lost none of its power. And that power comes from the purity of Hersey's reporting. Being able to make words dance is fine, even enviable. But it is the reporting that makes the music. . . . The tone is tense—not because of twirls and trickery, but because of the leanness and precision of Hersey's language. What adjectives are there are doing hard and necessary work.

WHAT TO READ NEXT

Hersey's 1950 novel, *The Wall*, is one of the most powerful and memorable works of fiction I have ever read. When *The Wall* was published, there was not yet a broad understanding of what had happened during the Holocaust, especially among many Americans. *The Diary of Anne Frank*, for instance, did not appear in English until 1952. Newspaper reports of the death camps in the *New York Times* and elsewhere had appeared after the war, but in postwar America there was not a complete grasp of the enormity of the mass deaths in Nazi camps. *The Wall* was one of the first novels to address the fate of the Jews to a large audience. Told through a fictional diary, it recounts the horrors of Warsaw's Jews, walled into a ghetto, and the hopelessly heroic attempt of a band of fighters to rise up against the Nazis.

For more on Hersey's nonfiction, investigate *The Algiers Motel Incident*, about the 1967 deaths of Black men at the hands of police authorities in Detroit; it has lost none of its timeliness.

For a complete history of the long road that ended in Hiroshima, I would point to *The Making of the Atomic Bomb* by Richard Rhodes; it is an extraordinary work of history. Also worth consideration is *Unconditional: The Japanese Surrender in World War II* (2020) by Marc Gallicchio, which frames the decision to drop the bomb in terms of the coming Cold War conflict with the Soviet Union.

The literature of World War II is, of course, vast. But I would single out *A Woman in Berlin*, an anonymously published account of what happened as the Red Army approached and then conquered Hitler's capital in 1945. Originally published in German in 2003, it is a harrowing and unforgettable look at war and its aftermath.

"Since Auschwitz we know what man is capable of.
And since Hiroshima we know what is at stake."

Man's Search for Meaning

— 1946 —
[FIRST ENGLISH TRANSLATION, 1959]

Viktor E. Frankl

Boston: Beacon Press, 2006; part 1 translated by Ilse Lasch; foreword by
Harold S. Kushner; afterword by William J. Winslade; 165 pages

EXCERPT

In psychiatry there is a certain condition known as "delusion of reprieve." The
condemned man, immediately before his execution, gets the illusion that he
might be reprieved at the very last minute. We, too, clung to shreds of hope
and believed to the last moment that it would not be so bad. Just the sight of
the red cheeks and round faces of those prisoners was a great encouragement.
Little did we know then that they formed a specially chosen elite, who for years
had been the receiving squad for new transports as they rolled into the station
day after day. They took charge of the new arrivals and their luggage, including

scarce items and smuggled jewelry. Auschwitz must have been a strange spot in this Europe of the last years of the war. There must have been unique treasures of gold and silver, platinum and diamonds, not only in the huge storehouses but also in the hands of the SS.

SUMMARY

First published in English under the title *From Death-Camp to Existentialism* and later renamed *Man's Search for Meaning*, this multimillion-copy-selling book is really two books, very different in content and tone. The first, "Experiences in a Concentration Camp," recounts the horrific ordeal of Viktor E. Frankl, a Viennese Jewish physician and psychiatrist who was arrested in September 1942 by the Nazis and deported to the death camps, along with his family—mother, father, and wife Tilly. Frankl's brother and sister-in-law were separately caught trying to escape and also deported. All but Frankl and his sister, Stella, who had earlier escaped Vienna, perished in the camps.

The second book, "Logotherapy in a Nutshell," offers an overview of the psychological approach Frankl developed—derived from the Greek word *logos* for "meaning"*—and which was named the "third school" of Viennese psychotherapy after Freud's Psychoanalysis (the "first school") and Alfred Adler's Individual Psychology (the "second school"). While Frankl had worked on these ideas before the Holocaust, his camp experiences gave them new intensity and purpose.

In the opening section Frankl recounts his hellish years in a series of camps—Theresienstadt, Auschwitz-Birkenau, Kaufering, and Türkheim, part of the Dachau complex. Clothed in rags, fed thin gruel, and beaten constantly, Frankl experienced unspeakable cruelty and witnessed violent death. Alongside these scenes of horror, Frankl delivers an explanation of

---

* In the entry on *Meditations* by Marcus Aurelius, a somewhat different sense of *logos* is provided as central to the philosophy of Stoicism. Many commentators describe Frankl's ideas as an expression of Stoicism, although Frankl does not mention *Meditations* or Stoicism in this book.

the psychological and philosophical attitudes he maintained for his survival, which he also shared with fellow prisoners. The brutal scenario of life in the camps, he writes, "tore open the human soul and exposed its depths." Frankl's philosophy and psychology are perhaps best summed up when he recounts:

> I told them that although there was still no typhus epidemic in the camp, I estimated my own chances of survival at about one in twenty. But I also told them that, in spite of this, I had no intention of losing hope and giving up. For no man knew what the future would bring, much less the next hour.

Liberated, Frankl closes the first part of the book by describing the complex array of emotions—joy, bitterness, anger, shame—that filled the survivors. Departing from the hellscape of the camps, he turns toward the future, emphasizing looking forward with purpose instead of delving into the past. "Logotherapy," he writes, "focuses on the meaning of human existence as well as on man's search for such a meaning. According to logotherapy, this striving to find a meaning in one's life is the primary motivational force in man."

Frankl's exploration of logotherapy is quite conceptual, in contrast to the harsh reality of the camps, and grounded in many years of psychiatric work. Frankl moves in the book's conclusion toward what he calls "Tragic Optimism." This means, in his words:

> an optimism in the face of tragedy and in view of the human potential which at its best always allows for: (1) turning suffering into a human achievement and accomplishment; (2) deriving from guilt the opportunity to change oneself for the better; and (3) deriving from life's transitoriness an incentive to take responsible action.

ABOUT THE AUTHOR: VIKTOR E. FRANKL

Viktor Emil Frankl was born in Vienna on March 26, 1905, son of an Austrian government official. An accomplished teenager who performed brilliantly in school, he pursued an early interest in medicine and psychiatry, including a course in Freudian theory. At sixteen, he wrote a letter to the "Father of Psychoanalysis" and began a correspondence with Freud that resulted in Frankl's publishing a paper in an international journal three years later, while still in his teens.

While studying at the University of Vienna Medical School, Frankl attended seminars taught by Alfred Adler, a leading Viennese psychiatrist who had earlier broken with Freud. According to the *New York Times*, Frankl "began to feel that Adler erred in denying that people had the freedom of choice and willpower to overcome their problems." After graduating from the University of Vienna Medical School in 1930, Dr. Frankl began to develop his own ideas about psychotherapy and the roots of what he would later call logotherapy, while he served as chief of the university's neurology and psychiatric clinic.

After the Nazis seized power in Austria in 1938, the Jewish Frankl was forced out of his practice and became director of a clinic serving only Jewish patients. In 1940, after receiving emigration papers, Frankl chose to remain in Vienna rather than abandon his elderly parents. In December 1941, he and nurse Tilly Grosser were among the last couples allowed to be wed at the National Office for Jewish Marriages. In one of the unspeakable acts demanded of Jews, the Nazis forced them to abort a child.

Fearing arrest, Tilly Frankl sewed the manuscript of the book Frankl was writing on his therapeutic theories into the lining of his coat. The coat and the rest of his belongings were taken from Frankl when he was deported to the first of the camps, but Frankl began reconstructing his manuscript on scraps of paper stolen for him by a fellow prisoner. These notes were later used in writing *Man's Search for Meaning*.

On April 27, 1945, Frankl was liberated from Türkheim, a subcamp of Dachau, by American forces. Frankl was eventually placed in charge of a hospital for displaced persons. After the war, he earned his doctorate in psychiatry, becoming director of the Vienna Neurological Policlinic in 1946, a position he held for twenty-five years. In 1947, after the Red Cross verified that his first wife was dead, he married Eleonore Schwindt; they would have one daughter. In 1946 his camp account was published in German, and in 1959 it was published in English as *From Death-Camp to Existentialism*. Over the years, it was followed by more than thirty books about Frankl's concepts, life experiences, and theoretical and clinical psychology.

In 1991, *Man's Search for Meaning* was named as one of the most influential books in America in a survey conducted for the Library of Congress. After becoming an internationally known lecturer and professor, with honorary degrees from some of the world's most prestigious universities, Frankl published his final book, *Man's Search for Ultimate Meaning*, in 1997. He died of heart failure on September 2, 1997, at the age of ninety-two.

It would be disingenuous to exclude from this biography the controversy that followed Frankl, both during his life and afterward. In 1988, he was criticized for accepting an award from Austrian president Kurt Waldheim, a former UN secretary-general, who had attempted to conceal his Nazi past. And a recent biographer of Frankl, Professor Timothy E. Pytell, revealed Frankl's prewar neurological experiments on suicidal patients, with Nazi permission: "As director, Frankl was given the opportunity to conduct experimental brain surgeries on suicidal patients. Reticent over the years about these experiments, he did not mention them in his original 1973 autobiographical statement."

To overlook Frankl's prewar experiments, which he himself referenced with a Canadian interviewer in 1981, would be misleading. These are weighty considerations, in which the circumstances of Frankl's life before his deportation and his later experiences in the camps must be balanced. As Professor David Mikics wrote in the journal *Tablet* in 2020, "Frankl was not a collaborator; he was a victim of the Shoah. But this does not entail that he should be immune to criticism. . . . We judge everyone caught up in history, and let us hope that we judge sympathetically, especially in difficult cases. Frankl was in some ways a heroic personage. He was not a saint, however. He was more interesting than most saints, far more interesting than his simplistic, feel-good version of psychotherapy would lead one to believe."

In the same article in Frankl's defense, Professor Anna Geifman counters Mikics: "But a judgment of survivor's reality from the outside is presumptuous and invalid. . . . Frankl accentuated that he was not telling others *why* life is worth living—only that in order to make it worth living they need to render it meaningful. Frankl does not supply the meanings; he helps his patients find their own."

Calling *Man's Search for Meaning* "one of the great books of our time," the late Rabbi Harold S. Kushner writes in a foreword to the current edition that "curing the soul by leading it to find meaning in life" forms the essence of Frankl's therapeutic approach.

Of course, "meaning" and "happiness" are not synonymous and should not be confused. According to this edition's afterword, Frankl once asked his students to guess what single sentence expressed the meaning of Frankl's own life. One student wrote: "The meaning of your life is to help others find the meaning of theirs." Frankl said, "That was it, exactly."

To read work that concerns the Holocaust is imperative today, primarily because of the rise of neo-Nazism, anti-Semitism, and, with these, Holocaust denials. The first half of *Man's Search for Meaning* serves as one of those epic reminders of the famous line by Heinrich Heine, now immortalized, at the scene of the Berlin book burnings of May 1933: "Where they burn books, they will, in the end, burn human beings too."

We can "never forget," and works like this keep memory alive.

Frankl's school of philosophy and psychiatry—Logotherapy—is, also, a widely admired approach to thinking about the world and an individual's personal and psychological reaction to it. The essence of Frankl's thinking—embodied in his book's title—is that the search for meaning in our lives must be an individual's prime motivating force. As Frankl's camp experience underscores, logotherapy holds that life has meaning in even the most horrific circumstances. Frankl's ideas focus on the individual's response to suffering, either through meaningful work or interaction with other people or in the attitude taken toward suffering.

On a highly practical level, Tim Sanders wrote in the *New York Times* of his use of logotherapy to overcome the flying anxiety of his fellow passengers by speaking to them of the purpose of their trips: "In one of my favorite books, 'Man's Search for Meaning,' the author and Nazi war camp survivor Viktor Frankl argues that when you have a sense of purpose in an effort, you don't suffer as much from its ups and downs. In the psychology field, he's known to be a logotherapist—one who prescribes meaning to alleviate mental anguish or anxiety. In my experience, logotherapy works like a charm when it comes to travel and life."

In a time buffeted by so many challenges, as ours is, finding the appropriate response is a key to spiritual and psychological survival. In an article on the benefits of logotherapy, medical journalist Maria Cohut writes: "In other words, creative activities that engage our talents, openness to finding pleasure and beauty in the world, and the ability to master our responses to circumstances beyond our control are good ways of living purposefully and becoming more resilient."

Some critics of the Logotherapy school dismiss it as a "feel-good" philosophy rather than a scientifically based form of therapy, which relies too much on a spiritual approach to life. Rollo May, a pioneer in "Existential Psychology" —the title of May's 1961 book—criticized logotherapy for its near authoritarianism, writing: "It seems that if the patient cannot find his goal, Frankl supplies him with one. This would seem to take over the patients' responsibility and . . . diminish the patient as a person."

However, Frankl's supporters and logotherapy adherents see it as a constructive alternative to other forms of psychotherapy—that in trying to find meaning and purpose in our actions we can eliminate mental anguish and anxiety.

WHAT TO READ NEXT

First published in 1946, *Yes to Life* collects lectures Frankl delivered shortly after his liberation. Another short, accessible book, it was first published in English in 2020. "So, fate is part of our lives and so is suffering;" he writes, "therefore, if life has meaning, suffering also has meaning. Consequently, suffering, as long as it is necessary and unavoidable, also holds the possibility of being meaningful."

"Frankl begins by considering the question of whether life is worth living through the central fact of human dignity," writes Maria Popova of the book. "Noting how gravely the Holocaust disillusioned humanity with itself, he cautions against the defeatist 'end-of-the-world' mindset with which many responded to this disillusionment, but cautions equally against the 'blithe optimism' of previous, more naïve eras that had not yet faced this gruesome civilizational mirror reflecting what human beings are capable of doing to one another."

The literature of the Holocaust is, of course, enormous and is discussed elsewhere in this collection under *Night* (see entry) and in my previous book *Great Short Books*, which included Art Spiegelman's graphic memoir *Maus* and Primo Levi's *If This Is a Man*.

As a counterpoint, read Rollo May, one of Frankl's critics and among the first and most influential of thinkers in psychotherapy to be influenced by European existentialists. May was the author of many books, including *The Courage to Create* (1975), which is included in this collection.

"That night, the soup tasted of corpses."

Night

— 1958 —

Elie Wiesel

*New York: Hill & Wang, 2006; a new translation by Marion Wiesel with a
new preface by the author; 115 pages*

OPENING WORDS/EXCERPT

They called him Moishe the Beadle, as if his entire life he had never had a
surname. He was the jack-of-all-trades in a Hasidic house of prayer, a *shtibl*. The
Jews of Sighet—the little town in Transylvania where I spent my childhood—
were fond of him. He was poor and lived in utter penury. As a rule, our towns-
people, while they did help the needy, did not particularly like them. Moishe the
Beadle was the exception. He stayed out of people's way. His presence bothered
no one. He had mastered the art of rendering himself insignificant, invisible.

———

And Moishe the Beadle, the poorest of the poor of Sighet, spoke to me for hours on end about Kabbalah's revelations and its mysteries. Thus began my initiation.

SUMMARY

Terrifying in its simple power, *Night* stands as one of the greatest testimonies of the Holocaust. It was written by Elie Wiesel, winner of the 1986 Nobel Peace Prize, a death camp survivor who would become perhaps the most prominent face of Holocaust witnesses in the world. With its emphasis on the degradation and terror of his experience and its soul-crushing impact on him, Wiesel's account offers a very different response from Viktor E. Frankl's "Tragic Optimism" (previous entry).

Wiesel briefly describes a life of Jewish orthodoxy and rigorous religious training in a small Romanian village before being deported. As a teenager, he was taken with his family—parents and three sisters—and loaded into railroad cars, eighty people per car, for transport to Auschwitz. There his mother and one of his sisters perished in the maw of the death camp's relentless fires.

Wiesel's account focuses on the time he and his father, Shlomo, were held in Buna-Monowitz, the slave labor camp connected to Auschwitz. As an observant young Jew, Wiesel eloquently and painfully describes how his experiences forced him to question his faith as he confronts absolute evil. After passing by the "notorious Dr. Mengele," the Angel of Death who metes out survival or doom with the flick of a baton at the "selection," Wiesel sees the flames of the crematoria. Wiesel realizes that he has survived the fires that consumed so many:

> The night had passed completely. The morning star shone in the sky. I too had become a different person. The student of Talmud, the child I was, had been consumed by the flames. All that was left was a shape that resembled me. My soul had been invaded—and devoured—by a black flame.

Father and son were transferred to Buchenwald, where his father died—his last word was "Eliezer," Elie's name—and from which Wiesel was liberated. Unlike *The Diary of Anne Frank*, first published in the United States in 1952, which ends before Anne Frank's deportation, *Night* offers a brutal, candid portrayal of the camp experience. That was one of the reasons it was turned down by many American publishing houses before its first U.S. publication in 1960.

Wiesel would later say, "Where Anne Frank's book ends, mine begins."

ABOUT THE AUTHOR: ELIE WIESEL

Born Eliezer Wiesel on September 30, 1928, in the small town of Sighet in the Carpathian Mountains of Romania, Wiesel spent his early years in a tight-knit Hasidic community. In 1940, Hungary annexed the territory and, while Hungary was allied to Germany, Hungarian Jews did not immediately face the terrors of the Holocaust. Then, in 1944, Hitler's forces moved into Hungary. Along with many of Hungary's Jews, the Wiesel family—Elie with his parents and three sisters, Beatrice, Hilda, and Tzipora—was deported to the Auschwitz extermination camp in Poland. Wiesel was tattooed with the number A-7713 on his left arm by the Germans. Wiesel's mother and younger sister, Tzipora, perished immediately in the gas chamber while his two older sisters, selected for slave labor, survived the camps. In 1945, Elie and his father were force-marched to Buchenwald, where Elie's father died.

Liberated by the U.S. Third Army on April 11, 1945, Wiesel went to France with hundreds of other Jewish orphans. Eventually, he would study at the Sorbonne, France's most prestigious university. Wiesel was later reunited with his two sisters, who believed him dead until one of them saw his photograph in a French newspaper.

Still in his teens, Wiesel began writing for French and Israeli newspapers, although not about his camp experience. In 1952, he was assigned to interview François Mauriac, a French Catholic novelist who'd won the Nobel Prize in Literature that year. A member of the French Resistance during the war, Mauriac discussed the plight of Jewish children loaded onto cattle cars with Wiesel. "I was one of them," Wiesel told him.

"It was then that I understood what had first appealed to me about this young Jew:," Mauriac later wrote, "the gaze of a Lazarus risen from the dead, yet still held captive in the somber regions into which he had strayed, stumbling over desecrated corpses."

With Mauriac's encouragement Wiesel wrote a lengthy account, in Yiddish, called *And the World Remained Silent*. Mauriac promised to write a preface to the book, which Wiesel later shortened and rewrote in French. After many rejections, the book found a French publisher who made further cuts and eventually published it in 1958 as *La Nuit*. It sold poorly and Wiesel's literary agent, George Borchardt, faced multiple rejections from American publishers, despite the success of Anne Frank's diary.

When Arthur Wang of Hill & Wang agreed to publish *Night* in 1959, Wiesel received an advance of one hundred dollars. Despite some admiring reviews, the book did not do well. "The Holocaust was not something people wanted to know about in those days, Mr. Wiesel told *Time* magazine in 1985."

Wiesel had, by then, moved to New York and continued to write other books, including fiction: *Dawn* (1961) and *Day* (1962), two short novels dealing with the aftermath of the Holocaust that are now considered, along with *Night*, the Night Trilogy. In 1969, he married Marion Erster Rose, who would translate his subsequent books. In 1972, he began teaching Judaic studies at the City University of New York.

A few years later, in 1976, Wiesel began teaching at Boston University. Holocaust studies had become more popular at the university level, but Wiesel's books were not yet widely adopted for the curriculum. Then, in 1978, President Jimmy Carter appointed Wiesel to chair a commission on the Holocaust. Wiesel wrote the commission's report, which eventually led to the creation of the United States Holocaust Memorial Museum, dedicated in April 1993 in Washington, D.C.

By his own account, Wiesel brought himself and *Night* into wider acclaim when he spoke out at a White House ceremony against President Ronald Reagan's 1985 visit to a military cemetery in Germany where members of the Nazi SS were buried: "That place, Mr. President, is not your place. Your place is with the victims of the SS."

In 1986, Wiesel was honored with the Nobel Peace Prize. In his acceptance speech, Wiesel spoke of addressing himself as that young boy in the camp:

> And then I explain to him how naïve we were, that the world did know and remained silent. And that is why I swore never to be silent whenever and wherever human beings endure suffering and humiliation. We must take sides. Neutrality helps the oppressor, never the victim. Silence encourages the tormentor, never the tormented.

In 2006, Oprah Winfrey selected *Night* for her book club and accompanied Wiesel to Auschwitz for a televised program. The book went onto the *New York Times* best seller list, where it remained for eighty weeks; it is now widely assigned in American schools. Wiesel returned to Buchenwald in 2009 with President Obama, whose great-uncle had been with the American army units that liberated the camps.

Elie Wiesel died on July 2, 2016, at the age of eighty-seven. His *New York Times* obituary read in part:

> There may have been better chroniclers who evoked the hellish minutiae of the German death machine. There were arguably more illuminating philosophers. But no single figure was able to combine Mr. Wiesel's moral urgency with his magnetism, which emanated from his deeply lined face and eyes as unrelievable melancholy.

WHY YOU SHOULD READ IT

Many of the valuable books cited in this collection are instructive, insightful, perhaps inspiring, and even provocative. Others cut closer to the bone, shaking our understanding of morality and conscience. *Night* is one of these. To read these books constitutes a profound personal challenge—a possible ethical awakening. We cannot read them without seriously considering what response we must make to the world.

In a time of increasing anti-Semitism, advancing authoritarianism, hateful political discourse fueled by mainstream politicians and abetted by willing broadcasters, writers, and social media, there is a Moral Imperative to read such books. They provide, as Joseph Conrad memorably put it, "that glimpse of truth for which you have forgotten to ask."

WHAT TO READ NEXT

The literature of the Holocaust is vast. Many American students are still assigned to read *Anne Frank: The Diary of a Young Girl*, which has been recently revised to reflect deletions made by her father, Otto Frank. If you have never read her book, it is a must read. German Jews who had fled to the Netherlands, the Frank family went into hiding in a secret apartment in Amsterdam in July 1942. They were arrested by the Nazis on August 4, 1944. Anne Frank and her sister, Margot, both died of typhus in early 1945; Anne's mother, Edith Frank, died in Auschwitz in January 1945; Otto Frank was liberated from Auschwitz by Soviet troops in January 1945. Recently, the book has been challenged or banned in certain school districts in the contemporary wave of school book bans. The book is sometimes challenged by parents and administrators who are made uncomfortable by its explicit descriptions of the Holocaust. They fear it might trigger uncomfortable feelings.

That, I suppose, is the point. *Night* remains, indisputably, a cornerstone of Holocaust literature, and should be read or reread.

The previous entry cited other essential testimonials to the Holocaust and the events preceding it. To these I would add *School for Barbarians: Education Under the Nazis* (1938) by Erika Mann, the daughter of the famed novelist Thomas Mann; it depicts the transformation of the German school system under the Nazis. She wrote: ". . . the German child is a Nazi child, and nothing else."

"A bill is coming in that I fear America is not prepared to pay."

The Fire Next Time

— 1963 —

James Baldwin

New York: Vintage International, 1993; 106 pages

EXCERPT

I became, during my fourteenth year, for the first time in my life, afraid—afraid of the evil within me and afraid of the evil without. What I saw around me that summer in Harlem was what I had always seen; nothing had changed. But now, without any warning, the whores and pimps and racketeers on the Avenue had become a personal menace. It had not before occurred to me that I could become one of them, but now I realized that we had been produced by the same circumstances. Many of my comrades were clearly headed for the Avenue, and my father said I was headed that way, too.

SUMMARY

What does the future hold for a nation that has deliberately and consistently suppressed its Black citizens? Will this "dishonored past" end in conflagration? One of the twentieth century's most profoundly influential writers, James Baldwin challenges us to examine these questions in this landmark book. It consists of two "letters" Baldwin published in book form in 1963, the centennial year of Lincoln's Emancipation Proclamation.

The first of these—"My Dungeon Shook"—is the shorter of the two. First published in the *Progressive* magazine in December 1962, it takes the form of a letter addressed to Baldwin's nephew, a teenage namesake. Lovingly written, it is a powerful warning to the next generation that calls up all that has been done to Black Americans over centuries. "This innocent country set you down in a ghetto in which, in fact, it intended that you should perish," Baldwin tells his nephew. "You were born where you were born and faced the future that you faced because you were black and *for no other reason* [emphasis in original]."

The second essay—"Down at the Cross"—appeared originally in the *New Yorker* in November 1962 as "Letter from a Region in My Mind." In it, Baldwin traces his personal journey, growing up in Harlem, becoming a teenage preacher, and eventually abandoning his Christian faith. He recounts his meeting with the charismatic Elijah Muhammad, who established the Nation of Islam and was mentor to both Malcolm X and Muhammad Ali. Baldwin listens, growing wary of Elijah Muhammad's pronouncements of "white devils." He writes: "The glorification of one race and the consequent debasement of another—or others—always has been and always will be a recipe for murder."

"Down at the Cross" is a more broadly open letter to America, a much longer jeremiad—a bitter lament and stark prophecy of doom. Near its conclusion he writes: "How can the American Negro past be used? It is entirely possible that this dishonored past will rise up soon to smite us all."

ABOUT THE AUTHOR: JAMES BALDWIN

Born on August 2, 1924, the oldest of nine children, Baldwin did not know his biological father. His mother, a cleaning woman, later married David Baldwin, a Baptist preacher described as an "unforgiving man with a terrible temper." James Baldwin grew up in Harlem at a time when there were few options for a young Black man. There was the "Avenue," described in the preceding excerpt, with its lures and dangers. And there was the church of David Baldwin, his stepfather.

In his teens, James Baldwin encountered a woman who was also pastor of a Harlem church: "It was my good luck—perhaps—that I found myself in the church racket instead of some other, and surrendered to a spiritual seduction long before I came to any carnal knowledge." Following an ecstatic epiphany, Baldwin emerged as a riveting teenage preacher—a "Young Minister"—who mesmerized congregations and became a bigger draw than his stepfather.

Baldwin's faith crumbled in time, a transformation he attributes to reading. Baldwin spent many hours as a child in New York's libraries and began writing at an early age. In junior high school, one of his teachers was Countee Cullen, a poet and key figure in the Harlem Renaissance; at DeWitt Clinton High School, Baldwin discovered Dostoevsky and edited the school magazine, *The Magpie*. His fellow editor was student Richard Avedon, who went on to achieve fame as a photographer; they later collaborated on a book.

It was in high school that Baldwin first questioned his Christianity. This led to a violent fracture with his stepfather after he brought home a best friend, a Jewish boy: "My father slammed me across the face with his great palm, and in that moment everything flooded back—all the hatred and all the fear, and the depth of a merciless resolve to kill my father rather than allow my father to kill me."

Working in a defense industry plant in New Jersey and later in a meatpacking factory to help support his family, Baldwin eventually left home and moved to Greenwich Village, then a bohemian enclave. With the encouragement of Richard Wright, whose 1940 novel, *Native Son*, was

the first best-selling book by a Black American, Baldwin found his calling
as a writer. His literary career was launched with a 1947 essay appearing in
the *Nation* magazine.

Using money from a literary fellowship, Baldwin moved to France in
1948 to escape the racism and homophobia of his home country. "I was
broke. I got to Paris with forty dollars in my pocket, but I had to get out
of New York," he told the *Paris Review* in a 1984 interview. "My luck was
running out. I was going to go to jail, I was going to kill somebody or be
killed. My best friend had committed suicide two years earlier, jumping
off the George Washington Bridge."

In 1949, Baldwin wrote an essay called "Everybody's Protest Novel,"
critical of Wright's *Native Son*, decrying Wright for what he considered
the perpetuation of stereotypical images of Black men. In 1953, Baldwin
published his own first novel, *Go Tell It on the Mountain*. Considered by
many critics his best work of fiction, it was followed by a collection of
essays, *Notes of a Native Son* (1955), which included the essay on Wright. A
second novel, *Giovanni's Room*, was set in Paris with white characters, and
dealt with bisexuality and coming out. Rejected by Baldwin's American
publisher, Alfred A. Knopf, which hoped for another novel set in Harlem,
the book was published by Dial Press in 1956.

As the Civil Rights Movement gathered momentum, Baldwin returned
often to the United States. In 1957, he was commissioned to write an
article on the movement and encountered Dr. Martin Luther King Jr.
for the first time. Baldwin soon became a major voice in the crusade.
Nobody Knows My Name: More Notes of a Native Son, a 1961 book of
essays, secured his place as a passionate spokesman for the Civil Rights
Movement. Following its publication, Dr. King wrote to Baldwin: "Your
analysis of the problem is always creative and penetrating. Your honesty
and courage in telling the truth to white Americans, even if it hurts, is
most impressive."

Baldwin achieved even greater prominence with the *New Yorker*'s
1962 publication of "Down at the Cross," the centerpiece essay in *The
Fire Next Time*. Its breadth and sense of urgency cemented Baldwin's
stature, garnering a place on the cover of *Time* magazine in May 1963. That

year, Baldwin also organized a meeting of other Black writers, civic leaders, and performers—including Harry Belafonte and Lena Horne—with then–attorney general Robert F. Kennedy. A few months later, Baldwin attended the August 1963 March on Washington but was not invited to speak.

James Baldwin was not to be silenced. Two years after his meeting with Robert F. Kennedy, Baldwin made his voice clearly heard. "From the point of view of the man in the Harlem barber shop, Bobby Kennedy only got here yesterday and now he is already on his way to the Presidency," he wrote in the *New York Times* in March 1965. "We were here for 400 years and now he tells us that maybe in 40 years, if you are good, we may let you become President."

Continuing to write essays and fiction into the 1980s, Baldwin returned to France, where he died of stomach cancer on December 1, 1987, at age sixty-three. Writing more than ten years after Baldwin's death, Hilton Als of the *New Yorker* commented: "He was at his best when he was writing about some aspect of life or politics that reflected his interior self: he contained a multitude of worlds, and those worlds were his true subject."

WHY YOU SHOULD READ IT

This is fairly simple. *The Fire Next Time* is a stark and searing testament to James Baldwin's place in twentieth-century American letters. In it, he delivers a riveting sermon that is part memoir, part history, and, finally, part somber warning to both Black Americans—like his own nephew—and white Americans, who Baldwin knew must be part of the solution to the nation's racial divide. The alternative was racial civil war.

Read it because it is not a time capsule—it is tellingly timely and, in many ways, the nation Baldwin described in 1963 still exists in 2023. America still manifests the gross inequities in race-based gerrymandering aimed to suppress the Black vote. These disparities also exist in the criminal justice system and in incarceration rates of Blacks and other minorities, and the continuing violence by police against Black Americans. And an increasingly open display of white Christian nationalism has resulted in mass shootings in racially motivated hate crimes. As Baldwin wrote:

White people hold the power, which means that they are superior to blacks (intrinsically, that is: God decreed it so), and the world has innumerable ways of making this difference known and felt and feared. Long before the Negro child perceives this difference, and even longer before he understands it, he has begun to react to it, he has begun to be controlled by it. Every effort made by the child's elders to prepare him for a fate from which they cannot protect him causes him secretly, in terror, to begin to await, without knowing that he is doing so, his mysterious and inexorable punishment.

Race remains the fault line in American society and politics. Baldwin saw it then. The times have changed. The problem has not.

WHAT TO READ NEXT

James Baldwin's body of work is large and profoundly topical. His voice is clearest in his essays, so look to *Notes of a Native Son* (1955) and *Nobody Knows My Name: More Notes of a Native Son* (1961). These books explore many of Baldwin's essential themes: sexuality, repression, artistic freedom, and being Black in a white world. Read more Baldwin.

In the earlier entry on *Civil Disobedience*, I suggested Dr. Martin Luther King Jr.'s *Why We Can't Wait*. I would reiterate that here. The period of the Civil Rights Movement led by Dr. King is also the subject of an award-winning trio of graphic novels titled *March*, written by the late John Lewis, who joined those Birmingham marches as a teenager. He was beaten, hospitalized, and jailed. Although aimed at younger readers, the trio of books vividly depict the period from the perspective of a man who eventually became a member of Congress and a tireless spokesperson for racial justice and democracy.

Finally, I recommend a book modeled on Baldwin's letter to his nephew. "Letter to My Son," by Ta-Nehisi Coates, appeared in the *Atlantic* on July 4, 2015, and opened with a quote from Baldwin. The letter was excerpted from Coates's book *Between the World and Me*, which went on to win the National Book Award and become a national best seller.

The book led many people to view Coates as Baldwin's natural successor, among them fellow writer Michael Eric Dyson. "By being himself, Coates is precisely the sort of writer that he needs to be—the sort of writer that we need, too, since every age gets the writers it deserves," wrote Dyson. "Ta-Nehisi Coates is an enormously gifted writer who, while feeding his hunger to eloquently tell the truth about race, has also fed a nation starving for that same truth."

"A hard task, dying, when one loves life so much."

A Very Easy Death

— 1964 —

Simone de Beauvoir

New York: Pantheon Books, 1965; translated from the French by Patrick O'Brian; 106 pages

OPENING WORDS

At four o'clock in the afternoon of Thursday, 24 October 1963, I was in Rome, in my room at the Hotel Minerva; I was to fly home the next day and I was putting papers away when the telephone rang. It was Bost calling me from Paris: "Your mother has had an accident," he said. I thought: she has been knocked down by a car; she was climbing laboriously from the roadway to the pavement, leaning on her stick, and a car knocked her down. "She had a fall in the bathroom: she has broken the neck of her femur," said Bost. He lived in the same building as my mother.

SUMMARY

Told with the economy and lyrical power of a finely compressed novella, this memoir recounts the emotional last few weeks in the life of the widowed mother of Simone de Beauvoir, one of the most consequential writers of the twentieth century. An accidental fall and its attendant physical limitations lead the seventy-eight-year-old Françoise to fret about being forced to surrender her apartment and with it her independence. But these worries are soon transformed by a far more dire complication—a diagnosis whose truth is withheld from the ailing woman.

Moving through the physical pain and personal anguish of her mother's final days, Beauvoir flashes back on her mother's life, as well as on the fraught relationship she and her sister had with their mother. In the midst of this intense family drama—one that is unhappily familiar to so many people—there are conflicts with doctors and hospitals over frightful decisions to be made. Through these reflections, Beauvoir combines regret and anger in describing the stark shift that comes when the child cares for the mother; finally, there is grief:

> I had grown very fond of this dying woman. As we talked in the half-darkness, I assuaged an old unhappiness; I was renewing the dialogue that had been broken off during my adolescence and that our differences and our likenesses had never allowed us to take up again. And the early tenderness that I had thought dead for ever came to life again, since it had become possible to slip into simple words and actions.

ABOUT THE AUTHOR: SIMONE DE BEAUVOIR

When the prominent French writer and philosopher Simone de Beauvoir died on April 14, 1986, noted American feminist Gloria Steinem said, "If any single human being can be credited with inspiring the current international woman's movement, it's Simone de Beauvoir." And in France, the headlines announcing her death read: "Women, you owe her everything!" These assessments were based on the impact of her most famous book, *The Second Sex*, a landmark work first published in France in 1949.

Introducing a 2010 restored and retranslated English edition of the book, journalist and social critic Judith Thurman wrote:

> While no one individual or her work is responsible for that seismic shift in laws and attitudes, the millions of young women who now confidently assume that their entitlement to work, pleasure, and autonomy is equal to that of their brothers owe a measure of their freedom to Beauvoir. *The Second Sex* was an act of Promethean audacity— a theft of Olympian fire—from which there was no turning back. It is not the last word on "the problem of woman," which, Beauvoir wrote, "has always been a problem of men," but it marks the place in history where an enlightenment begins.

Few intellectuals or writers attain the worldwide renown that Simone de Beauvoir achieved, in the breadth and depth of her works. As a writer of philosophy, a chief proponent of existentialism, a political scientist, a novelist, and the author of a landmark work of feminism, she was a towering figure in twentieth-century letters. Her fame was magnified significantly by her long and very public relationship with French writer-philosopher Jean-Paul Sartre. Internationally famed, the pair was inseparably linked through their writing, existential philosophy, and a highly complex relationship that involved multiple partners—for both of them, sometimes together.

Simone de Beauvoir was born in Paris on January 9, 1908, into a well-to-do family. After World War I, her father, Georges, a lawyer, lost much of his fortune. Her mother, Françoise, a devout Catholic and the daughter of a wealthy banker, was accustomed to living with servants but was eventually reduced to doing the housework. Yet Simone and her younger sister, Hélène, were sent to an excellent convent school and Simone even contemplated becoming a nun—among the few choices available to young women at the time.

A voracious reader and a brilliant student, she eventually went on to the elite French university the Sorbonne. In 1929, Beauvoir met Jean-Paul Sartre, then a slightly older student at the École normale supérieure, another elite Parisian institution. Together they crammed for a highly competitive postgraduate exam called the agrégation in philosophy. Sartre finished first and Beauvoir finished second, at twenty-one the youngest to ever take the exam. Biographers have suggested that—but for sexism—Beauvoir should have taken first place. Sartre and Beauvoir would spend most of their lives working together, although they did not live together and never married.

Between 1931 and 1943, she taught at several schools at the lycée level and began to write. Beauvoir's first novel, *She Came to Stay*, appeared in 1943. It concerns a couple whose relationship is destroyed by a young girl staying in their home and was based on a three-way love affair she and Sartre had with one of Beauvoir's former students. "In real life, this was a fraught love triangle that drew in more people until it became a love pentagon and eventually dissolved," writes Sarah Bakewell in a group portrait of wartime Paris's existentialist community.

During the war, Jean-Paul Sartre served a brief stint in the French army and was captured and released by the Germans, returning to Paris in 1941. He and Beauvoir then formed an underground group called Socialisme et Liberté with other writers. They later contributed to *Combat*, the clandestine resistance newspaper edited by Albert Camus (see entry), with whom they became friends.

Continuing their partnership, in 1945 Beauvoir and Sartre founded and began editing *Les Temps Modernes*, a monthly review that would eventually publish Richard Wright, Samuel Beckett, and Jean Genet, among other prominent avant-garde writers. In this prolific postwar period, Beauvoir wrote—among other works—two novels, *The Blood of Others* (1945) and *All Men Are Mortal* (1947); numerous essays; a book of philosophy called *The Ethics of Ambiguity* (1947); and a travel diary, *America Day by Day* (1948).

All the while, she was researching and writing her landmark work. In 1949, *The Second Sex* was published in France, appearing four years after Frenchwomen got the vote, but while birth control and abortion were still illegal. Beauvoir's essential argument—that women throughout history have been defined as inferior to men—was documented with an exhaustive array of evidence. As writer and critic Judith Thurman comments, "One is humbled to learn that this eight-hundred-page encyclopedia of the folklore, customs, laws, history, religion, philosophy, anthropology, literature, economic systems, and received ideas that have, since time began, objectified women was researched and composed in about fourteen months, between 1946 and 1949, while Beauvoir was also engaged with other literary projects, traveling widely, editing and contributing to Les Temps Modernes."

Published originally in two volumes, the book became a sensation and was soon placed on the Vatican's list of prohibited books. Its readership greatly expanded in 1953 when the first English edition was published by Alfred A. Knopf in America. This version had been condensed by its American translator, a retired zoology professor hired by Knopf who, according to Judith Thurman, lacked any background in French literature and philosophy. (A new English translation of the entire text of *The Second Sex* was published in 2009.)

Returning to fiction in 1954, Beauvoir wrote *Inseparable*—an autobiographical novel not published until 2021—and *The Mandarins*, for which she won France's chief literary award, the Prix Goncourt. A thinly disguised roman à clef, it included portraits of many people in the Beauvoir-Sartre circle. Not all were happy with the book, including Albert Camus, whose friendship with Beauvoir and Sartre had already bitterly fractured. Also angry was American novelist Nelson Algren, author of *The Man with the Golden Arm*, with whom Beauvoir had an affair before returning to Sartre.

"When I was growing up in the 60s, Simone de Beauvoir and Jean-Paul Sartre were a model couple, already legendary creatures, rebels with a great many causes, and leaders of what could be called the first postwar youth movement: existentialism—a philosophy that rejected all absolutes and talked of freedom, authenticity, and difficult choices," writes Beauvoir biographer Lisa Appignanesi. "It had its own music and garb of sophisticated black which looked wonderful against a cafe backdrop. Sartre and De Beauvoir were its Bogart and Bacall, partners in a gloriously modern love affair lived out between jazz club, cafe and writing desk, with forays on to the platforms and streets of protest. Despite being indissolubly united and bound by ideas, they remained unmarried and free to engage openly in any number of relationships."

Existentialism's "Bogart and Bacall" had a darker side, explicitly revealed when their multiple affairs and shared lovers became public, especially after private letters were published following their deaths. The woman who had been seduced as a teenager by the bisexual Beauvoir—her schoolteacher at the time—was later involved with Sartre. She wrote an account of the relationship, published in English in 1993 as *A Disgraceful Affair*.

Discussing the couple's complex relationship, critic and historian Louis Menand commented: "But it is clear now that Sartre and Beauvoir did not simply have a long-term relationship supplemented by independent affairs with other people. The affairs with other people formed the very basis of their relationship. The swapping and the sharing and the mimicking, the memoir-and novel-writing, right down to the interviews and the published letters and the duelling estates, was the stuff and substance of their 'marriage.' This was how they slept with each other after they stopped sleeping with each other."

Beauvoir's private life never slowed her prolific writing life. After *The Second Sex* and the fiction, Beauvoir wrote a series of highly praised autobiographical works, beginning with *Memoirs of a Dutiful Daughter* in 1958. Describing her adolescence and transformation into a rebellious writer and thinker, the memoir's themes reverberate in *A Very Easy Death*. Simone de Beauvoir died of pneumonia in April 1986, aged seventy-eight. Her ashes are buried with those of Sartre in Paris.

WHY YOU SHOULD READ IT

The simple answer is that the death of a parent is a nearly universal experience. And *A Very Easy Death* is profound. Written with restraint and an earthy honesty that is removed from the more philosophical abstractions of many of Beauvoir's other works, it is raw and powerful. While a therapist massages Beauvoir's bedridden mother, she writes:

The sight of my mother's nakedness had jarred me. No body existed
less for me: none existed more. As a child I had loved it dearly; as
an adolescent it had filled me with an uneasy repulsion: all this was
perfectly in the ordinary course of things and it seemed reasonable
to me that her body should retain its dual nature, that it should be
both repugnant and holy—a taboo. But for all that, I was astonished
at the violence of my distress.

The book is painful and often moving. Beauvoir brings a novelist's eye
for the details of its hospital settings, the coming and goings and doctors and
nurses, and the secretive conversations concealing the truth from Beauvoir's
dying mother.

A Very Easy Death is another stepping-stone book, an entrée into Beauvoir's works on philosophy and feminism. It hints at these other concerns
when, after her mother's death, Beauvoir writes: "There is no such thing
as a natural death: nothing that happens to a man is ever natural, since his
presence calls the world into question." That is the voice of Beauvoir the
existentialist responding to the most primal of experiences.

I must admit, however, that I read Beauvoir's dignified yet despairing
account before fully exploring the details of her relationship with Jean-Paul
Sartre. Having done so soured my view of a woman idolized by generations
of feminists and philosophers. Seducing and sharing a teenage student is
more than troubling.

Some may separate the author and very public figure of Beauvoir from
the private person. But what might be called the perversity of her relationship with Sartre complicates the reader's feelings about what might
otherwise be a profoundly moving narrative.

WHAT TO READ NEXT

If you are interested in the history of feminism, read the voluminous *The
Second Sex*. It remains one of the author's most notable achievements,
even though contemporary critics find it dated from the perspective of
the economic gains made by women since 1945 and in reflecting a largely

white point of view. But as Debra Bergoffen and Megan Burke comment, "Taken within the context of the feminist movement, this declaration of oppression was an event. It opened the way for the consciousness-raising that characterized second-wave feminism. It has and continues to validate the injustices experienced by girls and women."

Among Beauvoir's shorter works is the 1944 philosophical essay *Pyrrhus and Cineas*, reissued in a 2020 paperback titled *What is Existentialism?* It is a relatively accessible introduction to the school of philosophy that she and Sartre personified. Another is the relatively brief *The Ethics of Ambiguity*, Beauvoir's first postwar work. "Beauvoir speaks of the war as creating an existential rupture in time," write Debra Bergoffen and Megan Burke about living in Nazi-occupied Paris and its impact on Beauvoir. "She speaks of herself as having undergone a conversion. She can no longer afford the luxury of focusing on her own happiness and pleasure. The question of evil becomes a pressing concern. One cannot refuse to take a stand."

I plan to read Beauvoir's recently published posthumous novel, *Inseparable*, based on her childhood friendship with a girl called Zaza. In its introduction, novelist Margaret Atwood writes: "Without Zaza, without the passionate devotion between the two of them, without Zaza's encouragement of Beauvoir's intellectual ambition . . . would there have been a *Second Sex?* And without that pivotal book, what else would have not followed?"

For a brief introduction to the work of Jean-Paul Sartre, I point to *Existentialism Is a Humanism*, issued in English in 2007. Sartre writes: "You have seen that it [existentialism] cannot be considered a philosophy of quietism, since it defines man by his actions, nor can it be called a pessimistic description of man, for no doctrine is more optimistic, since it declares that man's destiny lies within himself." Awarded the Nobel Prize in 1964, Sartre chose to decline it.

Among Sartre's other notable works is the brief novel *Nausea*, which writer Sarah Bakewell calls an essential text of existentialism: "Although it is a novel, it's a novelization of philosophical ideas, so you approach the philosophy through one literary character's individual crisis and you approach that crisis through a sequence of ideas." Bakewell's own book, *At the Existentialist Café: Freedom, Being, and Apricot Cocktails*, provides a vivid group portrait of Beauvoir, Sartre, Camus, and others who made existentialism fashionable as well as a philosophy; it was named one of the Ten Best Books of 2016 by the *New York Times*.

"But this is how Paris was in the early days
when we were very poor and very happy."

A Moveable Feast

— 1964 —

Ernest Hemingway

New York: Scribner, 2003; 211 pages

OPENING WORDS

Then there was the bad weather. It would come in one day when the fall was over. We would have to shut the windows in the night against the rain and the cold wind would strip the leaves from the trees in the Place Contrescarpe. The leaves lay sodden in the rain and the wind drove the rain against the big green autobus at the terminal and the Café des Amateurs was crowded and the windows misted over from the heat and the smoke inside.

SUMMARY

Based on a set of notebooks that a struggling twentysomething Ernest Hemingway kept in post–World War I Paris, this memoir was published after the famed novelist's suicide in 1961. It is, in many ways, Hemingway at his best: simple yet robust descriptions of the streets, neighborhoods, cafés, and bars—there are many bars and lots of drinking—frequented by Hemingway during his European sojourn in the 1920s. Struggling to make his way with the short stories that eventually established his reputation, Hemingway fills these pages with the sights and smells of a time that has been greatly romanticized. But what a time.

And what a cast! It is replete with an extraordinary gallery of the remarkable people Hemingway encountered as he negotiated life among the so-called Lost Generation. In the demimonde he describes are many of the artists and writers who made this brief moment in time between world wars immortal. In the wake of World War I's mindless destruction, a new era of Modernism in writing and art had opened, and young Hemingway was in the thick of it.

Serving as bookends to Hemingway's vivid Paris tableau are the two people who figure most prominently in his recollections—Gertrude Stein, the center of this Parisian universe, and novelist F. Scott Fitzgerald, already famous but showing signs of the self-destructive behavior that doomed his career. More important, in Hemingway's riveting anecdotes of trips taken, meals eaten, and alcohol consumed, is the central character: Hemingway himself, accompanied by his first wife, Hadley Richardson, and their infant son, Jack, called Bumby. Hemingway's sketches of Paris do provide a feast—and a memorable one, at that.

ABOUT THE AUTHOR: ERNEST HEMINGWAY

Journalist, short story writer, novelist, and Nobel Prize laureate Ernest Miller Hemingway was a towering figure in twentieth-century letters. He left an indelible mark on succeeding generations of writers. Like his contemporaries Virginia Woolf and James Joyce, Hemingway changed how people wrote. Fellow Nobel Prize laureate Gabriel García Márquez, for instance, once described his admiration for the man famously called Papa, saying Hemingway "is the one who had the most to do with my craft." Joan Didion often described typing and retyping Hemingway paragraphs to hone her own writing skills.

Over an extraordinary career that spanned forty tempestuous years, Hemingway became a larger-than-life celebrity who witnessed several wars—as both participant and journalist—adored bullfighting and safaris, indulged in an insatiable appetite for excitement and life, and pioneered a literary style that influenced generations of writers to come. Born on July 21, 1889, in what is now Oak Park, Illinois, Hemingway was the second of six children. His mother, Grace Hall Hemingway, was a singer and music teacher who, by recent accounts, raised Ernest and his older sister, Marcelline, as twins until he was five, sometimes dressing him in girl's clothing. His father was a physician who instilled in Ernest a love of the outdoors, fishing, and hunting. Clarence Edmonds Hemingway would take his own life in 1928. (According to medical historian Dr. Howard Markel, "Seven of Hemingway's close family relations died by suicide, including his father, sister, brother and much later his granddaughter, the supermodel Margaux Hemingway.")

In Oak Park and River Forest High School, Hemingway wrote for and edited the school newspaper and yearbook, and he later worked as a cub reporter for the *Kansas City Star*. The newspaper's stylebook would mark his widely mimicked writing style: "Use short sentences. Use short first paragraphs. Use vigorous English."

After the United States declared war on Germany in 1917, Hemingway was rejected by the army for poor eyesight. Joining the Red Cross Ambulance Service instead, he was sent to Italy. Just before turning nineteen, Hemingway was badly wounded in a mortar attack. While recuperating in a Milan hospital, he fell in love with a Red Cross nurse, an experience later reflected in his 1929 novel, *A Farewell to Arms*—the wartime story of Frederic Henry, a wounded American ambulance driver, and English nurse Catherine Barkley.

After the war, Hemingway married Hadley Richardson in 1921, and they sailed to Paris, where he would write articles for the *Toronto Star*. Hemingway and Richardson, with their infant son, Jack, lived among the expatriate community that he vividly brings to life in *A Moveable Feast*. That community included poet Ezra Pound, who commissioned the stories that were published in the collection *In Our Time* (1925), which marked

Hemingway's literary arrival. It was followed by his first novel, *The Sun Also Rises* (1926), about aimless expatriates in France and Spain—a group very like the people in *A Moveable Feast*—confirming Hemingway's stature and giving him a taste of the success, and celebrity, he desperately craved.

In 1927, Hemingway divorced Richardson following an affair with Pauline Pfeiffer, a wealthy *Vogue* journalist who became the second of Hemingway's four wives. A few years later—in 1929—he published *A Farewell to Arms* and next he wrote *Death in the Afternoon* (1932), a nonfiction account of bullfighting, followed by *Green Hills of Africa* (1935) about big game hunting; both books cemented Hemingway's literary standing and rising celebrity.

Returning to Spain as a war correspondent in 1937 during the Spanish Civil War, Hemingway was an eyewitness to the battle in which Fascist forces defeated the Republican armies. While in Spain, he continued an affair with fellow journalist Martha Gellhorn, leading to another divorce and his third marriage, to Gellhorn. Hemingway's experience in wartime Spain was turned into *For Whom the Bell Tolls*, his 1940 novel about an American fighting against the Nazi-supported Fascists.

With Gellhorn, Hemingway traveled to China, then at war with Japan. When the United States entered World War II, Hemingway was dispatched to Europe as a war correspondent. Returning to Paris after its liberation, he then covered the Battle of the Bulge, the last major Nazi offensive of the war. The war years also brought an end to his stormy relationship with Gellhorn, herself a war correspondent of great talent and courage—she had gone to the Normandy beaches after D-Day, slipping onto a hospital ship disguised as a nurse. By that time, Hemingway had met *Time* correspondent Mary Welsh, who became his fourth wife in 1946.

But the years of injuries, alcoholism, and hard living had exacted a severe toll. Drinking heavily, overweight, and suffering from diabetes and depression, Hemingway struggled to write. When *The Old Man and the Sea* was published in 1952, the novella revived a flagging career and led to his 1954 Nobel Prize in Literature.

Returning to his Paris haunts a few years later, Hemingway made an astonishing discovery. As his friend and future biographer A. E. Hotchner described it:

In 1956, Ernest and I were having lunch at the Ritz in Paris with Charles Ritz, the hotel's chairman, when Charley asked if Ernest was aware that a trunk of his was in the basement storage room, left there in 1930. Ernest did not remember storing the trunk but he did recall that in the 1920s Louis Vuitton had made a special trunk for him. Ernest had wondered what had become of it.

. . . It was filled with a ragtag collection of clothes, menus, receipts, memos, hunting and fishing paraphernalia, skiing equipment, racing forms, correspondence and, on the bottom, something that elicited a joyful reaction from Ernest: "The notebooks! So that's where they were! Enfin!"

These notebooks became the source of *A Moveable Feast*, for which Hotchner provided the title, based on his recollection of an anecdote Hemingway had told him.

During an African safari, Hemingway was involved in a pair of plane crashes, leaving him bedridden and in severe pain. It has been suggested that the injuries he sustained, along with earlier concussions, may have damaged his brain. Still drinking heavily and often suffering from delusions, he underwent several rounds of electroshock therapy. But he had gone to work on the recovered notebooks. Between 1957 and the fall of 1960, he used those notes to write *A Moveable Feast*. The book was published posthumously in 1964, after Hemingway took his life with a shotgun at his home in Ketchum, Idaho, on July 2, 1961. He was sixty-one years old.

WHY YOU SHOULD READ IT

In September 2023, the *New York Times* reported that a four-page letter Ernest Hemingway wrote after his 1954 plane crashes in Africa sold at auction for more than $237,000. Just a curiosity? Or more testimony to the enduring allure of the writer called Papa? The subject of a recent PBS television documentary, Hemingway remains a larger-than-life figure in twentieth-century literature. *A Moveable Feast* is an important piece in understanding why.

This collection of books is a celebration of great ideas—and great writing. This is great writing—and helps fix Hemingway's place in the modern literary canon. So of course, read it for the masterful portraits Hemingway paints. By all means read it for its extraordinary view of an extraordinary moment in literary history. Certainly, read it for Hemingway's portraits of celebrated people in a now-legendary place and time. Who among us would not wish to sit at a café table nearby as Hemingway and James Joyce share a drink and talk about Ezra Pound and their mutual poverty? "He liked to listen to the actors, although he could not see them," writes Hemingway of Joyce, whose eyesight was notoriously poor. "He asked me to have a drink with him and we went to the Deux-Magots and ordered dry sherry although you will always read that he drank only Swiss white wine."

Hemingway's depictions of Gertrude Stein and F. Scott Fitzgerald, two of the most significant literary forces of the twentieth century, highlight *A Moveable Feast*. These alone are worth the price of admission. Stein, of course, offered her version of some of these events in *The Autobiography of Alice B. Toklas*. Hemingway provides a memorable counterpoint.

Also noteworthy here is the description of Hemingway and Fitzgerald making a car trip out of Paris together. They stop to eat and, of course, to drink:

> Downstairs I finished my dinner and thought about Scott. It was obvious he should not drink anything and I had not been taking good care of him. Anything that he drank seemed to stimulate him too much and then to poison him and I planned on the next day to cut all drinking to the minimum.

In the words of the late Joan Didion (see entry), Hemingway "was a writer who had in his time made the English language new, changed the rhythms of the way both his own and the next few generations would speak and write and think. The very grammar of a Hemingway sentence dictated, or was dictated by, a certain way of looking at the world, a way of looking but not joining, a way of moving through but not attaching, a kind of romantic individualism distinctly adapted to its time and source."

But a cautionary note: As I read Hemingway writing in the 1950s about the 1920s, I wondered how much his recollections as a young man were reshaped by the older, more famous Hemingway. In fact, in the preface to this material, written in 1960, Hemingway notes: "If the reader prefers, this book may be regarded as fiction."

In his depressed and somewhat tortured last years, Hemingway struggled to finish the memoir and the first edition of *A Moveable Feast* was edited and completed by his fourth wife and literary executor, Mary Hemingway. But Hemingway's friend and biographer A. E. Hotchner asserted that the book was Hemingway's writing: "These details are evidence that the book was a serious work that Ernest finished with his usual intensity, and that he certainly intended it for publication." It was published in 1964.

But the matter was not settled. A later edition appeared in 2009, edited by Seán Hemingway, Hemingway's grandson, reworked and published as *A Moveable Feast: The Restored Edition*. This revision has generated controversy since its appearance. Following its publication, biographer A. E. Hotchner wrote: "This new edition, also published by Scribner, has been extensively reworked by a grandson who doesn't like what the original said about his grandmother, Hemingway's second wife [Pauline Pfeiffer]."

Reviewing the revised edition, the late Christopher Hitchens (see entry) wrote of what he considered worthy restored sections of the book and concluded:

What is it exactly that explains the continued fascination of this rather slight book? Obviously, it is an ur-text of the American enthrallment with Paris. To be more precise, it is also a skeleton key to the American literary fascination with Paris (and contains some excellent tips for start-up writers, such as the advice to stop working while you still have something left to write the next day). There are the "wouldn't be without, even if you don't quite trust" glimpses of the magnetic Joyce and the personable Pound and the apparently wickedly malodorous Ford Madox Ford. Then there are the moments of amusingly uncynical honesty, as when Stein and Toklas met Ernest and Hadley and "forgave us for being in love and being married—time would fix that."

I read the 1964 original and will leave it to scholars to debate which of these dueling editions is definitive. Against this controversy, Hemingway's words in the closing chapter have added salience when he speaks to his regret over deceiving his first wife: "So you live day by day and enjoy what you have and do not worry. You lie and hate it and it destroys you and every day is more dangerous, but you live day to day as in a war."

Ernest Hemingway's reputation has undergone considerable revision, especially in light of some works now deemed racist and anti-Semitic. In *The Origin of Others* (see entry), Toni Morrison addresses what she calls Hemingway's "employment of colorism" that goes beyond his frequent use of the "N-word." Without looking past that blot, Hemingway's work and influence on generations of writers of many nations continue to demand we pay attention.

WHAT TO READ NEXT

There is no shortage of what to read next. Hemingway left a rich and varied reading list. If you are looking for more nonfiction, *Death in the Afternoon*, his 1932 account of the traditions and rituals of bullfighting, is not everyone's cup of tea, but it is still considered a classic. Besides the history of this spectacle, Hemingway discusses fear and courage—two themes that course powerfully through all of his work.

As for his fiction, the short story collections are ranked among Hemingway's best writing. But another cautionary note: I recently reread his much-admired short story "The Killers" and found it to be riddled with racial epithets.

"Just as the poet is a menace to conformity,
he is also a constant threat to political dictators."

The Courage to Create

— 1975 —

Rollo May

New York: W. W. Norton, 1994; 143 pages

OPENING WORDS

We are living at a time when one age is dying and the new age is not yet born.
We cannot doubt this as we look about us to see the radical changes in sexual
mores, in marriage styles, in family structures, in education, in religion, technology, and almost every other aspect of modern life. And behind it all is the
threat of the atom bomb, which recedes into the distance but never disappears.
To live with sensitivity in this age of limbo indeed requires courage.

SUMMARY

What is art? What makes an artist? What is the artist's greatest calling? Part
psychology class and part literary seminar, May's book explores the idea that
art, the imagination, and creativity are at the root of human experience.

To avert catastrophe—political, personal, or otherwise—we must value and elevate art and "seize the courage necessary to preserve our sensitivity, awareness, and responsibility" in the face of all the challenges posed by the modern world.

A former minister who pioneered what became known as existential and humanistic therapy, Rollo May sets out early to define his focal word: "Courage is not a virtue or value among other personal values like love or fidelity. It is the foundation that underlies and gives reality to all other virtues and personal values. Without courage our love pales into mere dependency. Without courage our fidelity becomes conformism."

Making distinctions between different types of courage, he briefly explores several varieties: physical, moral, social, and creative. But the central theme of the book's seven concise, essay-like chapters is the last of these, creative courage—which May calls the "most important courage of all."

Calling back to the oracles of Classical Greece and its philosophers in one chapter, May explores the importance of myths as universal truths, as he describes "the *creating of one's self*." He later describes the powerful sensation—the "Eureka moment" of creation:

> There is a curiously sharp sense of joy—or perhaps better expressed, a sense of mild ecstasy—that comes when you find the particular form required by your creation. Let us say you have been puzzling about it for days when suddenly you get the insight that unlocks the door—you see how to write that line, what combination of colors is needed in your picture, how to form that theme you may be writing for a class, or you hit upon the theory to fit your new facts. . . . I may have worked at my desk morning after morning trying to find a way to express some important idea. When my "insight" suddenly breaks through—which may happen when I am chopping wood in the afternoon—I experience a strange lightness in my step as though a great load were taken off my shoulders, a sense of joy on a deeper level that continues without any relation to the mundane tasks I may be performing at the time.

May finally relates this creative act to the strength and ability to change that can come when individuals confront their own anxieties. Creative courage is transformative—not only for individuals but for society.

ABOUT THE AUTHOR: ROLLO MAY

Born in Ada, Ohio, on April 21, 1909, Rollo May was the second oldest of six children and grew up in Marine City, Michigan. After his parents divorced and a sister was diagnosed with schizophrenia, May was often left by his mother to care for his younger siblings, which was a formative experience. He attended what is now Michigan State University, where he majored in English. But May transferred out, or was expelled by some accounts, after he and a friend started a campus magazine called the *Student*, which published an article critical of the state legislature. Shifting to Oberlin College in Ohio, May received a degree in English in 1930 with a minor concentration in Greek literature and history.

May then spent three years teaching at Anatolia College in Salonika, Greece. While there in 1932, he traveled to Vienna to hear lectures given by Alfred Adler, one of the most influential pioneers of psychotherapy. Adler had broken with colleague Sigmund Freud to develop a "second school" of Viennese psychotherapy usually called Individual Psychology.

Returning to the United States, May entered Union Theological Seminary in 1933. There he studied with the prominent German theologian Paul Tillich, obtaining his degree in 1938, the same year he married his first wife, Florence De Frees. Ordained as a Congregational minister, May served as pastor of a church in New Jersey but left the ministry after two years to pursue a degree in psychology.

While studying at Columbia University, May was diagnosed with tuberculosis in 1942 and spent more than a year in a sanatorium. During his treatment, he began to read the work of Danish religious philosopher Kierkegaard and other existentialists. Returning to Columbia, May earned his doctorate in clinical psychology, the first awarded by Columbia, and his dissertation was published in book form as *The Meaning of Anxiety* in 1950 (revised in 1977).

Teaching on the university level and developing his private practice as a psychotherapist, Rollo May emerged as a chief proponent of a new school of therapy based on his readings in existentialism. "In the 1950's, he was also one of the first thinkers in the field of psychotherapy to formulate a view of human nature that was not based on Freudian principles," Eric Pace wrote after May's death. "One of his main insights was a conviction that much of human behavior is motivated by a profound, underlying sense of anxiety, which he felt it was important to address in psychotherapy."

May was among the originators of the humanistic psychology movement, which moved away from the Freudian approach, which framed personal difficulties as residues of childhood trauma; or behaviorism, with its focus on an individual's response to the environment. Instead, humanistic psychology focuses on the ways in which people can grow. Finding these schools too pessimistic, key figures in the field of humanistic psychology, such as Abraham Maslow and Carl Rogers, proposed a hierarchy of human needs—physical safety, belongingness and love, and self-esteem, leading to "self-actualization," or the ability to fulfill one's potential. Moving from a concentration on analysis of the unconscious, the humanistic school offered far greater weight to free will, and emphasized the individual's ability to choose rather than being a victim of the past or of their environments. Flourishing in the 1960s, it later emerged as the "Human Potential Movement" and would influence new branches of therapy that offer paths for patients to control and determine their psychological well-being.

In the early 1970s, the discipline was described by writer David Dempsey in the *New York Times* as "a parallel movement that is to orthodox psychoanalysis what the Reformation was to Catholicism." Dempsey wrote: "This is an attempt to make the psyche available to the people in a language they can understand. Evangelical in spirit, the new 'human-potential' movement expresses itself in public soul-searching, encounter groups, body therapy, sensitivity sessions and similar forms of psychic petting designed to break down the invisible barriers that separate human beings from each other, and in so doing ease the alienation man feels within himself."

Hoping to take his work beyond numerous professional works on psychotherapeutic practice he had had written in the 1950s, May turned to writing for the general public, first with *Man's Search for Himself* (1953). His breakthrough book was *Love and Will* (1969), which became a major commercial success, was soon being studied at the university level, and won Phi Beta Kapa's Ralph Waldo Emerson Award for humane scholarship. It led to May being a sought-after speaker at such popular "human potential" meccas as the Esalen Institute in California. While the movement would later morph into the more wide-ranging "New Age" movement, May had taken psychoanalysis in a new direction.

In 1973, May wrote *Paulus: Reminiscence of a Friendship*, a memoir about his onetime professor, mentor, and friend theologian Paul Tillich, who died in 1965. Tillich's most famous work was *The Courage to Be* (1952) and May paid homage to Tillich with his title *The Courage to Create*.

For more than twenty years, May lectured at New York City's New School and served as a visiting professor at Harvard, Yale, Princeton, and other universities. He was presented with the Distinguished Career in Psychology Award by the American Psychological Association. After retiring from teaching, May continued to work in his private practice; he died at his home in Tiburon, California, of congestive heart failure on October 22, 1994.

WHY YOU SHOULD READ IT

The opening words of this book, speaking of an "age of limbo," are as appropriate in our time as they were when Rollo May wrote them nearly half a century ago. The "radical changes in sexual mores, in marriage styles, in family structures, in education, in religion, technology," he cites in his opening are—if anything—occurring in an even more radical fashion now than they were in the 1960s/1970s America he was discussing. That is certainly one reason his book still fits the times.

A celebration of the creative spirit and its central importance in shaping a life of meaning, Rollo May's book contains copious references to great works of literature, theater, and philosophy. Read it for May's fascinating range of insights into great works of art, especially those May cites as models of the courageous artist—among them Paul Cézanne, Samuel Beckett, James Joyce, and Aleksandr Solzhenitsyn.

Assessing May and other "humanistic psychologists," cultural critic Louis Menand writes: "As the psychologist and popular author Rollo May put it, creativity is not an aberrant quality, or something associated with psychic unrest—the tormented-artist type. On the contrary, creativity is 'the expression of normal people in the act of actualizing themselves.' It is associated with all good things: individualism, dignity, and humanity. And everyone has it. It just needs to be psychically unlocked."

May's examples of artistic courage are interspersed with insights he gathered during his long career as a psychotherapist. But May is not writing here for an academic audience or fellow therapists. His work illuminates these ideas and insights about the signature importance of embracing creativity in a style and language accessible to all. His emphasis, importantly, on creative courage as a form of resistance and rebellion makes the work worth reading today, in what is certainly an age of anxiety. Emphasizing the courage to create by artists and poets, May writes: "For they are the ones who threaten the status quo, which each society is devoted to protecting."

The relevance of May's work was underscored by his biographer, Robert Abzug, author of *Psyche and Soul in America: The Spiritual Odyssey of Rollo May* (2021): "His works lent historical breadth and reminders of traditional human virtues in a world where the technological innovations of big data, robotics, and artificial intelligence more and more have taken center stage—yet his was not a plea to turn back the clock. May appeals to those betwixt and between identities, whether of nationality, gender, or cultural aspiration, as well as to people who feel oppressed, alienated, and marginalized by modern society. . . . Love, courage, autonomy, integrity, freedom, responsibility, creativity—reading Rollo May's work today reminds us that these endangered values are perhaps even more important today to the crafting of a meaningful and fulfilling life as they were during May's own lifetime and for millennia past."

WHAT TO READ NEXT

Try Rollo May's first major success for a general audience, *Love and Will*. It was responsible for taking his ideas out of the world of professional psychiatry into a more popular form. Writing about the book at the height of May's fame in 1971, David Dempsey commented: "Although May's argument is complex and his style, at times, dense, the gist of his message is clear enough: man must reaffirm his basically human qualities and not simply cater to his biological needs. This means an emphasis on love rather than sex, on will (or 'intentionality,' as May refines the concept) rather than a passive running with life."

Among May's contemporaries was Erich Fromm, a German Jew who left for America in 1934 after the Nazi takeover. He cofounded the William Alanson White Institute, where Rollo May later taught. I suggest readers consider Fromm's many important titles. Two of the most influential and accessible are *Escape from Freedom* (1941) and *The Art of Loving: An Enquiry into the Nature of Love* (1956). Both are important short works.

One of the great influences on May was theologian Paul Tillich, whose book *The Courage to Be* would inspire May's title. In it, Tillich named three basic human anxieties: that we will die; moral anxiety; and the anxiety of meaninglessness—existential angst. Each of these, according to Tillich, demands a certain type of courage.

*"So successful has been the camera's role in beautifying the world
that photographs, rather than the world, have become
the standard of the beautiful."*

On Photography

— 1977 —

Susan Sontag

New York: Picador, 2001; 208 pages

OPENING WORDS

Humankind lingers unregenerately in Plato's cave, still reveling, its age-old
habit, in mere images of the truth. But being educated by photographs is
not like being educated by older, more artisanal images. For one thing, there
are a great many more images around, claiming our attention. The inventory
started in 1839 and since then just about everything has been photographed,
or so it seems. This very insatiability of the photographing eye changes the
terms of confinement in the cave, our world. In teaching us a new visual code,
photographs alter and enlarge our notions of what is worth looking at and what
we have a right to observe. They are a grammar, and even more importantly,
an ethics of seeing.

SUMMARY

Long before the advent of the ubiquitous camera-in-a-phone and the rise of the modern selfie, Susan Sontag was considering the import of photography on society and our lives. The proof is *On Photography*, which collects a series of essays that ran in the *New York Review of Books* from 1973 to 1977.

These collected essays demonstrate Sontag's extraordinary literary, philosophical, and artistic range—or "field of view," to borrow a photographic term. Reflecting on the evolution, artistry, and essential meaning of photography, she is equally versed in poetry and poets, such as Walt Whitman and Baudelaire, as she is in the pioneers of the camera such as Civil War photographer Mathew Brady and France's Eugène Atget, and modern masters such as Edward Steichen, Edward Weston, Berenice Abbott, and Diane Arbus.

One of Sontag's most celebrated essays examines Arbus, whose 1972 retrospective at New York's Museum of Modern Art was a record-setting milestone. Though she admired Arbus's craft, Sontag disdained the fascination Arbus exhibited for the extreme: nudists, giants, unsettling twins, and a wide range of unusual and sometimes grotesque characters: "For Arbus, both freaks and Middle America were equally exotic: a boy marching in a pro-war parade and a Levittown housewife were as alien as a dwarf or a transvestite: lower-middle-class suburbia was as remote as Times Square, lunatic asylums, and gay bars. . . . The subjects of Arbus's photographs are all members of the same family, inhabitants of a single village," wrote Sontag. "Only, as it happens, the idiot village is America."

The seven chapters in Sontag's book, plus a concluding anthology of quotations from notable photographers and other writers, trace photography's development and contemplate photography as a central, unignorable part of modern society. Photography, in Sontag's expansive view, does not simply just reflect the world. Photographs shape the way we look at the world.

In a stark moment in one of the essays, she writes:

One's first encounter with the photographic inventory of ultimate horror is a kind of revelation, the prototypically modern revelation:

a negative epiphany. For me, it was photographs of Bergen-Belsen and Dachau which I came across by chance in Santa Monica in July 1945. Nothing I have seen—in photographs or in real life—ever cut me as sharply, deeply, instantaneously. Indeed, it seems plausible to me to divide my life into two parts, before I saw those photographs (I was twelve) and after, though it was several years before I understood fully what they were about.

While photography has changed remarkably over the half century since these essays first appeared, the acuity of Sontag's insights into our long fascination with taking, and looking at, photographs is provocative. Like many great writers, she is forcing the reader to think. And the dazzling scope of Sontag's own thoughts and her ability to make connections between the everyday and the sublime have not been diminished by time: "Like guns and cars," she wrote, "cameras are fantasy machines whose use is addictive."

ABOUT THE AUTHOR: SUSAN SONTAG

A novelist, filmmaker, critic, activist, and very public intellectual, Susan Sontag made her most enduring mark as an essayist. At her death in 2004, the *New York Times* noted that she was, "one of the most lionized presences—and one of the most polarizing—in 20th-century letters."

Susan Sontag was born Susan Rosenblatt in Manhattan on January 16, 1933. Her father, Jack Rosenblatt, was a fur trader in China, and her mother, Mildred, often joined him there. Susan and her younger sister were left in the care of relatives or a nanny. After her father died of tuberculosis in China in 1939, Susan's mother moved the family to Tucson, Arizona, where she met Captain Nathan Sontag, a World War II veteran. They were later married, Susan took her stepfather's name, and the family relocated to Los Angeles.

Sontag graduated from high school before her sixteenth birthday and then spent a semester at the University of California, Berkeley. She transferred to the University of Chicago, studying literature and philosophy and graduating in 1951. While there, Sontag took a class with sociologist Philip Rieff, then a twenty-eight-year-old instructor. They married ten days after their meeting; Sontag was seventeen. In 1952, she gave birth to their son, David Rieff, later to become a writer and editor at the publishing house Farrar, Straus and Giroux, eventually editing some of his mother's work.

Moving to Boston when her husband took a teaching post at Brandeis, Sontag earned two master's degrees from Harvard, first in English literature in 1954 and another in philosophy the following year. She began studying for a doctorate in philosophy at Harvard but left to study abroad, first at Oxford and then at the Sorbonne in Paris. Sontag divorced Rieff in 1958 and landed in New York in 1959 with, in her words, "$70, two suitcases and a 7 year old." Sontag had also embarked on a relationship with the Cuban-born avant-garde playwright María Irene Fornés, whom she'd met in Paris, which continued after Sontag came to New York.

Back in America, student turned professor and new vistas opened. Teaching philosophy at City College, Sarah Lawrence, and Columbia, she became an editor at *Commentary*. She then wrote an experimental first novel, *The Benefactor*, published in 1963 by Farrar, Straus and Giroux, which has published all of her books.

In 1964, she made a resounding literary splash with an essay titled "Notes on 'Camp'"—published in the *Partisan Review*. In it, she argued that "popular art" and "high art" were both worthy of attention. Two years later, "Notes on 'Camp'" was included in Sontag's first essay collection, *Against Interpretation*, alongside pieces on Sartre, Camus, Ionesco, and modern French films. Reviewing it in the *New York Times*, Benjamin DeMott wrote: "Miss Sontag has written a ponderable, vivacious, beautifully living and quite astonishingly American book."

Becoming more politically vocal during the 1960s, Sontag opposed the war in Vietnam, made a controversial trip to Hanoi, and joined other writers in protesting a "war surtax" in 1968. She later made a controversial about-face declaring communism was "Fascism with a human face."

On Photography was published in 1977 and won the National Book Critics Circle Award for criticism. A year later, three long essays in the *New York Review of Books* were collected in the book *Illness as Metaphor*, in which she wrote about tuberculosis and cancer and how they were depicted in art and everyday language.

Sontag herself was being treated for breast cancer when she wrote this celebrated book. Her son, David Rieff, later wrote: "Part literary study, part polemic, it was a fervent plea to treat illness as illness, the luck of the genetic draw, and not the result of sexual inhibition, the repression of feeling, and the rest—that torrid brew of low-rent Wilhelm Reich and that mix of masochism and hubris that says that somehow people who got ill had brought it on themselves."

To her many admirers, her work was audacious and original. But she had critics as well. "Some branded Ms. Sontag an unoriginal thinker, a popularizer with a gift for aphorism who could boil down difficult writers for mass consumption," wrote Margalit Fox in Sontag's *New York Times* obituary. But Fox also noted: "No one ever called her dull." The same obituary quotes Mexican writer Carlos Fuentes, who compared Sontag to Erasmus, the Renaissance humanist. "Erasmus traveled with 32 volumes, which contained all the knowledge worth knowing," he said. "Susan Sontag carries it in her brain! I know of no other intellectual who is so clear-minded, with a capacity to link, to connect, to relate."

At the end of her life, Sontag was in a long-term relationship with the highly acclaimed photographer Annie Leibovitz, who had once photo-graphed Sontag for a vodka ad. She had become intellectual-as-celebrity, and readily identifiable. In Sontag's *New York Times* obituary, Margalit Fox wrote of her: "Through the decades her image—strong features, wide mouth, intense gaze and dark mane crowned in her middle years by a sweeping streak of white—became an instantly recognizable artifact of 20th-century popular culture."

After a bout of cervical cancer, Susan Sontag died of a form of leukemia at age seventy-one in New York on December 28, 2004. Her relationship with Leibovitz went unmentioned in many major obituaries, including those in the *New York Times* and *Los Angeles Times*.

"It seems that editors at what are, arguably, the nation's most respected (and liberal) newspapers believe that one personal detail cannot be men-tioned in even the most complete biographies—being a lesbian," author

Patrick Moore wrote in the *Los Angeles Times* shortly after her death. He concludes: "Susan Sontag was a brilliant, provocative writer who had vital, loving relationships with some of the most fascinating and creative women of her day. I believe that her intellectual accomplishments are even more compelling when one understands how her sexuality informed them. Sontag was often quoted as saying, 'Be serious, be passionate, wake up!' Let's hope that America's leading newspapers follow her advice."

WHY YOU SHOULD READ IT

I was taking a photography class at a community college when I was assigned Sontag's *Regarding the Pain of Others*, a shorter book published in 2003. A sequel of sorts to *On Photography*—which I had not yet read—it was my first reading experience of Sontag, and, frankly, it left me cold and unimpressed. I am sorry *On Photography* was not the assigned book—its writing is superlative and it remains one of the most influential works on the subject.

Whether or not you are interested in photography as art, as I am, read it because it is smart—very smart—opinionated, and thought-provoking. While familiarity with some of the writers and artists whose names cascade from Sontag's amazing intellectual catalog would be helpful, it is not a prerequisite to be familiar with names such as Steichen, Stieglitz, Weston, and Strand—to name a few. Many of the images she references can be readily accessed online.

"It was not a perfect book, as Sontag herself later agreed," writes Sontag biographer Benjamin Moser. "But it was a great book, its greatness residing not in its perfection but in its fecundity: its ability to provoke other thinkers, and to spur them to formulate new ideas of their own. It was the beginning of the conversation, not the end; and if we may never know whether it is possible to write about photography without reference to Susan Sontag, that is because hardly anyone has bothered to try."

Though the digital age has revolutionized picture taking, her comments still ring very true, as this more recent commentary attests: "While Sontag delved into a few photographers' careers, she was most prescient in her broader discussion of the medium's proliferation," Alina Chone writes in Artsy, an online art marketplace. "She referenced the camera's addictive nature, but warned that taking pictures only gives 'an appearance of participation'—our fevered adoption of Instagram today is the best evidence of her foresight. When we take a photo, we inherently distance ourselves from the world and people around us. Obsessive picture-taking is alienating—those with the most cluttered Instagram feeds, by Sontag's logic, may be the most isolated, regardless of what their sunny snapshots broadcast."

WHAT TO READ NEXT

To explore more Sontag, start with *Illness as Metaphor*, currently published together with a later book, *AIDS and Its Metaphors*, in which Sontag discussed the stigma of AIDS, as cancer patients had once been stigmatized. It is an important work in which she writes: "Illness is the night-side of life, a more onerous citizenship. Everyone who is born holds dual citizenship in the kingdom of the well and in the kingdom of the sick. Although we prefer to use only the good passport, sooner or later each of us is obliged, at least for a spell, to identify ourselves as citizens of that other place."

For other significant books on photography and photographs, I would single out *The Decisive Moment*, a 1952 classic work by French photographer Henri-Cartier Bresson; *Understanding a Photograph* by John Berger, author of *Ways of Seeing*; *The Family of Man*, the catalog of a landmark 1955 photographic exhibit at the Museum of Modern Art, edited by Edward Steichen, a great photographer who became director of MoMA's photography department; and last, *Let Us Now Praise Famous Men*, which combines the photography of Walker Evans with the writing of James Agee in a classic work of photojournalism documenting the Depression-era lives of sharecroppers.

"All the old questions—the original questions, sharply debated
at the beginning of Christianity—are being reopened:
How is one to understand the resurrection?"

The Gnostic Gospels

— 1979 —

Elaine Pagels

New York: Vintage Books, 1989; 182 pages

OPENING WORDS

"Jesus Christ rose from the grave." With this proclamation, the Christian
church began. This may be the fundamental element of Christian faith;
certainly it is the most radical. Other religions celebrate cycles of birth and
death: Christianity insists that in one unique historical moment, the cycle
reversed, and a dead man came back to life! For Jesus' followers this was
the turning point in world history, the sign of its coming end. Orthodox
Christians since then have confessed in the creed that Jesus of Nazareth,
"crucified, dead, and buried," was raised "on the third day." Many today
recite that creed without thinking about what they are saying, much less
actually believing it.

SUMMARY

"Jesus loves me—this I know / For the Bible tells me so," goes a familiar 1859 hymn sung by generations of Christian children in Sunday school.

For most of Christianity's two-thousand-year history, devout believers accepted the story of Jesus told in the New Testament's Gospels. It was the truth, the whole truth, and nothing but the truth; the Bible told them so. But biblical scholars have long debated the historical accuracy of those Gospels and their many translations, and while other early Christian writings were known to exist, conversations about them did not reach the ears of most of the faithful.

The discovery of a set of ancient texts in Egypt in 1945 changed that. At the heart of this book, for which biblical scholar Elaine Pagels won both the National Book Award and National Book Critics Circle Award, is the story of a set of alternative writings about the life of Jesus that raise fundamental questions about what is considered "Gospel Truth."

Recounting the roundabout path these books took from discovery in 1945 to the wider revelation of their contents in the 1970s, Pagels illuminates the import of the unearthing of these early writings and provides a fascinating history of how the first church leaders defined what was acceptable and what was "heresy." Eventually called the Gnostic Gospels, these very old documents raise profound questions about some of Christianity's fundamental tenets.

In a highly accessible style, Pagels explores the revolutionary impact on the origins of Christianity uncovered in these ancient texts. She examines many questions: What are Gnostic Gospels? Why were they hidden away? How did they come to light? And what do they mean?

Derived from the Greek *gnosis*, the word "gnostic" loosely means "those who have knowledge." "Gnostic" is used to describe an early Christian sect that stressed the idea of inner knowing for redemption and salvation, as opposed to the more traditional Christian idea that salvation comes through acceptance of Jesus Christ and his death and resurrection. Gnostics believed, for instance, that Jesus's rising from the dead was a spiritual act rather than an actual physical event.

Written in Coptic, a North African dialect, the Gnostic Gospels contain sayings and describe events similar to many of those in the New Testament. Pagels explores how these fifty-five texts are also very different: in one passage she cites, Jesus is described kissing Mary Magdalene on the lips. Suppressed by early church leaders who denounced the writings as heresy, these alternative stories, teachings, and sayings offer unique views of a different Jesus, potentially shaking the two-thousand-year-old foundations of established Christianity.

ABOUT THE AUTHOR: ELAINE PAGELS

Born on February 13, 1943, in Palo Alto, California, Elaine Hiesey was the daughter of nominal Protestants. They were, according to a review of Pagels's 2018 memoir, *Why Religion?*, "an aloof biologist father and a mother who played Chopin on the piano but could offer comfort only when her daughter pretended to be ill." In an act of adolescent defiance, young Elaine began attending an evangelical church, as David Remnick noted in the *New Yorker*, "partly out of curiosity, partly out of a teen-ager's search for the precise way to drive her parents crazy."

By 1960, she had abandoned the church and started skipping school to drink coffee in Menlo Park with a group that included a young Jerry Garcia, according to book reviewer Mark Epstein. "Her first brush with death came when Garcia and three friends had a deadly car accident, throwing him through the windshield and killing their 16-year-old mutual friend. Garcia credited the accident with giving him purpose—the moniker 'Grateful Dead' is said to spring from it—while Pagels began to ask the questions that form the backbone of this book. 'Where do the dead go? And how to go on living?'"

After receiving a B.A. in history from Stanford in 1964 and an M.A. in classics a year later, she briefly studied dance with the Martha Graham company. But then she decided to apply to Harvard for a doctoral degree in religion, where she encountered considerable sexism—the message she got was that women didn't study religion. While there, she married physicist Heinz Pagels, a research scientist, writer, and, eventually, the executive

director of the New York Academy of Science. After graduating with a
Ph.D. in religious studies in 1970, Elaine Pagels joined the faculty of Barnard
College. Four years later she was made chair of the religion department,
and in 1982 she left for a teaching post at Princeton.

By then, Elaine Pagels had written a number of books on early Christianity and the Gnostics. A reader of Coptic, Pagels was part of the international team of scholars that issued an English translation of the ancient texts
discovered at Nag Hammadi in Egypt in 1945. That work led to publication
in 1979 of *The Gnostic Gospels*, which became a popular best seller among
general readers as well as an academic audience.

Then, in the space of less than two years, her success and accomplishments were catastrophically shattered. After she and Heinz Pagels adopted
a daughter in 1986, their six-year-old son, Mark, died from a respiratory
ailment in 1987. After adopting another son, the family went on vacation
in Colorado, where Heinz Pagels died in a rock-climbing accident in 1988;
it was the same year Pagels published her highly praised book *Adam, Eve,
and the Serpent*.

These losses inspired Pagels to write *The Origin of Satan* in 1995. "For
people more religious—well, some might get angry at God, but that made
no sense to me," she told the *New Yorker*. "In the ancient Church, they got
mad at Satan. That seemed to make more sense. And so I had to ask, What
is Satan? What's the Devil?" A later book, *Beyond Belief: The Secret Gospel
of Thomas*, argues that this Gnostic Gospel was excluded from the Christian
canon because it presented a vision of Jesus totally at odds with the orthodoxy
of early Christian leaders who suppressed it and other "heretical" writings.

Winner of several prestigious awards, including a Rockefeller Fellow-
ship, a Guggenheim Fellowship, and the MacArthur Fellowship in 1981,
Pagels has written several other books exploring religion as well as a memoir,
Why Religion?: A Personal Story, published in 2018.

WHY YOU SHOULD READ IT

At #72 on the Modern Library's 100 Best Nonfiction list, *The Gnostic Gospels*
is a fascinating and eminently readable book that plumbs the depths of some

of the most basic questions about Christian beliefs and how one first-century school of Christian thought suppressed any others and eventually came to dominate Western history.

Read it first for the story of an archeological discovery as thrilling as an Indiana Jones movie. In 1945, an Egyptian farmer and his brother were digging near the town of Naj'Ḥammādī—more widely transliterated as Nag Hammadi—an area filled with caves in Upper Egypt. The men uncovered a large earthen jar and broke it open, hoping to find gold or other valuables. Instead, the brothers found some old papyrus pages, bound in leather. The men took them home, where their mother burned some of the books as kindling for a cook fire.

The intrigue deepened when the two men killed another man in a long-standing blood feud. With the police arriving to investigate the murder, one of the men who found the ancient documents turned them over to a local priest, fearing the police would discover them. Eventually, the Egyptian authorities got wind of the discovery and confiscated most of the books and placed them in Cairo's Coptic Museum. Meanwhile, another part of the find was smuggled out of Egypt and sold in America. The cat was out of the Coptic bag.

Learning of their existence, a biblical scholar traveled to Cairo and viewed photographs of the ancient manuscripts. In one of the first documents, he read this opening line: "These are the secret words which the living Jesus spoke, and which the twin, Judas Thomas, wrote down."

For Christians with a modicum of biblical knowledge and a Sunday school version of Jesus's life, the questions Pagels explores through these Gnostic Gospels may surprise and even rattle their faith. Her revelations portray an early form of Christian belief, one that was eventually overwhelmed by the church leaders who held power in the former Roman Empire and much of the Western world for centuries. For non-Christian readers, Pagels offers an important exploration of a set of beliefs that have dominated Western thought and, in no small measure, helped establish the second-place status of women in society.

"Through a careful reading of the fifty-two sacred texts that survived—they are Coptic translations of Greek originals, some as old as the four

Gospels—Pagels made it clear that early Christianity was far more complicated than anyone had ever imagined," writes the *New Yorker*'s David
Remnick. "A wildly diverse compendium of poems, chants, myths, gospels,
pagan documents, and spiritual instructions, the texts are distinct evidence
of fierce theological debate and of an alternative tradition within early
Christianity—a kind of mystical variant, much like the Zen tradition in
Buddhism, Kabbalah in Judaism, Sufism in Islam. What was more, Pagels
argued, the early Church Fathers, in their attempt to eliminate this more
experiential Christianity in favor of building an orthodox institution—
a universal, or catholic, church—declared the texts to be heretical."

WHAT TO READ NEXT

Of Pagels's other works, two of the most accessible and interesting are: the
1988 book *Adam, Eve, and the Serpent,* which explores the Eden story of
Creation in Genesis (see entry) and its impact on views of free will, how
sexuality came to be considered sinful, and the place of women through
history; and *The Origin of Satan,* which explores how Jewish and Christian
traditions transformed the concept of the Devil. "Characteristically brief
and lucid, it is an attempt to describe the evolving shape of the Devil
in the sacred Judeo-Christian literature and the rise of demonization, a
practice that has haunted two thousand years of history," writes David
Remnick. "For Pagels, demonization is a crucial and terrifying component
of Christianity. What began as a minority sect's rhetorical strategy, a way of
defining and asserting itself, became a majority religion's moral, and even
psychological, justification for persecution: first of Jews, then of Romans
and of heretics—of all opponents, real or imagined."

"Television's strongest point is that it brings personalities into our hearts,
not abstractions into our heads."

Amusing Ourselves to Death:
Public Discourse in the Age
of Show Business

— 1985 —

Neil Postman

New York: Penguin Books, 2006; with an introduction by Andrew Postman;
183 pages

EXCERPT

Today, we must look to the city of Las Vegas, Nevada, as a metaphor of our
national character and aspiration, its symbol a thirty-foot-high carboard picture of a slot machine and a chorus girl. For Las Vegas is a city entirely devoted
to the idea of entertainment, and as such proclaims the spirit of a culture
in which all public discourse increasingly takes the form of entertainment.
Our politics, religion, news, athletics, education and commerce have been
transformed into congenial adjuncts of show business, largely without protest
or even much popular notice. The result is that we are a people on the verge
of amusing ourselves to death.

SUMMARY

Originally published in 1985, when Apple's Macintosh was just a newborn, this powerful polemic warned of the threat that mass media—and specifically television—posed to our culture and politics. The book identified television programming, everything from MTV to *Sesame Street* and CNN, as the chief culprit in America's spiritual, cultural, and political decline. It came at a moment when the White House was occupied by a former movie star, who proved very adept in using television to project himself as the perfectly realized image of a president.

The late Neil Postman was not the first to decry the dangers of television and its effects on our democracy, let alone our minds and spirits. Television had its critics since the "tube" came to dominate the American landscape in the late 1950s; in his first speech as chairman of the Federal Communications Commission in 1961, Newton N. Minow famously decried what he called a "vast wasteland." A year later, historian and Librarian of Congress Daniel Boorstin condemned the dangers of public relations and celebrity worship in his landmark book *The Image: A Guide to Pseudo-Events in America* (1962; reissued 1992).

But well before the use of the personal computer, the smartphone, and social media combined to severely worsen these problems, Postman diagnosed the dangers in this thoughtful, accessible, and provocative book. Looking beyond the mere content presented on television screens, Postman explored how its central function—to entertain and to sell—was corrupting society in ways he considered alarming.

With its alluring visual images, television reduces everything—including politics, news, and history—to mere entertainment, Postman argued. While his book appeared soon after the fateful year of 1984—with its ominous Orwellian overtones—Postman believed that the more accurate and frightening prediction of what would come to pass was found in Aldous Huxley's *Brave New World*:

In the Huxleyan prophecy, Big Brother does not watch us, by his choice. We watch him, by ours. There is no need for wardens or gates or Ministries of Truth. When a population becomes distracted by trivia, when cultural life is redefined as a perpetual round of entertainments, when serious public conversation becomes a form of baby-talk, when, in short, a people become an audience and their public business a vaudeville act, then a nation finds itself at risk; culture-death is a clear possibility.

It is fair to say that we are living in the absolute fulfillment of that prophecy. Whether we can do anything about it is the $64 billion question of our times.

ABOUT THE AUTHOR: NEIL POSTMAN

Born on March 8, 1931, the educator, social critic, and media theoretician Neil Postman grew up in a Yiddish-speaking Brooklyn household. After attaining a B.S. from the State University of New York at Fredonia, he earned an M.A. in 1955 and a doctorate of education in 1958 from Columbia University's Teachers College. He taught for a year in California, before returning to New York to take a post at New York University's School of Education. There he later founded the school's Media Ecology program to study the effect of media and communications on people and, more specifically, how new information media create new cultures. He continued to teach at NYU for more than forty years.

In 1969, Postman and coauthor Charles Weingartner published *Teaching as a Subversive Activity*, which criticized rote learning and other traditional education methods. The book advocated instead for what is called inquiry-based education, in which the focus is on encouraging students to ask questions, an approach that seemed to work well for Socrates and Plato (see entry).

Over a long career, Postman wrote more than two hundred newspaper and magazine articles and more than twenty books, increasingly focused on the threat posed by the overwhelming presence of technology in modern life. According to Elaine Woo, in the *Los Angeles Times* writing after Postman's death, "Postman avoided computers; he wrote all of his

books in longhand, generally over bagels and coffee at a favorite diner in
Queens. He did not use a cell phone; he did not e-mail. He was probably,
by his own proud admission, 'one of the few people that you're likely
to . . . ever meet who is opposed to the use of personal computers in
school.'"

Woo also related how Postman had once rejected buying a car with
cruise control, asking why he would need such a feature: "The car salesman
mustered a reply after a moment, suggesting that cruise control was for
people who had trouble keeping their foot on the gas pedal. In his many
years of driving, Postman countered, stepping on the gas had never been
a problem. In his view, there usually was no good answer to his searingly
simple question. He always followed up with another zinger: 'Are you using
the technology, or is it using you?'"

Postman's 1982 book *The Disappearance of Childhood* argued that printing and literacy made it possible to separate adults—who could read—from
children, who could not. Not so television. TV eliminated that sharp divide
between childhood and adulthood because *watching* fundamentally differs
from *reading*. As Wolfgang Saxon wrote of Postman's contention, "It did
so . . . by steeping the minds of children in vast amounts of information
once reserved for their elders and subjecting them to all the desires and
conflicts of the adult world."

Perhaps his most influential book, *Amusing Ourselves to Death* was
followed in 1992 by *Technopoly: The Surrender of Culture to Technology*, in
which Postman was critical of what he called the deification of technology
as people surrendered their autonomy to the seeming advantages of technology's advances.

Many of Postman's books addressed education and the need to rethink
what American education is and does. That urgent question has only grown
more profound in an era of grotesque distortion, misinformation, conspiracy theories, partisan assaults on truth, history, and books—and the
increasingly sophisticated technology of artificial intelligence entering the
classroom.

Neil Postman died of lung cancer in October 2003 at the age of
seventy-two.

WHY YOU SHOULD READ IT

A book warning about television's dangers in the age of the internet, Instagram, and Tik Tok? Yes, perhaps now more than ever.

In this collection of works that are consequential, timely, relevant, well written, and force us to think, Postman's book remains a significant indictment of how the media—in the broadest sense—affects our lives and our politics. If anything, "death by amusement" is more threatening today than it was in 1985. Politics around the world, not just in contemporary America, has been swallowed up by a focus on entertainers of many stripes, such as the late Italian media tycoon turned prime minister Silvio Berlusconi.

Television's quick "sound bite," perfected by cable news, has been turned into the memes of social media—quick visuals that are intended as clickbait. Instead of thoughtful people of stature, the media—not television alone—has increasingly elevated showbiz value over seriousness. We have certainly arrived at that moment, cited in the opening lines earlier, when "a people become an audience and their public business a vaudeville act." A presidential hopeful, with no actual experience, can make a good media impression—"good copy" in old journalism jargon—and be rewarded with massive airtime and social media exposure before anyone critically addresses such a candidate's views, no matter how preposterous or dishonest.

Postman saw all of this coming. Written decades ago, his book offers a profound warning of the clear, present, and overwhelmingly dangerous power of media—not just old school television. What Postman saw in television has simply been amped up by new technology. His warning, drawn from Aldous Huxley in *Brave New World*, urges us to consider the toll that our media addiction is taking: that people were laughing in a mindless way, "but that they did not know what they were laughing about and why they had stopped thinking."

On their 1991 album *Nevermind*, Nirvana put it somewhat differently in "Smells like Teen Spirit": "I feel stupid and contagious / Here we are now, entertain us."

Let's be clear-eyed. So much is on the line. Dictators such as Mussolini and Hitler knew that controlling entertainment, like sports and films, and other forms of media, was central to their propaganda efforts. But because of new technology, the power emanating from media sources is more evident and pervasive than ever. Donald Trump became president of the United States for a variety of reasons that will be long debated. But certainly, many people may have voted for him simply because they believed that he was a successful businessman—and one who entertained millions. By many accounts, he was not. He just played one on television. He put his "reality TV" persona on steroids with the power of social media, largely nonexistent when Postman wrote this book. Early in the 2016 presidential primary campaign, the *New York Times* cited that candidate Trump had collected "$2 Billion Worth of Free Media," which was, according to reporters Nicholas Confessore and Karen Yourish, "about twice the all-in price of the most expensive presidential campaigns in history."

But the former president's political success and the current landscape of American politics are prime evidence of the fundamental warning that Neil Postman laid out about the public's desire to be entertained. In 1985, Postman wrote:

> This is the lesson of all great television commercials: They provide a slogan, a symbol or a focus that creates for viewers a comprehensive and compelling image of themselves. In the shift from party politics to television politics, the same goal is sought. We are not permitted to know who is best at being President or Governor or Senator, but whose image is best in touching and soothing the deep reaches of our discontent. . . . As Xenophanes remarked twenty-five centuries ago, men always make their gods in their own image. But to this, television politics has added a new wrinkle: Those who would be gods refashion themselves into images the viewers would have them be.

WHAT TO READ NEXT

At the top of this list, I place *Media Control: The Spectacular Achievements of Propaganda* (2nd edition, 2002) by Noam Chomsky, the noted linguistics professor, author, and outspoken activist. Much of Chomsky's academic writing is highly challenging. But this is a direct warning about the role of media in contemporary politics, written in very accessible style.

Criticism of mass media in all its forms, along with the omnipresent consumerism that it has created, has been the subject of many writers such as journalist Vance Packard, whose 1957 book, *The Hidden Persuaders*, revealed the sophisticated psychological techniques used to motivate consumers. I still recommend it. Historian Daniel Boorstin's *The Image*—cited earlier—is now somewhat dated, as it lacks reference to recent advances in technology. Nonetheless, it offers a fundamental text for understanding the media environment as it evolved and in which we now live.

Marshall McLuhan, the influential Canadian media critic and communications theorist, must also be counted as one of Postman's most significant predecessors. I recommend reading his valuable *The Medium Is the Massage*, a short book, filled with images as well as words. Produced with graphic designer Quentin Fiore and Jerome Agel in 1967, the book was supposed to be titled *The Medium Is the Message*, one of McLuhan's central concepts; it reflects his idea that television and other electronic media fundamentally re-formed our thought processes.

After a typesetter's error, however, McLuhan decided to go with the altered title. He opens the book with the words "The medium, or process of our time—electric technology—is reshaping and restructuring patterns of social interdependence and every aspect of our personal life. It is forcing us to reconsider and reevaluate practically every thought, every action, and every institution formerly taken for granted."

For me, Joe McGinniss's *The Selling of the President: 1968* was another extremely influential book. I still recommend it for its analysis of the 1968 presidential race, in which Richard Nixon's image was reshaped and he was "sold like a pack of cigarettes"—the image on the original jacket of the book. The fact that Roger Ailes, who would later lead Fox News, is a central player in the book adds to its currency.

More recently, the book *Affluenza: How Overconsumption Is Killing Us*, by John De Graaf, David Wann, and Thomas Naylor, addresses the degree to which consumerism has reshaped society and added to the problems of inequity facing the world that needs to look to a more sustainable future. I imagine Thoreau would agree.

Finally, cited briefly in my introduction is *The Shallows: What the Internet Is Doing to Our Brains*. A Pulitzer Prize finalist by Nicholas Carr, the book expands on his 2008 *Atlantic* magazine article that asked: "Is Google Making Us Stupid?"

"Why are we reading, if not in hope of beauty laid bare,
life heightened and its deepest mystery probed?"

The Writing Life

— 1989 —

Annie Dillard

New York: Harper Perennial, 2013; 111 pages

OPENING WORDS

When you write, you lay out a line of words. The line of words is a miner's pick, a woodcarver's gouge, a surgeon's probe. You wield it, and it digs a path you follow. Soon you find yourself deep in new territory. Is it a dead end, or have you located the real subject? You will know tomorrow, or this time next year.

SUMMARY

Best known for her Pulitzer Prize–winning *Pilgrim at Tinker Creek*, Annie Dillard started out writing poetry and moved on to nonfiction, and then eventually to novels. That's a literary hat trick. So, it is entirely appropriate that Dillard—who taught writing at the university level for many years—wrote this meditation on writing.

And it is a meditation, rather than a book of "advice" or "how to." It does not tell you much about proper grammar, or how a book should be structured, or how much dialogue should be included in a novel. It is, as the title suggests, about the writer's deep interior struggle to carve out the path she describes in the opening lines.

In seven concise, intense chapters, Dillard moves from the personal experience of writing—"I do not so much write a book as sit up with it, as with a dying friend," she writes—to the seemingly remote subject of stunt flying. Behind it all is the idea that writing is a demanding art. To read the insights of a writer so widely esteemed is to get a glimpse of the inner life of the artist at work:

> One of the few things I know about writing is this: spend it all, shoot it, play it, lose it, all, right away, every time.

ABOUT THE AUTHOR: ANNIE DILLARD

Winner of the Pulitzer Prize for General Nonfiction in 1975, Dillard was born Annie Doak on April 30, 1945, to Frank and Pam Doak in Pittsburgh, Pennsylvania. Attending public school until the fifth grade, she moved on to an all-girls private school and then went to Hollins College in Roanoke, Virginia, earning a B.A. in 1967. Dillard added an M.A. in 1968 with a thesis on Henry David Thoreau (see entry). While still a student at the school, she married her creative-writing teacher, Richard Dillard, in 1967.

In 1974 Annie Dillard published a first collection of poetry, *Tickets for a Prayer Wheel*, and, that same year, *Pilgrim at Tinker Creek*. A contemplation of the natural world, *Pilgrim at Tinker Creek* was born from journals Dillard began keeping in 1972 while exploring the area near Roanoke. Though it contained pieces she had earlier published in magazines, it was not a collection of essays but a unitary whole that invoked comparisons to Thoreau's *Walden*, achieving wide popular acclaim as well as a Pulitzer Prize.

"The book is a form of meditation, written with a headlong urgency, about *seeing*," novelist Eudora Welty wrote in a review. She added: "Annie Dillard had found the central metaphor for her book; it is the vision, the spiritual conception, that she will spend her days in solitude tramping the Roanoke creek banks and the Blue Ridge mountainside in search of herself."

After ten years of marriage, Dillard and her first husband divorced and she moved to Bellingham, Washington, becoming a writer-in-residence at Western Washington University, where she remained until 1978. While there, she married anthropology professor Gary Clevidence in 1976, with whom she had a daughter, Rosie, born in 1984. They divorced in 1988. Dillard then married Robert D. Richardson, a prizewinning literary biographer whom she met after writing him a letter praising his biography, *Henry Thoreau: A Life of the Mind*.

Annie Dillard's later books include *Holy the Firm* and *Teaching a Stone to Talk*, which continued to explore the themes of spirituality and the natural world she had written about in *Pilgrim at Tinker Creek*. "One way or another," writes Mary Cantwell, "Annie Dillard is forever thinking about God."

In 1987, Dillard published a best-selling autobiographical memoir, *An American Childhood*, and then turned to fiction with a first novel, *The Living*, set in the world of loggers in the Pacific Northwest. Her second novel, *The Maytrees*, is a compressed story about a married couple, set on post–World War II Cape Cod; it was chosen by the *New York Times* as one of the Top Ten Books of 2007.

Having joined the faculty of Wesleyan University in 1980, Dillard taught there until 2002, when she retired as professor emerita. In 2015, Dillard received the National Humanities Medal from President Obama.

WHY YOU SHOULD READ IT

"*The Writing Life* (1989) is an embarrassing nonfiction narrative fixed somewhat and republished by Harper Perennial 1998," professes writer Annie Dillard on her own website.

Ignore her self-deprecating description and read it. Even if you are not a writer, but, perhaps, especially if you are.

As a writer of many years, I must confess I never put too much stock in books about writing—with one exception. I keep *The Elements of Style* on my bookshelf, next to the dictionary and thesaurus—yes, they are physical books I use almost daily. *Elements* is a classic by William Strunk Jr. and E. B. White about the rules for writing rather than a meditation on writing. (Always remember: some rules are meant to be broken.)

Writing, I have always believed, is pretty much like ballet or basketball. Success in either does not usually come from reading a book about how to do a plié or a crossover dribble. And like ballet or basketball, writing only improves with steady, regular, and committed practice. Write it. Then write it again. Then write it again.

But over time, I have learned that there can be real beauty and wisdom in some books about writing. And this is one of them. It is filled with passages, many of which have little to do with the actual craft of writing, that are still teaching moments because they offer a glimpse of Dillard's pure, poetic prose.

In candor, not everyone agrees. In a 1989 *New York Times* review, writer Sara Maitland wrote of her admiration for Dillard and described *The Writing Life* as "full of joys." Maitland writes: "She knows so many things—stories and histories and facts and scraps—and she probes them for meaning so surely. . . . Unfortunately, the bits do not add up to a book."

I respectfully disagree. The bits are small gems, polished by Dillard's exceptional style. So, read and decide for yourself.

WHAT TO READ NEXT

In the realm of Dillard's other short works, consider *Teaching a Stone to Talk: Expeditions and Encounters*, a collection of writing about the natural world in which she finds deep meaning in what she encounters, from an eclipse to mangrove trees. Also consider *For the Time Being*, more nature writing, and *Holy the Firm*, a very short book about two years Dillard spent in solitude. All three books are about the natural world and all also explore profound spiritual themes.

Certainly, try Dillard's most notable work, the 1975 Pulitzer Prize winner, *Pilgrim at Tinker Creek*, the story of a year spent in Virginia's Roanoke Valley:

> I am sitting under a sycamore by Tinker Creek. I am really here, alive on the intricate earth under trees. But under me, directly under the weight of my body on the grass, are other creatures, just as real, for whom this moment, this tree, is "it." Take just the top inch of soil, the world squirming right under my palms. In the top inch of forest soil, biologists found "an average of 1,356 creatures present in each square foot, including 865 mites, 265 spring tails, 22 millipedes, 19 adult beetles and various numbers of 12 other forms. . . ." The chrysalids of butterflies linger here too, folded, rigid, and dreamless. I might as well include these creatures in this moment, as best I can.

Pilgrim at Tinker Creek was named to the Modern Library's 100 Best Nonfiction list (#89) and was ranked by readers at the New York Public Library on its 125th anniversary as one of the "125 Books We Love."

Dillard has also written two works of fiction, *The Living* and *The Maytrees*, novels I have not yet read but will add to the To-Be-Read list, and an acclaimed autobiography, *An American Childhood*, her evocative recollection of growing up and coming of age in Pittsburgh in the 1950s and 1960s.

For another take on writing, I recommend Stephen King's *On Writing: A Memoir of the Craft*. The book is part writing class and part delightful memoir by one of the most successful writers in modern times, who points out in a "Second Foreword" to *On Writing*: "This is a short book about writing because most books about writing are filled with bullshit."

As Stephen King himself would agree and points out in that same foreword, those looking for a guide to writing well are advised to turn to *The Elements of Style* by William Strunk Jr. and E. B. White. The book is based on a writing manual created in 1920 by Professor Strunk for his

Cornell students, one of whom was E. B. White. During his long career as a *New Yorker* writer and author of such classics as *Charlotte's Web*, White revised and added to Strunk's manual; it was reissued as *The Elements of Style* in 1959. A fundamental guide to clear, concise writing, it was named one of the "100 Most Important Nonfiction Books" by *Time* magazine. It is certainly on my list as well as on my bookshelf.

Finally, I have mentioned John McPhee's work several times throughout this collection. I'll further add *Draft No. 4*, a 2017 collection of eight McPhee essays on writing that initially appeared, in slightly different form, in the *New Yorker*.

*"Journalists who swallow the subject's account whole and publish it
are not journalists but publicists."*

The Journalist and the Murderer

— 1990 —

Janet Malcolm

New York: Vintage Books, 1990; 163 pages

OPENING WORDS

Every journalist who is not too stupid or too full of himself to notice what
is going on knows that what he does is morally indefensible. He is a kind of
confidence man, preying on people's vanity, ignorance, or loneliness, gaining
their trust and betraying them without remorse. Like the credulous widow who
wakes up one day to find the charming young man and all her savings gone,
so the consenting subject of a piece of nonfiction writing learns—when the
article or book appears—*his* hard lesson. Journalists justify their treachery in
various ways according to their temperaments.

SUMMARY

It is a curious coincidence that this selection by Janet Malcolm follows the work of Annie Dillard. They are two of the most significant writers of recent times, but their approaches to writing, and writing about writing, exist at different poles.

Positioned at #97 on the Modern Library's 100 Best Nonfiction Books of the Twentieth Century list, *The Journalist and the Murderer* is the late Janet Malcolm's dissection of a notorious case in which Dr. Jeffrey Mac-Donald, a Green Beret, was convicted of murdering his pregnant wife and two daughters nine years earlier.

Begun as a *New Yorker* series, Malcolm's book offers a great deal of courtroom testimony, but her focus is not on the actual crime. Malcolm is more interested in the unusual suit that followed Dr. MacDonald's conviction in a case that attracted almost as much attention as the 1979 murder trial.

In 1984, the imprisoned Jeffrey MacDonald sued author Joe McGinniss for fraud and breach of contract. He accused the writer of pretending that he believed in the doctor's innocence to gain his confidence and access to MacDonald's defense—and state of mind. Factoring into MacDonald's claim was Joe McGinniss's book *Fatal Vision*, published in 1983, which did not take MacDonald's side in the case. In fact, McGinniss claimed he had become convinced of the doctor's guilt.

With the earlier crime and this unusual suit as background, Janet Malcolm explores the uneasy relationship between journalists and their subjects. Ending with a hung jury—no spoiler, we learn that up front—the trial revealed that "five of the six jurors were persuaded that a man who was serving three consecutive life sentences for the murder of his wife and two small children was deserving of more sympathy than the writer who deceived him."

In the course of her own examination of the case, Malcolm would interview and correspond with both Joe McGinniss and the convicted Dr. MacDonald, as well as attorneys and other writers connected to both the murder trial and the 1984 fraud trial. She writes of being thrust into a situation not unlike the one she is trying to explore in this book. As Malcolm's own opening words describe the journalist's motus operandi, "He is a kind of confidence man, preying on people's vanity, ignorance, or loneliness, gaining their trust and betraying them without remorse. . . . Journalists justify their treachery in various ways according to their temperaments."

Like McGinniss and other journalists, Malcolm must enter into a similar kind of relationship with her interview subjects. She writes: "Unlike other relationships that have a purpose beyond themselves and are clearly delineated as such (dentist-patient, lawyer-client, teacher-student), the writer-subject relationship seems to depend for its life on a kind of fuzziness or murkiness, if not utter covertness, of purpose. If everybody put his cards on the table, the game would be over. The journalist must do his work in a kind of deliberately induced state of moral anarchy."

To be clear, Janet Malcolm is not reopening the murder case but using it to explore and expose the morality—or lack of it—of journalism as a calling. As Katherine Q. Seelye wrote in Malcolm's *New York Times* obituary, "Whatever Ms. Malcolm was writing about, her real subject was often the writing process itself—the slipperiness of truth, the perils of the writer-subject relationship, the ethical choices that writers are constantly called to make. One of the through lines in her work was a merciless view of journalism, never mind that she was one of its most prominent practitioners."

ABOUT THE AUTHOR: JANET MALCOLM

Born on July 8, 1934, in Prague, in what was then Czechoslovakia, Jana Klara Wienerová was the eldest daughter of a well-to-do Jewish family. Both parents were professionals: her father, Josef Wiener, a psychiatrist and neurologist; her mother, Hanna Taussigova Wiener, a lawyer. When Jana was almost five, the parents cobbled together a bribe sufficient to obtain an exit visa from Nazi officials. With Jana and her sister, Marie, a toddler, the family boarded a train bound for Hamburg, Germany—a photograph of their departure is included in Malcolm's posthumously published 2023 book, *Still Pictures*. There they were able to gain passage on one of the last civilian ships to leave Europe for America before the outbreak of World War II.

Upon their arrival in New York, the family name was changed to Winn and Jana Klara became Janet Clara. While Janet's father studied for the medical boards, the family lived with relatives in Brooklyn. In 1940, they moved to the Upper East Side of Manhattan, where there was a large working-class Czech population, and Janet's father became a respected doctor within that community. Her mother, who had taken the name Joan, worked for the Voice of America.

Janet spoke almost no English when she arrived but picked it up quickly. She attended Manhattan's High School of Music and Art and then the University of Michigan, where she wrote for the school paper, the *Michigan Daily*, and the campus humor magazine, *Gargoyle*. Before graduating with an English degree in 1955, she met and married Donald Malcolm, also a writer.

Moving to Washington, they both wrote for the *New Republic*. Then Donald Malcolm joined the staff of the *New Yorker* and the couple shifted to New York. Donald Malcolm would become the magazine's first off-Broadway drama critic and a book reviewer. Janet Malcolm's first piece in the *New Yorker*, where she would contribute for many years, was a six-stanza poem, "Thoughts on Living in a Shaker House," which appeared in 1963, the same year her daughter, Anne, was born.

Soon after, Donald Malcolm fell sick with an illness from which he never recovered, dying at the age of forty-three in 1975. By then, Janet Malcolm was regularly writing for the *New Yorker* on so-called women's topics such as Christmas shopping and children's books, and "About the House," a monthly column on interiors and design. She later became the magazine's photography columnist, her pieces collected in a 1980 book called *Diana & Nikon*.

Malcolm's signature style and approach emerged in the late 1970s, noted Katie Roiphe in an extended interview with Malcolm in the *Paris Review*: "She began to do the dense, idiosyncratic writing she is now known for when she quit smoking in 1978: she couldn't write without cigarettes, so she began reporting a long *New Yorker* fact piece, on family therapy, called 'The One-Way Mirror.' She set off for Philadelphia with a tape recorder—the old-fashioned kind, with tapes, which she uses to this day—and lined Mead composition notebooks with marbleized covers. By the time she finished the long period of reporting, she found she could finally write without smoking, and she had also found her form."

After her first husband's death, Janet Malcolm married Gardner Botsford, her *New Yorker* editor, in 1975. They worked together closely and she attributed much of her writing success to him. After Botsford's death in 2004, Malcolm worked with *New Yorker* editor Ann Goldstein, who has gone on to become a renowned translator, especially of the Italian novelist Elena Ferrante.

Before taking up the MacDonald-McGinniss case, Malcolm became involved in a long-running court case of her own, bringing her considerable notoriety. She and the *New Yorker* were sued for libel by Jeffrey Moussaieff Masson, the chief subject in a two-part 1983 magazine series and Malcolm's later book, *In the Freud Archives*. The case did not go to trial until 1993.

By then, *The Journalist and the Murderer* had appeared and Malcolm was again embroiled in questions about the relationship between writer and subject—which she addressed in the book's afterword: "I have been writing long pieces of reportage for a little over a decade. Almost from the start, I was struck by the unhealthiness of the journalist-subject relationship, and every piece I wrote only deepened my consciousness of the canker that lies at the heart of the rose of journalism."

After years of litigation, the Masson libel case was heard in 1993 and decided in 1994. According to the *New York Times*, "In the Masson suit, the jury ruled that while two of five disputed quotations that Ms. Malcolm had attributed to Mr. Masson were false and that one of those was defamatory, none were written with reckless disregard of the truth, the standard under which libel damages would have been allowed."

Katie Roiphe notes of Malcolm's case that "the courts ultimately found in her favor, in 1994, but the charges shadowed her for years, and both during the trial and afterward the journalistic community was not as supportive as one might have thought it would be." (Malcolm later asserted that she found the notebooks containing the contested quotes.)

Malcolm continued writing for the *New Yorker* and, over the next decades, produced many more articles on subjects ranging from Russian literature and Gertrude Stein to the popular hit Gossip Girls novels. Some of her journalism was republished in a number of successful books. "Malcolm's work, then, occupies that strange glittering territory between controversy and the establishment," wrote Katie Roiphe in 2011, "she is both a grande dame of journalism, and still, somehow, its enfant terrible."

Janet Malcolm died on June 16, 2021, of cancer, in a New York City hospital. She was eighty-six years old. In 2023, *Still Pictures*, a collection of short, autobiographical essays accompanied by old family photos, was published posthumously.

WHY YOU SHOULD READ IT

There is good reason that *The Journalist and the Murderer* became, as Harrison Smith wrote after Malcolm's death, "a dog-eared staple of journalism seminars and creative nonfiction classes." It provides an incisive look at its topic—the role of the journalist—as well as an object lesson in clear, concise writing. "When *The Journalist and the Murderer* came out in 1990," wrote Katie Roiphe, "it created a stir in the literary world; it antagonized, in other words, precisely those people it was meant to antagonize. But it is now taught to nearly every undergraduate studying journalism, and Malcolm's fiery comment on the relationship between the journalist and her subject has been assimilated so completely into the larger culture that it has become a truism."

As a writer, I read it with a student-like interest in the important questions of journalistic ethics Malcolm raises throughout. How writers uncover and represent truth—as reporters, critics, columnists, or historians—is a formidable challenge. This is what Katherine Q. Seelye described as "the slipperiness of truth" in her obituary of Malcom, cited earlier.

In assessing and questioning the writer's motives, Malcolm's work also demands that, as readers, we must also be more skeptical of what we read. The concept of "media literacy"—questioning the sources we read and hear—has taken on added urgency as we are confronted by the explosion of so-called fake news and manipulated images, already being alarmingly magnified by the growth of artificial intelligence. These are challenges that demand a sharpening of the critical approach we bring to a text of any kind presented as "truth." We must apply critical thinking even to those writers and sources we might presume to trust. Those are hard and important lessons, especially in a time when truth and facts have never seemed so elusive.

WHAT TO READ NEXT

As critic Charles Finch wrote in January 2023, Janet Malcolm and the late Joan Didion (see entry) were "the two most important long-form journalists this country has produced in the second half of the last century."

In the case of Malcolm, that leaves much to choose from. As Katie Roiphe wrote in the *Paris Review*:

> Her ten provocative books, including *The Journalist and the Murderer, Psychoanalysis: The Impossible Profession, The Silent Woman: Sylvia Plath and Ted Hughes, In the Freud Archives,* and *Two Lives: Gertrude and Alice,* are simultaneously beloved, demanding, scholarly, flashy, careful, bold, high-brow, and controversial. Many people have pointed out that her writing, which is often called journalism, is in fact some other wholly original form of art, some singular admixture of reporting, biography, literary criticism, psychoanalysis, and the nineteenth-century novel—English and Russian both.

Malcolm's 2007 book *Two Lives: Gertrude and Alice* was singled out earlier, in the entry on *The Autobiography of Alice B. Toklas.* I plan to go next with *In the Freud Archives,* another short book of nonfiction and the subject of the controversy involving Jeffrey Moussaieff Masson described earlier.

I would also add to the list Malcolm's acclaimed 2013 collection, *Forty-One False Starts: Essays on Artists and Writers.* In an introduction to the book, Ian Frazier concludes: "Her work has put her among the masters of modern nonfiction. . . . Over and over she has demonstrated that nonfiction—a book of reporting, an article in a magazine, something we see every day—can rise to the highest level of literature."

"To know love we have to tell the truth
to ourselves and to others."

All About Love: New Visions

— 2000 —

bell hooks

New York: William Morrow, 2018; 238 pages

OPENING WORDS

On my kitchen wall hang four snapshots of graffiti art I first saw on construction walls as I walked to my teaching job at Yale University years ago. The declaration, "The search for love continues even in the face of great odds," was painted in bright colors. At the time, recently separated from a partner of almost fifteen years, I was often overwhelmed by grief so profound it seemed as though an immense sea of pain was washing my heart and soul away.

SUMMARY

First published in 2000, this series of thirteen essays addresses a seemingly simple question: What is love?

With a conversational, candid approach, the prolific social critic and poet bell hooks explores "love" in all of its meanings, beyond its simplistic pop cultural expressions in books, movies, and songs—and in a sex-obsessed mass media. Her investigation begins from a very personal place—the breakup of her long-term relationship. Writing partly out of a sense of rejection while reflecting on her own sense of not being loved as a child, she prefaces the book:

> I feel our nation's turning away from love as intensely as I felt love's abandonment in my girlhood. Turning away we risk moving into a wilderness of spirit so intense we may never find our way home again. I write of love to bear witness both to the danger in this movement, and to call for a return to love. Redeemed and restored, love returns us to the promise of everlasting life. When we love we can let our hearts speak.

Each of the thirteen chapters briefly focuses on the specific elements that hooks explores as she seeks to define the essence of "love." In a personally candid examination of the concept of Love, hooks examines the various qualities—"Honesty," "Spirituality," "Community," "Loss," and "Healing" among them. In her introduction, hooks writes:

> Everyone wants to know more about love. We want to know what it means to love, what we can do in our everyday lives to love and be loved. . . . The strength of our desire does not change the power of our cultural uncertainty. Everywhere we learn that love is important, and yet we are bombarded by its failure.
>
> [Yet she concludes:] We still hope that love will prevail. We still believe in love's promise.

Setting out to define "love" and seeking the answer to the questions she has posed, hooks draws on an extraordinary spectrum of sources in each of these separate sections, seeking guidance from biblical scripture and Saint Teresa of Ávila to contemporary psychology and Buddhist monk Thich Nhat Hanh—as well as the deep-seated Christianity of her childhood and her attraction to Buddhism in later life. In fact, hooks would come to describe herself as a "Christian-Buddhist."

Intellectually provocative without lapsing into academic jargon, she presents a lively and compelling conversation about the meaning and power of love, emphasizing the need for honesty.

"To know love we have to tell the truth to ourselves and to others," she writes in the chapter on "Honesty." "Creating a false self to mask fears and insecurities has become so common that many of us forget who we are and what we feel underneath the pretense. . . . Lies and secrets burden us and cause stress. When an individual has always lied, he has no awareness that truth telling can take away this heavy burden. To know this, he must let the lies go. . . . To be loving we willingly hear each other's truth and, most important, we affirm the value of truth telling. Lies may make people feel better, but they do not help them to know love."

ABOUT THE AUTHOR: BELL HOOKS

Born Gloria Jean Watkins, the fourth of seven children in Hopkinsville, Kentucky, on September 25, 1952, bell hooks chose to use a pen name, a tribute to her maternal great-grandmother, Bell Blair Hooks. However, she spelled her name with lowercase letters to de-emphasize her individual identity. "Ironically, the spelling of her name became a matter of public fascination," noted Clyde McGrady in the *Washington Post*.

Her father was a World War II veteran in a segregated infantry unit who became a postal worker; and her mother a homemaker. Raised in a small city in the southwestern part of the state not far from the Tennessee border, she attended mostly segregated schools until integration arrived. As Clay Risen noted in the *New York Times* obituary of bell hooks, "her tight-knit Black community in Hopkinsville showed her the possibility of resistance from the margins, of finding community among the oppressed and drawing power from those connections—a theme to which she would return frequently in her work."

From early childhood, she was a reader, as her sisters recalled vividly in a statement released after her death late in 2021:

> Every night we would try to sleep, but the sounds of her writing or page turning caused us to yell down to Mom to make her turn the light off.
>
> There were many summer days that Gloria led the walk to the public library to checkout books. While Valeria and Gwenda would find one or two Nancy Drew or other fun books, Gloria always had at least ten books of a more serious nature (Shakespeare, *Little Women*, and other classics). . . . With her intense love for information, her ability to speed read was perfected. We will always remember Gloria as having a great thirst for knowledge, which she incorporated into her life's work.

Having traveled the great distance from rural Kentucky to Palo Alto, California, bell hooks graduated from Stanford in 1974 with a degree in English literature. While taking women's studies classes there as an undergraduate, she noted how Black women were generally left out of the conversation—that 1970s feminism was a largely white female preserve.

After Stanford, she received a master's in English from the University of Wisconsin and was teaching at the University of Southern California when she published her first book, *And There We Wept*, a collection of poetry, in 1978. She earned her doctorate in 1983, writing about the work of novelist Toni Morrison, who became the first Black woman to receive the Nobel Prize in Literature in 1993.

In 1981, hooks published the book she had begun drafting as a Stanford undergraduate. *Ain't I A Woman: Black Women and Feminism* was first published by a small press, its title borrowed from a speech (1851) by Sojourner Truth, the prominent abolitionist who demanded voting rights for Black women as well as men. In it, hooks wrote: "A devaluation of black womanhood occurred as a result of the sexual exploitation of black women during slavery that has not altered in the course of hundreds of years."

A succession of teaching posts, including at Yale University, followed as she continued to write, arguing that mainstream feminism—largely white—had sidelined the experience of Black women. In *Killing Rage: Ending Racism* (1995), hooks wrote: "It should have come as no surprise to any of us that those white women who were mainly concerned with gaining equal access to domains of white male privilege quickly ceased to espouse a radical political agenda which included the dismantling of patriarchy as well as an anti-racist, anti-classist agenda."

Over time, *Ain't I A Woman* became required reading in many university women's studies departments. "For me, reading 'Ain't I A Woman' was as if someone had opened the door, the windows, and raised the roof in my mind," wrote novelist Min Jin Lee, author of *Pachinko*, who took two classes with bell hooks at Yale. "I am neither white nor black, but through her theories, I was able to understand that my body contained historical multitudes and any analysis without such a measured consideration was limited and deeply flawed."

After moving to Greenwich Village and teaching at City College of New York and the New School, bell hooks returned to Kentucky for a teaching post at Berea College, a small liberal arts institution founded by an abolitionist in 1855 and open to Black and white students—the first nonsegregated, coeducational college in the South. Once housed in a one-room schoolhouse, it had been forced to close by proslavery supporters, reopening after the Civil War. Berea still charges no tuition, a policy begun in 1892.

On December 15, 2021, bell hooks died of kidney failure in her home in Berea; she was sixty-nine years old.

WHY YOU SHOULD READ IT

Remarkably, two decades after its publication and in the midst of the Covid pandemic, *All About Love* became a best seller, remaining on the *New York Times Book Review* nonfiction paperback list for 111 weeks as of February 4, 2024. This highly unusual publishing success—few books appear on best-seller lists so long after their publication—was one reason I was intrigued by the book. It had achieved unusual popular longevity. As a historian of books and publishing, I was interested in discovering the measure of that success.

I will confess that I had not read the work of bell hooks before embarking on this project, though I was familiar with her name and reputation as a writer whose previous titles included *Killing Rage*. Perhaps as an older white, straight man, I was not the "target reader" for someone whose early work addressed the intersection of racism and feminism. When I read about her after her death in 2021, however, I became fascinated by her life story and I decided to acquaint myself with this prominent voice in late twentieth-century American letters. Sometimes we really must read outside our comfort zones.

Perhaps anticipating a more academic approach, and aware of hooks's reputation for combative feminism, I was unprepared for the book's temperate, even tender tone. She makes frequent references to works I admired—such as *The Road Less Traveled* by M. Scott Peck. Her guiding principle, that loving means "to openly and honestly express care, affection, responsibility, respect, commitment, and trust," lays down a prescription that is comfortable without mawkish sentimentality.

"It is a warm affirmation that love is possible and an attack on the culture of narcissism and selfishness," one reviewer wrote. ". . . Her best points are simple ones. Community—extended family, creative or political collaboration, friendship—is as important as the couple or the nuclear family; love is an art that involves work, not just the thrill of attraction; desire may depend on illusion, but love comes only through painful truth-telling."

With its frequent references to those many writers hooks clearly admires and drew upon, such as Erich Fromm and the late Harold S. Kushner, *All About Love* is less a work of groundbreaking perception than a valuable aggregation—a collection of wisdom that a wise woman, open to learning since she walked to the library with her sisters as a child, has gleaned and distilled into a message still very much needed.

WHAT TO READ NEXT

For anyone who wants to explore more of the work of bell hooks, there are many choices. But the best follow-up may be *Ain't I a Woman: Black Women and Feminism*. Also about two hundred pages, it is the book that established her credentials and her voice. Her 1995 book, *Killing Rage: Ending Racism*, is slightly longer but also explores the idea that ending racism must go hand in hand with ending sexism. Its title essay starts in a tone very distinct from the voice in *All About Love*: "I am writing this essay sitting beside an anonymous white male that I long to murder," provoked by an incident of everyday sexism and racism that hooks had experienced with a friend.

Besides the extensive bell hooks catalog, *All About Love* itself offers a wealth of additional readings bell hooks drew upon. Among her many and most frequent references is *The Art of Loving* by Erich Fromm. Fromm's 1956 book is, I might argue, somewhat dated in terms of his cultural reference points. But hooks admired Fromm's approach to the act of loving as an active force and not just a question of personal pleasure. Commenting on Fromm's philosophy, she writes, "loving practice is not aimed at simply giving an individual greater life satisfaction. It is extolled as the primary way we end domination and oppression." This is a theme she returns to often.

Another of her touchstones is *The Road Less Traveled* by M. Scott Peck, an important and valuable popular work that has sold millions of copies since its 1978 publication. Peck speaks to the issues in *All About Love* and was clearly a significant influence on bell hooks.

Finally, bell hooks was a great admirer of Thich Nhat Hanh, the Vietnamese Buddhist monk who was highly influential in introducing Buddhist thought to the West. Thich Nhat Hanh, who died in 2022 at age ninety-five, is cited in this collection in the entry on *Tao Te Ching*.

While not singled out by hooks, *A Burst of Light and Other Essays* (1988) collects an important series of essays by Audre Lorde (1934–1992). A prominent Black poet and essayist, Lorde took on racism, sexism, and homophobia in her work and, in 1986, lesbian parenting. "Lesbians and

Gays of Color and the children of Lesbians and Gays of Color are in the forefront of every struggle for human dignity in this country today, and that is not by accident," Lorde wrote in 1986, while America was still in the midst of the AIDS crisis and decades before same-sex marriage became the law of the land. "At the same time, we must remember when they are children that they are children, and need love, protection, and direction."

"Then there's the question of how to make the best use of a fifteen-minute break when you have three or more urgent, simultaneous needs—to pee, to drink something, to get outside the neon and into the natural light, and most of all, to sit down."

Nickel and Dimed:
On (Not) Getting By in America

— 2001 —

Barbara Ehrenreich

New York: Picador, 2021; 20th anniversary edition; 221 pages

OPENING WORDS

Mostly out of laziness, I decide to start my low-wage life in the town nearest to where I actually live, Key West, Florida, which with a population of about 25,000 is elbowing its way up to the status of a genuine city. The downside of familiarity, I soon realize, is that it's not easy to go from being a consumer, thoughtlessly throwing money around in exchange for groceries and movies and gas, to being a worker in the very same place. I am terrified, especially at the beginning, of being recognized by some friendly business owner or erstwhile neighbor and having to stammer out some explanation of my project. Happily, though, my fears turn out to be entirely unwarranted: during a month of poverty and toil, no one recognizes my face or my name, which goes unnoticed and for the most part unuttered.

SUMMARY

How do people live on poverty wages?

In one of the most eye-opening journalistic works of recent times, veteran writer Barbara Ehrenreich reports on her three-month experiment in the world of the unskilled worker. Presenting herself as a homemaker needing to earn a living after a divorce, she joined the low end of the labor market in 1988 to see how the people who live and work in this world of low-paying work make ends meet.

Her experiment came during a time of relative American affluence but also political cruelty, as Clinton-era welfare reform—"workfare"—forced mothers with small children to seek jobs if they wanted to maintain their government assistance. Working for one month in three different parts of the country, Ehrenreich looked for the best-paying unskilled job she could find and also a place to live on her meager earnings. The result is this maddening, remarkable, often darkly funny look at the miseries and indignities of low-wage work in America.

As she lays out in the opening passage, Ehrenreich first sought work in her hometown, Key West. Filling out about twenty applications at supermarkets and hotels, she failed to get one of those jobs. Instead, she took up waitressing at a low-end restaurant, earning $2.43 an hour plus tips for an eight-hour shift. It was a start, but she needed a second waitress job to afford a decent place to stay.

The next destination was Maine, chosen for "its whiteness." Here she starts out as a "dietary aide" in a residential facility where many of the "guests" have Alzheimer's. At the same time, she joins Merry Maids, a cleaning service catering to affluent homeowners, for $6.65 an hour. Often backbreaking, the work is worsened by the harsh cleaning fluids she must use.

Finally, in Minnesota, she finds work at Walmart for $7 an hour. Balancing her descriptions of the extreme physical demands of these poverty-level jobs with the task of finding a decent place to live, Ehrenreich sees up close the daily struggles of her coworkers.

Ehrenreich's work was neither a stunt nor a do-gooder's well-meaning jaunt to assuage liberal guilt. As she writes, "So this is not a story of some death-defying 'undercover' adventure. Almost anyone could do what I did—look for jobs, work those jobs, try to make ends meet. In fact, millions of Americans do it every day, and with a lot less fanfare and dithering."

Written with great clarity beneath Ehrenreich's often bemused gaze, the book examines the trials faced by millions of such workers. Her anger sometimes boils over at a system that—now more than twenty years later—only continues to produce such grotesque inequities.

ABOUT THE AUTHOR: BARBARA EHRENREICH

Born on August 26, 1941, in Butte, Montana, Barbara Alexander was part of a working-class family. Her father, Benjamin Alexander, worked in the copper mines, like his father and other family members before him. Her mother, Isabelle Oxley, was a homemaker. But the family moved up the economic ladder when Barbara's father went to college, later earning a Ph.D. in metallurgy at Carnegie Mellon University in Pittsburgh. Barbara graduated from Reed College in 1963 and received a doctorate in cell biology from Rockefeller University in 1968. There she also met fellow graduate student John Ehrenreich, marrying him in 1967.

Barbara Ehrenreich never lost touch with her working-class roots. She knew family members who did dirty, dangerous work and had lost fingers on the job. As she recalled in *Nickel and Dimed*, "My father had been a copper miner; uncles and grandfathers worked in the mines or for the Union Pacific. So to me, sitting at a desk all day was not only a privilege but a duty: something I owed to all those people in my life, living and dead, who'd had so much more to say than anyone ever got to hear."

After college, she became a government budget analyst and then a staff member at a New York–based nonprofit tracking health policy. Moving to become an assistant professor in the health sciences program at the State

University of New York, Old Westbury, in 1971, she grew increasingly angry at what she observed during the social upheaval and political resistance of the 1960s and 1970s and she set out to write. Her first book, *Long March, Short Spring: The Student Uprising at Home and Abroad*, was written in 1969 with her husband, a clinical psychologist. The project grew out of their own opposition to the Vietnam War. Their second book, *The American Health Empire: Power, Profits and Politics*, published in 1970, described what they called the "medical-industrial complex."

In 1974, Ehrenreich left her teaching post to pursue full-time writing, selling articles to *Ms.* magazine and other journals. In a 1977 essay, she and her husband coined the term "professional-managerial class" ("PMC") to describe the teachers, social workers, middle managers, and other white-collar professionals who were separated from the blue-collar world but still far from America's wealthy elite. The Ehrenreichs divorced but continued to write articles together, and Barbara Ehrenreich produced a series of critically acclaimed books, including *Fear of Falling: The Inner Life of the Middle Class* and *The Worst Years of Our Lives: Irreverent Notes from a Decade of Greed*.

Then, as she writes in her introduction to *Nickel and Dimed*, over "a $30 lunch at some understated French country-style place," she met with *Harper's* editor Lewis Lapham. "I had the salmon and field greens, I think, and was pitching him some ideas . . . when the conversation drifted to one of my more familiar themes—poverty." After suggesting that someone should write about the women who were being forced into low-wage jobs by Clinton's welfare reform, she recalls, "But Lapham got this crazy-looking half smile on his face and ended life as I knew it, for long stretches at least, with the single word '*You.*'"

That was the birth of *Nickel and Dimed*, the work that became the turning point in her career. But she didn't just write. Ehrenreich lived a life of activism and involvement, as a member of the Democratic Socialists of America and as founder, advisor, or board member with such groups as the National Women's Health Network, the National Abortion Rights Action League, the National Writers Union, and the National Organization for the

Reform of Marijuana Laws. She also returned to the university, teaching at a variety of schools including New York University, Ohio State University as writer-in-residence, the University of Oregon, and the University of California, Berkeley.

Her writing always remained central, as she turned out a prodigious number of articles and books, including *Bright-sided: How the Relentless Promotion of Positive Thinking Has Undermined America*. Published in 2009, the book grew from her experience with breast cancer, first detailed in "Welcome to Cancerland: A Mammogram Leads to a World of Pink Kitsch," an award-winning 2001 *Harper's* article. She turned it into a book exploring the nation's "blithe sunniness." According to a *New York Times* interview with Ehrenreich, "The unrelenting message was 'that you had to be cheerful and accepting and that you would not recover unless you were. . . .' Most infuriating, she added, was the advice to 'consider your cancer a gift.'"

At the same time, Ehrenreich never relented in her focus on the essential themes of *Nickel and Dimed*—poverty, inequality, and the sharp injustices faced by America's struggling low-wage workers and others. In "Is It Now a Crime to Be Poor?," a 2009 op-ed that appeared in the *New York Times*, she wrote:

> The pattern is to curtail financing for services that might help the poor while ramping up law enforcement: starve school and public transportation budgets, then make truancy illegal. Shut down public housing, then make it a crime to be homeless. Be sure to harass street vendors when there are few other opportunities for employment. The experience of the poor, and especially poor minorities, comes to resemble that of a rat in a cage scrambling to avoid erratically administered electric shocks.

In 2018, Barbara Ehrenreich wrote her final book, *Natural Causes: An Epidemic of Wellness, the Certainty of Dying, and Killing Ourselves to Live Longer*. She died on September 1, 2022, in hospice, following a stroke she suffered shortly after her eighty-first birthday.

WHY YOU SHOULD READ IT

During the pandemic, we all learned the phrase "essential workers"—the people who had to go to work to keep the country functioning. There were the obvious ones—doctors, nurses, and EMTS. For these people, there was no Zooming in their pajamas. And many of them were cheered, for a time, as they left their hospital shifts.

But the category also included a great many people who received no applause—people who clean bathrooms, harvest food, stock shelves, fill warehouse orders with all those products the homebound were ordering online, and ring up grocery baskets, all the other "essential" jobs the rest of us need to go on living.

These are the people Barbara Ehrenreich wrote about in *Nickel and Dimed* in 2001, right after the "dot-com" bubble burst, giving the professional-managerial class a sharp and leveling lesson in economic shock. The book was reissued twenty years later, not long after the mortgage crisis and Great Recession provided the PMC another rude awakening from their seemingly comfortable lives.

Now, in the aftermath of the pandemic, Ehrenreich's richly detailed and acutely observed lessons are just as timely—and perhaps frustrating. "Here is a book that made a difference, and yet America refused to change," writes Matthew Desmond in a foreword to the 20th anniversary edition. "Until it does, *Nickel and Dimed* stands as an urgent and searing indictment of the American dream."

Read it because Barbara Ehrenreich is probably as close to an American George Orwell as any writer in recent times. Her work has been part of the national conversation about inequality for a long time. But the conversation must go on.

WHAT TO READ NEXT

Having read and reread *Nickel and Dimed*, I plan to move on to several other Ehrenreich works of particular interest: *Living with a Wild God: A Nonbeliever's Search for the Truth about Everything* is a 2014 book that explores an atheist's quest for truth and is in part a memoir of her own "mystical experiences" as a teen. *Bright-Sided: How Positive Thinking is Undermining America* is another relatively short book about a subject I find fascinating—America's long-term obsession with sunny optimism.

I would also recommend two books that focus on the issues raised by Ehrenreich, one written before and another after *Nickel and Dimed* was published. Michael Harrington's *The Other America: Poverty in the United States* is a classic in the field of sociology. First published in 1952, it was reissued in 2012.

The foreword to this edition of *Nickel and Dimed* was written by Matthew Desmond, author of the Pulitzer Prize–winning *Evicted: Poverty and Profit in the American City*. Published in 2016, it is a highly praised book, though not short, and named by the *New York Times* as one of the ten best nonfiction books of the decade.

At the other end of the political spectrum is *Capitalism and Freedom*, the work of Nobel Prize–winning economist Milton Friedman, among the most influential economists of the post–World War II era. Published in 1962 and reissued in an anniversary edition in 2002, it linked economic freedom to political freedom. With this series of essays and his later book *Free to Choose: A Personal Statement*, written with his wife, Rose Friedman, and which became a public television series, Friedman must be considered one of the most influential writers of the late twentieth century.

"Dante was a sectarian and a mystic but he was right to reserve one of the fieriest corners of his inferno for those who, in a time of moral crisis, try to stay neutral."

Letters to a Young Contrarian

— 2001 —

Christopher Hitchens

New York: Basic Books, 2005; 141 pages

OPENING WORDS

My dear X,

So then—you rather tend to flatter and embarrass me, when you inquire my advice as to how a radical or "contrarian" life may be lived. The flattery is in your suggestion that I might be anybody's "model," when almost by definition a single existence cannot furnish any pattern (and, if it is lived in dissent, should not anyway be supposed to be emulated). The embarrassment lies in the very title that you propose. It is a strange thing, but it remains true that our language and culture contain no proper word for your aspiration. The noble title of "dissident" must be earned rather than claimed; it connotes sacrifice and risk rather than mere disagreement, and it has been consecrated by many exemplary and courageous men and women.

SUMMARY

Styled on *Letters to a Young Poet* by Bohemian-Austrian poet Rainer Maria Rilke, this is a compendium of counsel in epistolary style. Rather than offering advice on how to write verse, as Rilke did, author and provocateur Christopher Hitchens sets out to address questions frequently posed by students at New York City's New School, where he taught, and other campuses where he spoke. These students wanted to know how they could change the world for the better and how to live, in Hitchens's words, "a life that would be, as far as possible, self-determined." Hitchens frames these through a correspondence with a single representative student.

It was a challenge well suited to Hitchens, a best-selling and prolific author, cultural critic, and gadfly. Hitchens was a highly skilled polemicist— an expert in aggressively attacking the opinions and principles of others. As he writes in one letter, "If you care about the points of agreement and civility, then, you had better be well-equipped with points of argument and combativity."

Well-equipped he was. As Hitchens demonstrates in this provocative series of essay-like letters, he despises hypocrites and does not suffer fools. And here he singles out many of them, from the powerful, to the sainted, to the celebrated: from Richard Nixon and Henry Kissinger to Mother Teresa, the Dalai Lama, and Princess Diana. He recaps some of his battles against what he calls "arbitrary authority or witless mass opinion."

His opening letter recalls the famous 1898 "J'Accuse . . . !" crusade of Émile Zola in his historic defense of Captain Alfred Dreyfus, a Jew wronged by the anti-Semitism of the French army, the French people, and the French Catholic Church. For Hitchens, Zola was among his role models—George Orwell was certainly another—who used words with withering power to prick the consciences of their countrymen.

With rapier wit and devastating audacity, Hitchens proffers his advice, skewering sacred cows along the way, blitzing religion and vapid New Age spirituality. His rapid-fire assault on politicians, spiritual gurus, crowned celebrities, and a host of other targets are well honed, soaked in history and literary precedent, and delivered with a sense of moral urgency—toward the cause of human rights and against autocrats and dictators of all stripes. Although this book was written at the beginning of the twenty-first century, his wisdom and clarity about the dangers of accepting authority could not be more prescient in this time of "moral crisis."

ABOUT THE AUTHOR: CHRISTOPHER HITCHENS

One of the most outspoken authors, journalists, critics, and polemicists of recent times, Christopher Eric Hitchens was born in Portsmouth, England, on April 13, 1949. His father was a commander in the Royal Navy whose ship sank a German battleship in World War II. His mother was a member of the Women's Royal Naval Service, known as the Wrens, who met her husband in 1945. With his father moving between naval assignments, Christopher Hitchens's early years involved stays at bases in Malta, Scotland, and other ports. His father later became a bookkeeper. His mother, according to Hitchens, insisted that he go to boarding school. As Hitchens reported it, she said "if there is going to be an upper class in this country, then Christopher is going to be in it."

At eight, Hitchens was sent off to first Devon and later a school in Cambridge. A gifted student, in 1968 he went to Oxford's Balliol College, where his politics and interests soon swung to the left. He joined in opposition to the Vietnam War and the spread of nuclear weapons, racism, and the vestiges of colonialism. Initially joining the Labour Party, Hitchens left over Prime Minister Harold Wilson's support for the Vietnam War and moved even further left, joining the International Socialists.

Graduating in 1970 with a degree in philosophy, politics, and economics, he wrote for the *Times Higher Education Supplement* in London. Hitchens later became a staff writer for the leftist weekly *New Statesman* and the *Evening Standard*, followed by stints as a foreign correspondent and foreign editor. "His work took him to Northern Ireland, Greece, Cyprus, Portugal, Spain and Argentina in the 1970s," wrote William Grimes, "generally to shine a light on the evil practices of entrenched dictators or the imperial machinations of the great powers."

In 1973, Hitchens's mother committed suicide after leaving her husband. Only after his father's death in 1987 did Hitchens learn that his mother was Jewish, a fact she had concealed from the family.

Hitchens moved to the United States in 1981, eventually landing in Washington, D.C., where he wrote for the liberal *Nation* magazine. He had also begun writing books based on his overseas assignments in Cyprus and elsewhere, his acid tone sharpened by his experiences in conflict zones. A key moment came when his friend novelist Salman Rushdie was threatened by Iran's Ayatollah Khomeini, who issued a fatwa—a formal religious order to Muslims around the world to kill Rushdie—over his satirical novel *The Satanic Verses* in 1989. Hitchens became an outspoken defender of Rushdie and audaciously addressed—given the dangerous threats to other people associated with Rushdie—what he called "Islamofascism." It was a term he did not coin but popularized. Hitchens also criticized others on the left for failing to sufficiently denounce the attacks on Rushdie.

His stature increasing, Hitchens began writing for the *Atlantic* and *Vanity Fair*, taking aim at the foibles of culture as well as religion and politics. As William Grimes later described this work, "He wrote a monthly review-essay for *The Atlantic* and, as a carte-blanche columnist at *Vanity Fair*, filed essays on topics as various as getting a Brazilian bikini wax and the experience of being waterboarded, a volunteer assignment that he called 'very much more frightening though less painful than the bikini wax.'"

Fearless and unpredictable, Hitchens was carving out an increasingly visible platform as a gadfly with a venomous sting. His withering gaze spared few personalities or politicians. He used his megaphone to expose and denounce what he saw as the hypocrisy of many public figures, notably among them Mother Teresa, the nun renowned for her work among the poor in Kolkata (formerly Calcutta), later sainted, and the subject of his 1995 book, *The Missionary Position: Mother Teresa in Theory and Practice*. Another central target was President Bill Clinton, subject of *No One Left to Lie To* (1999), for both his political policies and private indiscretions as an elected official. Hitchens also documented what he deemed the war crimes of President Nixon's foreign policy advisor and later secretary of state in *The Crimes of Henry Kissinger* (2001), the source of a documentary film of the same title.

Through his magazine work, books, and sharp opinions attacking these very prominent sacred cows, Hitchens became a very visible public intellectual. He frequently appeared on television, his eloquence and accented sarcasm demolishing debate opponents. It was rarely a fair fight.

After the September 11, 2001, attacks, Hitchens tacked sharply rightward, emerging as an enthusiastic supporter of the invasion of Saddam Hussein's Iraq. Wrote Peter Wilby in the *Guardian*: "Hitchens announced he was no longer on the left—while denying he had become any kind of conservative—and 'swore a sort of oath to remain coldly furious' until 'fascism with an Islamic face' was 'brought to a most strict and merciless account.'" In the U.S. 2004 presidential election, he endorsed President George W. Bush, who had ordered those attacks.

In 2007, Hitchens became a U.S. citizen. It was also the year he published his best-selling book *God Is Not Great: How Religion Poisons Everything*, a stinging denunciation of organized religion and a statement of his determined atheism. It was followed by a memoir, *Hitch-22*, published in 2010. While promoting the book, aggressively smoking during his interviews, Hitchens revealed a diagnosis of esophageal cancer, the same disease that had taken his father. He wrote and spoke about his illness during his last year. In *Vanity Fair*, Hitchens wrote: "In whatever kind of a 'race' life may be, I have very abruptly become a finalist."

Christopher Hitchens died on December 15, 2011, of pneumonia, a complication of esophageal cancer; he was sixty-two. A collection of writings, *Arguably: Essays*, published in the year he died, became a best seller and was ranked among the Top Ten Books of 2011 by the *New York Times*.

WHY YOU SHOULD READ IT

I miss Christopher Hitchens. We sorely need his voice today. While I may not have always agreed with him—I certainly thought his arguments for going to war in Iraq were mistaken—his thinking and writing are tours de force because they admonish us to gaze hard at the world around us and stand for something.

Generously sprinkled with references to Hitchens's literary predecessors—Émile Zola, Oscar Wilde, and George Orwell among them—as well as his many years of experience as journalist and war correspondent, this is a book of important lessons. Among these, two stand out: "The two worst things, as one can work out without leaving home, are racism and religion." And "Never be a spectator of unfairness or stupidity."

These collected letters of Christopher Hitchens offer his pure disdain for "the celebrity culture, and the spin-scum and the crooked lawyers and pseudo-statesmen and clerics" who "seemed to have everything their own way. . . . But their victory is not pre-determined."

Published at the opening of the twenty-first century, this is a work that speaks clearly and forcefully to our own moment of "moral crisis." *Letters to a Young Contrarian* reminds us this is no time to "stay neutral."

WHAT TO READ NEXT

Between his work as a journalist, essayist, and author, Hitchens left a large and impressive library. I would single out two of his titles, *Why Orwell Matters*, about one of the writers he most admired; and *God Is Not Great: How Religion Poisons Everything*, a best-selling book that dismantles organized religion. Among his other books I plan to add to my list are his works on two significant Thomases: *Thomas Jefferson: Author of America* (2005) and *Thomas Paine's Rights of Man: A Biography* (2007).

"Yes, it was war all right. Right away, the supermarkets were empty."

Persepolis:
The Story of a Childhood

— 2003 —

Marjane Satrapi

New York: Pantheon Books, 2003; 153 pages

OPENING WORDS

This is me when I was 10 years old. This was in 1980. And this is a class photo. I'm sitting on the far left so you don't see me. From left to right: Golnaz, Mahshid, Narine, Minna. In 1979, a revolution took place. It was later called "The Islamic Revolution." Then came 1980: The year it became obligatory to wear the veil at school. (*"Wear this!"*) We didn't really like to wear the veil, especially since we didn't understand why we had to.

SUMMARY

What was it like to live through Iran's Islamic Revolution as a child? To be forced to "take the veil" at ten? Or have your Nikes become a dangerous sign of rebellion?

The answers are found in this graphic memoir by an artist who experienced the Revolution and the beginning of Iran's devastating war with Iraq. Using comic book–style panels and spare dialogue, author and illustrator Marjane Satrapi recounts her memories of Teheran with a childlike whimsy that grows darker as she depicts the downfall of the pro-American Shah, and the Islamic uprising that brought to power the Ayatollah Khomeini.

With the Shah gone, ten-year-old Marji—as she is called—and her left-leaning parents initially celebrate the release of friends once held as political prisoners. But their joy is short-lived, as the Ayatollah's strict Islamic code ushers in a new era of repression, including veils for Marji and her friends.

Interspersed with occasional conversations with God—who resembles Karl Marx—Satrapi shows Marji acting out entirely typical adolescent behavior. Entering her teens, she acquires a taste for smuggled Iron Maiden posters, Nikes, Michael Jackson, and a jean jacket in a country that no longer tolerates such Western influences—or any whiff of rebellion. Simultaneously, Satrapi documents the opening of a long, destructive war with Saddam Hussein's Iraq. As the religious authorities continue to crack down and war comes close to home, the book closes with Marji, at fourteen, being dispatched to the safety of Europe.

ABOUT THE AUTHOR: MARJANE SATRAPI

Born in 1969 in Rasht, near the Caspian Sea, Marjane Satrapi grew up in Teheran under the rule of the Shah, installed as Iran's leader in 1953 after an American-led coup overthrew a Soviet-leaning prime minister. The daughter of an engineer and a dress designer, Satrapi was descended from aristocratic Iranian families on both sides, including a great-grandfather who was Persia's last emperor before being deposed in a coup.

Until she was ten, Marjane Satrapi grew up in the home of Westernized intellectuals with strong Marxist leanings. Her parents drank alcohol, drove an American car, and hoped an Islamic revolution would topple the Shah. Young Marjane was being educated in an elite French-language school in Teheran.

Change came abruptly and shockingly. When the Shah was overthrown in 1979, the family soon found itself living under a new reign of terror. Their once-comfortable Western lifestyle drew the attention of Iran's fundamentalist religious authorities. A hard-line Marxist, Marjane's uncle was arrested and executed. Then, in September 1980, missiles fell on Teheran as Iran was struck by neighboring Iraq under Saddam Hussein, beginning a deadly conflict lasting until 1988.

During the war years, Marjane's parents sent her to Austria to live with a friend—the point at which this first volume of Satrapi's *Persepolis* saga ends. The experience went badly and Satrapi was kicked out of a convent school. She spiraled downward, eventually living on the streets until she nearly died from bronchitis. At nineteen, Satrapi returned to Iran, studied art, and began working as an illustrator. She married a fellow artist, a war veteran, in 1991, but the marriage ended in divorce and she returned to Europe. In 1994, Satrapi took another art degree at the School of Decorative Arts in Strasbourg. She would remain in exile in France.

Life took a sharp turn when Satrapi was given a copy of Art Spiegelman's *Maus* as a birthday gift in 1995. Inspired, Satrapi published *Persepolis* in France in 2000, followed by *Persepolis 2* a year later. In 2003, *Persepolis: The Story of a Childhood* was published in the United States by Pantheon, publisher of the landmark *Maus* books. Its sequel, *Persepolis 2: The Story of a Return*, which recounts the events as Satrapi goes back to Iran, appeared in the United States in 2004. (The two books have since been combined in a single volume, *The Complete Persepolis*.)

In a harbinger of the recent book bannings in U.S. schools, Satrapi's books attracted national attention when the Chicago Public Schools ordered their removal from classrooms in 2013 over concerns about a single cartoon depicting torture. "They think kids are stupid," Satrapi said in an interview on the ban with the National Coalition Against Censorship (NCAC). "They are not babies. Children are not dumb." And as the NCAC notes, "Satrapi herself witnessed the depicted episodes of torture and violence as a young girl, the same age as the students who would be affected by the ban."

Continuing her rich examination of Iranian life, society, and traditions, Satrapi created two more graphic books: *Embroideries*, in which a ladies' afternoon tea becomes a conversation about love and sex; and *Chicken with Plums*, which recounts the story of her great-uncle, a musician whose instrument is broken by his wife, leaving him in despair. In 2007, Satrapi directed a film adaptation of her memoirs, also called *Persepolis*, which was nominated for an Academy Award for Best Animated Feature. Satrapi became the first woman to be nominated in the category. She later filmed *Chicken with Plums*, also as an animated feature.

Stretching her creative wings, Satrapi switched from making animated films to directing live-action movies with *The Voices*, a film about a serial killer starring Ryan Reynolds. In 2019, she directed a second live-action film, *Radioactive*, about the life of Marie Curie, based on a graphic novel by American artist Lauren Redniss.

At the time *The Voices* was released, Satrapi said she had abandoned the graphic novel form. "With that [*Persepolis*] and my second film, *Chicken With Plums*, I became the woman who makes films about Iran," she told the British newspaper *Guardian* in 2015. "Now I'm 44 years old. I need to break the frame I've made for myself in order to move on. I don't want to have any regrets once I have all the tubes in all the holes of my body. If I were to make Persepolis 2, I would feel like puking up over myself. And comics—no, I don't think I will go back."

WHY YOU SHOULD READ IT

I repeat: I chose books for their consequence, timeliness, literary value, and accessibility. *Persepolis* is another work in which I found all of these qualities eminently on display. It is also a work that is outside the admittedly Western focus of many of these selections. Obviously, it is important to expand our reading focus beyond American borders. In a recent account of young schoolgirls who are challenging Islamic authority in Iran by refusing to wear the required veil, I found such a significant example of consequence and timeliness. "The Islamist radicals who took charge shaped their project for Iranian society around women's subordination," wrote Azadeh Moaveni in the *New Yorker*. "The veiled schoolgirl, memorialized in Marjane Satrapi's graphic novel 'Persepolis,' became the symbol of a system designed to turn out model Islamic citizens by force." That is one reason *Persepolis* is here. Books inspire people to action. Satrapi's graphic document of resistance has found a new generation of young Iranian women.

Beyond that, *Persepolis* represents a moment of defiance in a contemporary theocracy and offers a picture of a country whose traditions and history remain obscure to many Americans. Satrapi and her books have been extolled for their unique approach to history and memoir. Writing in the *New Yorker*, Peter Schjeldahl commented:

> The best first-person graphic novel to date, 'Persepolis' (2003), and the second-best, 'Persepolis 2' (2004, both Pantheon), are by a woman, Marjane Satrapi. They suggest a number of rules for the form: have a compelling life, remember everything, tell it straight, and be very brave. . . . Her uncanny way of incorporating exposition, with nary a stumble in her pell-mell narrative momentum, immerses us in the lore of Iranian history and culture. Drawn in an inky and crude visual style that is as direct as a slap . . . It's a comic strategy that maintains buoyancy even in the face of the oppression, torture, and death of people dear to her, without for a moment treating the ordeals of others as secondary to her own.

Adding to the praise, Fernanda Eberstadt wrote in a *New York Times* review: "Like Spiegelman's 'Maus,' Satrapi's book combines political history and memoir, portraying a country's 20th-century upheavals through the story of one family. Her protagonist is Marji, a tough, sassy little Iranian girl, bent on prying from her evasive elders if not truth, at least a credible explanation of the travails they are living through."

Underlying this highly individualistic perspective on a turning point in modern history are profound ideas: Islamic fundamentalism versus Western

individualism versus Marxist ideology; coming-of-age and youthful rebel-
liousness versus family loyalties; and the reality of war in the eyes of a young
girl who sees a friend's bracelet in the wreckage of a bombed building.
Images and impressions like these are the reason that *Persepolis* cannot be
dismissed as a "comic book."

And it is a valuable history lesson. For many Americans, the mention
of Iran still conjures a single image: of captured American diplomats led
blindfolded out of the U.S. embassy in Teheran after the Shah's ouster. As
this hostage crisis led to a disastrous failed rescue operation under President
Jimmy Carter, the situation in Iran became an American political issue that
helped Ronald Reagan win the presidency in 1980. (The successful rescue
of several Americans from Teheran formed the backdrop of Ben Affleck's
2012 Academy Award–winning film *Argo*.)

Nearly half a century after the overthrow of the Shah in 1979, Iran
remains an intractable opponent of the United States. More recently, Iran
has become the scene of large public demonstrations against the regime's
Islamic morality police, following the death of a young woman who
allegedly broke the country's strict dress code. As described by Azadeh
Moaveni in the *New Yorker*:

> Last September, people rose up in fury at the killing of Mahsa Jina
> Amini, a young woman being held in police custody for allegedly
> flouting the dress code, and then stayed in the streets, demanding an
> end to clerical tyranny. Schoolgirls emerged as an unexpected source
> of defiant energy. In October, a video surfaced online of a throng of
> teen-agers on the streets of Tehran, stopping traffic, ripping up photos
> of Iran's first Supreme Leader, Ruhollah Khomeini, and chanting
> "Death to the dictator." Similar scenes erupted around the country,
> with crowds of girls and young women marching down boulevards
> and waving their veils in the air.

To many Americans, the country remains a cipher, obscured by simplistic media coverage and Iranian official censorship. Iran's recent history,
so entwined with American foreign policy debates and politics, is often

presented in black-and-white. And that is another reason *Persepolis* is worth reading. It makes a very human story out of a hard history. Home to a large, urban elite, Iran has been, as a *New York Times* review of *Persepolis* put it, "decimated by dictatorship and pauperized by decades of war."

In a brief introduction added after the original French publication and dated "Paris, September 2002," Satrapi described her country after the Shah's overthrow:

> Since then, this old and great civilization has been discussed mostly in connection with fundamentalism, fanaticism, and terrorism. As an Iranian who has lived more than half of my life in Iran, I know this image is far from the truth. This is why writing *Persepolis* was so important to me. I believe that an entire nation should not be judged by the wrongdoings of a few extremists. I also don't want those Iranians who lost their lives in prisons defending freedom, who died in the war against Iraq, who suffered under various repressive regimes, or who were forced to leave their families and flee their homeland to be forgotten.

WHAT TO READ NEXT

The obvious choice is the sequel, *Persepolis 2: The Story of a Return*. You might follow on with the author's other works: the adult graphic novels *Embroideries* and *Chicken with Plums* and a children's book, *Monsters Are Afraid of the Moon*.

Another excellent memoir of postrevolutionary Iran is worth consideration. *Reading Lolita in Tehran: A Memoir in Books* (2003) is Azar Nafisi's best-selling account of a university literature professor's experience in Iran before and after the Islamic Revolution. A celebration of reading and literature, it includes a memorable episode in which Professor Nafisi, responding to the criticism of one of her very devout Islamic students, agrees to put F. Scott Fitzgerald's *The Great Gatsby* "on trial"; the angry young man will act as "prosecutor." In a *New York Times* book review, critic Michiko Kakutani celebrated Nafisi's work:

It is a visceral and often harrowing portrait of the Islamic revolution
in that country and its fallout on the day-to-day lives of Ms. Nafisi
and her students. It is a thoughtful account of the novels they studied
together and the unexpected parallels they drew between those books
and their own experiences as women living under the unforgiving rule
of the mullahs. And it is, finally, an eloquent brief on the transformative powers of fiction—on the refuge from ideology that art can offer
to those living under tyranny, and art's affirmative and subversive
faith in the voice of the individual.

Another prominent feminist voice from the Islamic world is Egyptian
American journalist Mona Eltahawy in her provocative *Headscarves and
Hymens: Why the Middle East Needs a Sexual Revolution* (2015). It is a book-
length exploration of what the author describes as a war on women in the
Middle East, "a toxic mix of culture and religion that few seem willing or
able to disentangle lest they blaspheme or offend"—expanded from her
2012 *Foreign Policy* article "Why Do They Hate Us?"

"I could not give away the rest of his shoes. . . .
He would need shoes if he was to return."

The Year of Magical Thinking

— 2005 —

Joan Didion

New York: Vintage Books, 2007; 227 pages

OPENING WORDS

Life changes fast.
Life changes in the instant.
You sit down to dinner and life as you know it ends.
The question of self-pity.
Those were the first words I wrote after it happened.

SUMMARY

"Those were the first words I wrote after it happened."
   "It" was the heart attack that ended the life of novelist and screenwriter

John Gregory Dunne, writer Joan Didion's husband. "It" came as the couple
was having dinner in their Manhattan apartment. Didion and Dunne had
just returned from a nearby ICU, where their daughter, Quintana Roo
Dunne, was lying in a hospital bed, on a ventilator, with highly uncertain
prospects.

"This was the beginning of my year of magical thinking," Didion writes.

One of the most acclaimed American writers of recent times, Joan
Didion intimately brings the reader from this life-changing instant through
a year of grief and coping, skipping back and forth in time to present a portrait of an extraordinary marriage and literary collaboration of forty years.
Calling upon her great skills as a memoirist, journalist, and novelist—and
drawing upon a vast breadth of literary references—Didion calibrates the
emotional trauma that comes with losing a life partner.

She moves through this year of loss while navigating the ongoing uncertainty of her daughter's illnesses and dire health. In this national best seller
and National Book Award winner, Didion writes with the haunting clarity
and clear-eyed candor that made her one of the late twentieth century's
most admired writers:

> There have been a few occasions . . . on which I asked John point
> blank what to do. I said I needed his help. I said I could not do this
> alone. I said these things out loud, actually vocalized the words.
>
> I am a writer. Imagining what someone would say or do comes
> to me as naturally as breathing.
>
> Yet on each occasion these pleas for his presence served only to
> reinforce my awareness of the final silence that separated us.

ABOUT THE AUTHOR: JOAN DIDION

At her death in December 2021 at the age of eighty-seven from complications of Parkinson's disease, Joan Didion was one of the most influential,
admired, and widely imitated writers of our time.

Born in Sacramento, California, on December 5, 1934, she was a fifth-generation Californian whose ancestors had wisely broken off from the ill-fated and notorious Donner party in 1846. Her native California pulsed through much of her work—in both nonfiction and novels. California, wrote William Grimes in Didion's *New York Times* obituary, "provided her with her richest material. In sharp, knowing vignettes, she captured its harshness and beauty, its role as a magnet for restless settlers, its golden promise and rapidly vanishing past, and its power as a cultural laboratory."

Encouraged by her mother, Didion began to write in her childhood. "I wrote stories from the time I was a little girl, but I didn't want to be a writer. I wanted to be an actress," she told the *Paris Review* in 1978. "I didn't realize then that it's the same impulse. It's make-believe. It's performance. The only difference being that a writer can do it all alone." She says she learned writing by reading and copying out Hemingway, recalling in the same interview, "When I was fifteen or sixteen I would type out his stories to learn how the sentences worked. I taught myself to type at the same time."

While a student at the University of California, Berkeley, Didion won a stint as guest fiction editor at *Mademoiselle* and then took the top prize in an essay contest sponsored by *Vogue* in 1957. Turning down a proffered trip to Paris, she instead went to work for the magazine, moving from copy writer to associate features editor. Didion also began to contribute articles to other magazines, including the conservative *National Review*. In 1963, Didion published her first novel, *Run River*. A year later, she married John Gregory Dunne, then a writer at *Time*, and they later adopted a daughter they named Quintana Roo.

The couple began screenwriting together and collaborated on *Panic in Needle Park*, adapted from a novel about heroin addicts in New York, from which Al Pacino emerged as a star. (The film was produced by John Gregory Dunne's brother Dominick Dunne, later to achieve success as a novelist and true-crime writer.) They also adapted Didion's second novel, *Play It as It Lays*, and a rock-and-roll rewrite of the classic *A Star is Born*, starring Barbra Streisand and Kris Kristofferson. John Gregory Dunne had, in the meantime, published his novel *True Confessions* and Didion

and Dunne wrote the screenplay for the film, featuring Robert De Niro
and Robert Duvall as brothers—one a priest and the other a cop—in 1948
Los Angeles.

While the couple wrote for the movies, Didion continued her journalistic work. In 1967, on assignment for the *Saturday Evening Post*, she
went to the center of sixties hippiedom, San Francisco's Haight-Ashbury,
famed for its drugs and "free love." Using the fiction writer's techniques,
famously proclaimed "The New Journalism" in 1973 by fellow practitioner
Tom Wolfe, Didion wrote a dismissive account of what had become a
highly romanticized scene. The article was later collected with other essays
in the book *Slouching Towards Bethlehem* (1968). Didion's attitude toward
the hippie milieu reflected what was then a decidedly conservative bent.
"She wrote pieces about John Wayne, her favorite movie star, and, in the
1964 Presidential election, she voted for Barry Goldwater," Louis Menand
commented of Didion. "She adored Goldwater. It was hardly a surprise
that she found Haight-Ashbury repugnant."

A later collection, *The White Album* (1979), included pieces about
Charles Manson, The Doors, Janis Joplin, and the arrival of the shopping
mall, as well as her own nervous breakdown. Interviewing Didion in 1979 at
the time of the publication of *The White Album*—a reference to the Beatles
album of the same name—*New York Times* critic Michiko Kakutani wrote:

> And she has created, in her books, one of the most devastating and
> distinctive portraits of modern America to be found in fiction or
> nonfiction. . . . A gifted reporter with an eye for the telling detail—the
> frayed hem, the shaking hand—she is also a prescient witness, finding
> in her own experiences parallels of the times. The voice is always
> precise, the tone unsentimental, the view unabashedly subjective.
> She takes things personally.

By the late 1970s, Didion had shifted to writing for the *New York
Review of Books* and later the *New Yorker*—decidedly different venues from
William Buckley's *National Review* or the *Saturday Evening Post*. In one
important piece, "New York: Sentimental Journeys" (*New York Review of*

Books, January 17, 1991), she addressed the infamous case of the rape of a woman in Central Park and the five young men who were convicted of the crime. In pointing out the flawed manner in which the story was covered in the media, along with the commentary of elected officials and the tainted prosecution of the case, Didion anticipated the ultimate exoneration of the so-called Central Park Five in 2012.

Didion had by then passed a turning point, a shift that she had addressed in a 2003 book, *Where I Was From*, in which she surrendered the rugged individualism myth of her California upbringing. As Louis Menand writes, "Didion came to see the whole pioneer mystique as bogus from the start. The cultivation of California was not the act of rugged pioneers, she decided. It was the act of the federal government, which built the dams and the weirs and the railroads that made the state economically exploitable, public money spent on behalf of private business."

In the year that book was published, her daughter, Quintana, developed pneumonia that progressed to toxic shock. It was after Didion and John Gregory Dunne visited their daughter in the hospital on December 30, 2003, that Dunne suffered the fatal heart attack that opens *The Year of Magical Thinking*. Some twenty months later, in August 2005, Quintana Roo Dunne Michael died of acute pancreatitis. Didion wrote about her daughter's death in *Blue Nights* (2011), described by Michiko Kakutani as "a searing inquiry into loss and a melancholy meditation on mortality and time."

The Year of Magical Thinking was later transformed into a one-woman Broadway show starring Vanessa Redgrave. In 2017, Joan Didion was the subject of a documentary, *Joan Didion: The Center Will Not Hold*, produced and directed by actor-filmmaker Griffin Dunne, her nephew.

In an appreciative tribute written after Didion's death, critic Michiko Kakutani summarized her impact:

> She was uncannily attuned to the dark undercurrents of the day—the social fractures and divides that fueled carelessness and alienation. This is one reason Didion's work resonates so deeply with us today. Once again, we are living in times defined by chaos and uncertainty,

and what Didion called "the jitters" are settling in again, as we worry about Covid and climate change and police brutality and mass shootings at schools.

WHY YOU SHOULD READ IT

First, my own "True Confession." Reading *The Year of Magical Thinking* was my first encounter with Joan Didion. How that is possible I cannot answer. After all, Didion was, as critic Parul Sehgal described her in an appreciation, "the grand diagnostician of American disorder in essays of strong, unmistakable cadence, churning with floods and fire."

But I should also note the circumstances in which I read the book. Having escaped Covid for more than two years, I came down with a case in August 2022. Lying in bed and drinking Gatorade and ginger ale in isolation from my very attentive wife seemed like exactly the right moment to read Joan Didion. It was, for me, a straight-through, can't-put-it-down read.

Why? As a writer, also married for more than forty years to a writer, I certainly felt a personal connection to this story. It deepened when I read Didion obsessively did crossword puzzles—as I do. Although my bout of Covid was, fortunately, quite mild, the book also spoke to issues of marriage, mortality, and meaningfulness—of living life to its fullest. Didion's description of John Gregory Dunne's desire for an impulsive trip—"if he did not go to Paris in November he would never again go to Paris," Didion remembers—struck me as one of those "seize the day" moments. For me, these themes all resonated very powerfully.

But apart from these personal reverberations, the book is passionate and brilliantly written. As critic Robert Pinsky wrote:

> Didion's book is thrilling and engaging—sometimes quite funny—because it ventures to tell the truth. . . . As in Didion's previous writing, her sense of timing, sentence by sentence and in the arrangement of scenes, draws the reader forward. Her manner is deadpan funny, slicing away banality with an air that is ruthless yet meticulous. She uses few adjectives. The unshowy, nearly flat surface of her writing is

rippled by patterns of repetition: an understatement that, like Hemingway's, attains its own kind of drama. Repetition and observation narrate emotion by demonstrating it, so that restraint itself becomes poetic, even operatic.

When a book is really good, when it is so well tuned, it becomes unforgettable. We don't want to let it go. Near the end of *The Year of Magical Thinking*, Didion says she doesn't want to finish writing it. And we don't want to finish reading it. But as she writes, "I also know that if we are to live ourselves there comes a point at which we must relinquish the dead, let them go, keep them dead."

There is, after all, no point to keeping the shoes.

WHAT TO READ NEXT

With Joan Didion, there is a wealth of choices, in both her nonfiction and novels. Her two early collections of essays, *Slouching Towards Bethlehem* and *The White Album*, have achieved classic status. They are bookended by Didion's personal reappraisal in *Where I Was From*. Reviewing it, Thomas Mallon wrote: ". . . the more penetrating and idiosyncratic moments of 'Where I Was From' are the work of someone who can still be very much herself, someone who is even now, arguably, a great American writer."

"Eat food. Not too much. Mostly plants."

Food Rules:
An Eater's Manual

— 2009 —

Michael Pollan

New York: Penguin Books, 2011; illustrations by Maira Kalman; 207 pages

OPENING WORDS

Eat food.

These days this is easier said than done, especially when seventeen thousand new products show up in the supermarket each year, all vying for your food dollar. But most of these items don't deserve to be called food—I prefer to call them edible foodlike substances. They're highly processed concoctions designed by food scientists, consisting mostly of ingredients derived from corn and soy that no normal person keeps in the pantry, and they contain chemical additives with which the human body has not been long acquainted. Today much of the challenge of eating well comes down to choosing real food and avoiding these industrial novelties.

SUMMARY

The Bible has ten commandments. In *On Tyranny* (see entry), Timothy Snyder offers twenty lessons to save democracy. And in this slim—appropriately—volume about what we eat, writer Michael Pollan offers eighty-three rules. Sounds like a lot. But actually, they are quite simple and can be reduced to this simple seven-word mantra: "Eat food. Not too much. Mostly plants."

First published in 2009, with a mere sixty-four rules for better eating, this revised edition of *Food Rules* added nineteen commandments—some solicited from readers—about how to shop for food and eat well, more mindfully, and, most of all, more healthfully. Pollan has firm ideas. But he is not a doctrinaire scold prescribing a diet of sprouts and brown rice. His rules are laid out simply in a witty, charming, often funny manner.

The bonus feature in this edition is the whimsical illustrations provided by artist Maira Kalman, whom Pollan encountered at a TED Conference, where he had "the unenviable job" of following her as a speaker. He recalls hearing her opening lines to the audience:

> "I'm trying to figure out two very simple things," she began. "How to live and how to die. And I'm also trying to have some meals, and some snacks, yell at my children, and do all the normal things." Maira is a poet of all the normal things: life, death, and a nice snack.

With Kalman's drawings as a delightful accompaniment, Pollan organizes his rules under the three principles he espouses.

In the "Eat food" section, for instance, Rule #7 is "Avoid food products that contain ingredients that a third-grader cannot pronounce." This is a variation on a simpler rule: "Don't eat anything your great-grandmother wouldn't recognize as food." But my favorite may be #22: "It's not food if it arrived through the window of your car."

In section 2 about what to eat—"mostly plants"—Pollan cautions: "Don't eat breakfast cereals that change the color of the milk." (I see you, Froot Loops®.) And finally, in discussing how to eat ("Not too much"), the rules are also fairly simple, and may recall your mother—or father—saying, "Do all your eating at the table." Pollan writes in Rule #73: "No, a desk is not a table."

And in case you think this is all one big scold, Pollan finishes with—spoiler alert—Rule #83: "Break the rules once in a while."

ABOUT THE AUTHOR: MICHAEL POLLAN

Born in February 1955 on Long Island, New York, Michael Pollan is a journalist and writer whose various works on food and other things people put into their bodies have made him one of the most influential authors of our time. In 2010, *Time* magazine named Pollan one of the most influential people in the world in their annual ranking.

Having majored in English at Vermont's Bennington College and studied at Mansfield College, Oxford University, Pollan obtained his master's degree in English from Columbia University in 1981. A few years later, in 1984, Pollan was hired by *Harper's Magazine*, rising to executive editor before moving to become a contributing writer with the *New York Times Magazine* in 1987. In 1991, his first book, *Second Nature: A Gardener's Education*, collected his gardening articles.

Pollan's interest in vegetation and flowers blossomed into 2001's *The Botany of Desire*, which examined the history of four different plants—apples, tulips, cannabis, and the potato. Next came *The Omnivore's Dilemma: A Natural History of Four Meals*, which became a best seller and was named one of the best books of 2006 by both the *Washington Post* and the *New York Times*. Then he wrote *In Defense of Food: An Eater's Manifesto* (2008), which set forth his seven-word motto cited earlier.

As Pollan's output flowered, recognition came with it. He has received numerous awards, listed on his website: they include the James Beard Award for best magazine series in 2003; the John Burroughs prize for the best natural history essay in 1997; the 2003 Humane Society of the United States' Genesis Award for his writing on animal agriculture; the Nierenberg Prize for Science in the Public Interest by the Scripps Institution of Oceanography (2014); the Washburn Award for "outstanding contribution to public understanding of science" from the Boston Museum of Science; and the Lennon Ono Grant for Peace in 2010. His work has also been made into documentaries including a two-hour PBS special based on *The Botany of Desire*. He appeared in the Oscar-nominated 2008 documentary *Food Inc.*, which was partly based on *The Omnivore's Dilemma*. Pollan has also taught at University of California, Berkeley's Graduate School of Journalism and at Harvard as Professor of the Practice of Non-fiction.

His work took an unusual turn in 2018. After using certain psychedelic drugs such as LSD, he wrote *How to Change Your Mind*—named one of the best books of 2018 by the *New York Times*. Two years later, Pollan cofounded the UC Berkeley Center for the Science of Psychedelics and wrote *This Is Your Mind on Plants* (2021), which also explores mind-altering plants and fungi—including opium, caffeine, and mescaline—that have been used traditionally for centuries. Reviewing it, Rob Dunn wrote: "Pollan then turns to his own narratives of gardening and self-experimentation. As he does, he also masterfully elevates a series of big questions about drugs, plants and humans that are likely to leave readers thinking in new ways."

WHY YOU SHOULD READ IT

Consequence. Timeliness. Making us think.

So, I ask, what is more consequential, timely, and important to rethink than what and how we eat—and how what we eat affects how we live? Pollan succinctly and convincingly makes the case for this most basic piece of survival—eating properly. And it is a pure joy to read. What more can you ask of a book?

One of the most profoundly influential books in American history—and in my reading life—was Upton Sinclair's 1906 novel, *The Jungle*. A fictional exposé of the ills of the meatpacking industry in early twentieth-century America by a socialist and muckraking journalist, it led to the some of the nation's first laws to protect Americans from the food they eat. It spurred President Theodore Roosevelt to sign the Pure Food and Drug Act that same year. "I aimed at the public's heart," Sinclair later wrote, "and by accident hit its stomach."

Food Rules is a far cry from Upton Sinclair. But it is an important book that underscores the same principle: the food we eat and where it comes from are profoundly significant issues of health, politics, and business. We are what we eat. The American approach to food—or what is called food—on an industrial scale and its relationship to an obesity epidemic with many far-ranging impacts on health have been well-documented. Pollan's book takes on these issues with journalistic skills, presenting his findings in an accessible and joyful manner.

Since I am not a scientist, I will turn to *Scientific American* for one essential reason I chose this book and why it addresses such a serious matter: "As with most things related to people, the food we eat comes with a carbon cost. Soil tillage, crop and livestock transportation, manure management and all the other aspects of global food production generate greenhouse gas emissions to the tune of more than 17 billion metric tons per year, according to a new study," writes Andrea Thompson. "Animal-based foods account for 57 percent of those emissions, and plant-based ones make up 29 percent."

A recent UN publication reinforces this fact:

> What we eat, and how that food is produced, affects our health but also the environment.
>
> Food needs to be grown and processed, transported, distributed, prepared, consumed, and sometimes disposed of. Each of these steps creates greenhouse gases that trap the sun's heat and contribute to climate change. About a third of all human-caused greenhouse gas emissions is linked to food.

Certainly, one point of this entire collection of short nonfiction is to provide insight into how we all might live more consciously and thoughtfully. Think about it: Pollan's book is about mindfulness in the most important of ways—paying attention to how we shop, cook, eat, and share the food that keeps us alive. Aimed at the most basic necessity of life, his book accomplishes that. Pollan's advice is good for the planet and our well-being. *Buon appetito!*

WHAT TO READ NEXT

Food Rules was preceded by a much longer book, *The Omnivore's Dilemma: A Natural History in Four Meals*. Whether food is your interest or not, consider it, as it was selected one of the best books of 2006 by the *New York Times*, which said of Pollan: "He gracefully navigates within these anxieties as he traces the origins of four meals—from a fast-food dinner to a 'hunter-gatherer' feast—and makes us see, with remarkable clarity, exactly how what we eat affects both our bodies and the planet. Pollan is the perfect tour guide: his prose is incisive and alive, and pointed without being tendentious."

Another landmark in recent writing about food and commerce is Eric Schlosser's 2002 book, *Fast Food Nation: The Dark Side of the All-American Meal*. The basis for a documentary film of the same name, the book stands in the great American muckraking tradition as it explores how the fast-food industry altered how we eat, fueling an obesity epidemic as well as perpetuating other social ills.

There have been many notable books focusing on plants and food and their role in human history. I single out one favorite, Mark Kurlansky's *Cod: A Biography of a Fish That Changed the World* (1997), which offers a fascinating view of how this one fish altered history and the European arrival in North America. Another landmark in the genre is John McPhee's *Oranges*, which grew out of a 1966 *New Yorker* article on—you guessed it—oranges. McPhee is one of my favorite writers and a number of his books deserve a shout-out, including *The Survival of the Bark Canoe*, mentioned earlier, and *The Pine Barrens*, both quite short.

"If it is true that the full humanity of women is not our culture,
then we can and must make it our culture."

We Should All Be Feminists

— 2014 —

Chimamanda Ngozi Adichie

New York: Vintage Books, 2014; 52 pages

OPENING WORDS

Okoloma was one of my greatest childhood friends. He lived on my street and looked after me like a big brother: if I liked a boy, I would ask Okoloma's opinion. Okoloma was funny and intelligent and wore cowboy boots that were pointy at the tips. In December 2005, in a plane crash in southern Nigeria, Okoloma died. It is still hard for me to put into words how I felt. Okoloma was a person I could argue with, laugh with and truly talk to. He was also the first person to call me a feminist.

I was about fourteen.

SUMMARY

Based on a viral 2012 TEDx talk, this amusing and always provocative volume is by an award-winning, critically acclaimed, and best-selling Nigerian-born novelist and essayist. Chimamanda Ngozi Adichie zeroes in on the subject of sexism and the worldwide problem of sexual inequality.

Compact and compelling in its essential argument in favor of equity and equality between the sexes in all aspects of life, it presents the personal reflections of a highly accomplished writer whose thoughts range from the personal and comic to the poignant. Early on, Adichie describes how she was told by a journalist while on a book tour in Nigeria that she should not call herself a feminist: ". . . since feminists are women who are unhappy because they cannot find husbands. So I decided to call myself a Happy Feminist."

Adichie is then told that feminism is un-African and man hating: "At some point," she concludes, "I was a Happy African Feminist Who Does Not Hate Men And Who Likes To Wear Lip Gloss And High Heels For Herself And Not For Men."

While poking fun at the everyday sexism she experiences and witnesses in this good-natured way, her tone soon turns serious. Citing many personal experiences, she recounts the routine second-class citizenship of women in her native country and beyond. This is not about Nigeria—or Africa—but about the place of women in the world. Confronting these attitudes, she writes: "I am angry. We should all be angry. Anger has a long history of bringing about positive change."

A MacArthur Fellowship recipient, Chimamanda Ngozi Adichie delivers a provocative work that is, in the end, not an angry screed but a heartfelt and even gentle imploring plea: "*All* of us, women and men, must do better."

ABOUT THE AUTHOR: CHIMAMANDA NGOZI ADICHIE

Born on September 15, 1977, in Enugu, Nigeria, Chimamanda Ngozi Adichie is the fifth of six children raised in a Catholic family. Her father was a professor at the University of Nigeria, where her mother worked as the university's first female registrar. Her family resided in a university residence where the acclaimed novelist Chinua Achebe once lived. Achebe's 1958 book, *Things Fall Apart*, won him international fame, stands as the centerpiece of modern African literature, and is among the most important novels of the twentieth century. A voracious reader from childhood, Adichie discovered the book at a fairly young age, and it became a great influence on her. "He is a remarkable man. The writer and the man," Adichie said of Achebe in an interview with the BBC in 2007. "He's what I think writers should be."

After a year of study at a Nigerian medical college, Adichie chose to move to the United States, where her older sister was already in school. Studying for a time in Philadelphia, Adichie moved to Connecticut to care for her sister's son and earn money to pay her way through college. She graduated from Eastern Connecticut State University with a B.A. in communication and political science in 2001. While still a student, Adichie began her first novel, *Purple Hibiscus*, a coming-of-age story published in 2003 that collected several significant literary awards in the U.K. and put her on the publishing map.

Adichie went on to receive a master's in creative writing at Johns Hopkins University in 2003 and later a master's in African history from Yale in 2008. By then, her second novel, *Half of a Yellow Sun*, had also been published. Another highly regarded, prizewinning work, it was set during the brutal civil war between Nigeria and Biafra, begun in 1967, when the region of Biafra attempted to break away from Nigeria. Rooted in religious differences and tribalism, the conflict led to civilian massacres and the world saw horrific images of starving children—part of the estimated 2 million who perished from a famine caused by a Nigerian blockade. The conflict lasted until 1970 and Adichie's paternal grandfather died in a refugee camp during the war.

By 2008, Adichie was garnering more recognition, having received a MacArthur Fellowship, and then, in 2009, she published a critically acclaimed collection of short stories, *The Thing Around Your Neck*. That same year, she gave a TEDGlobal talk called "The Danger of a Single Story," which has been viewed more than 34 million times. Her most successful and acclaimed work to date came with publication in 2013 of *Americanah*, a much-admired novel telling of the struggles of a young Nigerian woman, Ifemelu, who moves to the United States and finds a certain amount of fame as a blogger writing about race and nationality.

Further elevating Adichie's status, *Americanah* won the National Book Critics Circle Award and was named to many best-of-the-year lists, including the *New York Times*'s 10 Best Books of 2013. According to the *Times*, "From the office politics of a hair-braiding salon to the burden of memory, there's nothing too humble or daunting for this fearless writer, who is so attuned to the various worlds and shifting selves we inhabit—in life and online, in love, as agents and victims of history and the heroes of our own stories." That same year, Beyoncé sampled Adichie's 2012 TEDx talk in a song called "Flawless." Adichie added to her considerable fame as the face of a British makeup brand. And in 2017, New Yorkers voted for *Americanah* as the first "One Book, One New York" initiative, encouraging all New York City residents to read the book together.

Her successful career in fiction and two viral TED talks—which have combined for more than 40 million views—have taken Adichie far beyond literary fame. In 2015, she was among *Time* magazine's 100 Most Influential People in the World and in 2017 *Fortune Magazine* named her one of the World's 50 Greatest Leaders.

"So in the past few years, she has become something of a star, flourishing at the unlikely juncture of fiction writing and celebrity," wrote Zoe Greenburg in the *New York Times* in 2017, at the publication of another work focusing on feminism, *Dear Ijeawele, or A Feminist Manifesto in Fifteen Suggestions*. "Her position was on full display during her visit to New York, where she started her book tour last week. She took the stage in front of a sold-out crowd at Cooper Union, and there was 'this kind of unanimous scream,' said Robin Desser, a Knopf editor who has worked with Ms. Adichie for 12 years."

In 2018, Adichie won the PEN Pinter Prize, given by the English branch of the writer's group. The award honors freedom of expression and promotes literature.

WHY YOU SHOULD READ IT

To be clear, we are not talking about a feminist manifesto here—nothing along the lines of, for instance, *The Second Sex* by Simone de Beauvoir (see entry). While there is rising anger in Adichie's plaintive cry, her simple call is for a better world for women—aided by men. It is short and sweet but never saccharine, with all of the complexity one would expect from a writer whose novels have won acclaim for addressing war, colonialism, racism, and sexism.

In a lengthy 2018 *New Yorker* profile that speaks to Adichie's range of concerns, but especially her views on sexual equality, Larissa MacFarquhar wrote:

> The kind of feminism she espoused in her *TEDx* talk—women should be permitted to hold positions of power; if a woman arrived alone at a hotel or a restaurant, she should not be assumed to be a prostitute—is not particularly controversial in America. But in Nigeria any feminism could be taken as a declaration of war against men. When it emerged that she had got married and, later, had a baby, many people in Nigeria were genuinely shocked: they hadn't realized that feminists did those things.

WHAT TO READ NEXT

Since *We Should All Be Feminists* appeared, Adichie has also written another short nonfiction book, *Dear Ijeawele, or A Feminist Manifesto in Fifteen Suggestions*, composed as a letter to a friend just before the birth of her own daughter. After the book was published, Zoe Greenburg noted in the *New York Times*: "The main proposition of 'Dear Ijeawele' is that feminism is a project that necessarily binds mothers and daughters, and that raising a daughter feminist has as much to do with what you tell yourself as what you tell her. Ms. Adichie's first of 15 suggestions places a mother's freedom and growth at the center of a daughter's feminist education."

Adichie herself told an interviewer for the British *Guardian*, "I don't think sexism is worse than racism, it's impossible even to compare. . . . It's that I feel lonely in my fight against sexism, in a way that I don't feel in my fight against racism. My friends, my family, they get racism, they get it. The people I'm close to who are not black get it. But I find that with sexism you are constantly having to explain, justify, convince, make a case for."

Written shortly after the death of her father, in 2021, Adichie's *Notes on Grief* in 2021 mourns his passing and celebrates his life. "It explores the brutality of those first desperate moments of grief," writes Leslie Gray Streeter in a *Washington Post* review, "this 'cruel kind of education' in this unasked-for new life."

While I have read neither of these, I plan to add both of them, along with *Americanah*, her highly praised third novel, to my To-Be-Read list.

Also not yet read is a critically praised recent book about women in the Islamic world. *It's Not About the Burqa: Muslim Women on Faith, Feminism, Sexuality and Race* is a 2021 collection of essays edited by Mariam Khan.

"Do not obey in advance."

On Tyranny: Twenty Lessons from the Twentieth Century

— 2017 —

Timothy Snyder

New York: Tim Duggan Books/Crown, 2017; 126 pages

OPENING WORDS

History does not repeat, but it does instruct. As the Founding Fathers debated our Constitution, they took instruction from the history they knew. Concerned that the democratic republic they envisioned would collapse, they contemplated the descent of ancient democracies and republics into oligarchy and empire. As they knew, Aristotle warned that equality brought instability, while Plato believed that demagogues exploited free speech to install themselves as tyrants. In founding a democratic republic upon law and establishing a system of checks and balances, the Founding Fathers sought to avoid the evil that they, like the ancient philosophers, called *tyranny* [original emphasis].

SUMMARY

How do we combat totalitarianism and preserve democracy? These are big questions for one small book to take on, but *On Tyranny* does just that in twenty succinct lessons.

Its author, Timothy Snyder, is a leading scholar in the areas of authoritarianism and modern European history—the history of Ukraine in particular. Each of his brief tutorials includes a pointed historical lesson, sharpened by a significant example. In #1, "Do not obey in advance," for example, Snyder points to the "anticipatory obedience" that took place after a 1932 German election led to Adolf Hitler becoming Germany's chancellor in a parliamentary-style government. Soon after, Germany was a one-party Nazi state.

When Hitler's Germany annexed Austria in 1938, Snyder writes, "it was the Austrians' anticipatory obedience that decided the fate of Austrian Jews. Local Austrian Nazis captured Jews and forced them to scrub the streets to remove symbols of independent Austria. Crucially, people who were not Nazis looked on with interest and amusement."

Snyder's twenty lessons may be brief, but that does not mean they are easy. Indeed, many are challenging: #2: "Defend institutions"; #6: "Be wary of paramilitaries";" #10: "Believe in truth" and the related #11: "Investigate." These might seem to be self-explanatory or, in the famous words of Thomas Jefferson "self-evident truths," but each lesson contains morals and powerful historical models well beyond the condensed wisdom Snyder expresses.

Others are slightly more cryptic, such as #12: "Make eye contact and small talk." Under the twentieth century's most repressive regimes, such as Germany, Italy, and the Soviet Union, small gestures—the smile, the handshake—often spoke volumes. "In the most dangerous of times, those who escape and survive generally know people whom they can trust," Snyder points out. "Having old friends is the politics of last resort. And making new ones is the first step towards change."

Perhaps he saves the hardest of all for last: #20: "Be as courageous as you can." Beneath that heading, Snyder writes: "If none of us is prepared to die for freedom, then all of us will die under tyranny."

ABOUT THE AUTHOR: TIMOTHY SNYDER

A teacher, historian, and public intellectual—and, increasingly, a voice of warning in a dangerous time—Timothy Snyder was born near Dayton, Ohio, on August 18, 1969. At this writing, he is the Richard C. Levin Professor of History at Yale University and a permanent fellow at the Institute for Human Sciences in Vienna.

Snyder received a degree in history and political science from Brown University, and then a doctorate in modern history from the University of Oxford. Numerous academic awards and fellowships followed, as Snyder produced scholarly histories and popular works, including the highly acclaimed *Bloodlands: Europe Between Hitler and Stalin*. As a reviewer in the *New York Times* wrote, Snyder's book "compels us to look squarely at the full range of destruction committed first by Stalin's regime and then by Hitler's Reich. Each fashioned a terrifying orgy of deliberate mass killing."

Speaking five European languages—and reading ten—Snyder has turned his expertise in Europe's bloody past into an international platform for discussing the accelerating threats to freedom and democracy around the world. His familiarity with Ukraine's history has proven especially timely since the Russian invasion of Ukraine in 2022, still ongoing at this writing.

Even before the Russian invasion, Snyder's expertise and his ability as a communicator had "established Mr. Snyder, 46, as a rising public intellectual," wrote Jennifer Schuessler of the *New York Times* in 2015, "unafraid to make bold connections between past and present, most notably in his full-throated defense of Ukraine in the face of what he has called Russian president Vladimir V. Putin's 'assault on European history.'"

WHY YOU SHOULD READ IT

Reading Snyder's book reminded me of an old saying, attributed to Mark Twain and his collaborator Charles Dudley Warner: "Everyone talks about the weather, but nobody does anything about it."

We might say the same thing about the modern authoritarian threat—both globally and in the United States, where voter suppression, anti-immigrant propaganda, censorship, nationalism, attacks on the press as "enemies of the state," and other typical tools of the authoritarian have become commonplace in recent times.

In this collection, Snyder does offer a way to do something about it.

"In recent years, he became something of a hero to liberals for a series of books particularly 'On Tyranny: 20 Lessons from the 20th Century,' which became something like a Bible for worried liberals early in the Trump era," notes journalist Ezra Klein. "These are books about what it feels like and what you do when your society is beginning to creep down or trip down the road to authoritarianism."

Why read it? If you care about the future of democracy, Snyder offers sound advice for protecting democratic ideals and the rule of law before they are extinguished. Once gone, they are much harder to resuscitate. And unlike the weather, we can do something about it.

WHAT TO READ NEXT

Many of Timothy Snyder's other works are far more scholarly than *On Tyranny*—and certainly not short books. Nonetheless, some are indispensable, including *Bloodlands: Europe Between Hitler and Stalin*. It is a powerful work presenting a complex view of the murderous period in Ukraine and eastern Europe that preceded World War II. I highly recommend it.

Snyder also collaborated on *Thinking the Twentieth Century* with the late Tony Judt, author of several highly acclaimed works of history. Judt's final work, published just before his death in 2010, is another brilliant book, *Ill Fares the Land*. Initially published after the 2008 financial crash, it was reissued in 2021. In it, Judt wrote:

The materialistic and selfish quality of contemporary life is not inherent in the human condition. Much of what appears "natural" today dates from the 1980s: the obsession with wealth creation, the cult of privatization and the private sector, the growing disparities of rich and poor. And above all, the rhetoric which accompanies these: uncritical admiration for unfettered markets, disdain for the public sector, the delusion of endless growth.

Many writers currently discussing the authoritarian threat cite Hannah Arendt, author of the seminal work *The Origins of Totalitarianism* (1951) and *Eichmann in Jerusalem: A Report on the Banality of Evil* (1963), in which Arendt reported on the trial in Israel of Nazi official Adolf Eichmann, one of the major organizers of the Holocaust. Both are long but important works. Much shorter, somewhat more accessible, and perhaps more timely are two of Arendt's books: *On Violence* (1970), an erudite essay on the violence and politics in a post–World War II, Cold War era, is still salient in a post–January 6 era as she writes: ". . . those who hold power and feel it slipping from their hands, be they the government or be they the governed, have always found it difficult to resist the temptation to substitute violence for it"; *On Lying and Politics* is an expansion of an essay written in 1971 in response to the publication of the Pentagon Papers and reissued in 2022 "No one has ever doubted that truth and politics are on rather bad terms with each other," Arendt opens, "and no one, as far as I know, has ever counted truthfulness among the political virtues."

"Race has been a constant arbiter of difference, as have wealth, class, and gender—each of which is about power and the necessity of control."

The Origin of Others

— 2017 —

Toni Morrison

Cambridge, MA: Harvard University Press, 2017; foreword by Ta-Nehisi Coates; 114 pages

EXCERPT

Finally, after a round of visits with other relatives, she entered our living room, tall, straight-backed, leaning on a cane she obviously did not need, and greeted my mother. Then, staring at my sister and me, playing or simply sitting on the floor, she frowned, pointed her cane at us, and said, "These children have been tampered with." My mother objected (strenuously), but the damage was done. My great-grandmother was tar black, and my mother knew precisely what she meant: we, her children, and therefore our immediate family, were sullied, not pure.

SUMMARY

One of America's most acclaimed writers, Nobel Prize laureate Toni Morrison opens this collection of essays with a memorable childhood recollection of a visit by her great-grandmother Millicent MacTeer—"the wise, unquestionable, majestic head of our family." Not understanding at such a young age the import of her great-grandmother's words—that Morrison had "been tampered with"—the author later came to see that she had been identified as "the Other."

"Othering"—in Morrison's brilliantly argued work—is the ancient human propensity to identify and classify groups of people as outsiders and, accordingly, as somehow lesser. As Morrison recognizes and defines it here, this powerful construction is part of a long history: ". . . our tendency to separate and judge those not in our clan as the enemy, as the vulnerable and the deficient needing control."

In Morrison's case it was the idea that she was "sullied" by white blood, an incongruous twist on America's once-prevalent "one-drop rule." Codified in state laws in many twentieth-century American states, the rule meant a single Black ancestor required legal designation as "Negro" or "Colored," with the loss of civil rights such a designation conveyed. These laws held sway until the Supreme Court's Loving decision in 1967 outlawed miscegenation.

Based on a series of lectures delivered at Harvard by Morrison in 2016, these essays offer a remarkably clear-eyed, perceptive, and damning survey of the "othering" of many different groups—for example, Jews, Catholics, and Orthodox immigrants coming to America, mostly from eastern and southern Europe. But Morrison focuses on how, in American history, the Other connects powerfully and inextricably to race. This racial divide is underscored in the opening essay, "Romancing Slavery."

In the course of the work, Morrison peppers her position with powerful references to historical documents and the literature of Harriet Beecher Stowe, William Faulkner, Flannery O'Connor, and Ernest Hemingway. She first offers a description of scientific racism—how southern enslavers, and later Americans in the eugenics field, attempted to "prove" the observation that "blacks are useful, not quite like cattle, yet not recognizably human." Morrison also describes how these questions of "othering" and race drove much of her own fiction, beginning with *The Bluest Eye*, eventually leading to what is widely acknowledged as her greatest work, *Beloved*.

In six highly concentrated and elegantly composed chapters, Morrison speaks to a question broader than race alone that continues to bedevil America and the globalized world. The "Other" remains at the heart of wars, global politics, and ethnic and racial hatred that are ultimately about power and control.

ABOUT THE AUTHOR: TONI MORRISON

Born Chloe Ardelia Wofford on February 18, 1931, Toni Morrison grew up in Depression-era Lorain, Ohio, the daughter of a welder and a homemaker. "Young Chloe grew up in a house suffused with narrative and superstition," Margalit Fox wrote in the *New York Times* after her death. "She adored listening to ghost stories; her grandmother ritually consulted a book on dream interpretation, from which she divined the day's selections when she played the numbers."

After joining the Roman Catholic Church, Chloe chose the baptismal name Anthony—the name from which her familiar nickname, Toni, emerged while she attended Howard University. After earning a master's in English literature at Cornell in 1955, Chloe Wofford taught at Houston's Texas Southern University and then at Howard, where she joined a writing workshop and began writing her own fiction.

She married Harold Morrison, an architect from Jamaica, in 1958 and they had two sons, Harold Ford and Slade. After the couple divorced, in 1964, Morrison moved to Syracuse, New York, finding work as a textbook editor. Eventually, she and her sons moved to New York, where she joined Random House as a book editor, working there for nearly two decades. As an editor, Morrison was determined to publish African American writers, and among the authors with whom she worked were activists Angela Davis and Huey Newton, novelist Gayle Jones, and Muhammad Ali, whose best-selling autobiography she edited.

While working at Random House, Morrison continued to pursue her own writing. A single mother raising two boys, she rose to write each day at 4 a.m. In 1970, *The Bluest Eye*, her first novel, was published; Morrison later spoke of her surprise at seeing what she considered a nickname, Toni Morrison, rather than her name, Chloe Wofford, on the cover. Set in Morrison's hometown of Lorain, it is the semi-autobiographical story of Pecola, a young Black girl who considers herself ugly and longs for the blue eyes she considers the symbol of whiteness and ideal beauty.

Winning admiring reviews, the book became a staple in university-level courses in African American history and literature. But when it began to be introduced to younger readers, *The Bluest Eye* emerged as a perennial target of bans and challenges. According to the American Library Association's Office for Intellectual Freedom (OIF), *The Bluest Eye* was America's tenth most banned and challenged book in the decade from 2010 to 2019 and the third most challenged in 2022.

Her second novel, *Sula* (1973), a multigenerational novel, was followed by her first significant commercial success, *The Song of Solomon* (1977). The book won the National Book Critics Award and became a main selection of the Book-of-the-Month Club, the first novel by a Black writer to be so honored since Richard Wright's *Native Son* in 1940.

During her work as an editor, as she relates in *The Origin of Others*, Morrison came across an 1856 newspaper clipping about an enslaved mother who killed her child. This became the genesis for *Beloved*, published in 1987 and awarded the Pulitzer Prize for Fiction. Following its publication, Morrison left Random House to join the faculty at Princeton University.

In 1993, Toni Morrison was awarded the Nobel Prize in Literature, the first African American woman so honored.

Toni Morrison died of complications from pneumonia in a Bronx hospital at the age of eighty-eight on August 5, 2019. Her death brought a tremendous outpouring of grief and tributes from the literary world. Among those voicing homage to Morrison was novelist Chimamanda Ngozi Adichie (see entry):

Reading Ms. Morrison, you knew she gloried in the joy of language, sentence by sentence, that she dared even to invent her own syntax, and as a reader you trusted her to lead you. She was a lucid thinker in her nonfiction, curious and knowledgeable and reasonable, and in her fiction she showed a compassionate and moving familiarity with the contradictions of human beings. She was Black and she didn't apologize for her Blackness, and she didn't pander and she didn't temper the painful reality of Black American history, in a country that often seemed keen to minimize it. . . . I remember her queenliness, a particular presence that came from a mix of her confidence, her gorgeous silver dreads, and her quite simply being Toni Morrison. And I remember her laughter, joyous and mischievous, a sound so free of restraint, and so uninterested in being false.

WHY YOU SHOULD READ IT

As I write this, slavery is again being "romanced" by those who would obscenely profess that enslavement conveyed some "benefits" to the enslaved by providing them with "skills." In 2023, the state of Florida introduced a controversial set of educational standards professing that violence was historically committed against *and by* (my emphasis) African Americans—ignoring the overwhelmingly vast record of American violence against Black individuals and whole communities over centuries.

Morrison would undoubtedly be horrified, but perhaps not at all surprised, at this turn of events. In this book, Morrison cites a mere handful of the assaults on Black people in the twentieth century—a much longer history documented earlier in this collection by *On Lynchings*. Morrison includes the story of a Black veteran returning home from the Pacific after World War II, who was beaten and left blinded by South Carolina policemen. These are all sickening reminders of the reality of violence against Black Americans. As she writes, "These are just some—there are many, many more, all dreadful—but these are representative, I think, of the circumstances, the real danger for blacks (no longer slaves) in the twentieth century."

So read Morrison because she sets the record straight. Because she tells the unflinching truth, with historical facts—and "facts are stubborn things," as John Adams once said. Let us be crystal clear on this stubborn fact: slavery conveyed no benefits. It was a brutal, murderous crime against humanity. And any effort to cover up or diminish the legacy of enslavement in American history must be denounced in no uncertain terms.

"To understand why we find ourselves here again, we are fortunate to have Toni Morrison, one of the finest writers and thinkers this country has ever produced," writer Ta-Nehisi Coates comments in a foreword to the book. "Her work is rooted in history and pulls beauty from some of its own most grotesque manifestations. But that beauty is not fantasy, and so it should not be surprising that she ranks among those who understand the hold that history has on us all."

In my introduction, I wrote about the key attributes that I sought for books I selected: consequence, timeliness, literary value, and accessibility. Morrison's slim volume is the paradigm of these qualities. If we are to learn, to question assumptions, to challenge our own preconceptions, and, finally, to think, Morrison's work brings us to that place.

WHAT TO READ NEXT

While this is a collection of nonfiction recommendations, it would be impossible to discuss what next to read with respect to Toni Morrison without directing readers to her novels. Among these are *The Bluest Eye* and *Sula*, cited earlier. Both are short works of fiction that plumb many of the issues Morrison discusses in these essays. And all paths in reading Morrison ultimately bring us to her masterpiece, *Beloved*. In 2006, it was selected as "The Best Work of American Fiction of the Last 25 Years" by hundreds of critics, writers, and editors surveyed by the *New York Times*.

In an appreciation written after Morrison's death, *New York Times* critic Dwight Garner commented: "Morrison had a superfluity of gifts and, like few other writers of her era, bent language to her will. Her prose could be lush, or raw and demotic, or carefree and eccentric, often on a single page. She filtered folklore, biblical rhythms, dreams, choral voices and a steep awareness of history into her work. In the best of her 11 novels—these include 'The Bluest Eye' (1970), 'Sula' (1973) and 'Song of Solomon' (1977)—she transmuted the basic matter of existence into profound works of art." Garner concludes with this praise: "This writer enlarged the American imagination in ways we are only beginning to understand."

These books, along with many of Morrison's other works of fiction, continue to stand at the epicenter of the current wave of partisan book censorship in this country. They are not attacked because they are "obscene" or "pornographic." They are despised by these book banners because they reveal stubborn truths that many want to conceal. All the more reason to read Toni Morrison.

"The choices that we'll make—that we are making right now, without being necessarily aware of them—will determine the future of life for our children and their children and all other species on earth for generations to come."

Under a White Sky:
The Nature of the Future

— 2021 —

Elizabeth Kolbert

New York: Crown, 2022; 207 pages plus notes

OPENING WORDS

Rivers make good metaphors—too good, perhaps. They can be murky and charged with hidden meaning, like the Mississippi, which to Twain represented "the grimmest and most dead-earnest of reading matter." Alternatively, they can be bright and clear and mirror-like. Thoreau set off for a week on the Concord and Merrimack Rivers and within a day found himself lost in reflection over the reflections he saw playing on the water. Rivers can signify destiny, or coming into knowledge, or coming upon that which one would rather not know. "Going up that river was like traveling back to the earliest beginnings of the world, when vegetation rioted on the earth," Conrad's Marlow recalls. They can stand for time, for change, and for life itself.

SUMMARY

Pulitzer Prize–winning journalist Elizabeth Kolbert raises two fundamental questions in this provocative book: Can we change nature? And do we have time?

Kolbert, a staff writer at the *New Yorker*, where portions of her book originally appeared, knows well and understands better than most the threat posed to our planet by climate change and other human impacts on the Earth and the environment. In this work, she sets off on an odyssey in search of possible responses to the mess made by centuries of technology, industry, and other human impacts.

In a series of relatively short chapters, she looks for the people who are attempting to use science and technology to reverse the damage before it is too late. One of these attempts, an elaborate project Kolbert calls "solar geoengineering," might alleviate the impact of global warming but change the color of the sky. "White would become the new blue," she writes—hence, her title.

The opening chapter describes the effort of the Army Corps of Engineers and others to manage the silver carp, an invasive species plaguing waters near Chicago. Voracious feeders, they basically wipe out other species of fish—with the irony being that these carp were introduced to American waters in an attempt to clean up sewage treatment plants and water polluted by chemical waste, an idea suggested by Rachel Carson (see entry), author of the landmark environmental work *Silent Spring*.

The carp helped clear the waters of chemicals and toxins, but their numbers soon exploded, with devastating results for the stock of other desirable native fish. The Law of Unintended Consequences at work.

In other chapters, Kolbert describes the area around New Orleans, devastated by storms in recent years, where people have been trying to control nature for centuries. The results, as the catastrophic hurricanes and flooding of recent years indicate, are anything but successful. "A Mississippi that's been harnessed, straightened, regularized, and shackled can still exert a godlike force," Kolbert writes of America's legendary river.

Moving to Iceland, Kolbert meets engineers who are looking for ways to deal with carbon dioxide in the atmosphere by turning such emissions into stone. In Australia, she encounters researchers attempting to create a "super coral" that can survive rising sea temperatures.

"This has been a book," Kolbert writes in conclusion, "about people trying to solve problems created by people trying to solve problems." The problems are real and very daunting, and the solutions are as elusive as the problems are enormous. But Kolbert makes a steady, engaging guide through what increasingly feels like a bleak quest for answers.

ABOUT THE AUTHOR: ELIZABETH KOLBERT

Born in 1961, Elizabeth Kolbert grew up in the Bronx before her family moved to Larchmont, New York, in Westchester County. After graduating from high school and studying literature at Yale, she was awarded a Fulbright Scholarship in 1983. While studying in Hamburg, Germany, she began work as a "stringer," or freelance contributor, for the *New York Times*.

In time, Kolbert joined the newspaper on its Metro desk, which covers news of New York City and its neighboring communities. In 1988, she moved to Albany, New York's state capital, as the bureau chief. She then became a columnist, writing "Metro Matters" from 1997 to 1998.

A move to the *New Yorker* as a staff writer in 1999 came with an increased focused on science and environmental issues. Her three-part series on global warming, "The Climate of Man," won the 2006 National Magazine Award for Public Interest. In the series, she wrote about the decades of research into climate change and warned "in the same way that global warming has gradually ceased to be merely a theory, so, too, its impacts are no longer just hypothetical. Nearly every major glacier in the world is shrinking; those in Glacier National Park are retreating so quickly it has been estimated that they will vanish entirely by 2030."

This series raised screaming alarm bells on the environmental emergency Kolbert described. It was turned into a highly regarded book, *Field Notes from a Catastrophe: Man, Nature, and Climate Change*, published in 2006. In 2010 she was awarded a Guggenheim Fellowship, and in 2015 Kolbert wrote *The Sixth Extinction: An Unnatural History*, a book exploring the seemingly unthinkable—a human-led mass extinction. For this work, Kolbert won the Pulitzer Prize for General Nonfiction, and the book became a national best seller, winning many other accolades. In 2021, *Under a White Sky* was named one of the ten best books of the year by the *Washington Post*, among many other honors.

Kolbert's recent work might be summed up best in a line she wrote in a 2020 *New Yorker* piece, after observing unprecedented wildfires raging across Australia: "The world is in danger, and we need to act immediately to survive."

While continuing her work for the *New Yorker*, Elizabeth Kolbert is also a visiting fellow at Williams College and lives in Williamstown, Massachusetts, with her husband and children.

WHY YOU SHOULD READ IT

As I have reiterated, I established four standards, besides length, for the books I would include in this collection: consequence, timeliness, literary value—meaning the writing was pleasurable or profound—and accessibility. *Under a White Sky* is another of the most perfect exemplars of hitting all four out of the park. Kolbert does it by exploring science right now, and she does it with prose as clear as our current catastrophe is dire. That settles the question of timeliness and consequence.

Will the same human ingenuity and innovation that created the Industrial Revolution and modern world largely responsible for the climate crisis we live in bring about any solutions?

That is an awfully big question. And not everyone is convinced. During a 2021 interview with Kolbert on his *New York Times* podcast, Ezra Klein says of *Under a White Sky* ". . . this book's existence is evidence of how badly that fight is going. This is a book about what we are going to need to contemplate in the coming years that we don't want to. It's a book about taking responsibility for how irreversibly we have altered the natural world; how often we have tried to control it, and then watched those attempts at control fail; how often the best most scientific minds of the age have come up with some brilliant solution, implemented it, and then watched calamity result."

WHAT TO READ NEXT

This is fairly simple. Elizabeth Kolbert's previous books *Field Notes from a Catastrophe* and the Pulitzer Prize–winning *The Sixth Extinction* should go on your To-Be-Read list.

In the latter, she writes of the disappearance of mastodons, auks, and ammonites—creatures that are already gone—and a mass spawning of coral on the Great Barrier Reef, colorfully calling it "synchronized group sex," the kind of phrase that sets Kolbert's writing apart. But her true focus is on humans and whether we are causing an event so catastrophic—like the asteroid that wiped out the dinosaurs—that life on earth will suddenly and drastically contract. That would be—for all of us—the "Sixth Extinction."

What Is Not Here
and What I Learned

Are we there yet? Not quite. But here's the good news: no pop quiz!

Having made it this far, whether or not you've read fifty-two books in fifty-two weeks, the journey isn't over. It has only just begun. I have always contended that my books offer the first word and not the last word on any given topic. I also subscribe to the belief that "education is not the filling of a pail, but the lighting of a fire." *

This is clearly not the bonfire of burning books—it is the flame of reading, learning, thinking, and knowing. We should invest in these pursuits as a lifelong activity. Yes, read as if your life depended on it. Because it might!

As I wrote in my introduction and repeatedly emphasized throughout this book, I had several key considerations for whether or not a book made the grade in this collection. Consequence, timeliness, literary value, and accessibility were the major considerations. But the precursor to these

---

* Over the years, many including me, have attributed this quote to the great Irish poet William Butler Yeats. "It ain't necessarily so." There is no evidence Yeats said or wrote such a thing. As scholar Robert Strong wrote about his unsuccessful attempt to source this widely quoted wisdom to Yeats, "And don't be afraid to challenge prominent people and published sources if you find evidence they might be wrong." *Irish Times,* October 15, 2013. Good advice in all matters. https://www.irishtimes.com/news/education/education-is-not-the-filling-of -a-pail-but-the-lighting-of-a-fire-it-s-an-inspiring-quote-but-did-wb-yeats-say-it-1.1560192.

factors was certainly length, which meant that an enormous number of books—including many highly consequential books—were left at the starting gate.

I think immediately of David McCullough's *Mornings on Horseback*, about a young Theodore Roosevelt; *The 900 Days*, Harrison Salisbury's epic narrative of the World War II siege of Leningrad that helped spark my fascination with history; Stanley Karnow's *Vietnam: A History*, the classic account of that war; *No Ordinary Time*, Doris Kearns Goodwin's masterful narrative of FDR and Churchill in the World War II White House; Akhil Reed Amar's *America's Constitution: A Biography* and his *The Bill of Rights*; and Annette Gordon-Reed's *The Hemingses of Monticello*, the sweeping story of an extraordinary family of enslaved people and their role in Thomas Jefferson's life.

These are profoundly influential books that remain in my personal library, alongside the works of Ron Chernow, John Hope Franklin, Barbara Tuchman, and Isabel Wilkerson, among many others. My personal list of the best and most influential nonfiction books and best nonfiction writers is substantial. I could go on to name a pantheon of favorite writers, all important to a life lived in books. But here is the point: the length of a book shouldn't frighten anyone who has interest and time. Many of the greatest works of history, biography, and memoir, while sizable, are also true page-turners.

While I was making the very difficult choices of which books I would include, I also made another clear decision: what not to include. I made the judgment to eliminate what might be called evil books. These are books of propaganda—many of them of great historical consequence—that spread vicious, hateful, and destructive lies and ideas. Of course, both *The Protocols of the Elders of Zion*—the most notorious and widely distributed work of anti-Semitism in modern times—and *Mein Kampf* fall into this category. At 939 pages in its 1939 American edition, Hitler's book was excluded on the basis of length alone. But it would never be a choice of mine, even though its dreadful impact on history is undeniable.

Even excluding such vile books, there were still far too many choices to fit into a single volume of great short nonfiction. As you have read in the "What to Read Next" section of each entry, I have already included scores of alternative and additional selections worth reading.

But, to echo Gertrude Stein, a year is a year is a year. And as it is also said, time and tide wait for no man. Nor does my editor! I had to omit a considerable number of very worthy books in the interests of space and time. Many books are called; few are chosen. For instance, among my very difficult decisions were five titles I read and enjoyed a great deal—books on the bubble, I will call them. I would like to have included full entries on these, and others, if space permitted. All of them inspired the sort of challenge to thinking, distinctive voices, and stimulating perceptions that I sought for this collection. So, in brief, here are "Five Easy Pieces," another handful for your consideration:

- *When Bad Things Happen to Good People* by Harold S. Kushner (New York: Anchor Books, 2004; 164 pages)

"One of the most important things that any religion can teach us is what it means to be human."

Born out of the loss of the late Rabbi Harold S. Kushner's young son to a cruel disease, this multimillion-copy seller sets out to answer a question that has plagued people since the time of the biblical Job and even earlier: Why do bad things happen to good people? In everyday language, Kushner offers some comforting answers.

- *Fun Home: A Family Tragicomic* by Alison Bechdel (Boston: Houghton Mifflin Harcourt/Mariner Books, 2007; 232 pages)

"Our home was like an artists' colony. We ate together, but otherwise were absorbed in our separate pursuits."

A landmark in the field of graphic literature, Bechdel's memoir in cartoon panels is anything but a comic. Relating her young life with a very idiosyncratic father, his untimely death, and her coming out, it is a "tragicomic"—as she describes it—and a generational milestone in queer literature.

- *Longitude* by Dava Sobel (New York: Bloomsbury, 2007; foreword by Neil Armstrong; 184 pages)

"Sauerkraut. That was the watchword on Captain James Cook's triumphant second voyage, which set sail in 1772."

This is a fascinating exploration of the quest to accurately measure the imaginary lines called longitude, a matter of life and death for sailors in a bygone era, written by one of the best science writers of recent times. At the center of this account of the race to solve a very old problem is the riveting story of one persistent man who changed the history of navigation, and the considerable intrigue surrounding his achievement.

- *I Feel Bad About My Neck and Other Thoughts on Being a Woman* by Nora Ephron (New York: Vintage Books, 2008; 137 pages)

"Until around 1910, people exercised all the time, but they didn't think of it as exercise—they thought of it as life itself."

A delightful collection of essays by a columnist, journalist, novelist, and film director who understood that making fun of things is serious business. As *New York Times* columnist Gail Collins wrote in praise of the late Nora Ephron, "Pointing out how ridiculous the status quo is breaks its spell and gives us the freedom to dream up something better. Imagine what she'd say now about library book banning or the latest abortion battle or—oh, wow—the governor of Florida's war on Disney."

So, this demands a true confession. Perhaps my chief regret with regard to books missing from this compilation is the relative absence of humor writing. Great satirists and humorists from Mark Twain to Calvin Trillin, Fran Lebowitz, and David Sedaris have a unique way of laughing at the absurdity, stupidity, and even cruelty of the world. Funny can be serious business.

- *My Stroke of Insight: A Brain Scientist's Personal Journey* by Jill Bolte Taylor (New York: Plume, 2009; 206 pages)

"I was like a newborn unable to make sense of the sensory stimulation in the physical space around me."

An accomplished neuroscientist, Taylor suffered a nearly fatal stroke and tells the story of what happened, how she recovered, and the surprising things she learned from this life-altering experience. Taylor takes us on a journey through the workings of the brain before making a sharp turn into the spiritual awakening she describes as a result of her debilitating stroke.

There you have it—five "bonus books" in addition to the others already cited. In carefully choosing and reading the entries in this book and explaining why you should read them, I have learned a great deal, because I was made to think. I won't recap all of those lessons here—many are already discussed in the "Why You Should Read It" section of each entry. But I will take the liberty of quickly sorting out what were, for me, among the most important things I gleaned during this year of reading nonfiction—briefly.

First, I must humbly acknowledge that I learned once again how much I don't know. The arrogance of certainty is a constant danger in our times—all too frequently on display in American politics and religion. One of the most important features of many of these selections is that they demand we relinquish, or at least relax, what may be deeply held personal ideas and beliefs.

Great books and great writers force us to test those tenets, if you will, and that is a very healthy exercise. If you are a person of faith, for instance, challenging cherished convictions can be a powerful means to strengthen those beliefs. A faith that won't withstand some sincere questions, as I have written elsewhere, is not a very powerful faith. While I have explored many faith-based texts here, I must admit, I was not brought around—I didn't "find religion." Or, in my case, rediscover it. Raised in a very traditional yet progressive Protestant church, I long ago surrendered my Sunday school faith and today remain largely in the camp of Voltaire, Paine, Camus, Hitchens, and others in rejecting organized religion. However, I have also learned to keep an open mind—another important lesson of these great short books.

On a more personal level, many of these books forced me to examine some of my own actions and choices. Yes, Michael Pollan. I will try to "Eat food. Not too much. Mostly plants."

More seriously, many of these readings demanded that I look at how I must "be" in this world. How do I balance the need to retreat away from our chaotic, often despairing times into the private spirituality of the natural world—as Thoreau and Annie Dillard counsel—against the need to "transgress unjust laws" in society as Thoreau also advised? How to become part of bell hooks's "beloved community"? I have come out of this year of reading briefly with a strengthened conviction that I must act justly and walk humbly in a moment when fundamental freedoms and basic rights are under assault. Reading Timothy Snyder's admonitions on opposing tyranny provided an important challenge. In our "War of Ideas," democracy is very much on the firing line.

The stakes could not be higher. Given the political issues and deep division in this country, I am concerned about the health and fate of our system of government. As a historian, I do not write those words lightly. Many of the books in this collection underscore the grave threats we have faced in the past from racism, sexism, and fascism, and they offer stark evidence of the great cost of remaining silent. Today's "War of Ideas" is about the growing menace of authoritarianism that might end democracy as we know it. As Thomas Paine eloquently put it nearly 250 years ago, "Tyranny, like hell, is not easily conquered." And as Christopher Hitchens wrote, "Dante was a sectarian and a mystic but he was right to reserve one of the fieriest corners of his inferno for those who, in a time of moral crisis, try to stay neutral."

All of the hazards we face—political, moral, spiritual—demand choices. And against this backdrop of current events is the more existential threat of climate catastrophe. Some of the writers I admire and include—Neil Postman, Michael Pollan, and Elizabeth Kolbert to name a few—compel me to continually examine my choices, from what I watch and eat to how I conduct my life. We can turn away from the truths that these writers bring forth. That is a choice. Or we can seek meaningful action in the way we respond to the world.

Apart from these challenges, I came away from my "Year of Reading—Briefly" with two other concise lessons. Like Marcus Aurelius, I will "learn to ask of all actions, 'Why are they doing that?' Starting with . . . [my] own."

And like the Sisyphus of Camus, I will continue to keep pushing the stone up the hill. Because in the end, I believe, there is no other choice.

My Ten Favorite Great Short Nonfiction Books (in chronological order)

1. *Stung with Love* by Sappho
   Age weighs heavily on me, and the knees
   Buckle that long ago, like fawns, pranced nimbly.

   I groan much but to what end? Humans simply
   Cannot be ageless like divinities.

2. *Narrative of the Life of Frederick Douglass* by Frederick Douglass
   "Though conscious of the difficulty of learning without a teacher, I set out with high hope, and a fixed purpose, at whatever cost of trouble, to learn how to read."

3. *Civil Disobedience* by Henry David Thoreau
   "Unjust laws exist: shall we be content to obey them, or shall we endeavor to amend them, and obey them until we have succeeded, or shall we transgress them at once?"

4. *Homage to Catalonia* by George Orwell
   "Human beings were trying to behave as human beings and not as cogs in the capitalist machine."

5. *Under the Sea-Wind* by Rachel Carson
   "There the young were to be born of the darkness of the deep sea and the old eels were to die and become sea again."

6. *Hiroshima* by John Hersey
   "There, in the tin factory, in the first moment of the atomic age, a human being was crushed by books."

7. *The Fire Next Time* by James Baldwin
   "The glorification of one race and the consequent debasement of another— or others—always has been and always will be a recipe for murder."

8. *A Year of Magical Thinking* by Joan Didion
   "Life changes in the instant.
   You sit down to dinner and life as you know it ends."

9. *On Tyranny* by Timothy Snyder
   "Be as courageous as you can. . . . If none of us is prepared to die for freedom, then all of us will die under tyranny."

10. *Under a White Sky* by Elizabeth Kolbert
    "The choices that we'll make—that we are making right now, without being necessarily aware of them—will determine the future of life for our children and their children and all other species on earth for generations to come."

52 More of the Great Short Books That Make Us Think

I would like to propose 52 more titles you might find interesting.

So, get busy. You have your work cut out for you.

Ain't I a Woman Sojourner Truth

Anatomy of an Illness
    Norman Cousins

Aspects of the Novel E. M. Forster

*The Autobiography of Benjamin
    Franklin*
    Benjamin Franklin

Black Skin, White Masks
    Frantz Fanon

The Book of Tea Kazuko Okakura

Books and Islands in Ojibwe Country
    Louise Erdrich

Brunelleschi's Dome Ross King

Cape Cod Henry David Thoreau

Civilization and Its Discontents
    or *The Future of an Illusion*
    Sigmund Freud

Dark Night of the Soul
    St. John of the Cross

Fear and Loathing in Las Vegas
    Hunter Thompson

Fear and Trembling
    Søren Kierkegaard

The Four Agreements
    Don Miguel Ruiz

From the Back of the Bus
    Dick Gregory

Games People Play Eric Berne

Gather Together in My Name
    Maya Angelou

Girl, Interrupted Susanna Kaysen

God and Man at Yale
    William F. Buckley Jr.

Holidays on Ice David Sedaris

How the Irish Saved Civilization
  Thomas Cahill
*How to Stop a Conspiracy: An Ancient
  Guide to Saving a Republic (The
  War against Catiline)*
  Sallust
The Last Best Hope George Packer
The Last Supper Rachel Cusk
Letters to a Young Poet
  Rainer Maria Rilke
The Little Virtues (1962)
  Natalia Ginzburg
Men Explain Things to Me
  Rebecca Solnit
Mere Christianity C. S. Lewis
Metropolitan Life Fran Lebowitz
The Moral Sayings of Publius Syrius
  Publius Syrius
The Naked Ape Desmond Morris
*Notes of James Madison on the
  Constitutional Convention*
  James Madison
On Living and Dying Well Cicero
Operating Manual for Spaceship Earth
  Buckminster Fuller

The Peregrine J. A. Baker
The Perfect Storm Sebastian Junger
*The Protestant Ethic and the "Spirit"
  of Capitalism*
  Max Weber
The Renaissance: A Short History
  Paul Johnson
The Screwtape Letters C. S. Lewis
Seduction and Betrayal
  Elizabeth Hardwick
Selected Works Juana Inés de la Cruz
Self Reliance Ralph W. Emerson
Slow Days, Fast Company
  Eve Babitz
A Small Place Jamaica Kincaid
Three Rings Daniel Mendelsohn
Tomorrow Is Now
  Eleanor Roosevelt
The Truce Primo Levi
The True Believer Eric Hoffer
A Vindication of the Rights of Woman
  Mary Wollstonecraft
Waiting for God Simone Weil
Ways of Seeing John Berger
A Year in Provence Peter Mayle

Acknowledgments

"What soon grows old?" asked Aristotle. "Gratitude." On this, I must disagree with the Greek sage.

Every book I have ever written comes with the recognition that it is the work of many hands. Of course, any errors are mine alone. But I am exceedingly grateful to all those who have had a hand in this book.

I start with all those who shaped my love of reading and passion for books: my parents, teachers, many personal and professional friends, booksellers, and librarians who guided my path to a life in books.

For my work on *The World in Books,* I am especially grateful to the New York Public Library, in particular the librarians at the Hudson Park and Jefferson Market branches in Manhattan's West Village. I am in debt as well to my friends at Three Lives & Co., my neighborhood independent bookstore, for their assistance and shared passion for books and reading.

Every book demands a true collaboration between author and publisher. So let me first thank my Scribner editor Sally Howe for supporting this project in the first place and for her thoughtful and important contributions to this work. Sally is a passionate reader, questioner, and thinker. To partner with an editor in possession of these essential attributes is, in my opinion, a gift to any writer.

I am also deeply grateful to many others at Scribner who form such an excellent team: Nan Graham, Jaya Miceli, Sydney Newman, Stuart Smith, Hope Herr-Cardillo, Meryll Preposi, Madison Thân, Colin Harrison, Ashley Gilliam Rose, Georgia Brainard, Annie Craig, Rafael Taveras,

Hilda Koparanian, Elisa Rivlin, and Barbara Wild. A special shout-out to Mark LaFlaur for his careful work on production of the manuscript. And I add my praise to Sam Kerr, the artist commissioned by Scribner, for his wonderful author portraits.

I close these notes of gratitude—No, Aristotle, gratitude never grows old—with thanks to my family: my grandchildren Kit and Archer, who give me great joy; to my daughter Jenny Davis, whose editorial suggestions and literary insights were immensely valuable; and my son Colin Davis who has always stood by me, offering welcome words of encouragement and support when the work days were long. Lastly, to my wife Joann Davis. I am forever grateful to her for the life in books we have shared.

Notes

ix *6. Do not overwrite:* William Strunk Jr. and E. B. White, *The Elements of Style*, New York: Penguin Books, 2005, 105.

ix *Why are we reading:* Annie Dillard, *The Writing Life*, New York: Harper Perennial, 2013, 72.

ix *Dead writers and living Gods:* Amit Majmudar, foreword to *Godsong: A Verse Translation of the Bhagavad Gita, with Commentary*, trans. Amit Majmudar, New York: Alfred A. Knopf, 2018, xxiv.

INTRODUCTION

xv *No to decadence and moral corruption!:* Unsigned and undated article, "Book Burning," *Holocaust Encyclopedia*, United States Holocaust Memorial Museum, https://encyclopedia.ushmm.org/content/en/article/book-burning?series=198.

xvi *decadence and moral decay:* Unsigned and undated article, "Fire Oaths," *Holocaust Encyclopedia*, United States Holocaust Memorial Museum, https://encyclopedia.ushmm.org/content/en/article/fire-oaths.

xvi *Where they burn books, they will also ultimately burn people:* Heinrich Heine, cited in unsigned and undated article, "Book Burning."

xix *Over the last few years:* Nicholas Carr, *The Shallows*, New York: W. W. Norton, 2010, 5–6.

xx *who inscribed above the entrance to a library:* Ceridwen Dovey, "Can Reading Make You Happier?" *New Yorker,* June 9, 2015, https://www.newyorker.com/culture/cultural-comment/can-reading-make-you-happier?itm_content=footer-recirc.

xx *Try deep reading (on paper):* Dana G. Smith, "How to Focus Like It's 1990," *New York Times,* January 9, 2023, https://www.nytimes.com/2023/01/09/well /mind/concentration-focus-distraction.html?searchResultPosition=5.

THE EPIC OF GILGAMESH

1 *Bitterly Gilgamesh wept: The Epic of Gilgamesh,* trans. N. K. Sandars, New York: Penguin Books, 1972, 97.

2 *I will proclaim to the world the deeds of Gilgamesh:* Ibid., 61.

3 *His lust leaves no virgin:* Ibid., 62.

3 *the first queer love story:* Robert Macfarlane, "A Fireball from the Sands," *New York Review of Books,* October 20, 2022, https://www.nybooks.com /articles/2022/10/20/a-fireball-from-the-sands-gilgamesh/.

4 *The poem we call* Gilgamesh*:* Michael Schmidt, *Gilgamesh: The Life of a Poem,* Princeton, NJ: Princeton University Press, 2019, 116.

5 *One reason for the epic's appeal: Gilgamesh: A New Translation of the Ancient Epic,* trans. Sophus Helle, New Haven, CT: Yale University Press, 2021, 2.

6 *Why does* Gilgamesh *continue:* Macfarlane, "Fireball."

THE BOOK OF GENESIS

7 *The man said, "The woman whom you gave . . .":* Genesis 3:12, *The New Oxford Annotated Bible* (New Revised Standard Version), ed. Bruce M. Metzger and Roland E. Murphy, New York: Oxford University Press, 1991, 5.

7 *In the beginning:* Genesis 1:1–5, *New Oxford Annotated Bible,* 2.

9 *The printing press had now become the collaborator:* Daniel J. Boorstin, *The Seekers: The Story of Man's Continuing Quest to Understand His World,* New York: Vintage Books, 1999, 114–115.

11 *all the families of the earth:* Genesis 12:3, *New Oxford Annotated Bible,* 16.

11 *a long robe with sleeves:* Genesis 37:3 note, *New Oxford Annotated Bible,* 48.

12 *The J and E authors interpreted the saga*: Karen Armstrong, *The Bible: A Biography,* New York: Atlantic Monthly Press, 2007, 14–16.

14 *in the image of God he created them:* Genesis 1:27, *New Oxford Annotated Bible,* 3.

14 *The woman whom you gave:* Genesis 3:12, *New Oxford Annotated Bible,* 5.

TAO TE CHING (THE BOOK OF THE WAY)

17 *Who knows doesn't talk:* Ursula K. Le Guin with J. P. Seaton, *Tao Te Ching: A Book about the Way and the Power of the Way,* Boulder, CO: Shambhala, 1997, 67.

18 *The way you can go:* Ibid., 3.

18 *emphasized inner freedom: Tao Te Ching: The Tao and the Power,* trans. John Minford, New York: Viking, 2018, vii.

18 *Over and over Lao Tzu says* wei wu wei: Le Guin, *Tao Te Ching,* 6.

19 *A good athlete can enter:* Stephen Mitchell, foreword to *Tao Te Ching: A New English Version,* trans. Stephen Mitchell, New York: Harper Perennial Modern Classics, 2006, viii.

19 *Wise souls don't hoard:* Le Guin, *Tao Te Ching,* 96.

19 *Nothing about it is certain:* Ursula K. Le Guin, introduction to Le Guin, *Tao Te Ching,* ix.

20 *the profound modesty:* Le Guin, *Tao Te Ching,* 7.

20 *The West has no:* Alan Watts, *The Way of Zen,* New York: Vintage Books, 2019, 11.

20 *it is now recognized as one of five faiths:* Eleanor Albert and Lindsay Maizland, "Religion in China," Council on Foreign Relations, September 25, 2020, https://www.cfr.org/backgrounder/religion-china.

21 *Do not impose on others:* Confucius, *The Analects,* trans. D. C. Lau, New York: Penguin Books, 1979, 135.

21 *Some people live as though they are already dead:* Thich Nhat Hanh, *You Are Here,* Boulder, CO: Shambhala, 2009, 9.

STUNG WITH LOVE: POEMS AND FRAGMENTS

22 *You will have memories:* Sappho, *Stung with Love: Poems and Fragments,* trans. Aaron Poochigian, New York: Penguin Books, 2009, 39.

23 *Sweet mother, I can't take shuttle in hand:* Ibid., 7.

23 *You will have memories:* Ibid., 39.

23 *We are left to wonder:* Aaron Poochigian in Sappho, *Stung with Love,* 38.

24 *The greatest problem for Sappho studies:* Daniel Mendelsohn, "Girl, Interrupted: Who Was Sappho?," *New Yorker,* March 9, 2015, https://www.newyorker.com/magazine/2015/03/16/girl-interrupted.

25 *the seventh-century-B.C. lyric genius:* Ibid.

25 *No other woman from early antiquity has been so talked about:* Judith Schalansky, "What We Know of Sappho," *Paris Review*, December 8, 2020, https://www.theparisreview.org/blog/2020/12/08/what-we-know-of-sappho/.

25 *ugly, being dark in complexion:* Ibid.

26 *a women's circle in Mytilene:* Ibid.

26 *However exalted her reputation:* Mendelsohn, "Girl, Interrupted."

27 *There are not many surviving literary works:* Schalansky, "What We Know of Sappho."

27 *As a poet, she was inventive:* Sarah B. Pomeroy, *Goddesses, Whores, Wives, and Slaves: Women in Classical Antiquity*, New York: Schocken Books, 1995.

28 *We know that the letters Emily Dickinson:* Schalansky, "What We Know of Sappho."

THE ART OF WAR

29 *Warfare is the art of deception:* Sun Tzu, *The Art of War*, trans. Michael Nylan, New York: W. W. Norton, 2020, 43.

29 *Late 6th century BCE:* Michael Nylan, introduction to Sun Tzu, *The Art of War*, 10.

29 *Arms are a vital matter:* Sun Tzu, *The Art of War*, 41.

30 *Know the enemy and your own:* Ibid., 107.

30 *perhaps the most profound message:* Nylan, introduction to Sun Tzu, *The Art of War*, 25.

31 *Nylan dismisses the "hero narrative":* Ibid., 10.

31 *A thousand four-horse light chariots:* Sun Tzu, *The Art of War*, 47.

31 *As featured on* The Sopranos*:* https://www.amazon.com/Art-War-As-Featured-Sopranos/dp/1932407170.

32 *Europe first discovered Sun Tzu:* Fumio Ota, "Sun Tzu in Contemporary Chinese Strategy," *Joint Force Quarterly* 73 (Second Quarter 2014), https://ndupress.ndu.edu/Portals/68/Documents/jfq/jfq-73/jfq-73_76-83_Ota.pdf?ver=2014-03-26-120732-250.

32 *Like the general public:* Nylan, introduction to Sun Tzu, *The Art of War*, 15.

32 *It's a smart book:* https://www.businessinsider.com/best-lessons-and-summary-of-the-art-of-war-by-sun-tzu-2015-3?op=1#on-tactics-all-warfare-is-based-on-deception-4.

33 Karl von Clausewitz, *On War*, cited in John Bartlett, *Bartlett's Familiar Quotations*, 16th ed., Justin Kaplan, General Editor, Boston: Little, Brown, 1992, 393.

THE SYMPOSIUM

34 *So if I had my way:* Plato, *The Symposium*, trans. Christopher Gill, New York: Penguin Books, 1999, 8.

35 *Then Agathon, who happened to be lying:* Ibid., 7.

35 *they then poured libations:* Ibid., 7.

35 *A marked feature:* Christopher Gill, introduction to Plato, *The Symposium*, xiii.

36 *And why is reproduction the object:* Plato, *The Symposium*, 44.

36 *People like that:* Ibid., 46–47.

38 *The Socrates of Plato's works:* Elizabeth Watson Scharffenberger, introduction to Plato, *Republic*, trans. Benjamin Jowett, New York: Barnes & Noble Classics, 2004, xxix.

38 *So a halo of ambiguity:* Daniel J. Boorstin, *The Seekers: The Story of Man's Continuing Quest to Understand His World*, New York: Vintage Books, 1999, 28–29.

39 *To attain a successful life:* Luc Ferry, *A Brief History of Thought*, New York: Harper Perennial, 2011, 39.

40 *The* Symposium, *together with:* Christopher Gill, introduction to Plato, *The Symposium*, xv.

41 *Socrates proceeds to ask:* Ferry, *Brief History of Thought*, 159.

42 *In a democracy fond of:* Martha C. Nussbaum, *Not for Profit*, Princeton, NJ: Princeton University Press, 2010, 47–48.

42 *Is it that life has its value:* M. M. McCabe interviewed by Nigel Warburton, "The Best Books on Socrates," Five Books website, April 22, 2016, https://fivebooks.com/best-books/socrates/.

43 *The* Republic *is really exploring:* Melissa Lane interviewed by Nigel Warburton, "The Best Plato Books," Five Books website,, July 14, 2014, https://fivebooks.com/best-books/plato-melissa-lane/.

43 Not for Profit *focuses on:* Nussbaum, *Not for Profit*, xvii.

43 *Every year I witness Socrates:* Roosevelt Montás, *Rescuing Socrates*, Princeton, NJ: Princeton University Press, 2021, 11–12.

THE POETICS (HOW TO TELL A STORY)

44 *In stories, what is impossible:* Aristotle, *How to Tell a Story: An Ancient Guide to the Art of Storytelling for Writers and Readers,* trans. Philip Freeman, Princeton, NJ: Princeton University Press, 2022, 177.

45 *In this book we are going to discuss:* Ibid., 3.

45 *These words can be limiting:* Philip Freeman in "Notes" in Aristotle, *How to Tell a Story,* 213.

46 *Homer deserves praise:* Aristotle, *How to Tell a Story,* 173.

47 *Even his works attacking Plato's theory:* Daniel J. Boorstin, *The Seekers: The Story of Man's Continuing Quest to Understand His World,* New York: Vintage Books, 1999 58.

47 *Aristotle had arrived from northern Greece:* Charles Freeman, *The Reopening of the Western Mind: The Resurgence of Intellectual Life from the End of Antiquity to the Dawn of the Enlightenment,* New York: Alfred A. Knopf, 2023, 189.

48 *he would not let the Athenians:* Philip Freeman in Aristotle, *How to Tell a Story,* viii.

48 *at least 130:* Edith Hall, *Aristotle's Way: How Ancient Wisdom Can Change Your Life,* New York: Penguin Books, 2019, 15.

48 *Rules are what makes (sic) art beautiful:* Aaron Sorkin, cited by Philip Freeman in Aristotle, *How to Tell a Story,* xv.

49 *I read and loved Plato's dialogues:* Roosevelt Montás, *Rescuing Socrates,* Princeton, NJ: Princeton University Press, 2021, 66–67.

49 *Aristotle's overwhelming influence:* Boorstin, *The Seekers,* 71.

50 *When you read Aristotle:* Hall, *Aristotle's Way,* 13.

THE BHAGAVAD GITA

51 *Know what your duty is: Bhagavad Gita: A New Translation,* trans. Stephen Mitchell, New York: Harmony Books, 2000, 51.

52 *The whole universe, all things:* Ibid., 133.

52 *almost 100,000 couplets:* Wendy Doniger, "Mahabharata," *Encyclopedia Britannica,* accessed April 27, 2023, https://www.britannica.com/topic/Mahabharata.

53 *After Hamlet:* Parul Sehgal, "In 'Godsong,' a New Poem That's 2,000 Years Old," *New York Times,* March 20, 2018, https://www.nytimes.com/2018/03/20/books/godsong-bhagavad-gita-amit-majmudar-review.html?searchResultPosition=21.

53 *But there is general scholarly consensus: Bhagavad Gita*, 14.

53 *Did Krishna "really" sing it?:* Amit Majmudar, foreword to *Godsong: A Verse Translation of the Bhagavad Gita, with Commentary*, trans. Amit Majmudar, New York: Alfred A. Knopf, 2018, xvii.

54 *We waited until the blast had passed:* Richard Rhodes, *The Making of the Atomic Bomb*, New York: Simon & Schuster, 1986, 676.

54 *I am death, shatterer of worlds: Bhagavad Gita*, 138.

54 *Ralph Waldo Emerson and Henry David Thoreau:* Stephen Mitchell, notes to the introduction to *Bhagavad Gita*, 199.

54 *second only to the Divine Comedy:* Ibid., 209.

55 *The author of the Mahabharata has not established:* Mohandas K. Gandhi, "The Message of the Gita," in *Bhagavad Gita*, 212.

55 *Know what your duty is: Bhagavad Gita*, 51.

55 *Gandhi eventually translated the* Gita *from its original Sanskrit:* Uma Majmudar, "Mahatma Gandhi and the Bhagavad Gita," American Vedantist website, December 6, 2014, accessed April 27, 2023, https://americanvedantist.org/2014/articles/mahatma-gandhi-and-the-bhagavad-gita/.

55 *No other book or scripture:* Ibid.

56 *The Gita imagined a relationship:* Amit Majmudar, foreword to *Godsong*, xiii.

56 *My parents, both Hindus, had taught me:* Sunita Puri, "The Lesson of Impermanence," *New York Times*, March 7, 2019, https://www.nytimes.com/2019/03/07/well/live/palliative-care-end-of-life-death.html?searchResultPosition=14.

THE GOSPEL ACCORDING TO LUKE

58 *Do not judge:* Luke 6:37–38, *The New Oxford Annotated Bible*, New Revised Standard Version, ed. Bruce M. Metzger and Roland E. Murphy, New York: Oxford University Press, 1991, 88.

59 *In the sixth month the angel Gabriel was sent:* Luke 1:26–33, *New Oxford Annotated Bible*, 78.

61 *The Christian scriptures were written:* Karen Armstrong, *The Bible: A Biography*, New York: Atlantic Monthly Press, 2007, 66–67.

62 *in a manger:* Luke 2:7, *New Oxford Annotated Bible*, 80.

62 *You are my Son, the Beloved:* Luke 3:22, *New Oxford Annotated Bible*, 83.

62 *carried up into heaven:* Luke 24:51, *New Oxford Annotated Bible*, 123.

64 *In the beginning was the Word*: John 1:1–2, *New Oxford Annotated Bible*, 125.

MEDITATIONS

65 *Learn to ask:* Marcus Aurelius, *Meditations*, trans. Gregory Hays, New York: Modern Library, 2003, 143.

66 *When you wake up:* Ibid., 17.

66 *For every action:* Ibid., 101–102.

67 *The basic assumption:* Robert Hughes, *Rome: A Cultural, Visual, and Personal History*, New York: Vintage Books, 2012, 43.

68 *Marcus himself was no doubt aware:* Gregory Hays, introduction to Marcus Aurelius, *Meditations*, xiv.

69 *composed to provide:* Ibid., xxxvii.

69 *And this too:* Marcus Aurelius, *Meditations*, 96.

69 *Need little, / want less:* Ursula K. Le Guin with J. P. Seaton, *Tao Te Ching: A Book about the Way and the Power of the Way*, Boulder, CO: Shambhala, 2019, 23.

70 *Life is long enough:* Seneca, *On the Shortness of Life: Life Is Long If You Know How to Use It*, trans. C. D. N. Costa, New York: Penguin Books, 2005, 1–2.

THE QUR'AN

71 *We gave Moses the Scripture: The Qur'an*, trans. M. A. S. Abdel Haleem, New York: Oxford University Press, 2016, 11.

71 *This is the Scripture in which there is no doubt:* Ibid., 4–5.

73 *God does not burden any soul:* Ibid., 33.

73 *This translation is intended to go:* M. A. S. Abdel Haleem, introduction to *The Qur'an*, xxix.

73 *the Quran was revealed:* Karen Armstrong, *Islam: A Short History*, New York: Modern Library, 2002, 4–5.

74 *was meticulous in ensuring that the Qur'an was recorded:* Haleem, introduction to *The Qur'an*, xv.

74 *The Hajj pilgrimage to the Ka'ba:* Ibid., x.

75 *There was also spiritual:* Armstrong, *Islam*, 3.

75 *The young Muhammad was well-liked:* Karen Armstrong, *Muhammad: A Prophet for Our Time*, New York: HarperOne, 2006, 25.

76 *Muhammad was transported:* Bruce B. Lawrence, *The Koran in English: A Biography*, Princeton, NJ: Princeton University Press, 2017, 11.

78 *Historians have attributed:* Peter Manseau, "Why Thomas Jefferson Owned a Qur'an," *Smithsonian*, January 31, 2018, https://www.smithsonianmag .com/smithsonian-institution/why-thomas-jefferson-owned-qur-1-180967 997/.

78 *The Qur'an stresses:* Haleem, introduction to *The Qur'an*, xviii.

79 *Hence Muhammad never:* Armstrong, *Islam*, 10.

79 *He was also creating:* Ibid., 4.

80 *We can no longer afford to indulge:* Armstrong, *Muhammad*, 7.

80 *a highly readable, unbiasedly comparative and elegantly insightful study of the Quran:* Mustafa Akyol, "Illuminating Islam's Peaceful Origins," *New York Times*, December 26, 2018, https://www.nytimes.com/2018/12/26 /books/review/illuminating-islams-peaceful-origins.html?searchResultPosi tion=5.

VITA NUOVA

81 *Let me say that whenever she appeared:* Dante, *Vita Nuova*, trans. Virginia Jewiss, New York: Penguin Books, 2022, 33.

81 *Nine times already since my birth:* Ibid., 3.

82 *The encounter:* Virginia Jewiss, introduction to Dante, *Vita Nuova*, vii.

82 *From then on:* Dante, *Vita Nuova*, 3.

82 *In the Middle Ages:* Joseph Luzzi, *Botticelli's Secret*, New York: W. W. Norton, 2022, 29.

83 *My lady carries Love:* Dante, *Vita Nuova*, 79.

84 *Exile would make him:* Luzzi, *Botticelli's Secret*, 33.

85 The Divine Comedy *became:* Ibid., 35.

85 *it was not published in English until 1843:* Virginia Jewiss, introduction to Dante, *Vita Nuova*, xx.

86 *a work of capital importance for the discipline of the emotions:* Ibid.

86 *Fixing a date:* William Manchester, *A World Lit Only by Fire*, New York: Back Bay Books, 1993, 25–26.

86 *Midway on our life's journey:* Dante, *The Inferno of Dante: A New Verse Translation*, trans. Robert Pinsky, New York: Farrar, Straus and Giroux, 1994, 3.

87 *The* Divine Comedy *is, of course, deeply rooted:* Charles Freeman, *The Reopening of the Western Mind: The Resurgence of Intellectual Life from the End of Antiquity to the Dawn of the Enlightenment*, New York: Knopf, 2023, 249.

UTOPIA

89 *The prospective bride:* Thomas More, *Utopia*, New York: Penguin Books, 2003, 84.

90 *Utopia was originally not:* Thomas More, *Utopia*, New York: Penguin Books, 2003, 50.

90 *its meaning . . . should be borne in mind throughout:* Paul Turner, "Introduction" in *Utopia*, New York: Penguin Books, 2003, xii.

91 *They never force people:* Thomas More, *Utopia*, New York: Penguin Books, 2003, 59.

91 *by mutual consent:* Thomas More, *Utopia*, New York: Penguin Books, 2003, 85.

94 *Some have argued:* Charles Freeman, *The Reopening of the Western Mind: The Resurgence of Intellectual Life from the End of Antiquity to the Dawn of the Enlightenment*, New York: Alfred A. Knopf, 2023, 467.

THE PRINCE

96 *Therefore one must be a fox:* Niccolò Machiavelli, *The Prince*, trans. George Bull, New York: Penguin Books, 2004, 74.

96 *From this arises the following question:* Ibid., 71.

97 *a man of low:* Ibid., 2.

98 *And here it has to be noted that men:* Ibid., 10.

98 *Machiavelli has long enjoyed:* Ross King, *Machiavelli: Philosopher of Power*, New York: HarperCollins, 2007, 234–235.

100 *The bust of Machiavelli in the Palazzo Vecchio:* Ondine Cohane, "In Tuscany, Following the Rise and Fall of Machiavelli," *New York Times,* December 4, 2014, https://www.nytimes.com/2014/12/07/travel/in-tuscany-following-the-rise-and-fall-of-machiavelli.html?searchResultPosition=6.

101 *In the ensuing chaos:* Claudia Roth Pierpont, "The Florentine," *New Yorker,* September 8, 2008, https://www.newyorker.com/magazine/2008/09/15/the-florentine.

102 *A prince should also show esteem:* Machiavelli, *The Prince*, 98.

102 *The jaded Machiavelli:* Charles Freeman, *The Reopening of the Western Mind: The Resurgence of Intellectual Life from the End of Antiquity to the Dawn of the Enlightenment,* New York: Alfred A. Knopf, 2023, 471.

103 *The key to some of the ambiguities:* King, *Machiavelli,* 236–237.

103 *Wherever a sovereign usurped:* Pierpont, "The Florentine."

THE SOVEREIGNTY AND GOODNESS OF GOD

105 *I had often before this said:* Mary Rowlandson, *The Sovereignty and Goodness of God,* ed. Neal Salisbury, Boston: Bedford/St. Martin's, 1997, 70.

106 *On the tenth of February 1675:* Ibid., 68.

108 *I remember in the night season:* Ibid., 111.

109 *it was translated:* Library of Congress, "Bible Collection," https://www.loc .gov/exhibits/bibles/other-bibles.html.

109 *It is a powerful rendering:* Neal Salisbury, preface to Rowlandson, *Sovereignty and Goodness of God,* vii.

110 *Plymouth Colony lost close to 8 percent:* Nathaniel Philbrick, *Mayflower,* New York: Viking, 2006, 332.

110 *Step by painful step:* Elaine Showalter, "Dark Places," *New York Times,* June 6, 2013, https://www.nytimes.com/2013/06/09/books/review/tradi tion-of-captivity-narratives.html.

111 *To say that the United States is a colonialist settler-state:* Roxanne Dunbar-Ortiz, *An Indigenous Peoples' History of the United States,* Boston: Beacon Press, 2014.

TREATISE ON TOLERATION

112 *Lies have dominated people:* Voltaire, *Treatise on Toleration,* trans. Desmond M. Clarke, New York: Penguin Books, 2016, 57.

112 *Reason is gentle and humane:* Ibid., 30.

112 *The law of intolerance is therefore:* Ibid., 34.

113 *If an innocent Huguenot could be so:* Desmond M. Clarke, introduction to Voltaire, *Treatise on Toleration,* x.

114 *I sow a seed that may:* Voltaire, *Treatise on Toleration,* 132.

114 *Voltaire is an anagram of "Arouet":* Unsigned, "About Voltaire," Voltaire Foundation website, https://www.voltaire.ox.ac.uk/about-voltaire/.

115 *praised the innovative and creative energy:* Clarke, introduction to Voltaire, *Treatise on Toleration,* x.

116 *Voltaire wanted to write a book:* Nicholas Cronk, introduction to *Voltaire: A Pocket Philosophical Dictionary*, trans. John Fletcher, New York: Oxford University Press, 2011, vii.

116 *the book was promptly condemned in Paris:* Ibid.

116 The Treatise *was much more like:* Ibid., xi.

117 *The free communication of ideas:* "Declaration of the Rights of Man—1789," Yale Law School/Avalon Project Documents in Law, History and Diplomacy, https://avalon.law.yale.edu/18th_century/rightsof.asp.

117 *Should those who teach their works*: Laurie Shrage, "Confronting Philosophy's Anti-Semitism," *New York Times*, March 18, 2019, https://www.nytimes.com/2019/03/18/opinion/philosophy-anti-semitism.html.

117 *Let no one do any:* Voltaire, *Treatise on Toleration*, 99.

117 *a statue honoring Voltaire in Paris was defaced:* Kim Willsher, "Où est Voltaire? Mystery of Parisian Statue Solved," *Guardian*, February 20, 2022, https://www.theguardian.com/world/2022/feb/20/ou-est-voltaire-mystery-of-parisian-statue-solved.

118 *Man was born free:* Jean-Jacques Rousseau, *Of the Social Contract and Other Political Writings*, ed. Christopher Bertram, trans. Quinton Hoare, New York: Penguin Books, 2012, 10.

118 *Just as Voltaire sought:* Daniel J. Boorstin, *The Seekers: The Story of Man's Continuing Quest to Understand His World*, New York: Vintage Books, 1999, 202.

THE AGE OF REASON

120 *My own mind is my own church:* Thomas Paine, *The Age of Reason: Being an Investigation of True and Fabulous Theology*, Mineola, NY: Dover, 2004, 21–22.

121 *I believe in one God, and no more:* Thomas Paine, Ibid.

121 *Reprinted in countless editions:* Eric Foner, introduction to Thomas Paine, *Rights of Man*, New York: Penguin: 1984, 20.

122 *When the church mythologists established:* Paine, *Rights of Man*, 32.

122 *The Almighty . . . is the great mechanic:* Ibid., 193.

123 *Of more worth is one honest man:* Thomas Paine, *Common Sense*, Mineola, NY: Dover, 1997, 17.

123 *It also revealed Paine:* Foner, introduction to Paine, *Rights of Man*, 9.

124 *These are the times that try men's souls:* Thomas Paine, "The American Crisis Number 1, 1776," in *Common Sense, The Crisis, & Other Writings from the American Revolution,* ed. Eric Foner, New York: Library of America, 2015.

125 *Monopolies of every kind marked:* Thomas Paine, quoted in Kevin Grimm, "Thomas Paine," George Washington's Mount Vernon, accessed April 28, 2023, https://www.mountvernon.org/library/digitalhistory/digital-encyclopedia /article/thomas-paine/#note1.

125 *The bones then were passed:* Heather Thomas, "The Bones of Thomas Paine," *Headlines & Heroes* blog, Library of Congress, April 2, 2019.

126 *with the assistance of some old stories:* Paine, *Age of Reason,* 42.

126 *More than any other individual:* Foner, introduction to Paine, *Rights of Man,* 22.

NARRATIVE OF THE LIFE OF FREDERICK DOUGLASS, AN AMERICAN SLAVE

128 *You have seen how a man was made a slave:* Frederick Douglass, *Narrative of the Life of Frederick Douglass, an American Slave,* New Haven, CT: Yale University Press, 2001, 50.

128 *I was born in Tuckahoe:* Ibid., 13.

129 *Before he commenced whipping Aunt Hester:* Ibid., 16.

131 *In six years, twenty-one editions of the book had been published in the United States:* John W. Blassingame, introduction to Douglass, *Narrative,* xxiv.

132 *We are striking the rebels with our soft white hand:* "Confronting a President: Douglass and Lincoln," Frederick Douglass National Historic Site, National Parks Service, https://www.nps.gov/frdo/learn/historyculture /confronting-a-president-douglass-and-lincoln.htm.

133 *What business has the world:* Brandon Zang, "Why Was Frederick Douglass's Marriage to Helen Pitts Controversial?," *Encyclopedia Britannica,* https:// www.britannica.com/story/why-was-frederick-douglasss-marriage-to-helen -pitts-controversial.

134 *I therefore hate the:* Douglass, *Narrative,* 81.

THE COMMUNIST MANIFESTO

136 *The history of all hitherto:* Karl Marx and Friedrich Engels, *The Communist Manifesto,* trans. Samuel Moore, New York: Penguin Books, 2011, 64.

136 *A spectre is haunting Europe:* Ibid., 63.

137 *Freeman and slave, patrician and plebian:* Ibid., 64.

137 *By bourgeoisie is meant the class:* Ibid., 64.

138 *The proletarians have nothing to lose:* Ibid., 104.

140 *one of the four best-selling books:* Unsigned, "Seven Facts about Karl Marx," Deutschland.de, accessed April 28, 2023, https://www.deutschland.de/en /topic/knowledge/200-years-of-karl-marx-seven-facts.

140 *Unlike Marxism, the illiberal:* Anne Applebaum, *Twilight of Democracy*, New York: Doubleday, 2020, 22.

141 *Marx hates capitalism:* Marshall Berman, introduction to Marx and Engels, *The Communist Manifesto*, 3.

141 *Labor is prior to and independent of capital:* Abraham Lincoln, "December 3, 1861: First Annual Message," Presidential Speeches, UVA / Miller Center, accessed April 28, 2023, https://millercenter.org/the-presidency/presidential -speeches/december-3-1861-first-annual-message.

142 *to secure the maximum profit:* Daniel J. Boorstin, *The Seekers: The Story of Man's Continuing Quest to Understand His World*, New York: Vintage Books, 1999, 229.

142 *Capital is only the fruit of labor:* Lincoln, "December 3, 1861: First Annual Message."

142 *A revolution is not a dinner party: Quotations from Chairman Mao Tse-Tung*, Eastford, CT: Martino Fine Books, 2018, 6–7.

CIVIL DISOBEDIENCE

144 *Unjust laws exist:* Henry David Thoreau, "Civil Disobedience," in *Walden and Civil Disobedience*, New York: Penguin Books, 2017, 278.

145 *I heartily accept the motto:* Ibid., 271.

146 *There will never be a really free:* Ibid., 292.

147 *The law will never make men free:* Henry D. Thoreau, "Slavery in Massachu-setts," Henry David Thoreau online, accessed April 28, 2023, https://www .thoreau-online.org/slavery-in-massachusetts-page4.html.

147 *I hear many condemn:* Henry David Thoreau, "A Plea for Captain John Brown," Yale Law School/Avalon Project Documents in Law, History and Diplomacy, accessed April 28, 2023, https://avalon.law.yale.edu/19th_century /thoreau_001.asp.

148 *The country knows not yet:* Ralph Waldo Emerson, "Thoreau," *Atlantic*,

August 1862, accessed April 28, 2023, https://www.theatlantic.com/magazine/archive/1862/08/thoreau/306418/.

149 *When I went to Morehouse:* Martin Luther King, Jr., *The Autobiography of Martin Luther King, Jr.*, New York: Warner Books, 1998, 14.

149 *Thoreau the rebel, intransigent muse:* Rebecca Solnit, "The Thoreau Problem," *Orion Magazine*, undated, accessed April 28, 2023, https://orion magazine.org/article/the-thoreau-problem/.

149 *You head for the hills to enjoy:* Ibid.

149 *Thoreau's writings have renewed significance:* Kristen Case, "Introduction to Civil Disobedience," in Thoreau, *Walden and Civil Disobedience*, xvi.

149 *The mass of men:* Thoreau, *Walden and Civil Disobedience*, 7.

150 *I went to the woods:* Ibid., 72.

150 *The happiest man:* Ralph Waldo Emerson, *Nature*, New York: Penguin Books, 2008, 44.

150 *This book expands on:* Unsigned, "Letter from Birmingham Jail," King Encyclopedia, Stanford University/Martin Luther King, Jr. Research and Education Institute, https://kinginstitute.stanford.edu/encyclopedia/letter-birmingham-jail.

INCIDENTS IN THE LIFE OF A SLAVE GIRL:
WRITTEN BY HERSELF

151 *I want to add my testimony:* Harriet Jacobs, *Incidents in the Life of a Slave Girl: Written by Herself*, New York: Modern Library, 2021, 8.

152 *I was born a slave:* Ibid., 11.

152 *fall of 1813:* "Notes" in Jacobs, *Incidents*, 244.

152 *Reader, be assured:* Ibid., 7.

153 *My master began to whisper:* Ibid., 37.

153 *Making this decision:* Tiya Miles, introduction to Jacobs, *Incidents*, viii.

153 *These brats will bring me:* Jacobs, *Incidents*, 97.

155 *At her request:* Lydia Maria Child, "Introduction by the Editor," in Jacobs, *Incidents*, 9.

155 *she encountered the destitute widow:* Sam Roberts, "Jean Fagan Yellin, Who Uncovered a Slavery Tale's True Author, Dies at 92," *New York Times,* July 28, 2023, https://www.nytimes.com/2023/07/28/books/jean-fagan-yellin-dead.html?action=click&module=Well&pgtype=Homepage&section=Obituaries.

156 *Publication of this book:* Jean Fagan Yellin, "Commentary," in Jacobs, *Incidents*, 280.

156 *Jacobs's narrative is a bold:* Henry Louis Gates Jr., "To Be Raped, Bred or Abused," *New York Times*, November 22, 1987, accessed April 28, 2023, https://archive.nytimes.com/www.nytimes.com/books/00/09/10/nnp/jacobs-slave.html.

157 *say students should learn that enslaved people "developed skills":* Lori Rosza, "Florida Approves Black History Standards Decried as 'Step Backward,'" *Washington Post*, July 19, 2023, https://www.washingtonpost.com/nation/2023/07/19/florida-black-history-standards/.

157 *I read the first annotated edition:* Tiya Miles, introduction to Jacobs, *Incidents*, xi.

ON LYNCHINGS

158 *The entire system of the judiciary:* Ida B. Wells-Barnett, *On Lynchings*, Garden City, NY: Dover, 2014, 59.

159 *Wednesday evening May 24th, 1892:* Ibid., 7.

159 *Nobody in this section of the country believes:* Caitlin Dickerson, "Ida B. Wells," *New York Times*, March 9, 2018, https://www.nytimes.com/interactive/2018/obituaries/overlooked-ida-b-wells.html.

160 *If this work can contribute in any way:* Wells-Barnett, *On Lynchings*, 3.

160 *Nothing is more definitely settled:* Ibid., 28.

162 *Her goal was to question a stereotype:* Dickerson, "Ida B. Wells."

162 *Despite her ebbing influence:* Ibid.

162 *For her outstanding and courageous reporting:* "Ida B. Wells," The Pulitzer Prizes, https://www.pulitzer.org/winners/ida-b-wells.

163 *She carefully chronicled names, date, locations:* Michael D. Shear, "Biden Signs Bill to Make Lynching a Federal Crime," *New York Times*, March 29, 2022, https://www.nytimes.com/2022/03/29/us/politics/biden-signs-anti-lynching-bill.html.

163 *The Spires Bolling House in Holly Springs:* Ida B. Wells-Barnett Museum, https://idabwellsmuseum.org/.

164 *This is not merely an escalation of the "history wars":* Unsigned, "AHA Statement Opposing Florida House Bill 999 (March 2023)," American Historical Association, March 3, 2023, https://www.historians.org/news-and-advocacy/aha-advocacy/aha-statement-opposing-florida-house-bill-999-(march-2023).

165 *It is about how easily we condemn:* Bryan Stevenson, *Just Mercy*, New York: One World, 2014, 14.

165 *Subsequently, the NAACP marginalized:* Paula J. Giddings, *Ida: A Sword Among Lions*, New York: Amistad, 2008, 7.

THE SOULS OF BLACK FOLK

166 *We have no right:* W. E. B. Du Bois, *The Souls of Black Folk*, New York: Penguin Books, 1996, 47.

167 *Herein lie buried many things:* Ibid., 1.

167 *It is a peculiar sensation:* Ibid., 5.

168 *Every chapter in Du Bois's book:* Donald Gibson, introduction to Du Bois, *Souls*, xxi.

168 *programme of industrial:* Du Bois, *Souls*, 36.

168 *these weird old songs in which the soul of the black slave:* Ibid., 204.

168 *Your country?:* Ibid., 214–215.

169 *In a wee wooden schoolhouse:* Ibid., 4.

171 *When W. E. B. Du Bois Made a Laughingstock:* Ian Frazier, "When W. E. B. Du Bois Made a Laughingstock of a White Supremacist," *New Yorker*, August 26, 2019, https://www.newyorker.com/magazine/2019/08/26/when-w-e-b-du-bois-made-a-laughingstock-of-a-white-supremacist.

172 *One idea he insistently taught:* Martin Luther King, Jr., cited in Frazier, "When W. E. B. Du Bois Made a Laughingstock."

174 *These two giants:* Unsigned website article, "Booker T. Washington and the 'Atlanta Compromise,'" National Museum of African American History and Culture, accessed April 28, 2023, https://nmaahc.si.edu/explore/stories/booker-t-washington-and-atlanta-compromise.

THE WORLD I LIVE IN

175 *The silence and darkness:* Helen Keller, *The World I Live In,* ed. Roger Shattuck, New York: New York Review Books, 2003, 29–30.

175 *I have just touched my dog:* Ibid., 9.

176 *Helen is a miracle:* William Gibson, "Looking Back at 'The Miracle Worker' on TV," *New York Times*, October 14, 1979, https://www.nytimes.com/1979/10/14/archives/looking-back-at-the-miracle-worker-on-tv-keller.html.

176 *Most people measure their happiness:* Keller, *World*, 127–128.

177 *reverted nearly to the state of a seriously wounded, untamed animal:* Roger Shattuck, introduction to Keller, *World*, viii.

177 *Four months after Annie's arrival:* Shattuck, introduction to Keller, *World*, ix.

178 *Dear Comrade:* "To Eugene V. Debs," Helen Keller Reference Archive, first published April 29, 1919, *New York Call*, in *Helen Keller: Her Socialist Years*, ed. Philip S. Foner, New York: International, 1967, https://www.marxists.org /reference/archive/keller-helen/works/1910s/19_04_29.htm.

179 *She was a member of the Socialist Party:* Olivia B. Waxman, "Co-Founding the ACLU, Fighting for Labor Rights and Other Helen Keller Accomplishments Students Don't Learn in School," *Time,* December 15, 2020, https://time .com/5918660/helen-keller-disability-history/.

179 *Keller donated her German:* "Helen Keller," Holocaust Encyclopedia, United States Holocaust Memorial Museum, accessed April 26, 2023, https://ency clopedia.ushmm.org/content/en/article/helen-keller.

179 *Once, in daylight:* Anne Dillard, *The Writing Life*, New York: Harper Perennial, 2013, 30.

180 *The reason why we find:* Shattuck, introduction to Keller, *World*, xxxiii.

180 *She noticed the close relationship between disability and poverty:* Sascha Cohen, "Helen Keller's Forgotten Radicalism," *Time,* June 26, 2015, https://time .com/3923213/helen-keller-radicalism/.

A ROOM OF ONE'S OWN

181 *Like most uneducated Englishwomen:* Virginia Woolf, *A Room of One's Own*, New York: Harcourt Brace & Co., 1981, 108.

182 *But, you may say, we asked you to speak about women and fiction:* Ibid., 3–4.

182 *His face expressed horror and indignation:* Ibid., 6.

183 *She was as adventurous:* Ibid., 47.

183 *Chloe liked Olivia:* Ibid., 82.

183 *it is fatal for anyone who writes:* Ibid., 104.

184 *Her mother died when she was thirteen:* Nigel Nicolson, *Virginia Woolf*, New York: Viking Penguin, 2000, 2.

185 *It was a pacifist's statement:* Ibid., 157.

186 *women are poor because, instead:* Mary Gordon, foreword to Woolf, *Room*, x.

186 *It stated the case with overwhelming force:* Nicolson, *Virginia Woolf*, 110.

186 *Woolf is concerned with the fate of women of genius:* Gordon, foreword to Woolf, *Room*, viii.

186 *Intellectual freedom depends upon:* Woolf, *Room*, 108.

187 *the nursemaid will heave coal:* Ibid., 40.

187 *Human happiness, the happiness of writers:* Gordon, foreword to Woolf, *Room*, xiii.

187 *travel and adventure, and research:* Woolf, *Room*, 110–111.

188 *It is not* what *you say:* Mary Beard, *Women & Power: A Manifesto*, New York: Liveright, 2017, 36–37.

189 *I wanted to work out how I would explain:* Ibid., x–xi.

THE AUTOBIOGRAPHY OF ALICE B. TOKLAS

190 *I may say that only three times:* Gertrude Stein, *The Autobiography of Alice B. Toklas*, New York: Vintage Books, 1990, 5.

191 *This was the year 1907:* Ibid., 6.

192 *Stein wrote* The Autobiography*:* Janet Malcolm, *Two Lives: Gertrude and Alice*, New Haven, CT: Yale University Press, 2007, 8–9.

193 *Dear Professor James, I am sorry:* Ibid., Malcolm, 14; Alice P. Albright, "Gertrude Stein at Radcliffe," *Harvard Crimson*, February 18, 1959, https://web.archive.org/web/20180418012645/http://www.thecrimson.com/article/1959/2/18/gertrude-stein-at-radcliffe-most-brilliant/?page=2.

193 *The walls of their atelier:* James R. Mellow, "The Stein Salon Was the First Museum of Modern Art," *New York Times,* December 1, 1968, https://archive.nytimes.com/www.nytimes.com/books/98/05/03/specials/stein-salon.html.

194 *committed supporter of Philippe Pétain:* Barbara Will, "The Strange Politics of Gertrude Stein," *Humanities*, March/April 2012, https://www.neh.gov/humanities/2012/marchapril/feature/the-strange-politics-gertrude-stein.

194 *How had the pair of elderly Jewish lesbians:* Malcolm, *Two Lives*, 6.

195 *You know what I am going to do:* Stein, *Autobiography*, 252.

HOMAGE TO CATALONIA

197 *This war, in which I played:* George Orwell, *Homage to Catalonia*, New York: Mariner Books, 2015, 195.

197 *Together with all this:* Ibid., 4.

198 *The whole experience of being hit:* Ibid., 143–144.

199 *for mysterious reasons:* Anna Funder, "Looking for Eileen: How George Orwell Wrote His Wife out of His Story," *Guardian*, July 30, 2023, https://www .theguardian.com/books/2023/jul/30/my-hunt-for-eileen-george-orwell -erased-wife-anna-funder.

200 *only six hundred copies:* Caroline Moorehead, *Martha Gellhorn: A Twentieth-Century Life,* New York: Picador, 2003, 127.

201 *a vivid account of the experiences:* Paul Preston, "George Orwell's Spanish Civil War Memoir Is a Classic, but Is It Bad History?," *Guardian*, May 6, 2017, https://www.theguardian.com/books/2017/may/06/george-orwell -homage-to-catalonia-account-spanish-civil-war-wrong.

201 *The Spanish war and other events:* George Orwell, *Why I Write,* New York: Penguin Books, 2005, 8.

201 *I did try very hard:* Ibid., 9.

202 *He told the truth:* Lionel Trilling, introduction Orwell, *Homage to Catalonia,* xliv.

202 *But the British ruling class:* Orwell, *Why I Write,* 33.

203 *The upshot of this:* Robert McCrum, "100 Best Nonfiction Books: #39—The Road to Wigan Pier (1937)," *Guardian*, October 24, 2106, accessed April 29, 2023, https://www.theguardian.com/books/2016/oct/24/road-wigan-pier -george-orwell-100-best-nonfiction-books.

A CHILL IN THE AIR: AN ITALIAN WAR DIARY, 1939–1940

204 *Yet so great is his personal:* Iris Origo, *A Chill in the Air: An Italian War Diary, 1949–1940,* New York: New York Review Books, 2017, 66.

204 *The train is packed:* Ibid., 23.

206 *Went to bed not daring:* Ibid., 82.

206 *We know:* Ibid., 83.

206 *In the autumn of 1940:* Ibid., 168.

206 *to grow up free from all this national feeling:* Lucy Hughes-Hallett, introduction to Origo, *A Chill in the Air,* 6.

208 *Here she demonstrates the same keen eye:* Alexander Stille, "Living with Fascism in Italy," *New York Times*, September 21, 2018, https://www.nytimes .com/2018/09/21/books/review/iris-origo-chill-in-the-air.html?searchResult Position=7.

209 *Trenchant, intelligent, and written with a cool head:* Cynthia Zarin, "Not

a Moment Too Soon: Iris Origo's War Diary," *New Yorker*, August 1, 2018, https://www.newyorker.com/culture/culture-desk/not-a-moment-too-soon-iris-origos-war-diary.

209 *The people Origo encounters:* Stille, "Living with Fascism."

UNDER THE SEA-WIND

210 *There the young were to be born:* Rachel Carson, *Under the Sea-Wind*, New York: Penguin Books, 2007, 153.

210 *The Island lay in shadows: Ibid.*, 9.

212 *I can remember no time:* Rachel Carson, quoted in Linda Lear, *Rachel Carson: Witness for Nature*, Boston: Mariner Books, 2009, 8.

213 *As the Depression deepened:* Jill Lepore, "The Right Way to Remember Rachel Carson," *New Yorker*, March 19, 2018, https://www.newyorker.com/magazine/2018/03/26/the-right-way-to-remember-rachel-carson.

213 *It left readers swooning:* Ibid.

213 *Conscious of the role of alliteration:* Linda Lear, introduction to Carson, *Under the Sea-Wind*, xiii.

215 *Since the late nineteen-forties:* Rachel Carson, "Silent Spring–I," *New Yorker*, June 9, 1962, https://www.newyorker.com/magazine/1962/06/16/silent-spring-part-1.

216 *scientist-poet of the sea:* Lepore, "Right Way to Remember."

216 *Carson's most enduring literary themes:* Lear, introduction to Carson, *Under the Sea-Wind*, x.

216 *To stand at the edge of the sea:* Carson, *Under the Sea-Wind*, 2007, 4.

THE MYTH OF SISYPHUS

218 *The gods had condemned:* Albert Camus, *The Myth of Sisyphus*, trans. Justin O'Brien, New York: Vintage International, 2018, 119.

218 *There is but one truly serious: Ibid.*, 3.

219 *A world that can be explained: Ibid.*, 6.

220 *His family had no electricity:* Sarah Bakewell, *At the Existentialist Café: Freedom, Being, and Apricot Cocktails*, New York: Other Press, 2016, 147.

221 *Inspired by an authentic moral engagement:* Anders Österling, "Presentation Speech," 1957 Nobel Prize Award Ceremony, https://www.nobelprize.org/prizes/literature/1957/ceremony-speech/.

222 *The fundamental subject:* Albert Camus, preface to *The Myth of Sisyphus*.

222 *Camus represents also the philosophical movement called Existentialism:* Österling, "Presentation Speech."

222 *Thus I draw from the absurd:* Camus, *The Myth of Sisyphus*, 64.

223 *There's definitely an element of Stoicism:* Sarah Bakewell interviewed by Nigel Warburton, "The Best Books on Existentialism Recommended by Sarah Bakewell," Five Books website, June 2, 2013, https://fivebooks.com/best-books/existentialism-sarah-bakewell/.

HIROSHIMA

224 *There, in the tin factory:* John Hersey, *Hiroshima*, New York: Vintage Books, 2020, 21.

224 *At exactly fifteen minutes past eight:* Ibid., 3.

225 *A hundred thousand people:* Ibid., 4.

225 *After publishing "Hiroshima":* Jon Michaud, "Eighty-Five from the Archive: John Hersey," *New Yorker*, June 8, 2010, accessed Aril 29, 2023, https://www.newyorker.com/books/double-take/eighty-five-from-the-archive-john-hersey.

226 *in a prose so stripped of mannerism, sentimentality, and even minimal emphasis:* Roger Angell, "Hersey and History," *New Yorker*, July 23, 1995, https://www.newyorker.com/magazine/1995/07/31/hersey-and-history.

226 *What everybody knows about John Hersey:* Nicholas Lemann, "John Hersey and the Art of Fact," *New Yorker*, April 22, 2019, accessed April 29, 2023, https://www.newyorker.com/magazine/2019/04/29/john-hersey-and-the-art-of-fact.

226 *Born on June 17, 1914, in Tientsin:* Richard Severo, "John Hersey, Author of 'Hiroshima,' Is Dead at 78," *New York Times*, March 25, 1993, accessed April 29, 2023, https://www.nytimes.com/1993/03/25/obituaries/john-hersey-author-of-hiroshima-is-dead-at-78.html?searchResultPosition=1.

226 *The scholarship boys cleaned classrooms:* John Hersey interviewed by Jonathan Dee, "John Hersey, The Art of Fiction No. 92," *Paris Review*, Summer-Fall 1986, accessed April 29, 2023, https://www.theparisreview.org/interviews/2756/the-art-of-fiction-no-92-john-hersey.

227 *Mr. Hersey later recalled that:* Severo, "John Hersey, Author of 'Hiroshima.'"

227 *He was wonderfully important to me:* Hersey interviewed by Dee, "John Hersey, The Art of Fiction No. 92."

227 *rather seriously deranged:* Ibid.

228 *Kennedy, who had been on the Harvard:* John Hersey, "Survival," *New Yorker*, June 10, 1944, https://www.newyorker.com/magazine/1944/06/17/survival.

228 *Hersey traveled through China:* Michaud, "Eighty-Five from the Archive."

229 *Hersey had received his own call:* Nicholas Lemann, "John Hersey and the Art of Fact," *New Yorker*, April 22, 2019, accessed April 29, 2023, https://www.newyorker.com/magazine/2019/04/29/john-hersey-and-the-art-of-fact.

229 *I don't think I have an impulse:* Hersey interviewed by Dee, "John Hersey, The Art of Fiction No. 92."

229 *But it has lost none of its power:* Jacqui Banaszynski, "The Enduring Power of John Hersey's 'Hiroshima,' the First 'Nonfiction Novel,'" Nieman News, August 6, 2020, https://nieman.harvard.edu/stories/the-enduring-power-of-john-herseys-hiroshima-the-first-nonfiction-novel/.

MAN'S SEARCH FOR MEANING

231 *Since Auschwitz we know:* Viktor E. Frankl, *Man's Search for Meaning*, part 1 translated by Ilse Lasch; foreword by Harold S. Kushner; afterword by William J. Winslade, Boston: Beacon Press, 2006, 154.

232 *In psychiatry there is a certain condition:* Ibid., 10.

232 *Frankl's brother and sister-in-law were caught:* "Viktor Frankl Biography," Viktor Frankl Institute, https://www.viktorfrankl.org/biography.html.

233 *tore open the human soul:* Frankl, *Man's Search for Meaning*, 87.

233 *I told them:* Ibid., 82.

233 *"Logotherapy," he writes, "focuses":* Ibid., 98–99.

233 *an optimism in the face of:* Ibid., 137–138.

234 *Frankl "began to feel that Adler erred":* Holcomb B. Noble, "Dr. Viktor E. Frankl, Psychiatrist of the Search for Meaning, Dies at 92," *New York Times*, September 4, 1997, https://www.nytimes.com/1997/09/04/world/dr-viktor-e-frankl-of-vienna-psychiatrist-of-the-search-for-meaning-dies-at-92.html?searchResultPosition=1.

234 *The Nazis forced them to abort a child:* "Viktor Frankl Biography."

235 *In 1991,* Man's Search for Meaning *was named:* Esther B. Fein, "Book Notes," *New York Times*, November 20, 1991, https://www.nytimes.com/1991/11/20/books/book-notes-059091.html.

235 *As director, Frankl was given:* Timothy E. Pytell, "Redeeming the Unredeemable: Auschwitz and Man's Search for Meaning," *Holocaust and Genocide Studies* 17, no. 1 (2003): 89–113, muse.jhu.edu/article/43137.

235 *Frankl's prewar experiments:* Timothy Pytell, "Is It OK to Criticize a Saint? On Humanizing Viktor Frankl," *Psychology Today*, March 31, 2017, https://www.psychologytoday.com/us/blog/authoritarian-therapy/201703/is-it-ok-criticize-saint-humanizing-viktor-frankl.

236 *Frankl was not a collaborator:* Anna Geifman and David Mikics, "The Life of Viktor Frankl," *Tablet*, December 10, 2020, https://www.tabletmag.com/sections/arts-letters/articles/viktor-frankl-geifman-mikics-exchange.

236 *curing the soul:* Harold S. Kushner, foreword to Frankl, *Man's Search for Meaning*, xi.

236 *The meaning of your life is to help others:* William J. Winslade, afterword to Frankl, *Man's Search for Meaning*, 164–165.

237 *In one of my favorite books:* Tim Sanders, "A Chatterer's Guide to Easing Anxiety," *New York Times*, October 27, 2008, https://www.nytimes.com/2008/11/27/travel/27iht-25flier.18204176.html.

237 *In other words, creative activities that engage:* Maria Cohut, "Searching for Purpose: Logotherapy Might Help," *Medical News Today*, February 2, 2018, https://www.medicalnewstoday.com/articles/320814.

237 *It seems that if the patient cannot find his goal:* Rollo May, cited in Timothy Pytell, "The Case against Viktor Frankl," *Psychology Today*, April 14, 2016, https://www.psychologytoday.com/us/blog/authoritarian-therapy/201604/the-case-against-viktor-frankl.

237 *So, fate is part of our lives:* Viktor E. Frankl, *Yes to Life*, Boston: Beacon Press, 2020, 40.

238 *Frankl begins by considering:* Maria Popova, "Yes to Life in Spite of Everything: Viktor Frankl's Lost Lectures on Moving Beyond Optimism and Pessimism to Find the Deepest Source of Meaning," *The Marginalian*, May 17, 2020, https://www.themarginalian.org/2020/05/17/yes-to-life-in-spite-of-everything-viktor-frankl/.

NIGHT

239 *That night, the soup tasted of corpses:* Elie Wiesel, *Night*, trans. Marion Wiesel, New York: Hill & Wang, 2006, 65.

239 *They called him Moishe the Beadle:* Ibid., 3.

239 *And Moishe the Beadle:* Ibid., 5.

240 *The night had passed completely:* Ibid., 37.

241 *Where Anne Frank's book ends:* Rachel Donadio, "The Story of 'Night,'" *New York Times*, January 20, 2008, https://www.nytimes.com/2008/01/20/books/review/Donadio-t.html.

241 *It was then that I understood:* François Mauriac, foreword to Wiesel, *Night*, xviii–xx.

242 *The Holocaust was not something people wanted:* Joseph Berger, "Elie Wiesel, Auschwitz Survivor and Nobel Peace Prize Winner, Dies at 87," *New York Times*, July 2, 2016, https://www.nytimes.com/2016/07/03/world/europe/elie-wiesel-auschwitz-survivor-and-nobel-peace-prize-winner-dies-at-87.html.

242 *That place, Mr. President:* Donadio, "The Story of 'Night,'" https://www.nytimes.com/2008/01/20/books/review/Donadio-t.html.

243 *And then I explain to him how naïve we were:* Elie Wiesel, "Nobel Peace Prize Acceptance Speech," *Night*, 118.

243 *There may have been better chroniclers:* Berger, "Elie Wiesel" https://www.nytimes.com/2016/07/03/world/europe/elie-wiesel-auschwitz-survivor-and-nobel-peace-prize-winner-dies-at-87.html.

244 Erika Mann, *School for Barbarians: Education under the Nazis*, Mineola, NY: Dover Publications, 19.

THE FIRE NEXT TIME

245 *A bill is coming in:* James Baldwin, *The Fire Next Time*, New York: Vintage International, 1993, 103.

245 *I became, during my fourteenth year:* Ibid., 16.

246 *This innocent country set you down:* Ibid., 7.

246 *The glorification of one race:* Ibid., 82.

246 *How can the American Negro past:* Ibid., 103.

247 *unforgiving man with a terrible temper:* Hilton Als, "The Enemy Within," *New Yorker*, February 9, 1998, https://www.newyorker.com/magazine/1998/02/16/the-enemy-within-hilton-als.

247 *It was my good luck:* Baldwin, *The Fire Next Time*, 29.

247 *My father slammed me across the face:* Ibid., 37.

248 *I was broke:* Jordan Elgrably, "James Baldwin, The Art of Fiction No. 78," *Paris Review*, Spring 1984, https://theparisreview.org/interviews/2994/the-art-of-fiction-no-78-james-baldwin.

248 *Your analysis of the problem:* Unsigned, "Baldwin, James Arthur," King Encyclopedia, Stanford University/Martin Luther King, Jr. Research and Education Institute, https://kinginstitute.stanford.edu/encyclopedia/baldwin-james-arthur.

249 *From the point of view of the man:* James Baldwin, "The American Dream and the American Negro," *New York Times,* March 7, 1965, https://archive.nytimes.com/www.nytimes.com/books/98/03/29/specials/baldwin-dream.html.

249 *He was at his best:* Als, "The Enemy Within."

250 *White people hold the power:* Baldwin, *The Fire Next Time,* 25–26.

251 *By being himself:* Michael Eric Dyson, "*Between the World and Me:* Baldwin's Heir?," *Atlantic,* July 23, 2015, https://www.theatlantic.com/politics/archive/2015/07/james-baldwin-tanehisi-coates/399413/.

A VERY EASY DEATH

252 *A hard task, dying:* Simone de Beauvoir, *A Very Easy Death,* trans. Patrick O'Brian, New York: Pantheon Books, 1965, 79.

252 *At four o'clock in the afternoon:* Ibid., 9.

253 *I had grown very fond of this dying woman:* Ibid., 76.

253 *If any single human being can be credited:* Unsigned obituary, "Simone de Beauvoir, Author and Intellectual, Dies in Paris at 78," *New York Times,* April 15,1986, https://www.nytimes.com/1986/04/15/obituaries/simone-de-beauvoir-author-and-intellectual-dies-in-paris-at-78.html?searchResultPosition=11.

254 *Women, you owe her everything!:* Cited by Lisa Appignanesi in "Did Simone de Beauvoir's Open 'Marriage' Make Her Happy?," *Guardian,* June 10, 2005, https://www.theguardian.com/world/2005/jun/10/gender.politicsphilosophyandsociety.

254 *While no one individual or her work:* Judith Thurman, "Introduction to Simone de Beauvoir's 'The Second Sex,'" *New York Times,* May 27, 2010, https://www.nytimes.com/2010/05/30/books/excerpt-introduction-second-sex.html.

255 *In real life, this was a fraught love triangle:* Sarah Bakewell, *At the Existentialist Café: Freedom, Being, and Apricot Cocktails,* New York: Other Press, 2017, 108.

256 *One is humbled to learn:* Thurman, "Introduction."

257 *When I was growing up:* Appignanesi, "Did Simone de Beauvoir's 'Open 'Marriage' Make Her Happy?"

257 *But it is clear now:* Louis Menand, "Stand by Your Man," *New Yorker*, September 18, 2005, https://www.newyorker.com/magazine/2005/09/26/stand-by-your-man.

258 *The sight of my mother's nakedness:* Beauvoir, *A Very Easy Death*, 19–20.

258 *There is no such thing:* Ibid., 106.

259 *Taken within the context of the feminist movement:* Debra Bergoffen and Megan Burke, "Simone de Beauvoir," *Stanford Encyclopedia of Philosophy*, Stanford University, Spring 2023 ed., ed. Edward N. Zalta and Uri Nodelman, https://plato.stanford.edu/archives/spr2023/entries/beauvoir/.

259 *Beauvoir speaks of the war:* Ibid.

259 *Without Zaza:* Margaret Atwood, introduction to Simone de Beauvoir, *Inseparable*, New York: Ecco, 2021, xvi–xvii.

259 *You have seen that it:* Jean-Paul Sartre, *Existentialism Is a Humanism*, trans. Carol Macomber, New Haven, CT: Yale University Press, 2007, 39–40.

260 *Although it is a novel:* Sarah Bakewell interviewed by Nigel Warburton, "The Best Books on Existentialism Recommended by Sarah Bakewell," Five Books website, June 2, 2013, https://fivebooks.com/best-books/existentialism-sarah-bakewell/.

A MOVEABLE FEAST

261 *But this is how Paris was:* Ernest Hemingway, *A Moveable Feast*, New York: Scribner, 2003, 211.

261 *Then there was the bad weather:* Ibid., 3.

262 *is the one who had the most to do with my craft:* Gabriel García Márquez, "Gabriel García Márquez Meets Ernest Hemingway," *New York Times*, July 26, 1981, https://archive.nytimes.com/www.nytimes.com/books/99/07/04/specials/hemingway-marquez.html.

263 *Seven of Hemingway's close family relations:* Dr. Howard Markel, "How Mental Health Struggles Wrote Ernest Hemingway's Final Chapter," PBS Newshour, July 21, 2020, https://www.pbs.org/newshour/health/how-mental-health-struggles-wrote-ernest-hemingways-final-chapter.

265 *In 1956, Ernest and I were having lunch:* A. E. Hotchner, "Don't Touch 'A Moveable Feast,'" *New York Times*, July 19, 2009, https://www.nytimes.com/2009/07/20/opinion/20hotchner.html.

265 *In September 2023:* Clair Moses, "Hemingway Survived Two Plane Crashes. A Letter about Them Just Sold for over $237,000," *New York Times*, September 5, 2023, https://www.nytimes.com/2023/09/05/books/hemingway -plane-crash-letter-auction.html.

266 *He liked to listen to the actors:* Hemingway, *A Moveable Feast*, 128.

266 *Downstairs I finished my dinner:* Ibid., 174.

266 *was a writer who had in his time:* Joan Didion, "Last Words," *New Yorker*, October 25, 1998, https://www.newyorker.com/magazine/1998/11/09 /last-words-6.

267 *If the reader prefers:* Ernest Hemingway, preface to *A Moveable Feast*, ix.

267 *These details are evidence:* Hotchner, "Don't Touch 'A Moveable Feast.'"

267 *This new edition, also published:* Ibid.

267 *What is it exactly that explains:* Christopher Hitchens, "Hemingway's Libidinous Feast," *Atlantic*, June 2009, https://www.theatlantic.com/magazine /archive/2009/06/hemingways-libidinous-feast/307425/.

268 *So you live day by day:* Hemingway, *A Moveable Feast*, 210.

268 *employment of colorism:* Toni Morrison, *The Origin of Others*, Cambridge, MA: Harvard University Press, 2017, 43.

THE COURAGE TO CREATE

269 *Just as the poet:* Rollo May, *The Courage to Create*, New York: W. W. Norton, 1994, 73.

269 *We are living at a time:* Ibid., 11.

270 *Courage is not a virtue:* Ibid., 13.

270 *the creating of one's self:* Ibid., 99.

270 *There is a curiously sharp sense of joy:* Ibid., 122–123.

272 *In the 1950's:* Eric Pace, "Rollo May Is Dead at 85; Was Innovator in Psychology," *New York Times*, October 24, 1994, https://www.nytimes.com/1994 /10/24/obituaries/dr-rollo-may-is-dead-at-85-was-innovator-in-psychology .html.

272 *a parallel movement that is to orthodox psychoanalysis:* David Dempsey, "Love and Will and Rollo May," *New York Times*, March 28, 1971, https://www .nytimes.com/1971/03/28/archives/love-and-will-and-rollo-may-dr-may-is -the-prime-mover-of-the-new.html?searchResultPosition=19.

274 *As the psychologist and popular author Rollo May:* Louis Menand, "The

Origins of Creativity," *New Yorker*, April 17, 2023, https://www.newyorker
.com/magazine/2023/04/24/the-cult-of-creativity-samuel-weil-franklin-book
-review.

274 *For they are the ones who threaten:* May, *The Courage to Create*, 27.

274 *His works lent historical breadth:* Robert Abzug interviewed by Stephen
Diamond, "Wounded Healer: Rollo May's Psycho-Spiritual Odyssey," *Psychology Today*, February 1, 2021, https://www.psychologytoday.com/us/blog
/evil-deeds/202102/wounded-healer-rollo-mays-psycho-spiritual-odyssey.

275 *Although May's argument is complex:* Dempsey, "Love and Will and Rollo May."

ON PHOTOGRAPHY

276 *So successful has been the camera's role:* Susan Sontag, *On Photography*, New
York: Picador, 2001, 85.

276 *Humankind lingers unregenerately in Plato's cave:* Ibid., 3.

277 *For Arbus, both freaks and Middle America:* Ibid., 45, 47.

278 *One's first encounter:* Ibid., 19–20.

278 *Like guns and cars:* Ibid., 14.

278 *one of the most lionized:* Margalit Fox, "Susan Sontag, Social Critic with
Verve, Dies at 71," *New York Times*, December 28, 2004, https://www.nytimes
.com/2004/12/28/books/susan-sontag-social-critic-with-verve-dies-at-71.html
?searchResultPosition=21.

279 *$70, two suitcases and a 7 year old:* Ibid.

279 *Miss Sontag has written a ponderable:* Benjamin DeMott, "Against Interpretation," *New York Times*, January 23, 1966, https://web.archive.org/web
/20170714133425/https://www.nytimes.com/1966/01/23/books/booksspecial
/sontag-interpretation.html.

279 *Fascism with a human face:* Unsigned, "Susan Sontag Provokes Debate on
Communism," *New York Times*, February 27, 1982, https://archive.nytimes
.com/www.nytimes.com/books/00/03/12/specials/sontag-communism.html.

280 *Part literary study, part polemic:* David Rieff, "Why I Had to Lie to My Dying
Mother," *Observer*, May 18, 2008, https://www.theguardian.com/books/2008
/may/18/society.

280 *Some branded Ms. Sontag:* Fox, "Susan Sontag."

280 *Erasmus traveled with 32 volumes:* Carlos Fuentes, quoted in Fox, "Susan
Sontag."

280 *Through the decades her image:* Fox, "Susan Sontag."

281 *It seems that editors:* Patrick Moore, "Susan Sontag and a Case of Curious Silence," *Los Angeles Times*, January 4, 2005, https://www.latimes.com /archives/la-xpm-2005-jan-04-oe-moore4-story.html.

281 *It was not a perfect book:* Benjamin Moser, *Sontag: Her Life and Work*, New York: Ecco, 2019, 349–350.

282 *While Sontag delved into a few:* Alina Cohen, "Susan Sontag's Radical Views Still Shape How We See Photography," Artsy.net, June 13, 2019, https://www .artsy.net/article/artsy-editorial-susan-sontags-radical-views-shape-photo graphy.

282 *Illness is the night-side of life:* Susan Sontag, *Illness as Metaphor and AIDS and Its Metaphors*, New York: Picador, 1990, 3.

THE GNOSTIC GOSPELS

283 *All the old questions:* Elaine Pagels, *The Gnostic Gospels*, New York: Vintage Books, 1989, 150.

283 *Jesus Christ rose from the grave:* Ibid., 3.

285 *an aloof biologist:* Mark Epstein, "A Scholar of Religion Confronts Her Own Grief," *New York Times*, December 4, 2018, https://www.nytimes .com/2018/12/04/books/review/why-religion-elaine-pagels.html?searchResult Position=4.

285 *partly out of curiosity:* David Remnick, "The Devil Problem," *New Yorker*, April 3, 1995, https://www.newyorker.com/magazine/1995/04/03/the-devil -problem.

285 *Her first brush with death:* Epstein, "A Scholar of Religion."

286 *For people more religious:* Remnick, "The Devil Problem."

287 *These are the secret words:* Elaine Pagels, introduction to *The Gnostic Gospels*, xiii–xv.

288 *Through a careful reading of the fifty-two:* Remnick, "The Devil Problem."

288 *Characteristically brief and lucid:* Ibid.

AMUSING OURSELVES TO DEATH: PUBLIC DISCOURSE IN THE AGE OF SHOW BUSINESS

289 *Television's strongest point:* Neil Postman, *Amusing Ourselves to Death: Public Discourse in the Age of Show Business*, New York: Penguin Books, 2006, 123.

289 *Today, we must look to the city:* Ibid., 3–4.

290 *vast wasteland:* Newton N. Minow, quoted in "The Scathing Speech That Made Television History," *Time*, May 9, 2016, https://time.com/4315217 /newton-minow-vast-wasteland-1961-speech/.

291 *In the Huxleyan prophecy:* Postman, *Amusing Ourselves to Death*, 155–156.

292 *Postman avoided computers:* Elaine Woo, "Neil Postman, 72; Author Warned of Technology Threats," *Los Angeles Times*, October 12, 2003, https://www .latimes.com/archives/la-xpm-2003-oct-12-me-postman12-story.html.

292 *The car salesman mustered a reply:* Ibid.

292 *It did so . . . by steeping the minds of children:* Wolfgang Saxon, "Neil Postman, 72, Mass Media Critic, Dies," *New York Times*, October 9, 2003, https://www .nytimes.com/2003/10/09/nyregion/neil-postman-72-mass-media-critic-dies .html?searchResultPosition=3.

293 *but that they did not know:* Postman, *Amusing Ourselves to Death*, 163.

293 *I feel stupid and contagious:* Nirvana, "Smells Like Teen Spirit," written by David Grohl, Krist Novoselic, and Kurt Cobain, on *Nevermind* (1991). (BMG Rights Management, Kobalt Music Publishing Ltd., 1991.)

294 *about twice the all-in price of the most expensive presidential campaigns in history:* Nicholas Confessore and Karen Yourish, "$2 Billion Worth of Free Media for Donald Trump, "*New York Times*, March 15, 2016, https://www .nytimes.com/2016/03/16/upshot/measuring-donald-trumps-mammoth-ad vantage-in-free-media.html.

294 *This is the lesson:* Postman, *Amusing Ourselves to Death*, 135.

295 *The medium, or process, of our time:* Marshall McLuhan and Quentin Fiore, *The Medium Is the Massage*, Berkeley, CA: Gingko Press, 1996, 8.

THE WRITING LIFE

297 *Why are we reading:* Annie Dillard, *The Writing Life*, New York: Harper Perennial, 2013, 72.

297 *When you write, you lay out a line of words:* Ibid., 3.

298 *I do not so much write a book:* Ibid., 52.

298 *One of the few things I know:* Ibid., 78.

298 *While still a student at the school, she married:* Mary Cantwell, "A Pilgrim's Progress," *New York Times*, April 26, 1992, https://archive.nytimes.com/www .nytimes.com/books/99/03/28/specials/dillard-pilgrim.html.

299 *The book is a form of meditation:* Eudora Welty, "Meditation on Seeing,"

New York Times, March 24, 1974, https://archive.nytimes.com/www.nytimes
.com/books/99/03/28/specials/dillard-tinker.html.

299 *One way or another:* Cantwell, "A Pilgrim's Progress."

299 *The Writing Life (1989) is an embarrassing:* Annie Dillard, "Books by Annie
Dillard," Annie Dillard website, accessed April 26, 2023, https://www.annie
dillard.com/books-annie-dillard.html.

300 *She knows so many things:* Sara Maitland, "'Spend It All, Shoot It, Play It,
Lose It,'" *New York Times*, September 17, 1989, https://www.nytimes.com
/1989/09/17/books/spend-it-all-shoot-it-play-it-lose-it.html?searchResult
Position=13.

301 *I am sitting under a sycamore by Tinker Creek:* Annie Dillard, *Pilgrim at Tinker
Creek*, New York: Harper Perennial, 2013, 95.

301 *This is a short book:* Stephen King, *On Writing: A Memoir of the Craft*, New
York: Scribner, 2010, ix.

THE JOURNALIST AND THE MURDERER

303 *Journalists who swallow:* Janet Malcolm, *The Journalist and the Murderer*, New
York: Vintage Books, 1990, 144.

303 *Every journalist who is not too stupid:* Ibid., 3.

304 *five of the six jurors:* Ibid., 6.

305 *He is a kind of confidence man:* Ibid., 3.

305 *Unlike other relationships:* Ibid., 143.

305 *Whatever Ms. Malcolm was writing about:* Katherine Q. Seelye, "Janet
Malcolm, Provocative Journalist with a Piercing Eye, Dies at 86," *New York
Times*, June 17, 2021, https://www.nytimes.com/2021/06/17/business/media
/janet-malcolm-dead.html.

307 *She began to do the dense, idiosyncratic:* Katie Roiphe, "Janet Malcolm, The Art
of Nonfiction No. 4," *Paris Review*, Spring 2011, https://www.theparisreview
.org/interviews/6073/the-art-of-nonfiction-no-4-janet-malcolm.

307 *I have been writing long pieces:* Malcolm, *The Journalist and the Murderer*,
158.

307 *In the Masson suit:* Seelye, "Janet Malcolm."

307 *the courts ultimately found in her favor:* Roiphe, "Janet Malcolm."

307 *Malcolm later asserted that she found the notebooks containing:* David Stout,
"Malcolm's Lost Notes and a Child at Play," *New York Times*, August 30,

1995, https://www.nytimes.com/1995/08/30/arts/malcolm-s-lost-notes-and
-a-child-at-play.html.

308 *Malcolm's work, then, occupies:* Roiphe, "Janet Malcolm."

308 *a dog-eared staple:* Harrison Smith, "Janet Malcolm, Elegant and Incisive Writer for the New Yorker, Dies at 86," *Washington Post*, June 17, 2021, https:// www.washingtonpost.com/local/obituaries/janet-malcolm-dead/2021/06/17 /b548b5d8-cd23-11ea-bc6a-6841b28d9093_story.html.

308 *When* The Journalist and the Murderer *came out:* Roiphe, "Janet Malcolm."

309 *the two most important long-form journalists:* Charles Finch, "Janet Malcolm Remembers," *New York Times*, January 15, 2023, https://www.nytimes.com /2023/01/08/books/review/still-pictures-janet-malcolm.html.

309 *Her ten provocative books:* Roiphe, "Janet Malcolm."

309 *Her work has put her:* Ian Frazier, introduction to Janet Malcolm, *Forty-One False Starts*, New York: Farrar, Straus and Giroux, 2013, xv.

ALL ABOUT LOVE: NEW VISIONS

310 *To know love we have to tell the truth:* bell hooks, *All About Love: New Visions*, New York: William Morrow, 2018, 48.

310 *On my kitchen wall hang four snapshots:* Ibid., xv.

311 *I feel our nation's turning away from love:* Ibid., x–xi.

311 *Everyone wants to know more about love:* Ibid., xxvii.

312 *To know love we have to tell the truth:* Ibid., 48–49.

312 *Ironically, the spelling of her name:* Clyde McGrady, "Why bell hooks Didn't Capitalize Her Name," *Washington Post*, December 15, 2021, https://www .washingtonpost.com/lifestyle/2021/12/15/bell-hooks-real-name/.

313 *her tight-knit Black community:* Clay Risen, "bell hooks, Pathbreaking Black Feminist, Dies at 69," *New York Times*, December 15, 2021, https://www .nytimes.com/2021/12/15/books/bell-hooks-dead.html?searchResultPosition=1.

313 *Every night we would try to sleep:* hooks family statement, cited in Sam Gillette, "Remembering bell hooks: Kamala Harris, Ibram X. Kendi and Others Mourn the Black Feminist Author," *People*, December 16, 2021, https://people .com/human-interest/black-feminist-author-bell-hooks-dead-kamala-harris -ibram-x-kendi-others-pay-tribute/.

314 *A devaluation of Black womanhood:* bell hooks, *Ain't I A Woman: Black Women and Feminism*, New York: Routledge, 2015, 53.

314 *It should have come as no surprise:* bell hooks, *Killing Rage: Ending Racism*, New York: Holt Paperbacks, 1995, 99.

314 *For me, reading 'Ain't I A Woman':* Min Jin Lee, "In Praise of bell hooks," *New York Times*, February 28, 2019, https://www.nytimes.com/2019/02/28 /books/bell-hooks-min-jin-lee-aint-i-a-woman.html.

315 *It is a warm affirmation:* Elise Harris, "That 4-Letter Word," *New York Times*, January 30, 2000, https://www.nytimes.com/2000/01/30/books/that-4-letter -word.html.

316 *I am writing this essay:* hooks, *Killing Rage*, 8.

316 *loving practice is not aimed at simply giving:* hooks, *All About Love*, 76.

317 *Lesbians and Gays of Color:* Audre Lorde, *A Burst of Light and Other Essays*, Garden City, NY: Ixia Press, 2017, 38.

NICKEL AND DIMED: ON (NOT) GETTING BY IN AMERICA

318 *Then there's the question:* Barbara Ehrenreich, *Nickel and Dimed: On (Not) Getting By in America*, 20th anniversary ed. New York: Picador, 2021, 163–164.

319 *Mostly out of laziness:* Ibid., 11.

320 *So this is not a story:* Ibid., 6.

320 *My father had been:* Ibid., 2.

321 *a $30 lunch at some understated French country-style place:* Ibid., 1–2.

322 *The unrelenting message was:* Patricia Cohen, "Author's Personal Forecast: Not Always Sunny, but Pleasantly Skeptical," *New York Times*, October 9, 2009, https://www.nytimes.com/2009/10/10/books/10ehrenreich.html.

322 *The pattern is to curtail financing:* Barbara Ehrenreich, "Is It Now a Crime to Be Poor?," *New York Times*, August 8, 2009, https://www.nytimes.com /2009/08/09/opinion/09ehrenreich.html.

323 *Here is a book that made a difference:* Matthew Desmond, foreword to Ehrenreich, *Nickel and Dimed*, xvi.

LETTERS TO A YOUNG CONTRARIAN

325 *Dante was a sectarian:* Christopher Hitchens, *Letters to a Young Contrarian*, New York: Basic Books, 2005, 127.

326 *My dear X:* Ibid., 1.

326 *a life that would be:* Ibid., xiii.

326 *If you care about the points:* Ibid., 21.

327 *If there is going to be an upper class in this country:* Cited in William Grimes, "Christopher Hitchens, Polemicist Who Slashed All, Freely, Is Dead at 62," *New York Times*, December 16, 2011, https://www.nytimes.com/2011/12/16/arts/christopher-hitchens-is-dead-at-62-obituary.html; Peter Wilby, "Christopher Hitchens Obituary," *Guardian*, December 16, 2011, https://www.theguardian.com/books/2011/dec/16/christopher-hitchens-obituary.

328 *His work took him:* Grimes, "Christopher Hitchens."

328 *He wrote a weekly review-essay:* Ibid.

329 *Hitchens announced he was no longer on the left:* Wilby, "Christopher Hitchens Obituary."

329 *In whatever kind of a "race":* Christopher Hitchens, "Topic of Cancer," *Vanity Fair*, August 4, 2010, https://www.vanityfair.com/culture/2010/09/hitchens-201009.

330 *The two worst things:* Hitchens, *Letters*, 107.

330 *Never be a spectator:* Ibid., 140.

330 *the celebrity culture:* Ibid., xii.

PERSEPOLIS: THE STORY OF A CHILDHOOD

331 *Yes, it was war all right:* Marjane Satrapi, *Persepolis: The Story of a Childhood*, New York: Pantheon Books, 2003, 87.

331 *This is me when I was 10 years old:* Ibid., 3.

334 *They think kids are stupid:* Dan Sohval, "'Persepolis' Banned in Chicago Public Schools," National Coalition Against Censorship blog, March 28, 2013, https://ncac.org/news/blog/persepolis-banned-in-chicago-public-schools.

334 *With that [Persepolis] and my second film:* Ryan Gilbey, "Marjane Satrapi: The Persepolis Director Escapes Her Comfort Zone," *Guardian*, March 20, 2015, https://www.theguardian.com/film/2015/mar/20/marjane-satrapi-the-voices.

335 *The Islamist radicals who took charge:* Azadeh Moaveni, "The Protests inside Iran's Girls' Schools," *New Yorker*, August 7, 2023, https://www.newyorker.com/magazine/2023/08/14/the-protests-inside-irans-girls-schools.

335 *The best first-person graphic novel:* Peter Schjeldahl, "Words and Pictures," *New Yorker*, October 9, 2005, https://www.newyorker.com/magazine/2005/10/17/words-and-pictures.

335 *Like Spiegelman's 'Maus,' Satrapi's book:* Fernanda Eberstadt, review of *Persepolis,* by Marjane Satrapi, *New York Times,* October 21, 2021, https://www.nytimes.com/2021/10/21/books/review/marjane-satrapi-persepolis.html?searchResultPosition=2.

336 *Last September, people rose up in fury:* Moaveni, "Protests."

337 *decimated by dictatorship:* Eberstadt, review of *Persepolis.*

337 *Since then, this old and great:* Marjane Satrapi, introduction to *Persepolis,* unpaged.

338 *It is a visceral and often harrowing portrait:* Michiko Kakutani, "Book Study as Insubordination under the Mullahs," *New York Times,* April 15, 2003, https://www.nytimes.com/2003/04/15/books/books-of-the-times-book-study-as-insubordination-under-the-mullahs.html?searchResultPosition=2.

THE YEAR OF MAGICAL THINKING

339 *I could not give away the rest of his shoes:* Joan Didion, *The Year of Magical Thinking,* New York: Vintage Books, 2007, 37.

339 Life changes fast: Ibid., 3.

340 *This was the beginning:* Ibid., 33.

340 *There have been a few occasions:* Ibid., 196.

341 *provided her with her richest material:* William Grimes, "Joan Didion, 'New Journalist' Who Explored Culture and Chaos, Dies at 87," *New York Times,* December 23, 2021, https://www.nytimes.com/2021/12/23/books/joan-didion-dead.html.

341 *I wrote stories from the time:* Joan Didion interviewed by Linda Kuehl, "Joan Didion, The Art of Fiction No. 71," *Paris Review,* Fall-Winter 1978, https://www.theparisreview.org/interviews/3439/the-art-of-fiction-no-71-joan-didion.

342 *She wrote pieces about John Wayne:* Louis Menand, "Out of Bethlehem," *New Yorker,* August 17, 2015, https://www.newyorker.com/magazine/2015/08/24/out-of-bethlehem.

342 *And she has created, in her books:* Michiko Kakutani, "Staking Out California," *New York Times,* June 10, 1979, https://www.nytimes.com/1979/06/10/books/didion-calif.html.

343 *Didion came to see the whole pioneer:* Menand, "Out of Bethlehem."

343 *a searing inquiry into loss:* Michiko Kakutani, "In Loss, a Mother Explores Dark Questions and Bright Memories," *New York Times,* October 31, 2011,

https://www.nytimes.com/2011/11/01/books/blue-nights-by-joan-didion
-review.html.

344 *She was uncannily attuned:* Michiko Kakutani, "Didion's Prophetic Eye
on America," *New York Times,* December 24, 2021, https://www.nytimes
.com/2021/12/24/opinion/joan-didion-books.html.

344 *the grand diagnostician of American disorder:* Parul Sehgal, "Joan Didion
Chronicled American Disorder with Her Own Unmistakable Style," *New
York Times,* December 23, 2021, https://www.nytimes.com/2021/12/23/books
/death-of-joan-didion.html.

344 *if he did not go to Paris in November:* Didion, *Year,* 80.

345 *Didion's book is thrilling and engaging:* Robert Pinsky, "'The Year of Magical
Thinking': Goodbye to All That," *New York Times,* October 9, 2005, https://
www.nytimes.com/2005/10/09/books/review/the-year-of-magical-thinking
-goodbye-to-all-that.html.

345 *I also know that if we are:* Didion, *Year,* 225–226.

345 *the more penetrating and idiosyncratic moments:* Thomas Mallon, "On Second Thought," *New York Times,* September 28, 2003, https://www.nytimes
.com/2003/09/28/books/on-second-thought.html.

FOOD RULES: AN EATER'S MANUAL

346 *Eat food. Not too much:* Michael Pollan, *Food Rules: An Eater's Manual,* New
York: Penguin Books, 2011, 17.

346 *Eat food. These days this is easier:* Ibid., 45.

347 *Eat food. Not too much:* Ibid., 17.

347 *I'm trying to figure out two very simple things:* Ibid., 30.

347 *Avoid food products:* Ibid., 58.

347 *Don't eat anything your great-grandmother:* Ibid., 46.

347 *It's not food if it arrived:* Ibid., 84.

347 *Don't eat breakfast cereals:* Ibid., 118.

348 *No, a desk is not:* Ibid., 180.

348 *Break the rules:* Ibid., 206.

348 Time *magazine named Pollan:* Alice Waters, "Michael Pollan: The 2010 Time
100," *Time,* April 29, 2010, https://content.time.com/time/specials/packages
/article/0,28804,1984685_1984745_1984934,00.html.

349 *He has received numerous awards:* "About Michael Pollan," Michael Pollan
website, https://michaelpollan.com/about/.

349 *partly based on* The Omnivore's Dilemma*:* Ibid.

349 *Pollan has also taught:* Ibid.

349 *named one of the best books of 2018:* Unsigned, "The 10 Best Books of 2018," *New York Times*, November 29, 2018, https://www.nytimes.com/2018/11/29 /books/review/best-books.html.

349 *Pollan then turns to his own narratives:* Rob Dunn, "Michael Pollan Explores the Mind-Altering Plants in His Garden," *New York Times,* July 8, 2021, https://www.nytimes.com/2021/07/08/books/review/this-is-your-mind -on-plants-michael-pollan.html?searchResultPosition=1.

349 *I aimed at the public's heart:* Sinclair Lewis, quoted in *The Jungle*, Dickinson University/Theodore Roosevelt Center, https://www.theodore rooseveltcenter.org/Learn-About-TR/TR-Encyclopedia/Reading-and-Writing /The-Jungle.

350 *As with most things related to people:* Andrea Thompson, "Here's How Much Food Contributes to Climate Change," *Scientific American*, September 13, 2021, https://www.scientificamerican.com/article/heres-how-much-food -contributes-to-climate-change/.

350 *What we eat:* United Nations, "Food and Climate Change: Healthy Diets for a Healthier Planet," https://www.un.org/en/climatechange/science/climate -issues/food.

351 *He gracefully navigates within these anxieties:* Unsigned, "The Ten Best Books of 2006," *New York Times*, December 10, 2006, https://archive.nytimes.com /www.nytimes.com/ref/books/review/20061210tenbestbooks.html.

WE SHOULD ALL BE FEMINISTS

352 *If it is true that the full humanity:* Chimamanda Ngozi Adichie, *We Should All Be Feminists*, New York: Vintage Books, 2015, 46.

352 *Okoloma was one of my greatest childhood friends:* Ibid., 7–8.

353 *since feminists are women who are unhappy:* Ibid., 9.

353 *At some point:* Ibid., 10.

353 *I am angry:* Ibid., 21.

353 *All of us, women and men:* Ibid., 48.

354 *He is a remarkable man:* Sean Murray, "The New Face of Nigerian Literature," BBC News, June 8, 2007, http://news.bbc.co.uk/2/hi/africa/6731387 .stm.

355 *been viewed more than 34 million times:* "The Danger of a Single Story," TEDGlobal, posted October 2009, https://www.ted.com/talks/chimamanda _ngozi_adichie_the_danger_of_a_single_story.

355 *From the office politics of a hair-braiding salon:* Unsigned, "The 10 Best Books of 2013," December 4, 2013, https://www.nytimes.com/2013/12/15 /books/review/the-10-best-books-of-2013.html.

355 *So in the past few years:* Zoe Greenburg, "Chimamanda Ngozi Adichie's Blueprint for Feminism," *New York Times*, March 15, 2017, https://www .nytimes.com/2017/03/15/books/chimamanda-ngozi-adiche-dear-ijeawele .html?searchResultPosition=1.

355 *In 2018, Adichie won the PEN Pinter Prize:* "Chimamanda Ngozi Adichie wins PEN Pinter Prize," *Irish Times*, June 12, 2018, https://www.irishtimes .com/culture/books/chimamanda-ngozi-adichie-wins-pen-pinter-prize -1.3527676.

356 *The kind of feminism she espoused:* Larissa MacFarquhar, "Chimamanda Ngozi Adichie Comes to Terms with Global Fame," *New Yorker*, May 28, 2018, https://www.newyorker.com/magazine/2018/06/04/chimamanda-ngozi -adichie-comes-to-terms-with-global-fame.

356 *The main proposition of:* Greenburg, "Chimamanda Ngozi Adichie's Blueprint."

357 *I don't think sexism is worse:* Chimamanda Ngozi Adichie, quoted in Lisa Allardice, "Chimamanda Ngozi Adichie: 'This Could Be the Beginning of a Revolution,'" *Guardian*, April 28, 2018, https://www.theguardian.com /books/2018/apr/28/chimamanda-ngozi-adichie-feminism-racism-sexism -gender-metoo.

357 *It explores the brutality:* Leslie Gray Streeter, "Chimamanda Ngozi Adichie Writes Her Way through Grief," *Washington Post*, May 11, 2021, https:// www.washingtonpost.com/entertainment/books/chimamanda-ngozi -adichie-notes-on-grief/2021/05/06/d62246a2-ae96-11eb-ab4c-986555a1c511 _story.html.

ON TYRANNY: TWENTY LESSONS FROM THE TWENTIETH CENTURY

358 *Do not obey:* Timothy Snyder, *On Tyranny: Twenty Lessons from the Twentieth Century*, New York: Tim Duggan Books/Crown, 2017, 17.

359 *History does not repeat:* Ibid., 9–10.

359 *it was the Austrians' anticipatory obedience:* Ibid., 18–19.

360 *In the most dangerous of times:* Ibid., 81–82.

360 *If none of us is prepared to die:* Ibid., 115.

360 *compels us to look squarely:* Joshua Rubenstein, "The Devils' Playground," *New York Times,* November 26, 2010, https://www.nytimes.com/2010/11/28 /books/review/Rubenstein-t.html.

360 *established Mr. Snyder, 46:* Jennifer Schuessler, "Timothy Snyder's 'Black Earth' Puts Holocaust, and Himself, in Spotlight," *New York Times,* September 7, 2015, https://www.nytimes.com/2015/09/08/books/timothy -snyders-black-earth-puts-holocaust-and-himself-in-spotlight.html?search ResultPosition=4.

361 *In recent years:* Ezra Klein, "Transcript: Ezra Klein Interviews Timothy Snyder," *New York Times,* March 15, 2022, https://www.nytimes.com/2022/03/15 /podcasts/transcript-ezra-klein-interviews-timothy-snyder.html?search ResultPosition=1.

362 *The materialistic and selfish quality:* Tony Judt, *Ill Fares the Land,* New York: Penguin Books, 2021, 2.

362 *those who hold power:* Hannah Arendt, *On Violence,* New York: Harcourt Brace Jovanovich, 1970, 87.

362 *No one has ever doubted that truth:* Hannah Arendt, *On Lying and Politics,* New York: Library of America, 2022, 3.

THE ORIGIN OF OTHERS

363 *Race has been a constant arbiter:* Toni Morrison, *The Origin of Others,* Cambridge, MA: Harvard University Press, 2017, 3.

363 *Finally, after a round of visits:* Ibid., 2.

364 *our tendency to separate and judge:* Ibid., 3.

365 *blacks are useful:* Ibid., 5.

365 *Young Chloe grew up:* Margalit Fox, in "Toni Morrison, Towering Novelist of the Black Experience, Dies at 88," *New York Times,* August 6, 2019, https://www.nytimes.com/2019/08/06/books/toni-morrison-dead .html.

366 *According to the American Library Association's Office for Intellectual Freedom:* "Top 100 Most Banned and Challenged Books:2010-2019," Office for Intel-

lectual Freedom/American Library Association, undated webpage, https://www.ala.org/advocacy/bbooks/frequentlychallengedbooks/decade2019.

367 *Reading Ms. Morrison:* Chimamanda Ngozi Adichie, cited in "Remembering Toni Morrison," *New York Times*, https://www.nytimes.com/2019/08/06/books/remembering-toni-morrison.html?action=click&module=RelatedLinks&pgtype=Article.

367 *These are just some:* Morrison, *The Origin of Others*, 63.

368 *To understand why we find ourselves here again:* Ta-Nehisi Coates, foreword to Morrison, *The Origin of Others*, xvii.

369 *Morrison had a superfluidity:* Dwight Garner, "Toni Morrison, A Writer of Many Gifts Who Bent Language to Her Will," *New York Times,* August 6, 2019 https://www.nytimes.com/2019/08/06/books/toni-morrison-death.html.

UNDER A WHITE SKY: THE NATURE OF THE FUTURE

370 *The choices that we'll make:* Elizabeth Kolbert, *Under a White Sky: The Nature of the Future*, New York: Crown, 2022, 206–207.

370 *Rivers make good metaphors:* Ibid., 3.

371 *White would become:* Ibid., 181.

371 *A Mississippi that's been harnessed:* Ibid., 60.

372 *This has been a book:* Ibid., 200.

372 *in the same way that global warming:* Elizabeth Kolbert, "The Climate of Man—I," *New Yorker*, April 25, 2005, https://www.newyorker.com/magazine/2005/04/25/the-climate-of-man-i.

373 *The world is in danger:* Elizabeth Kolbert, "What Will Another Decade of Climate Crisis Bring?," *New Yorker,* January 5, 2020, https://www.newyorker.com/magazine/2020/01/13/what-will-another-decade-of-climate-crisis-bring.

374 *this book's existence is evidence:* Ezra Klein, "Transcript: Ezra Klein Interviews Elizabeth Kolbert about Geoengineering," *New York Times*, February 9, 2021, https://www.nytimes.com/2021/02/09/podcasts/ezra-klein-podcast-elizabeth-kolbert-transcript.html?searchResultPosition=4.

AFTERWORD

377 *One of the most important things:* Harold S. Kushner, *When Bad Things Happen to Good People*, New York: Anchor Books, 2004, 81.

377 *Our home was like an artists' colony:* Alison Bechdel, *Fun Home: A Family Tragicomic,* Boston: Houghton Mifflin Harcourt/Mariner Books, 2007, 134.

378 *Sauerkraut:* Dava Sobel, *Longitude,* New York: Bloomsbury, 2007, 138.

378 *Until around 1910:* Nora Ephron, *I Feel Bad about My Neck and Other Thoughts on Being a Woman,* New York: Vintage Books, 2008, 45.

378 *Pointing out how ridiculous:* Gail Collins, "America Is Really Very Funny: Gail Collins on The Most of Nora Ephron," *New York Times,* June 202, 2023, https://www.nytimes.com/interactive/2023/06/20/opinion/gail-collins-the-most-of-nora-ephron.html?smid=em-share.

379 *I was like a newborn:* Jill Bolte Taylor, *My Stroke of Insight: A Brain Scientist's Personal Journey,* New York: Plume, 2009, 75.

380 *eat food. Not too much:* Michael Pollan, *Food Rules: An Eater's Manual,* New York: Penguin Books, 2011, 17.

380 *Dante was a sectarian:* Christopher Hitchens, *Letters to a Young Contrarian,* New York: Basic Books, 2005, 127.

381 *learn to ask:* Marcus Aurelius, *Meditations,* New York: Modern Library, 2002, 143.

APPENDIX I

383 *Age weighs heavily on me:* Sappho, *Stung with Love: Poems and Fragments,* trans. Aaron Poochigian, New York: Penguin Books, 2009, 45.

383 *Though conscious of the difficulty:* Frederick Douglass, *Narrative of the Life of Frederick Douglass, an American Slave,* New Haven, CT: Yale University Press, 2001, 32.

383 *Unjust laws exist:* Henry David Thoreau, "Civil Disobedience," in *Walden and Civil Disobedience,* New York: Penguin, 2017, 278.

383 *Human beings were trying to behave:* George Orwell, *Homage to Catalonia,* New York: Mariner Books, 2015, 4.

384 *There the young were to be born:* Rachel Carson, *Under the Sea-Wind,* New York: Penguin Books, 2007, 153.

384 *There, in the tin factory:* John Hersey, *Hiroshima,* New York: Vintage Books, 2020, 21.

384 *The glorification of one race:* James Baldwin, *The Fire Next Time,* New York: Vintage Books, 1993, 82.

384 Life changes in the instant: Joan Didion, *The Year of Magical Thinking*, New York: Vintage Books, 2007, 3.

384 *Be as courageous as you can:* Timothy Snyder, *On Tyranny: Twenty Lessons from the Twentieth Century*, New York: Tim Duggan Books/Crown, 2017, 115.

384 *The choices that we'll make:* Elizabeth Kolbert, *Under a White Sky: The Nature of the Future*, New York: Crown, 2021, 206–207.